DECOLONIZING GOD

The Bible in the Modern World, 16

Series Editors
J. Cheryl Exum, Jorunn Økland, Stephen D. Moore

DECOLONIZING GOD

THE BIBLE IN THE TIDES OF EMPIRE

Mark G. Brett

SHEFFIELD PHOENIX PRESS

2009

Copyright © 2008, 2009 Sheffield Phoenix Press
First published in hardback 2008
First published in paperback 2009

Published by Sheffield Phoenix Press
Department of Biblical Studies, University of Sheffield
45 Victoria Street, Sheffield S3 7QB

www.sheffieldphoenix.com

The earlier versions of chs.3, 4 and 5 were, in order, published as:
'The Loss and Retrieval of Ancestral Religion—in Ancient Israel and in Australia'
in M. Parsons (ed.), *Text and Task: Scripture and Mission* (Milton Keynes:
Paternoster, 2005), pp.1-19.

'Israel's Indigenous Origins: Cultural Hybridity and the Formation of Israelite Ethnicity'
Biblical Interpretation 11 (2003), pp.400-412.

'Genocide in Deuteronomy: Postcolonial Variations on Mimetic Desire' in M. O'Brien
and H. Wallace (eds), *Seeing Signals, Reading Signs* (London: Continuum, 2004),
pp.76-90.

Paternoster, E.J. Brill and Continuum have all provided permission to re-use this
material, for which I am grateful.

A CIP catalogue record for this book
is available from the British Library

Typeset by Vikatan Publishing Solutions, Chennai, India
Printed by Lightning Source

ISBN 978-1-906055-37-0 (hardback)
ISBN 978-1-906055-89-9 (paperback)

ISSN 1747-9630

מה העדת והחקים והמׁשפטים (Deut. 6.20)

FOR ANUSHA, MATTHEUS AND LIAM

CONTENTS

Acknowledgments   ix

Introduction   1

Chapter 1
THE BIBLE AND COLONIZATION   7

Chapter 2
ALIENATING EARTH AND THE CURSE OF EMPIRES   32

Chapter 3
ANCESTORS AND THEIR GIFTS   44

Chapter 4
PIGS, POTS AND CULTURAL HYBRIDS   62

Chapter 5
DEUTERONOMY, GENOCIDE AND THE DESIRES OF NATIONS   79

Chapter 6
DISSIDENT PROPHETS AND THE MAKING OF UTOPIAS   94

Chapter 7
EXILE AND ETHNIC CONFLICT   112

Chapter 8
JESUS, NON-VIOLENCE AND THE CHRIST QUESTION   132

Chapter 9
PAUL AND HYBRID CHRISTIAN IDENTITIES   153

Chapter 10
POSTCOLONIAL THEOLOGY AND ETHICS   178

Bibliography   205
Index of References   225
Index of Authors   229
Index of Subjects   234

ACKNOWLEDGMENTS

The content of this book has arisen from conversations over the past twenty years with Indigenous colleagues and students from Burma, North-East India, the Pacific and Australia. I would especially like to acknowledge Edea Kidu, Anna May Say Pa, R.L. Hnuni, Inotoli Zhimomi, Pothin Wete, Peniamina Leota, Djiniyini Gondarra, Graham and Grant Paulson, and Mark Yettica-Paulson.

While this remains a 'whitefella' book, the questions posed have also been shaped in no small measure by my work with Native Title Services Victoria and with the Victorian Traditional Owner Land Justice Group. Chris Marshall and Mick Dodson, among others, have helped to sustain my hope that another kind of social imagination may yet be possible in Australia.

I am grateful to a number of people who were kind enough to comment on parts of the manuscript in earlier stages of its production: Deborah Bird Rose, Diana Lipton, Gershon Hepner, Norman Habel, Gerald West, Fernando Segovia, Stephen Fowl, Duncan Reid, Philip Chia, Merryl Blair, Howard Wallace, Kynan Sutherland, Fred Morgan, Gordon Preece and Mark Lindsay. I owe a special debt of gratitude to Tamara Eskenazi, Keith Dyer, Robert Francis and Bill Ashcroft who worked their way through all of the chapters in draft and whose critiques provided great encouragement.

Finally, however, this work would not have been possible without my wife Ilsa's ability to get to the heart of things, and whose mindfulness has steadily untied the knots in my soul.

INTRODUCTION

Our past is sedimented in our present,
and we are doomed to misidentify ourselves
as long as we can't do justice to where we come from.[1]

Charles Taylor

The argument of this book oscillates between ancient and modern contexts without suggesting, in line with current solipsistic fashions, that readers can only ever recreate the past in their own image. I presume, for example, that it is quite possible to distinguish between ancient and modern versions of colonialism or imperialism, and in modern times, we can discern important differences between what happened in eighteenth-century North America and our experience in nineteenth-century Australia. Those differences are sometimes significant, as this book will show, but there are also important analogies between the various experiences of colonial expansion, and the implications of those analogies need rigorous scrutiny. In particular, the implications are worth reflecting on in contexts where the after-effects of Christendom have not yet subsided.

Robert Francis, a White River Band Cherokee theologian, recently suggested that decolonization will require a long process of *reducing dependency* on colonial order—theologically, psychologically and economically.[2] The reduction of this dependency is not just a matter for Indigenous communities who are revitalizing their cultures and economies. It is also a matter for all communities who derive their identity—even indirectly—from the Bible, and who are exploring the significance of postcolonial spirituality and politics.

Part of this process will include a reconsideration of biblical traditions, both their production and reception, in order to discover less distorted habits of thinking and acting that may be brought to the unfinished business of reconciliation with Indigenous people. In the case of Australia, for example, the legal basis for ownership of lands and natural resources rests for the most part on illegitimate actions taken in the nineteenth century

1. Charles Taylor, *A Secular Age* (Cambridge, MA: Belknap Press, 2007), p. 29.
2. Robert Francis, 'From Bondage to Freedom', unpublished paper, August 2007.

by colonial agents of the British Crown.[3] The recognition of past wrongs and the restoration of mutually respectful relationships are projects that have barely begun. A critical theology requires the praxis of repentance and genuine dialogue with Indigenous people. Moreover, the construction of Australian national identity needs to free itself from legal and economic dependence on historic injustices.

In Chapter 1, 'The Bible and Colonization', I provide a series of sketches illustrating how biblical texts were embedded in the discourses of colonialism. The focus is on Australia, with selected comparisons and contrasts from the Americas, Africa, India and Aotearoa New Zealand. It becomes clear that there were favorite biblical texts that appeared regularly in different contexts, which were used both to legitimate and to mitigate the devastating effects of colonization. Generations of Europeans became intoxicated with their ideas of racial superiority and civilization, and the Bible was caught up in the destructive consequences.

Most biblical traditions, however, as the subsequent chapters demonstrate, were produced by people who were themselves subject to the shifting tides of ancient imperial domination—whether in the form of imperial administration exercised largely at a distance, or in the form of threatening colonies of migrating populations.[4]

Chapter 2, 'Alienating Earth and the Curse of Empires', notes how the divine command in Gen. 1.28 to 'subdue the earth' was frequently cited, from the sixteenth century onwards, both as a reason for imperial expansions and as a warrant for linking property rights to cultivation. I argue that this hermeneutical hubris actually inverted the communicative intentions of the biblical primeval narratives as we now have them.

One virulent strain of agrarian ideology that developed in Australia helped to shape the legal assumptions of *terra nullius* ('land belonging to no one') that deprived Indigenous groups of 'native title' rights even up until 1992. Unlike the land rights legislation that dates from the 1970s—which provides land to Aboriginal people in the form of a 'grant' from the Crown—it

3.   This issue is discussed in Chapter 1, but for a recent analysis of the legal predicament of land title in Australia see Samantha Hepburn, 'Feudal Tenure and Native Title: Revising an Enduring Fiction' *Sydney Law Review* 27/1 (2005), pp. 49–86.

4.   See, for example, Carolyn R. Higginbotham, *Egyptianization and Elite Emulation in Ramesside Palestine: Governance and Accommodation on the Imperial Periphery* (Leiden: E.J. Brill, 2000); Eckart Otto, *Das Deuteronomium: Politische Theologie und Rechtsreform in Juda und Assyrien* (Berlin: de Gruyter, 2000); Charles Carter, *The Emergence of Yehud in the Persian Period* (Sheffield: Sheffield Academic Press, 1999); Claire L. Lyons and John K. Papadopoulos (eds.), *The Archaeology of Colonialism* (Los Angeles: Getty Research Institute, 2002).

was in 1992 that the Federal Court of Australia finally recognized that Indigenous law and custom might actually qualify the Crown's jurisdiction. The initial act of court recognition had a sting in the tail, however, as illustrated in this excerpt from the judgement:

> The common law can, by reference to the traditional laws and customs of an Indigenous people, identify and protect the native rights and interests to which they give rise. However, when the tide of history has washed away any real acknowledgment of traditional law and any real observance of traditional customs, the foundation of native title has disappeared... Once traditional native title expires, the Crown's radical title expands to a full beneficial title, for then there is no other proprietor than the Crown.[5]

The phrase 'the tide of history' has echoed notoriously through subsequent legal judgements that have denied particular Indigenous groups their native title on the grounds that the local system of law and custom has not, in the eyes of the Court, been continuously maintained.[6]

The formality of legal language here obscures the agency of successive colonial governments who adopted policies specifically designed *to undermine Indigenous laws and to sever the connections between Aboriginal groups and their traditional countries.* The presumptive and self-serving logic of the Crown in this legal history is clearly open to a theological critique. One of the key arguments of this book is that such a critique can be inferred from the Bible's reiterated opposition to the tides of imperial sovereignties that washed over the ancient Levant. The 'tide of history' can be further analysed in terms of the tides of empire.

In Chapter 3, 'Ancestors and their Gifts', I argue that the Hebrew Bible reflects substantial changes of law and custom, without suggesting that the Crown (whether an Israelite or a foreign monarch) could extinguish the land

5. *Mabo vs. Queensland [No 2]* (1992) 175 CLR 1, Justice Brennan at 66. See further Lisa Strelein, *Compromised Jurisprudence: Native Title Cases since Mabo* (Canberra: Aboriginal Studies Press, 2006); James F. Weiner, 'Diaspora, Materialism, Tradition: Anthropological Issues in the Recent High Court Appeal of the Yorta Yorta', *Land, Rights, Laws: Issues of Native Title*, Issues Paper 18 (2002) available at www.aiatsis.gov. au/rsrch/ntru/ntpapers/IPv2n18/pdf.

6. The requirement of 'continuity' arises from the tension between two positions held within Australian jurisprudence: (1) that the Courts do not recognize two parallel law-making systems and hence can only recognize the Aboriginal laws and customs that existed *when British sovereignty was first asserted*; and (2) that in order to recognize native title *today*, there must be proof of a normative system that has had continuous vitality since the assertion of British sovereignty. See Strelein, *Compromised Jurisprudence*, pp. 121, 129.

rights passed on from the ancestors to various clans. On the contrary, there is an assumption that Israelite clans had indefinite claims on particular pieces of land, in spite of periods of dislocation or exile. Indeed, 'redemption' meant primarily the restoration of alienated kin and ancestral country.

Chapter 4, 'Pigs, Pots and Cultural Hybrids', describes the broad agreement that now exists among archaeologists that the populations of the early Iron Age Palestine (c. 1200 to 1000 BCE) were overwhelmingly Indigenous. The evidence from language, clothing, hair styles, housing and pottery indicates that the early Israelites can be seen as a rural group of Canaanites. Israelite cultural identity was not imposed from outside, as was the case in the Philistine colonies. It first developed through a fissure in Canaanite culture in the rural setting of the central hill country. In the course of time, a view of Yahwist religion emerged that made the worship of other gods incompatible with Israelite identity, even though many aspects of culture continued to be shared with Indigenous neighbours.

Chapter 5, 'Deuteronomy, Genocide and the Desires of Nations', focuses on the call for genocide of the people of Canaan, particularly as it is expressed in Deuteronomy 20. I argue that this shocking text was produced in the context of the seventh century BCE—long after the arrival of Yahwism in Canaan—as part of a discourse that grouped non-Yahwist Israelites with 'foreign' Canaanites. This and other parts of Deuteronomy were modelled on Assyrian treaty documents that demanded exclusive loyalty to the imperial king, but Deuteronomy's authors resisted the dominant imperial culture of the time by asserting that they had their own treaty or covenant with a higher sovereignty—their God Yahweh. This example of subversive 'mimicry' is ironically quite different from the oppressive history of Deuteronomy's use when it was co-opted historically by Christian groups in order to legitimate colonization.[7] The contrast between 'Israelite' and 'Canaanite' arguably wrought far more damage in the modern period than it ever did in Judah of the seventh century BCE.

Chapter 6, 'Dissident Prophets and the Making of Utopias', addresses the utopian visions of Israel's prophets that envisaged a universal peace in which Israel 'possessed' other nations. The classical prophets often condemned the rich for misappropriating land, and one of the basic principles of the prophetic books is that the boundaries of the nations should be respected. This chapter examines the question whether the prophetic tradition is able to hold together the tensions between the early teaching on social justice and the later visions of utopia.

---

7.   On the idea of mimicry in postcolonial studies, see the classic discussion in Homi Bhabha, *Location of Culture* (London: Routledge, 1994), pp. 102–22.

Chapter 7, 'Exile and Ethnic Conflict', accepts the view that the most ethnically self-conscious biblical theology, in Ezra and Nehemiah, had its roots historically not in strategies of social control invented by the ruling classes, but rather, in a pattern of cultural resistance adopted by minority Israelites struggling to survive in exile in Babylon. In the subsequent period of restoration under Persian administration, however, the ethnocentrism of Ezra and Nehemiah is less justifiable, and indeed, the idea in Ezra 9 of Israel as a 'holy seed' conflicts with the Priestly purity regulations in the Torah that relate to strangers. Ezra and Nehemiah may be comparable, it is suggested, with some anti-colonial movements in modern contexts where 'nativist' elites promoted social visions that were blind to particular groups within their own society.

Chapter 8, 'Jesus, Non-Violence and the Christ Question', argues that the teachings of Jesus reflect a prophetic resistance to the oppressive economic conditions of peasant life and a rejection of the Roman imperial system. Nothing in the life and death of Jesus, however, corresponds to the violent motifs generated by Israel's messianic imagination. This chapter discusses the tension between the non-violent Jesus and the traumatic visions of divine judgment in the Gospels. It also examines the 'other worldly' spirituality of John's Gospel, which threatens to undermine the legitimacy of all territorially based cultural traditions and apparently opens the way to a global religious imperialism.

Chapter 9, 'Paul and Hybrid Christian Identities', suggests that a key question for the apostle Paul was how Gentiles come to share in the life of Israel without, at the same time, subjecting themselves to the dictates of Jewish ethnicity. On this issue, Paul is a radical thinker, but his letters also have an ambiguous history of reception that includes tolerance of slavery in the Christian tradition, and by implication, within modern colonial regimes. The argument in this chapter does not attempt to dispel the ambiguities in Paul's writings, but rather, proposes an approach to Paul that locates the tensions in his thought against the political background of the Roman Empire. This approach throws light on the place of cultural hybridity in Paul's theology, and enables a fresh consideration of the history of his influence.

Chapter 10, 'Postcolonial Theology and Ethics', summarizes the implications of the previous discussion for contemporary Christian theology and ethics. God will not be decolonized, I suggest, by embracing a postmodern 'free market' of endlessly plastic religious identities. The argument locates itself within Christian tradition and links cultural, political, environmental and economic theology to an ethics of solidarity—beginning with restraint on the part of the powerful, and orientated around the root metaphors of friendship and hospitality.

The arguments in this book presume no particular critical theory or 'hermeneutic'. I do however presume that it is possible to have a genuine conversation with the classic biblical texts, and that this conversation requires neither full understanding nor full agreement with 'biblical theologies'. Even if we ask only a single question of a text, and rigorously apply a certain method of reading, it is usually the case that a number of alternative interpretations are plausible—not a limitless number, but there are still interpretive choices to be made.[8] In order to address the complexity of the postcolonial issues, a number of different questions and methods are needed, and the degree of indeterminacy increases proportionally. In presenting the broad range of hypotheses in this book, the Australian context within which I work has been crucial in shaping the interpretive choices that are made, but the proposals here should be seen as an invitation to further conversation and praxis.

8. See, e.g., Charles Cosgrove, 'Towards a Postmodern *Hermeneutica Sacra*', in C.H. Cosgrove (ed.), *The Meanings We Choose: Hermeneutical Ethics, Indeterminacy and the Conflict of Interpretations* (London: T. & T. Clark, 2004), pp. 39–61.

1

The Bible and Colonization

> The conceptual leap that accompanies the advent of the state in the sixteenth century is the invention of sovereignty.[1]
>
> *William Cavanaugh*

> It became a fundamental maxim, and necessary principle (though in reality a mere fiction) of our English tenures, "that the king is the universal lord and original proprietor of all the lands in his kingdom; and that no man doth or can possess any part of it, but what has, mediately or immediately, been derived as a gift from him, to be held upon feodal services." For this being the real case in pure, original, proper feuds, other nations who adopted this system were obliged to act upon the same supposition, as a substruction and foundation of their new polity, though the fact was indeed far otherwise.
>
> *William Blackstone,*
> *Commentaries on the Laws of England (1765–1769), Book II, Chap. 4*

Introduction

In his painting 'And on the Eighth Day', the Australian Aboriginal artist Lin Onus presents a visual satire on the first chapter of the Bible: English angels arrive bearing sheep, fencing wire, a gun, a Bible, and disinfectant. 'On the sixth day', the artist commented, 'God created the earth, on the seventh day he rested, and on the eighth day he stuffed it up for Aboriginal people'.[2] Lin Onus's commentary is manifestly true of colonial ideology: the land needed to be fenced in, subjugated with a gun, civilized with a Bible,

---

1. William T. Cavanaugh, 'Killing for the Telephone Company: Why the Nation-State is Not the Keeper of the Common Good', *Modern Theology* 20 (2004), pp. 250, 243–74.

2. Quoted in Margo Neale, *Urban Dingo: The Art and Life of Lin Onus 1948–1996* (Brisbane: Queensland Art Gallery, 2000), p. 21 (see p. 90 for a reproduction of the painting). Cf. Paul Carter's suggestion that Albert Namatjira's landscapes may have 'mimicked the iconography of Bible illustrations' in order to 'mock our self-absorption' (Carter, *The Lie of the Land* [London: Faber & Faber, 1996], pp. 45–46).

and disinfected of unwanted elements. Traditional country was appropriated unjustly, even according to international law of the day.[3] Its prior inhabitants were either killed or denied their rights, and far from bringing disinfectants, the colonists brought diseases that killed Aboriginal people in breathtakingly large numbers. Governor Philip reported that in 1789, a year after settlement in Sydney cove, about half of the Indigenous population died from a smallpox epidemic.[4] These events in late eighteenth and early nineteenth-century Australia were reiterating patterns that can be found in most histories of colonization.

What this chapter sets out to provide is not so much the historical details of colonization projects from the sixteenth century onwards, nor history enhanced by social theory or psychology, but a series of sketches illustrating how biblical texts were implicated in the language of colonialism. It will become clear that there were favorite texts, which appear with relentless regularity in different contexts, but they were deployed in significantly different ways, both to legitimate and to mitigate the devastating effects of colonization. The Bible has also figured in resistance to colonialism, and in anti-imperial expressions of nationalism, and these factors need to be considered as well. In short, this chapter will identify key texts, themes and questions that need to shape any 'postcolonial' re-reading of the Bible. It will focus on Australian experience but show how some aspects of this experience are by no means unique.

The settlement of Australia was, however, distinguishable from many other colonial projects in at least one respect. Settlers in North America, South Africa and New Zealand, for example, did not generally deny that the Indigenous peoples were the original owners of the land, a denial that became the standard legal ideology in the Australian colonies. In the late seventeenth century, the Puritans in North America configured themselves as a 'chosen people' with a divinely given mission—a 'New Israel' confronting the prior inhabitants of the promised land with an Israelite right of conquest. Biblical narratives and laws were sometimes drawn on to demonstrate that Native Americans had been disinherited by divine decision.[5] But official legal ideology in North America was never founded on biblical discourse alone; it was blended from notions of 'civilization' and the superior rights of European culture. In the nineteenth century, the legal

3. Henry Reynolds, *The Law of the Land* (Melbourne: Penguin, 2nd edn, 1992).

4. John Harris, *One Blood: 200 Years of Aboriginal Encounter with Christianity* (Sutherland: Albatross, 2nd edn, 1994), p. 41.

5. See Susan Niditch, *War in the Hebrew Bible* (Oxford: Oxford University Press, 1993), pp. 3–5.

writer James Kent was able to claim colonial legitimacy in North America 'in consequence of the superior genius of the Europeans, founded on civilization and Christianity, and of their superiority in the means and act of war'.[6] The combined forces of civilization, Christianity and rights of conquest were pitted against the Native Americans, and through a long period of conflict, numerous treaties were signed.

In contrast, the *South Australian Constitution Act* of 1834 asserted that prior to British settlement the land of the colony was 'waste and unoccupied', an expression of the *terra nullius* ideology which was not legally overturned in Australia, astonishingly, until the Mabo native title judgment in 1992. The idea of *terra nullius* ('land belonging to no one') was not so much a doctrine as a network of assumptions, which when linked to a feudal doctrine of land tenure that recognized no sovereignty other than the British Crown, yielded Australia's peculiar history in relation to land rights.[7]

It would have been difficult to make the Puritan rhetoric of a 'New Israel' plausible in the early penal colonies of Australia. The settlers were much more likely, if they exercised their biblical imagination at all, to see themselves in *exile* rather than in a new 'promised land'.[8] Moreover, there is no evidence to show that the early explorer diaries configure Aborigines as Canaanites; on the contrary, there are many examples where Indigenous practices are seen to be analogous with Israelite ones.[9] The explorers often spoke of a generalized providence, but the genre of the divine underwriting could sometimes be mistaken for a curse, as when the unfamiliar land and its creatures were seen as a kind of creation in reverse—'wrong-footed' perhaps being an appropriate rendering of 'Antipodean'. The first book of poetry printed in the colonies reiterated the old theological tradition that the Antipodes somehow escaped God's original blessing, with only the kangaroo being a clue that perhaps there was wonder here that European eyes might yet perceive[10]:

6. James Kent, *Commentaries on American Law* (Boston: Little, Brown, 11th edn, 1867), p. 485.

7. Reynolds, *The Law of the Land*, pp. 4, 12, 32; Samantha Hepburn, 'Feudal Tenure and Native Title: Revising an Enduring Fiction', *Sydney Law Review* 27/1 (2005), pp. 49–86.

8. Deborah Bird Rose, 'Rupture and the Ethics of Care in Colonized Space', in T. Bonyhady and T. Griffiths (eds.), *Prehistory to Politics* (Melbourne: Melbourne University Press, 1996), p. 205; cf. Peter Beilharz, *Imagining the Antipodes: Culture, Theory and the Visual in the Work of Bernard Smith* (Cambridge: Cambridge University Press, 1997), pp. 97–99.

9. Roland Boer, *Last Stop before Antarctica: The Bible and Postcolonialism in Australia* (Sheffield: Sheffield Academic Press, 2001), pp. 63–72, 115.

10. Barron Fields, 'Kangaroo' (1819), quoted in Boer, *Last Stop*, p. 117.

Kangaroo! Kangaroo!
Thou spirit of Australia,
That redeems from utter failure,
From perfect desolation,
And warrants the creation
Of this fifth part of the earth;
Which would seem an afterbirth,
Not conceived at the beginning
(For GOD blessed his work at first
And saw that it was good),
But emerged at the first sinning,
When the ground therefore was curst—
And hence this barren wood!

The idea of Indigenous Australians as Canaanites seems to have made an occasional appearance in material from the mid-nineteenth century, but the theme did not have the systemic influence that it did amongst the Puritans or the Boers. An article written by Rev. J. Campbell, for example, appeared in the *Brisbane Courier* of 1864, noting sermons by Charles Kingsley which referred to Aborigines as being like 'Canaanites of old to be swept off the face of the earth'. But the ideas are mentioned only to be refuted.[11]

More significant for the Australian colonists was a widely spread conviction of their racial superiority, given biblical sanction in mission history by an interpretation of the 'curse of Ham' in Gen. 9.20–27 which saw the text as a universal curse on black peoples that condemned them to slavery. This tradition of interpretation has a long and complex history, prior to modern versions of colonialism and including medieval Muslim justifications of black slavery, but in Australian mission history it seems to have mutated into a claim about racial inferiority rather than a sanction for slavery as such.[12]

There is overwhelming evidence, however, that Australian colonists used Aboriginal people for forced labour in the nineteenth century. Indigenous labour was still exploited in the early twentieth although the language of 'slavery' was not normally used. To mention just one example from Northern Queensland, the Aboriginal Protector Walter Roth reported in a letter written to the Home Secretary in 1898 that forced labour was

11.   See R. Evans, K. Saunders, K. Cronin, *Race Relations in Colonial Queensland: A History of Exclusion, Exploitation and Extermination* (St Lucia: University of Queensland Press, 2nd edn, 1988), p. 69, and the tangential references in Harris, *One Blood*, p. 31.

12.   Harris, *One Blood*, pp. 49, 657–58; W.M. Evans, 'From the Land of Canaan to the Land of Guinea: The Strange Odyssey of the "Sons of Ham"', *American Historical Review* 85 (1980), pp. 15–43; David M. Goldenberg, *The Curse of Ham: Race and Slavery in early Judaism, Christianity, and Islam* (Princeton: Princeton University Press, 2003).

referred to as 'shanghaiing' or 'press-ganging', and its history was 'one long record of brutal cruelty, bestiality and debauchery'.[13] Missionaries did not support such abuse, but the 'curse of Ham' tradition was too conveniently compatible with it.

Outside missionary circles, the major sources of racism came from the social and natural sciences of the day that served to reinforce popular prejudice and economic interest. Indigenous people were caught in an ideological pincer movement. A theory of cultural evolution and progress had long been circulating in modern Europe, and when the English sociologist Herbert Spencer coined the phrase 'survival of the fittest' in 1850, it was just the phrase he coined, not the idea. In the same year, the geologist Charles Lyell had confidently observed that 'few future events are more certain than the speedy extermination of the Indians of North America or the savages of New Holland'. The appearance of Darwin's *Origin of Species* in 1859 was a high profile scientific event, but it also served to consolidate diverse cultural themes from the previous century. And it provided an excellent means for Europeans to relieve themselves of their 'weight of charity' towards Indigenous peoples.[14]

Darwin caused a theological controversy, but in the wider context of cultural debates, popular ideas of social evolution could now be given a biological foundation. The idea that humans were descended from apes had the crucial qualification, both in scientific and in popular opinion, that black peoples were closer to apes than whites. The social Darwinist H.K. Rusden was able to write in the *Melbourne Review* of 1876:

> The survival of the fittest means that might—widely used—is right. And thus we invoke and remorselessly fulfill the inexorable law of natural selection when exterminating the inferior Australian.[15]

13. Quoted in Evans, Saunders, Cronin, *Race Relations in Colonial Queensland*, p. 105; R. and C. Berndt, *End of an Era: Aboriginal Labour in the Northern Territory* (Canberra: Australian Institute of Aboriginal Studies, 1987), based on research in the 1940s; Deborah Bird Rose, *Reports from a Wild Country: Ethics for Decolonisation* (Sydney: UNSW Press, 2004), pp. 66–72.

14. Marvin Harris, *The Rise of Anthropological Theory* (London: Routledge & Kegan Paul, 1968), pp. 97, 117; J.A. Barnes, 'Anthropology in Britain before and after Darwin', *Mankind* 5/9 (1960), pp. 37–74; Evans, Saunders, Cronin, *Race Relations in Colonial Queensland*, pp. 12–13.

15. Quoted in Evans, Saunders, Cronin, *Race Relations in Colonial Queensland*, pp. 81–82.

As the historian Robert Kenny has recently observed, the idea of natural selection provided the colonists with 'a new version of the right of conquest'.[16]

The Christian missions in nineteenth-century Australia often stated their intention to protect Indigenous people from the worst excesses of the settlers—especially murder and the abuse of Aboriginal women—but in many cases, the published opinions of the clergy differed little from the most extreme expressions of racism. The Aborigines were 'almost on the level with the brute', suggested John Harper from the Wesleyan Missionary Society. Also a Wesleyan, Joseph Orton asserted in 1836 that they were 'far below the brute creation'. The Presbyterian John Dove argued in a scientific journal: 'such is the depth of their degradation that they have reached the level of the beasts, every thought bearing upon the nature of rational beings has now been erased from their breasts'.[17] These ideas were endemic within white society, regardless of religious or anti-religious dispositions, but as we shall see below Christian opinion was deeply divided on Indigenous issues.

Savage Brutes and Canaanites in the Sixteenth Century

Notions of social evolution were given a new weight by the nineteenth-century sciences, but the association of Indigenous people with animals belongs also to a much earlier Christian tradition, for example, in justifications provided for the Spanish Conquistadors in South America. Representative of this tradition in the sixteenth century is the 'Treatise on the Just Causes of the War against the Indians' (1550), written by Juan Ginés de Sepúlveda:

> It is just and natural that prudent, wise, and humane people have dominion over those who do not have those qualities…(therefore) the Spaniards have a perfect right to rule over these *barbarians of the New World* and adjacent islands, who in prudence, intelligence, virtue, and humanity are as inferior to the Spaniards as *children* are to adults and *women* to men, having between them as great a difference as that between *savage and cruel peoples* and the most merciful peoples…and I would even say between monkeys and human beings.

In a series of binary contrasts, 'the Spaniard' is linked to the 'higher' qualities: intelligent, virtuous, adult, male, merciful, and human, while

---

16.   Robert Kenny, *The Lamb Enters the Dreaming: Nathanael Pepper and the Ruptured World* (Melbourne: Scribe, 2007), p. 295.

17.   Thomas Dove, 'Moral and Social Characteristics of the Aborigines of Tasmania', *Tasmanian Journal of the Natural Science* 1/4 (1842), pp. 247–54, 249. Harper, Orton and Dove quoted in Harris, *One Blood*, pp. 30–32.

the 'barbarian' is linked to the 'lower' qualities: stupid, libidinous, childish, female, cruel and animal.

That the higher order should rule over the lower order is a matter not of 'natural selection', as Darwinism would later have it, but of 'Natural Law' as derived from the most distinguished classical authorities, especially Aristotle, Augustine and Aquinas. The argument culminates with a blatant sanctification of force:

> What is natural and just is that the soul rules over the *body*, that reason presides over the *appetite*…therefore that *wild beasts* be subdued and subjected to the dominion of humanity. Therefore the man rules over the *woman*, the adult over the *child*, the father over his *sons and daughters*, that is to say, the most powerful and perfect over those who are *weakest and most imperfect*.[18]

Sepúlveda's philosophical argument from Natural Law was blended with Catholic theories of 'just war' and with biblical references designed to illustrate the unity of reason and revelation on the issue of colonization. The legitimacy of slavery was easily demonstrated from a number of biblical texts, the right of governments to punish sin was inferred from Romans 13, and a differential treatment of enemies in war was found in Deuteronomy 20—the Indigenous peoples being compared with idolatrous Canaanites who suffered under Joshua's conquest of the promised land.[19]

This reading of the Bible and Catholic tradition had its notable opponents, such as the Dominican Bartolomé de las Casas (1474–1564), whose defence of the native populations led him to oppose the Spanish colonial practice of the *encomienda* (from the Spanish *encomendar*, to entrust) which entailed the granting of Indigenous lands to Spanish overlords. A typical *encomienda* from 1514 decreed that its holder was entrusted with the Indigenous population 'to make use of them' in agrarian labour and to 'teach them about our holy Catholic faith', which in practice was a license for often violent exploitation.[20] Las Casas used Catholic tradition and biblical material in defence of the 'Indians', arguing for example that the Gospels emphasized a 'gentle spirit' rather than violence (Mt. 11.29-30), and he

18. Juan Ginés de Sepúlveda, *Tratado sobre las justas causas de la guerra contra los indios* (Mexico City: Fondo de Cultura Económica, 1979), pp. 85, 101, 153, quoted in Pablo Richard, 'Biblical Interpretation from the Perspective of Indigenous Cultures of Latin America (Mayas, Kunas and Quechuas)', in M.G. Brett (ed.), *Ethnicity and the Bible* (Leiden: Brill, 1996/2002), pp. 298-301.

19. See also T. Todorov, *The Conquest of America* (New York: Harper & Row, 1984), pp. 146-60.

20. Louis N. Rivera, *A Violent Evangelism: The Political and Religious Conquest of the Americas* (Louisville: Westminster/John Knox, 1992), pp. 114-18.

supported an alternative system called the *reducción*, in which Indigenous people could live in separated towns under missionary supervision. Towards the end of his life, he prophesied judgment on Spain for the corruption of its divine election.[21] 'They think', he wrote, 'that the victories they have over the innocent Indians whom they are assaulting are given them by God because their evil wars are just, as if they are rejoicing and giving praise and thanks to God for their tyrannies'.

Yet Las Casas could still see providence at work in the divine choice of Columbus as an 'apostle in these Indies'. 'Christopher', he wrote, 'a name one should know signifies *Christum ferens,* which means carrier or bringer of Christ'.[22] And indeed, Columbus had gone to great lengths to explain his own mission in his *Book of Prophecies* in 1501–1502, in terms derived particularly from Isaiah 41–66: the distant islands were waiting for their redemption, after which the 'wealth of nations' could be brought to Jerusalem—meaning that the king of Spain could conquer Jerusalem and rebuild the temple.[23]

This is the language and reasoning of a Catholic empire, and it is very different from the Puritan theology of seventeenth-century Massachusetts and Connecticut, where the allegory between Israel and New England evoked a different permutation of the logic of extermination for the prior inhabitants. The Protestant 'national allegory' was forged especially in the sixteenth century with both England and Holland each self-consciously made in the image of ancient Israel, with stories of liberation from Roman Catholic oppression standing in parallel with Israel's escape from Egyptian bondage. Both Queen Elizabeth and William of Orange were configured as 'Moses' in the nation-building myths, the covenant makers of England and The Netherlands.[24]

These grand Protestant allegories of a 'chosen nation' probably have little relevance for understanding the ideology of the Australian penal colonies, although the Dutch version may have had some significance amongst the early Boers in South Africa. Amongst the meager evidence from the

---

21.   Bartolomé de las Casas, *The Only Way to Draw All People to a Living Faith* (ed. Helen Rand; New York: Paulist, 1992), pp. 194–95.

22.   Las Casas, quoted in Rivera, *A Violent Evangelism*, pp. 58–59.

23.   D.C. West and A. Kling (eds.), *The Libro de las Profecías of Christopher Columbus* (Gainesville: University of Florida Press, 1991), pp. 68–71.

24.   See, e.g., W. Haller, *The Elect Nation: the Meaning and Relevance of Foxe's Book of Martyrs* (New York: Jonathan Cape, 1963); C. Cherry, *God's New Israel: Religious Interpretations of American Destiny* (Chapel Hill: University of North Carolina Press, rev. edn, 1998); W. Verboom, 'The Netherlands as the Second Israel', in E.A.J.G. Van der Borght *et al.* (eds.), *Faith and Ethnicity*, II (Zoetermeer: Meinema, 2002), pp. 93–108.

mid-nineteenth century, we find the missionary doctor David Livingstone recording with horror that some Afrikaners guilty of killing more than a hundred people in a 'bloody slave-hunt' in 1852 invoked Deut. 20.10–14 and the 'Divine Law of Joshua', providing themselves with biblical warrants for exterminating Indigenous people.[25] Such warrants, or pretexts, are not in themselves evidence for the developed covenantal allegory amongst the Boers that was later to come to expression especially in the Afrikaner nationalism of the 1880s, and more pervasively still in the 1930s.[26] In the South African context, the focus shifted during the nineteenth century to a policy calling for the separation of the races, and Joshua's extermination theology faded from view.

The Nineteenth Century and Humanitarian Concern

In Australian colonial history of the nineteenth century, one can find some analogies to the Spanish administrative practices of the *encomienda* and the *reducción*, although no direct theological influences can be discerned. Las Casas finds a kind of counterpart, for example, in the Baptist minister John Saunders who warned the readers of *The Colonist* in 1838 of divine displeasure at the shedding of Aboriginal blood:

> Let the Hawkesbury and Emu Plains tell their history, let Bathurst give her account, and the Hunter render her tale, not to mention the South… The spot of blood is upon us, the blood of the poor and defenceless, the blood of the men we wronged before we slew, and too, too often, a hundred times too often, innocent blood… We have, therefore, reason to dread the approach of the Lord when he cometh out of his place to punish the inhabitants of the earth for their iniquity: 'For the earth also shall disclose her blood, and shall no more cover her slain'.[27]

In 1845, the Catholic Bishop Polding expressed his view to a committee of the New South Wales Legislative Council that Aboriginal resistance

---

25. In I. Schapera (ed.), *David Livingstone: South African Papers 1849–1853* (Capetown: Van Riebeeck Society, 1974), pp. 84–85; cf. p. 20.

26. A. du Toit, 'Puritans in Africa? Afrikaner "Calvinism" and Kyperian Neo-Calvinism in Late Nineteenth-Century South Africa', *Comparative Studies in Society and History* 27 (1985), pp. 209–40. Livingstone claims to have found such a national allegory in 1849 complete with A.H. Potgieter (1792–1852) being seen as a second Moses—'notwithstanding his Satanic tricks' (Schapera, *David Livingstone*, pp. 20, 84).

27. Cited in Reynolds, *Law of the Land*, pp. 91–92, from *The Colonist* 17, 20 October, 1838. Saunders is quoting from Isa. 26.21.

must be attributed to the bad feeling and want of confidence
naturally caused by the mode in which possession has been taken of
their country—occupation by force, accompanied by murders, ill-
treatment, ravishment of their women, in a word, to the conviction
on their minds that the white man has come for his own advantage,
without any regard to their rights—Feeling this burning injustice
inflicted by the white man, it is not in the nature of things that
the black man should believe the white man better than himself,
or suppose the moral and religious laws, by which the white man
proposes the black man to be governed, to be better than those of
his own tribe.[28]

What has sometimes been insufficiently recognized is that the views of
people like Saunders and Polding echoed concerns that emanated from
the Colonial Office in London in the 1830s and 1840s. A group of powerful evangelical Anglicans in the British parliament, supported by some
influential Quakers, had tirelessly worked for the abolition of slavery in
the early nineteenth century, and especially after the *Emancipation Act*
of 1833, this group focused their humanitarian attention on Aboriginal
people in the colonies. In the understanding of these Parliamentarians,
the twin causes of Christianity and 'civilization' (almost inevitably linked
in this period) were being damaged by injustices done to Indigenous peoples in the name of the empire. Following in the footsteps of William
Wilberforce in the campaign against slavery, it was especially Thomas
Buxton, James Stephen and Lord Glenelg who concerned themselves
with the native peoples of Southern Africa, the Caribbean, Australia and
New Zealand.

Buxton's lobbying resulted, for example, in Lord Glenelg's famous
despatch to Governor D'Urban of the eastern Cape in December 1835
renouncing the annexation of Queen Adelaide Province on the grounds
that 'the original justice is on the side of the conquered, not the victori-
ous party'.[29] Expressing related concerns to the South Australian colonial
Commission in same month, Lord Glenelg stated:

Before His Majesty can be advised to transfer to his subjects the
Property in any part of the land of Australia, he must have at least
some reasonable assurance that he is not about to sanction any act
of injustice toward the Aboriginal natives of that part of the Globe.
In drawing the line of demarcation for the New Province...the

---

28.   Reynolds, *Law of the Land*, pp. 159–60, quoting from the *NSW Legislative Council
Votes and Proceedings*, 1845, p. 9.
29.   Quoted in Reynolds, *Law of the Land*, p. 98 from the *British Parliamentary Papers*
1836, 39, 279.

> Commissioners therefore must not proceed any further than those
> limits within which they can show, by some sufficient evidence,
> that the land is unoccupied and that no earlier and preferable title
> exists.[30]

It was this kind of thinking which lay behind the settlement of New Zealand, and the Treaty of Waitangi in 1840 was a natural consequence, but the *South Australian Constitution Act* of 1834 had already denied the possibility of native title by declaring that the land was 'waste and unoccupied'.

The ideology of *terra nullius* could thus be used to outwit the pious reformers at the centre of the empire, and the colonial administrators often simply denied that the Indigenous people 'occupied' the land in any relevant sense. Already in 1848, a Western Australian official was able to explain the tensions between the Colonial Office in London and the administrators in Australia:

> The wishes and intentions of the home government towards them
> [the Indigenous peoples] have been frequently frustrated, evaded,
> misrepresented and successfully counteracted, opposed, not openly
> in the face of positive instructions, but encountered by a dead weight
> of indisposition towards them by a covert opposition, a persevering
> system of obstruction, a pulling back of the wheels of Government
> which has proved sufficient to hinder any efforts that have been
> made to upraise the Aborigines.[31]

This point can also be illustrated by an example arising from Thomas Buxton's Select Committee inquiry into the treatment of 'Native Inhabitants of British Settlement', conducted during 1835–36. Following the report of this enquiry, the New South Wales parliament introduced legislation in 1839 allowing Aborigines to give evidence in court on an 'affirmation of truth' rather than an oath sworn on the Christian Bible. The legislation was soon overruled on the grounds that to allow 'heathens' to give evidence would be 'contrary to the principles of British Jurisprudence'.[32] Murder trials were dismissed when Aboriginal witnesses were thought incapable of understanding the nature of an oath. In Queensland, the status of Aboriginal testimony remained ambiguous until a Commission in 1874 identified such blatant miscarriages of justice that the Attorney General recommended Aboriginal witnesses should be allowed at least in cases against the notorious 'native police'. The matter was controversial, but the Queensland legislative assembly finally did pass a bill in 1876 allowing an 'affirmation of truth' to

30. Quoted in Reynolds, *Law of the Land*, p. 106.
31. Quoted in Reynolds, *Law of the Land*, pp. 158–59.
32. L. Skinner, 'Law and Justice for the Queensland Colony', *Royal Historical Society of Queensland Journal* 9/3 (1971–72), p. 100.

replace the Christian oath.[33] In short, the British parliamentary reformers of the 1830s were quite capable of understanding the role of the Bible in legal processes as a symbol of truth that transcends the conflicts of human interest, but in the hands of the colonial courts, the Bible often became merely an instrument for underwriting white power.

There is no doubt that Thomas Buxton's group were motivated by religious convictions, but it is important to recognize that in spite of their explicit evangelicalism and their links to the missionary societies, their language is often shaped by moral ideas which are not especially biblical. For example, following Buxton's Select Committee inquiry of 1835–36, he expressed the view that all native peoples have 'an *inalienable* right to their own soil', an idea which cannot be derived straightforwardly from the Bible.[34] Similarly, William Ellis, a representative from the London Missionary Society, put his view to the Select Committee that colonization should never have involved 'the expulsion or annihilation' of the people whose land is seized.

> It has been our custom to go to a country, and because we were stronger than the inhabitants, to take and retain possession of the country, to which we had no claim, but to which they had the most *inalienable* right, upon no other principle than that we had the power to do so. This is a principle that can never be acted upon without insult and offense to the Almighty, the common parent of the human family, and without exposing ourselves, sooner or later, to the most disastrous calamities and indelible disgrace.[35]

This argument clearly contradicts Sepúlveda's sanctification of force in the sixteenth century. What Ellis and Sepúlveda have in common is an underlying concept of natural law, but their applications of that concept are entirely different. Expressions of natural law have a long and complex history—in the modern period intertwined with theories of universal human rights—and it is this non-biblical tradition that produced the idea that rights could be 'inalienable'. While there are some important analogies between biblical laws and human rights, the confluence of these legal ideas in the nineteenth century is very different from what we find in Sepúlveda. The Conquistadors and the Puritans—because they could see themselves as

---

33.   R. Kidd, *The Way We Civilize: Aboriginal Affairs—The Untold Story* (St Lucia: University of Queensland Press, 1997), pp. 3, 26. On the 'native police', see Evans, Saunders and Cronin, *Race Relations in Colonial Queensland*, pp. 55–66.

34.   Buxton quoted in Reynolds, *Law of the Land*, p. 85. On the indirect relationship between the Bible and human rights, see especially Eckart Otto, 'Human Rights: The Influence of the Hebrew Bible', *Journal of Northwest Semitic Languages* 25 (1999), pp. 1–14.

35.   William Ellis, quoted in Reynolds, *Law of the Land*, p. 95 from the *British Parliamentary Papers* 1837, p. 510.

a 'new Israel'—were able at times to disregard the land rights of Indigenous people with warrants drawn from Deuteronomy and Joshua. It is precisely these problematic biblical texts that could help create the idea that *some* Indigenous people are not worthy of their land, or to put the point more generally, the Hebrew Bible provided arguments to suggest that some people groups do not hold their land by inalienable right.

In short, there is a considerable difference between the logics of imperialism produced in Catholic Spain of the sixteenth century and in the British empire of the nineteenth. 'Enlightened' Christian thinking in the nineteenth century was more likely to presume that Indigenous people have certain rights—regardless of their culture's moral or religious characteristics—and these rights need not be harmed by appropriate cultural contacts which may include peaceful negotiations and the payment of compensation for land. Under these conditions, it was held that the benefits of civilization and Christianity could flow freely.

This approach to colonization was articulated quite succinctly in 1830 by an American House of Representatives Committee on Indian Affairs, justifying the transformation of Indigenous rights 'of soil and sovereignty' into the creation of Indian reservations:

> The rigor of the rule of their exclusion from these rights (the rights of soil and sovereignty) has been mitigated, in practice, in conformity with the doctrines of those writers upon natural law, who, while they admit the superior rights of agriculturalists over the claims of savage tribes in the appropriation of wild lands, yet, upon the principle that the earth was intended to be a provision for all mankind, assign to them such portion as, when subdued by the arts of the husbandman, may be sufficient for their subsistence. To the operation of this rule of natural law may be traced all those small reservations to the Indian tribes within the limits of most of the old states.[36]

There were a great number of 'writers on natural law' at the time, but among the most influential was John Locke. His *Two Treatises of Government* (1690) was widely read in the eighteenth century, and it displaced the older models of political philosophy that had focussed much more attention on sanctions drawn directly from the Bible.[37] It was Locke's thought that was to have more influence in Australia than the learned theological debates of the sixteenth century. He also fabricated a significant theory of property which had direct bearing on the legal problems encountered in colonization.

---

36. A.H. Snow, *The Question of Aborigines* (Washington, DC: Government Printing Office, 1919), p. 76.

37. H. Graf Reventlow, *The Authority of the Bible and the Rise of the Modern World* (London: SCM Press, 1984).

Locke noted that God commanded humankind to 'subdue the earth', a biblical allusion to Gen. 1.28, a text with a long history of sanctioning the despoiling of nature.[38] But Locke goes far beyond the biblical text to infer that there was an original 'state of nature' when people were equal and property was held in common. The divine command of Gen. 1.28 is then blended with an agrarian ideology which could be applied potentially not just to Adam and Eve but to colonizers in the outer reaches of the British empire:

> Whatsoever, then, he removes out of the state that nature had pro-
> vided and left it in, he hath mixed his labour with, and joined to it
> something that is his own, and thereby makes it his property.[39]

It is a seemingly small extrapolation from this kind of argument to the notion of *terra nullius*, which could claim that no one actually possessed land until agrarian labour was added to the earth. A Sydney barrister expressed exactly this view in *The Colonist* in 1838, arguing that Aborigines 'had no right to the land' since 'it belonged to him who first cultivated it'.[40]

Interestingly, David Livingstone used another version of this argument *against* the colonizing Boers in South Africa, suggesting that because they were nomadic cattle farmers they were not superior to the Indigenous people they enslaved. Livingstone also invoked Gen. 1.28 as a 'divine charter':

> Such being the charter on which all primitive lands may be held,
> it seems plain that the man who subdues or cultivates a portion of
> the earth has a better title to it than he who only hunts over it. He
> bestows his labour upon it, and thus it is his property.[41]

The encroachments of the 'vagrant Boers', Livingstone argued,

> differ essentially from those of the Americans and other civilized
> communities inasmuch as they cultivate less of the soil than do
> the aborigines whom they expel. Indeed, it is not land they seek to
> appropriate so much as cattle and slaves.[42]

---

38.   Geoffrey Bolton, *Spoils and Spoilers: Australians make their Environment 1788–1980* (Sydney: Allen & Unwin, 2nd edn, 1992), p. 11; Anne Pattel-Gray, *The Great White Flood: Racism in Australia* (Atlanta: Scholars Press, 1998), p. 124; Peter Harrison, '"Fill the Earth and Subdue It": Biblical Warrants for Colonization in Seventeenth-Century England', *Journal of Religious History* 29/1 (2005), pp. 3–24.

39.   See Reynolds, *The Law of the Land*, pp. 23–29, citing the fourth edition of Locke, *Two Treatises of Government* (1713), p. 15.

40.   R. Windeyer in *The Colonist*, 27 October, 1838.

41.   In Schapera, *David Livingstone*, p. 76.

42.   In Schapera, *David Livingstone*, p. 77; cf. the references to 'vagrant Boers' on pp. 16, 18, 19.

But Livingstone was also able to see certain problems with the doctrine of cultivation, since if it were consistently applied, 'it would strip Earl Grey of his broad acres around Alnwick Castle' and other English landlords of their deerparks. Instead of recommending a revolution in England, he argued that there are certain 'ancestral rights' which imply that land can be held 'untilled', and 'we must admit that the claims of even savages must be held sacred. If we deprive them, without compensation, of any of the resources by which they subsist, we are guilty of robbery'.[43] Thus one could say, even on the grounds of this very English reasoning, that the Indigenous people of the colonies held their land by ancestral rights well known in the House of Lords.

The agrarian ideology of the nineteenth century was therefore susceptible of several different interpretations, as further comparisons with the American context can illustrate. The American Supreme Court made a number of famous decisions that could have provided an alternative model for the Australian colonies (and one which was more in line with what the London Colonial Office was demanding in the 1830s). In a series of cases between 1810 and 1835, Chief Justice John Marshall ruled that the Indian nations had legal rights to the soil based on prior possession, and that native title did not depend on any particular mode of land-use or settlement: 'their hunting grounds were as much their actual possession as the cleared fields of the whites'.[44] The American pattern at the time was characterized by negotiated treaties and compensation—although one critic asserted in 1885 that the government had failed to fulfill the obligations of a single one of them.[45]

Aboriginal reserves were also created in the Australian colonies in the second half of the nineteenth century, but in Australia the reserves were usually thought to be the product of white generosity, rather than the recognition of a prior right to land and water. In both countries, the frequent violence of frontier expansion gave way to a quieter cultural strangling on the reservations and missions. And in both, there were consistent patterns of exploiting Aboriginal labour, just as was the case in Latin America and South Africa.

Nineteenth-century missionaries, however, generally did not themselves receive great financial benefits from their work. Protestantism, in a more indirect sense, has been seen as one catalyst in the massive social changes wrought by capitalism (e.g., by converting the sin of usury into a positive

---

43. In Schapera, *David Livingstone*, pp. 76–77.
44. Quoted in Reynolds, *Law of the Land*, p. 46.
45. H.B. Whipple's preface to Helen Hunt Jackson, *A Century of Dishonour* (Cambridge: Cambridge University Press, 1885).

necessity and in providing a work ethic), but the relationships between missions and mercantile interests were complex, and at times conflicted. Missionaries in India did make the case that when the Hindus received the benefits of civilization, then this could only improve the British economy. William Ward of Serampore College wrote, for example, in 1820:

> But let Hindost'han receive that higher civilization she needs, that cultivation of which she is so capable; let European literature be transfused into all her language, then the ocean, from the ports of Britain to India, will be covered with our merchant vessels; and from the centre of India moral culture and science will be extended all over Asia, to the Burman empire and Siam, to China, with all her millions, to Persia, and even to Arabia.[46]

At the time when Ward advanced this argument, the East India Company was refusing to carry missionaries on British ships because they feared that religious meddling might undermine the mercantile interests, and it was only after a change to the Company's charter in 1833 that the happy intersection of business and mission was accepted as a realistic possibility.

It is clear, however, that the East India Company did not begin with the logic of Christopher Columbus; they did not provide a grand theological scheme to legitimate the expansion of their markets. Ward's prediction was based on the assumed superiority of European literature in general, of which he took the Bible to be a part—even though not a single line of it was first composed in the colonizing nations of Europe. Fifteen years after Ward's prediction, a colonial administrator who chaired the 'Committee of Public Instruction' in Bengal, T.B. Macaulay, produced a notorious 'Minute on Education' which argued that the study of English literature would produce 'a class of persons, Indian in blood and colour, but English in taste, in opinion, in morals and intellect'[47] (precisely the kind of assimilationism which Afrikaner nationalism characteristically rejected). Commentators in India were to see this as the most damaging form of colonialism. In his influential book *The Intimate Enemy: Loss and Recovery of Self under Colonialism*, Ashis Nandy argues that the East India Company 'had not actually intended to govern India but just to make money there, which of course they did with

---

46. William Ward, *A View of the History, Literature, and Mythology of the Hindus*, III (London: Black, Kingsbury, Parbury, & Allen, 1820), p. liii; see further J.S. Dharmaraj, *Colonialism and Christian Mission: Postcolonial Reflections* (Delhi: ISPCK, 1993), p. 53; R.S. Sugirtharajah, *Asian Biblical Hermeneutics and Postcolonialism* (Sheffield: Sheffield Academic Press, 1998), pp. 86–98.

47. Benedict Anderson, *Imagined Communities* (London: Verso, 2nd edn, 1991), pp. 90–91.

predictable ruthlessness'. But when key figures in the 1820s began 'to ascribe cultural meanings to the British domination, colonialism proper can be said to have begun'. This is the well-meaning project that 'colonizes minds in addition to bodies and it releases forces within the colonized societies to alter their cultural priorities once for all'.[48]

Ward and Macaulay have often been singled out for critique, but their views were not unusual. Even the leading intellectual John Ruskin became an elegant spokesperson for the manifest 'destiny' of English colonial rule. In his 1870 Slade Lectures in Oxford, Ruskin delivered a Romantic hymn to the pure England that he could perceive through the smog—the 'unholy clouds'—of her industrialized cities:

> And this is what she must do, or perish: she must found colonies as fast and as far as she is able…seizing every piece of fruitful waste ground she can set her foot, and there teaching these her colonists that their chief virtue is to be fidelity to their country, and that their first aim is to be to advance the power of England by land and sea: and that, though they live off a distant plot of ground, they are no more to consider themselves therefore disenfranchised from their native land, than the sailors of their fleets do…and England, in these her motionless navies (or, in the true and mightiest sense, motionless *churches*, ruled by pilots on the Galilean lake of all the world), is to 'expect every man to do his duty'… But that they may be able to do this, she must make her own majesty stainless; she must give them thoughts of their home of which they can be proud. The England who is to be mistress of half the earth…must guide the human arts, and gather the divine knowledge, of distant nations, transformed from savageness to manhood, and redeemed from despairing into peace.[49]

This was Ruskin's version of the civilizing mission. It was a secularized and Romantic one, rather than the fulfillment of biblical prophecy, as Columbus had it. Nor was its 'gathering of divine knowledge' compatible with William Carey's call to preach the gospel to 'all nations' in his seminal pamphlet *An Inquiry into the Obligations of Christians to use Means for the Conversion of the Heathen* (1792), taking his starting point from Matthew 28.19.[50] It was especially Carey's influence that led to the founding of the mission societies in London in the early nineteenth century. These were all very different logics

---

48. Ashis Nandy, *The Intimate Enemy: Loss and Recovery of Self under Colonialism* (Delhi: Oxford University Press, 1983), pp. xi, 6.

49. Quoted in E. Said, *Culture and Imperialism* (London: Chatto & Windus, 1993), pp. 123–25.

50. R.S. Sugirtharajah, *Postcolonial Reconfigurations* (London: SCM Press, 2003), pp. 17–21.

that were used to sanction imperialism, yet one would have to say that their impact on Indigenous people in the colonies were often disturbingly similar.

The Bible and Resistance to Colonialism

Such were the delusions of empire that T.B. Macaulay could write in 1836 that 'No Hindu who has received an English education ever remains sincerely attached to his religion'.[51] Mahatma Gandhi took a different view. European civilization, he suggested, was shot through with violence and materialism and therefore of little value to Hindus. He always insisted in debates with his Christian comrades that religious conversion was problematic, since it tore the fabric of social relations. But Jesus' 'Sermon on the Mount' in Matthew 5, he wrote, 'went straight to my heart'. It was this text that awakened him to the value of 'passive resistance', and it provoked a re-interpretation of non-violence within Hinduism.[52] Gandhi's hybrid mix of the Sermon on the Mount and Hindu spirituality shaped his vocation to lead a mass movement against British rule in India. (In a fascinating circulation of biblical influences, the Baptist minister Martin Luther King Jr was to be inspired by Gandhi's example to lead his own non-violent struggle against the American legacies of the 'curse of Ham'.)

These examples of the Bible as a shaper of resistance illustrate the fact that missionaries could not ultimately control the reception of scripture, especially once it was rendered in vernacular languages. There were notable converts, like Olaudah Equiano (1745–1797) who argued in orthodox Christian terms against slavery, and the Pequot Methodist William Apess (1798–1839) who defended the equality of Native Americans on biblical grounds.[53] The Bible was often used in ways that dismayed the proponents of orthodoxy. Ironically, the Indian convert Pandita Ramabai (1858–1922) stood firmly on a key Protestant principle when she emphasized in her debates with conservative Christians that her faith rested on the Bible itself, and not on church authorities.[54]

---

51.   Quoted in Anderson, *Imagined Communities*, p. 91.

52.   Quoted in M.M. Thomas, *The Acknowledged Christ of the Indian Renaissance* (London: SCM Press, 1969), pp. 198–209; see further, Nandy, *The Intimate Enemy*, pp. 51–57.

53.   Olaudah Equiano, *The Interesting Narrative and Other Writings* (London: Penguin, [1789] 1995); Barry O'Connell (ed.), *On our Own Ground: The Complete Works of William Apess, A Pequot* (Amherst: University of Massachusetts Press, 1992).

54.   A.B. Shah, *The Letters and Correspondence of Pandita Ramabai* (Bombay: Maharashtra State Board for Literature and Culture, 1977); Sugirtharajah, *The Bible and the Third World*, pp. 97–105.

Historians have described a diversity of social effects generated by the reception of the Bible in Africa, including slave rebellion in Guyana and the formation of national consciousness in Nigeria. For example, the vernacular Yoruba Bible in Western Nigeria provided a common written language that transcended the varieties of spoken dialects to help form a single people. In this case, the vernacular Bible provided a common language, even when Islamic Yoruba were in the majority—since Islam does not use a vernacular Koran in worship and is theologically opposed to the separation of Muslim nations.[55] The Bible has had a significant role to play, then, not only in the formation of early European Protestant nationalisms, but also in the nationalist struggles of the twentieth century.

In the 1920s, translation of the Sermon on the Mount into the Gikuyu language had started to foment social struggles in Kenya. Matthew 5.4— 'Blessed are the meek, for they shall inherit the earth'—became an argument that the *ahoreri* ('meek', the 'quiet' ones without land and livestock) would *gaya* the earth ('divide', 'inherit'). The legitimacy of the 'loudly' wealthy—the elders with land and livestock—was therefore put into question by biblical authority, and younger people were given a voice within a new religious framework.

This is just one example of how the vernacular translations of the Bible in Africa became a catalyst for social change. African churches became divided between those who stood for the status quo, and the more independently minded who read the Bible for themselves and drew their own conclusions. Amongst the Gikuyu there was the notable example of Bildad Kaggia, a Pentecostal trade union leader whose translations of the Bible helped to form the intellectual roots of the Mau Mau rebellion against the British. A focus of the rebellion was a condemnation of the wealthy (including Christians) for failing, on biblical standards, to share their wealth with the poor.[56]

In Aotearoa New Zealand, a Maori prophet named Te Kooti (d. 1893) had also appropriated the scriptural patterns in great detail in shaping resistance

55. Adrian Hastings, *The Construction of Nationhood: Ethnicity, Religion and Nationalism* (Cambridge: Cambridge University Press, 1997), pp. 150–58; Patrick Harries, 'The Roots of Ethnicity', *African Affairs* 87 (1988), pp. 25–52; Brian Stanley, *The Bible and the Flag: Protestant Missions and British Imperialism in the Nineteenth and Twentieth Centuries* (London: Apollos, 1990), pp. 86–87.

56. See Derek Peterson, 'The Rhetoric of the Word: Bible Translation and Mau Mau in Colonial Central Kenya', in B. Stanley (ed.), *Missions, Nationalism and the End of Empire* (Grand Rapids: Eerdmans, 2003), pp. 165–79; Bildad Kaggia, *Roots of Freedom 1921–1963: The Autobiography of Bildad Kaggia* (Nairobi, 1975); J. Lonsdale, 'Kikuyu Christianities', *Journal of Religion in Africa* 29/2 (1999), pp. 206–29.

to the British rule and in founding the Ringatu faith. This Indigenous religion identified with the Israelites in their bondage to Egypt (Britain), the struggle of the exodus and the covenants with the Israelite ancestors. Te Kooti saw the gospel of Christ as potentially connecting the world of the supreme Maori divinity Io to that of the whites, but the social realities of injustice stood in the way. Even the conquest texts from Joshua 23 were turned back on the British to insist that the colonial government would be expelled from the land. Te Kooti's identification with Moses was embodied in many textual links, including the tradition that no one knows where either leader is buried (Deut. 34.6).[57]

In the Ringatu faith, the Bible was seen as *tapu*, a Maori conception of the holy. Special 'houses for the covenant' were built alongside the meeting-houses, and family copies of the scriptures were kept in the roof space of homes or on a separate shelf. It was often deemed necessary to wash after touching the Bible 'to lift the *tapu*'.[58] These practices were signs of traditional culture accommodating a new sacred literature, analogous perhaps to the cases in South Africa, and amongst the Miskitu in Nicaragua, where the Bible was initially absorbed into practices of divination.[59]

One would need to remember, however, that the Bible had already shaped ethnic identities long before the invention of modern colonialism. For example, the Orthodox church of Ethiopia traces its ancestry back to Solomon's son Menelik and to an Israelite model of land, people, monarchy and religion.

Such 'Israelite' models have played a relatively insignificant role in Australian Indigenous history. Nevertheless, biblical faith presented a form of sovereignty higher than government and it thus provided a foothold for Indigenous resistance—evidenced for example in the historic campaigns of Christian Aboriginal leaders like William Cooper and Douglas Nicholls. The majority of Indigenous people indicated in the 2001 census that they were Christians, and it should not therefore be surprising that when the body of Eddie Mabo was moved to his island home in 1996 (his grave on the mainland had been daubed with swastikas) the combined island choir celebrated with a Moses hymn. 'Koiki led the people of Murray islands from the bondage of *terra nullius*', they said.

57.   Judith Binney, *Redemption Songs: A Life of the Nineteenth-Century Maori Leader Te Kooti Arikirangi Te Turuki* (Melbourne: Melbourne University Press, 1997), pp. 70–72, 115, 210, 219, 287, 502.

58.   Binney, *Redemption Songs*, p. 525.

59.   Jean and John Comaroff, *Of Revelation and Revolution: Christianity, Colonialism, and Consciousness in South Africa* (Chicago: University of Chicago Press, 1991), p. 229; Susan Hawley, 'Does God Speak Miskitu?', in M.G. Brett (ed.), *Ethnicity and the Bible* (Leiden: Brill, 1996), pp. 315–42.

Mama namarida Mose mara memegle e naose gair mara omaskir Israil le.
You sent Moses your servant to lead the people of Israel from Egypt.[60]

Legacies of Colonialism

In many ways, it is difficult to generalize about the missions in Australia, and certainly there are numerous instances of violence and abuse in mission history that need to be considered case by case. Profiteering was not one of their habitual sins. Nevertheless, there were systemic factors of colonialism that can be shown to have had devastating effects on Indigenous people, and the responsibility on these issues would have to be shared between government and the missions. Some of these systemic factors can be attributed to ethnocentric misunderstandings widely shared amongst Europeans, or religious prejudices, and some are more related to failures of social imagination characteristic of the British class system.

For example, the legally sanctioned removal of 'problem' individuals was a practice common to both Australian and British governments in the mid-nineteenth century. Social commentators of the time were able to decry the vagrants or 'nomads' of British society who could be distinguished from 'civilized man' by a lack of 'regular labour' and by a 'looseness of his notions as to property'[61] (David Livingstone's attack on 'vagrant Boers' in South Africa is part of this genealogy of ideas). The British state had powers to remove destitute children, along with those who were 'vicious or in moral danger', and reform schools were created in response to these social problems in industrialized cities. Children could be apprenticed out from the age of ten—lest they became dependant on charity—and their wages were controlled by the state until they were twenty-one. The majority of the convicts transported to Australia also came from the lower classes, and one of the early chaplains to the colony in New South Wales, Samuel Marsden, was able to observe:

> The number of Catholic convicts is very great…and these in general composed the lowest class of the Irish nation: who are the most

60. Merrill Findley, *The Age*, June 1, 1996. On William Cooper and Douglas Nicholls, see especially Bain Attwood and Andrew Markus, *Thinking Black: William Cooper and the Australian Aborigines' League* (Canberra: Aboriginal Studies Press, 2004), p. 5, and the detailed discussion in Bain Attwood, *Rights for Aborigines* (Sydney: Allen & Unwin, 2003); cf. Lyndsay Head, 'The Pursuit of Identity in Maori Society; in A. Sharp and P. McHugh (eds), *History, Power and Loss* (Wellington: Bridget Williams, 2001), pp.97–121.

61. Kidd, *The Way We Civilize*, pp. 21–23, citing G. Pearson, *The Deviant Imagination* (London: Macmillan, 1975), p. 153.

wild, ignorant and savage race that were ever favoured with the
lights of civilization.[62]

The construction of civilization, through these Anglican eyes, therefore
located poor Irish Catholics on the border of what is acceptable. The
Indigenous 'nomads' of the colonies apparently shared with vagrant
Catholics inferior notions of labour and property.

In Australia, the criteria for lack of civilization were similar to those in
Britain, but here the distinction was rendered even clearer by a lack of clothing. Missionary progress could be measured not just by conversions but by
clothing and by 'productive' labour. Some clergy insisted that the graces
of Christianity could only be built on the prior foundations of civilization,
while others argued that the faith itself could engender the required changes.
Lutheran missionary Christopher Eipper insisted, for example, 'The gospel it
was that changed the lazy Hottentot into an industrious subject: the gospel
it will be that works a change in the habits of the individual Australian'.[63]
Missionaries were therefore determined not only to protect Aboriginals from
exploitation in the wider society, and to inculcate the Christian faith, but also
to engender the prefabricated patterns of 'civilized behaviour'.

Following the logic of British reform and industrial schools, the
Queensland *Industrial and Reformatories Schools* Act of 1865 authorized the
removal of any vagrant child, any child living with thieves, drunkards or
prostitutes, and any *Aboriginal* child—apparently all were deviant persons
in their own way. Under the control of the state, such children could be
sent for domestic service or farming work. The 1897 *Aboriginal Protection*
act carried forward the purposes of the 1865 'reform school' legislation by
clarifying the status of *all* Aboriginal people as wards of the state (a full
century would have to pass before they were declared citizens of Australia).
Only 'half-castes' over the age of sixteen, not living with an Indigenous
group, escaped legal definition as 'Aboriginal'.[64] Living directly under police
authority, Indigenous people could be moved between the missions, or
sent out to work just as the earlier *Industrial and Reformatories Schools* Act
had decreed, and wages for all Aboriginal people were a matter of discre-
tion—usually paid in the form of clothing and food. It was not until 1914
in Queensland that minimum wages were determined for Aborigines, but
these were controlled by the state and a large portion withheld in government trust funds. The recovery of lost Aboriginal wages in Queensland and
elsewhere is still the subject of legal dispute.

62. Quoted in Harris, *One Blood*, p. 79.
63. Harris, *One Blood*, pp. 79–82, 528–33.
64. Kidd, *The Way We Civilize*, pp. 18–20, 47–48.

From 1914, the Chief Protector of Aborigines in Queensland was John Bleakley, a committed Anglican. In his reflections on nearly three decades in this role, he argued that not only did the missions 'protect the child races from the unscrupulous white, but they help to preserve the purity of the white race'. The Aborigines were like children who first had to be 'socialized' before they could be 'Christianized': 'they must first be made good citizens and taught the sound doctrine of self-respect and self-reliance'[65]—this from the man who presided over the system of withholding wages on the grounds that Indigenous people could not really be trusted with their own money. There is an uncanny consistency between what Bleakley wrote in 1961 and what John Eliot, a Puritan missionary in Massachusetts, tells us about his response in 1650 to a group of Indian people who expressed interest in baptism: 'I declared unto them how necessary it was that they should first be Civilized, by being brought from their scattered and wild form of life, unto civil Cohabitation and Government'.[66]

An ironic feature of Bleakley's argument is that self-respect and self-reliance are indeed virtues that Indigenous Christians affirm, even though the systematic degrading of Aboriginal culture in many of the mission administrations undermined exactly these qualities. Reflecting on the history of missions amongst Native Americans, George Tinker (an Osage/Cherokee theologian) argues that the overall effect of most of the missions was cultural genocide—more subtle than extermination, but no less devastating. In spite of good intentions, 'the missionary-mandated rejection of their culture and its values and structures of existence necessarily resulted in the denial of self and the inculcation of self-hatred'. Those who did convert remained 'second class' church members. 'Indian people today still suffer a loss of self-esteem and a general level of self-deprecation that derive from the forced alienation of Indian people from their history, their culture, and their land'.[67]

In a number of Australian Aboriginal communities, a pattern of respecting both traditional culture and Christian faith has developed. At one notable meeting on Elcho Island (in the Northern Territory) in 1992, an Aboriginal minister from the Uniting Church addressed some visiting white missionaries: 'In the old days, we followed you. We kept our heads down because we were ashamed. Now we walk with our heads up and we look at you in the

65. J.W. Bleakley, *The Aborigines of Australia* (Brisbane: Jacaranda Press, 1961), p. 124.
66. Quoted in George E. Tinker, *Missionary Conquest: The Gospel and Native American Genocide* (Minneapolis: Fortress Press, 1993), p. 36.
67. Tinker, *Missionary Conquest*, pp. 40–41.

eye and say, "We can be brothers and sisters together"'.[68] When Djiniyini
Gondarra made this speech, he was speaking perhaps more from faith than
from experience, and yet, this breath-taking generosity of spirit can often be
encountered amongst Indigenous Christians.

One of the leaders of the church on Elcho Island at the time was David
Burrumarra, a traditional elder of the Warramiri clan, a land rights advocate,
and an informant for generations of anthropologists in Northern Australia.
An incident in the 1940s illustrates the tensions in his lived experience:
when a whirlwind destroyed his house but left other houses standing, clan
members said that this was because he had been neglecting the Warramiri
ceremonies, while the missionaries suggested it was because he was straying
from God.[69] Burrumarra summarized his own perspective on these tensions
with typical brevity:

> I believe in both ways, the traditional and the Christian life, but we
> have so many questions. That's why we talk and discuss meanings.
> We search for the purpose of life in our history and in the land itself.
> And now we have the Bible as well.

'Do the ceremony properly', he advised the younger generation, 'for your
homeland and for yourself. Understand the land and everything in it so
you can manage it properly'. In his view, these are 'the real human rights'.[70]
Burrumarra was the custodian of a great number of traditions, which he said
he handed on carefully, lest people become 'drunk' with an idea. He once
commented that he would like to tell more stories, 'but how can I, they are
my backbone'.[71]

Burrumarra's philosophy of education, and his understanding of
Christianity, contain significant clues for the shaping of postcolonial spirituality. Aboriginal Christianity offers both a sense of inter-ethnic connected-
ness *and* an acknowledgement of cultural differences that do not need to
be shared in every respect. Australian Aboriginal traditions allow for the
possibility of many 'chosen peoples' and 'promised lands', each with mutually
respected jurisdictions. In this kind of worldview, the identity and spirit of a
people is so nourished by their land that the conquest of another country

---

68.   Djiniyini Gondarra, quoted in Ian McIntosh, *The Whale and the Cross:
Conversations with David Burrumarra* (Darwin: Historical Society of the Northern
Territory, 1994), p. 112.

69.   R.M. Berndt, *An Adjustment Movement in Arnhem Land* (Paris: Mouton, 1962),
p. 34.

70.   McIntosh, *The Whale and the Cross*, pp. 77–78; cf. Deborah Bird Rose, *Reports
from a Wild Country*, pp. 179–92.

71.   McIntosh, *The Whale and the Cross*, pp. 70, 72.

does not make sense. This model does not suggest a 'vacuous cultural relativism that decrees all cultures to be equally valid', as the anthropologist David Turner has put it, but it does at least provide an alternative to those European nationalisms that could not conceive of a land as sacred 'unless it could put forward a unique claim in the global economy of salvation'.[72] Thus, in the last chapter of this book, we will examine the character of Christian spirituality if it were to be shaped more by David Burrumarra than by Christopher Columbus or John Ruskin. This theological task is relevant not just to those who are developing Indigenous theology but also to those who still imagine that their own construction of the gospel applies globally.[73]

Conclusion

In the history of colonization, it is clear that generations of Europeans became intoxicated with their ideas of racial superiority and civilization, and the Bible was caught up in the destructive consequences. Biblical texts were often used as colonial instruments of power, exploited with pre-emptive and self-interested strategies of reading. But as we shall see, most biblical texts were produced by authors who were themselves subject to the shifting tides of ancient empires. Mindful of the cultural dynamics that shaped the biblical materials, this book sets out to provide fresh interpretations of key texts and themes thrown up by the history of colonization, in the hope that the decolonization of God might still be possible.

72. Eric Hobsbawm, *Nations and Nationalism since 1780* (Cambridge: Cambridge University Press, 1990), p. 49, here discussing Russian nationalism. See David Turner, *Life before Genesis: A Conclusion* (New York: Peter Land, 2 edn, 1987), p. ii; cf. Eve Mangwa D. Fesl, 'Religion and Ethnic Identity: A Koori View', in A.W. Ata (ed.), *Religion and Ethnicity: An Australian Study* (Melbourne: Spectrum, 1989), p. 9.

73. See the discussion in Stephen B. Chapman, 'Imperial Exegesis: When Caesar Interprets Scripture', in W. Avram (ed.), *Anxious about Empire: Theological Essays on the New Global Realities* (Grand Rapids: Brazos, 2004), pp. 91–102.

2

ALIENATING EARTH AND THE CURSE OF EMPIRES

> Therefore the land mourns, and every one who dwells therein shall
> languish, with the beasts of the field, and the birds of the heavens,
> and indeed the fish of the sea shall be taken away.
>
> *Hosea 4.3*

As we have seen, one of the most significant biblical texts in the development of colonialism was Gen. 1.28, a single verse within the Bible's
complex theologies of creation. The divine command in this verse to 'subdue the earth' was frequently cited from the seventeenth century onwards
both as a reason for imperial expansions and as a warrant for linking the
cultivation of land to property rights.[1] Agrarian ideologies developed in
various permutations, and the most virulent strain in Australia shaped
the legal fiction of *terra nullius*, one of the many permutations of 'empty
land' ideology. In this chapter, we will re-examine the literary context of
Gen. 1.28 in order to show that this text provides no warrant at all for
colonialism; it is more likely that the *reverse* is true. Taken as a whole, the
literature of Genesis 1–11 undermines all imperial intentions. Moreover,
the 'curse of Ham' episode in Genesis 9—notoriously a part of the colonialist history of missions—is similarly best understood in terms of this
anti-imperial interpretation.

Subdue the Earth?

The broader context of Genesis 1–11 provides a mix of traditions that bring
together stories of creation, crimes, consequences, and re-adjustments—all
in the 'primordial time' before ordinary life conditions begin. Primordial
time (as in the Dreaming of Aboriginal Australians[2]) is not just ordinary,

---

1. See especially Peter Harrison, '"Fill the Earth and Subdue It": Biblical Warrants
for Colonization in Seventeenth Century England', *Journal of Religious History* 29/1
(2005), pp. 3–24.

2. See Deborah Bird Rose, 'Consciousness and Responsibility in an Australian
Aboriginal Religion', in W.H. Edwards (ed.), *Traditional Aboriginal Society* (Melbourne:
Macmillan, 2nd edn, 1998), pp. 239–51.

historical time, since it bears directly on the shape of current experience. The narratives of Genesis 1–11 do not simply string together episodes that may be of antiquarian interest; they configure the human and non-human condition. And these chapters need to be read *as narratives*. It would be a mistake to imagine that Genesis 1 contains all we need to know about the divine intentions for creation, since that would neglect the unfolding of the story which reveals divine regret at the increasing levels of violence within the created order.

The statement about divine intentions in Gen. 1.28 suggests that the first humans should 'be fruitful and multiply, fill the earth and subdue it'.

> And God said, 'Let us make humankind in our image,
>   according to our similitude,
> and let them rule over the fish of the sea and the birds
>   of the heavens, over the
> livestock, over all the earth, and over all the creatures
>   that move on the earth'.

> So God created the human in his image,
> in the image of God he created him,
> male and female he created them.

> And God blessed them and said to them,
> 'Be fruitful and increase in number, fill the earth and subdue it,
> rule over the fish of the sea and the birds of the heavens
> and over every living creature that moves on the earth' (1.26–28).

In the immediate context, humans and animals were to be vegetarian (1.29–30), and this expectation necessarily qualifies the idea of 'subduing the earth' in v. 28. But later when the vegetarian ideal is relinquished— after the flood story—the divine imperative is truncated in God's speech to Noah: 'be fruitful and multiply and fill the earth' (9.1). The licence to 'subdue' the earth is not reiterated, and this is just one of the many nuances that needs to be considered in any understanding of what 'subduing the earth' might mean its wider narrative context.[3] At the very least, this phrase needs to be read alongside the other expressions of the divine perspective in Genesis 1–11.

Moreover, by the end of the Tower of Babel story in ch. 11, the earth is already 'filled', at least in the sense that ethnic groups have covered the 'whole earth'. No more human expansion would appear to be necessary. In the original state of things, 'the whole earth had one language' (11.1), but after the dispersal of humanity, the narrator explains that the tower

---

3.   See Anne Gardner, 'Ecojustice: A Study of Genesis 6.11–13', in Habel and Wurst, *The Earth Story in Genesis*, pp. 117–29.

was given the name Babel (playing on the Hebrew word *balal*, 'to confuse') because God '*confused* the language of the whole earth; and from there Yahweh scattered them abroad over the face of the whole earth' (11.9). The divine intervention in this narrative re-affirms the first vocation to fill the earth,[4] leaving the peoples simply with the task of procreating. So when the procreation formula appears again after this point in Genesis (as it does in 28.3, 35.11, and 48.4), it is shortened to 'be fruitful and multiply'; both 'filling the earth' and 'subduing it' are missing, presumably because they are no longer necessary.

So any colonialist warrant to 'subdue' the earth stands on an insecure footing in the biblical narrative, especially if this warrant is taken to mean that one privileged civilization should expand itself over the face of the earth. There is no suggestion in the primordial time of Genesis 1–11 that a particular culture can claim superiority. On the contrary, the whole point of the Tower of Babel story is that this attempt to grasp the cultural high ground, with a tower reaching 'up to the heavens' (11.4), is delusory and against God's intentions. No culture is represented as having divine favour, and when the people are dispersed they are shaped into a diversity of languages and cultures. Only Noah emerges as a person of complete integrity (6.9), and at the beginning of the flood narrative, it is said that 'all flesh' has corrupted itself with violence (6.12).

The new divine expectations established after the flood reflect the developments that have taken place within primordial time: when asked to be vegetarians at the beginning of the story, the humans lapsed into violence. Humans may now eat animals, but only on condition that their blood is drained (9.3–6)—probably as a reminder that this was not the original ideal.[5] When the procreation formula is repeated at this point in the narrative, the humans are commanded by God to be 'fruitful' and 'multiply on the earth' (9.7), but again, subjugation is not mentioned. Animals were also called on to be fruitful and multiply in Gen. 1.22 and 24. Now that the shedding of blood permitted, it is only under conditions of respectful restraint.

Humans and animals, it should be noted, share the same blood that gives 'life' (9.4). At other points, life is symbolized not by blood but by 'spirit' (*ruach* in 6.17 and 7.15). Psalm 104.29–30 also speaks of spirit as a life force given by Yahweh to the whole created order:

---

4.   Umberto Cassuto, *Commentary on the Book of Genesis. I. From Adam to Noah, Genesis 1–6.8* (Jerusalem: Magnes, [1944] 1961), p. 226; cf. Bernhard Anderson, *From Creation to New Creation* (Minneapolis: Fortress Press, 1994), pp. 173–78.

5.   Cassuto, *Genesis*, pp. 58–59.

When you hide your face, they are troubled;
when you take away their *breath* (*ruach*),
   they die and return to their dust.
When you send out your *spirit* (*ruach*), they are created;
and you renew the *face of the land* (*peney adamah*).

In regards to their life/blood/spirit, there is no sharp distinction between the species (ironically a perspective that accords more with the cultural assumptions of Indigenous Australians than with their colonizers). According to 9.3–6, all living creatures with blood flowing in their veins are to be held accountable for life, and God goes on to establish a covenant with 'every living creature', 'all flesh', in 9.8–17.

It is not that there are two covenants here—one perhaps with the species who is to 'subdue the earth', and another covenant with all the rest.[6] There is just *one*, summarized in 9.13 as a covenant with 'the earth'. This naturally covers the species *made* from the earth, both animals (2.19; cf. 1.24) and humans (2.7), and we may infer that they all belong to the same lineage system as the 'generations of the earth' (2.4). The sign of this first covenant in the Bible is divine restraint: the 'bow' in the clouds ('rainbow' in English translations) signifies a weapon of destruction turned *away* from the earth. The scope of the promise includes all living things, not just humankind, and one might infer that a species made in the image of God (1.26–28) should also exercise its responsibility in a reluctance to use violence. In short, this symbol of the rainbow stands against a violent subjection of the earth.

The principle of accountability for bloodshed is already stated in the earlier chapters of Genesis. In the first story of murder, for example, Cain kills his brother Abel and then is confronted by God:

> And Yahweh said, 'What have you done? The voice of your brother's blood is crying out to me from the land. And now you are cursed from the land, which has opened its mouth to receive your brother's blood from your hand. When you work the land, it will no longer yield to you its strength' (4.10–12).

This is a remarkable divine speech if we take it 'literally'. The land responds on behalf of it own kin: in 2.7 it was said that the human (*adam*) is made from the land (*adamah*), and here in 4.10 the land therefore cries out for its murdered child. The land will no longer yield, or be subdued (once again, the perspective of the text accords well with Indigenous perspectives that link 'kin and country' into a single kinship system). Cain will

---

6.   John Olley, 'Mixed Blessings for Animals', in Habel and Wurst, *The Earth Story in Genesis*, pp. 130, 136; cf. Wali Fejo, 'The Voice of the Earth: An Indigenous Reading of Genesis 9', *The Earth Story in Genesis*, pp. 140–46.

be driven away from 'the face of the land' (*peney ha-adamah*, 4.14), which seems to mean that he has to turn from the cultivator's lifestyle, and as a consequence, he or his son Enoch founds the first city (4.17). He cannot 'face' the land, because of the crime he has committed against the 'earth community' and its kinsman Abel.

Cain becomes a man of the city in 4.17 perhaps because urban culture provided an escape from the 'face' of the land. The builders of the Tower of Babel exhibit a very similar logic. They say to themselves, 'Let us build ourselves a city, and a tower with its head in the heavens, and let us make a name for ourselves; otherwise we shall be scattered upon the face of the whole earth' (11.4). The verbal parallel between the two stories is suggestive.[7]

Cain's speech

'you have driven me out this day from
upon the face of the land
al peney ha adamah (4.14)

The tower builders' speech

'otherwise we shall be scattered
upon the face of the whole earth
al peney kol ha arets (11.4)

In both cases, the outcome is a resolve to take up urban life.

Cain is presented not only as the founder of the first city, but his descendants are also associated with the beginning of urban crafts in 4.21–22, and in Lamech's case, with the escalation of violence (4.23–24). These comparisons between Cain's story and the Tower of Babel illustrate how the primordial stories of Genesis 1–11 often throw a negative light on urban 'civilization'. A key question arises: who can face the earth with integrity and listen to its voice? As we shall see, Noah can, but there are very few others.

Ironically, Cain's original vocation as a 'servant of the land' (4.2) corresponds to the divine expectations stated in the narratives of Genesis 2–3. Gen. 2.4–5 raises the needs of the land before those of the human: 'there was no human to work the land'. The Hebrew word for 'work' here (*'abad*) is otherwise most commonly translated as 'serve', in the sense of 'work for'. A more pointed translation would therefore be: 'there was no human to *serve* the land'. The same vocabulary is used in 2.15: 'And Yahweh God took the human and put him in the Garden of Eden to *serve* it and to *take care* of it', ironically reversing the human vocation to *rule* and *subdue* the earth

---

7. See Günter Wittenberg, 'Alienation and "Emancipation" from the Earth', in Habel and Wurst, *The Earth Story in Genesis*, pp. 110–12.

in Gen. 1.28. After the expulsion from Eden, this vocation is repeated in regards to the land outside the Garden: 'Therefore Yahweh God sent him [the human] out from the Garden of Eden to serve the land from which he was taken' (3.23). In initially becoming a cultivator in 4.3, Cain was apparently therefore doing nothing other than was divinely expected.

Yet a significant problem arises in ch. 4 if we were to assume that cultivation is God's preferred form of cultural life. Cain brings an offering to Yahweh from his field, while his brother offers choice animals from his flock. Abel's work as a shepherd is not divinely mandated in the previous narrative, but God nevertheless accepts Abel's offering and not Cain's. The reasons for the divine choice here are unclear, but at least we can be sure that there is no attempt in the narrative to elevate cultivation of the land as a culturally superior form of life. In other words, the colonialist doctrine that links cultivation to a divine mandate to 'subdue the land' has failed to appreciate (assuming that there were actually attempts to do so) the complexity of the Genesis creation narratives.

The human vocation to 'rule' and 'subdue' the earth in Genesis 1 is juxtaposed with so many qualifications, and alternative formulations, that one needs to examine carefully why that particular formulation is in the text at all. There is good reason to think that the use of the verb 'rule' (*radah*) alludes to the royal ideologies spread throughout the neighbouring cultures of the day, and certainly, the phrase 'image of God' was commonly associated with pharaohs and kings in the literature of ancient Egypt and Mesopotamia.[8] Although there is a passing allusion to the 'image of God' in Gen. 5.1, the idea plays no role elsewhere in the Hebrew Bible. Indeed, in the hymn to leviathan in Job 41, it is specifically said that the great beast of the sea cannot be subdued (v. 9) and that 'he is king over all the children of pride' (v. 34). In short, the book of Job contests the idea that humankind can ever be fully successful in being king over all the earth, and surely it was not just the readers of Job who would have wondered how a mere human could subdue the sea monsters mentioned in Gen. 1.21.

When humanity as a whole is exhorted to rule over the other living creatures, this can be read as a polemical undermining of a status that is otherwise associated with kings and empires. Royal ideology often claimed that the fertility of the earth depended upon the stability and order brought by a king. Psalm 72, for example, interweaves the expectation that the ideal king is one who defends the weak and afflicted (vv. 2, 4, 12–14) with the claim that this rule is characterized by prosperity and fertility (vv. 3, 6–7, 16–17).

8.   Phyllis Bird, *Missing Persons and Mistaken Identities: Women and Gender in Ancient Israel* (Minneapolis: Fortress Press, 1997), pp. 134–38.

If, however, the health of the created order does not depend upon kings, but upon responsibilities given to all of humanity, then the democratization of human 'rule' in Gen. 1.27–28 can be seen as polemical and anti-monarchic. Indeed, there is an anti-monarchic tone to the whole of Genesis, which accumulates as the narrative unfolds.[9]

There is nevertheless a harsh tone to the verb 'subdue' in Gen. 1.28, which may not be reduced solely to an anti-monarchic polemic. The strength of this term may also reflect fears about the wild animals that presented serious threats to human well-being (threats which would perhaps have remained unfounded had animals remained vegetarian as 1.29–30 suggests). Thus, the representation of even the utopian beginning of Genesis 1 may be marked by a significant tension that betrays the realities of daily experience in the ancient world.

Apart from Noah's apparent equanimity in the face of wild animals (7.14), the literature of ancient Israel provides evidence that they were feared. The theme is taken to almost comical lengths in Amos 5.19 where a day of judgment is compared to serial encounters with the face of death:

> It will be as if someone fled from a lion and met a bear,
> entered the house and rested his hand on the wall
> only to have a serpent bite him.

Conversely, prophetic announcements of hope often entail the utopian removal of such threats, such as in Isa. 65.25 where the lion finally turns to eating straw and the serpent to eating dust (cf. Gen. 3.14).

The prophecies of Hosea are particularly relevant since that book uses strikingly similar vocabulary to Gen. 1.27–28 when it suggests that Israelite violence and faithlessness has brought death to 'the beasts of the field, the birds of the heavens, and the fish of the sea' and therefore 'the land mourns' (Hos. 4.3; cf. Jer. 4.23–28). The point of this prophetic text is that the wholesale destruction of other species is an image of horror, not a rightful 'subduing', and as a consequence the earth mourns for her kin.

In Hos. 2.18, God promises the security of a new covenant: 'I will make for them a covenant on that day with the beasts of the field, the birds of the heavens, and the creatures that move on the land'. In other words, a holistic vision of human restoration entails both the end of war—also mentioned in Hos. 2.18—and the removal of threats from the natural world.[10]

---

9.   See Mark G. Brett, *Genesis: Procreation and the Politics of Identity* (London: Routledge, 2000).

10.   The vision of a peacefully interconnected created order is not peculiar to Hosea; it is a characteristic feature of prophetic hope in the Hebrew Bible. See Donald Gowan, *Eschatology in the Old Testament* (Edinburgh: T. & T. Clark, 1986), pp. 97–120.

In speaking of the need to 'subdue' the earth, the first creation story perhaps reflects a tension between the primal utopia and a human fear of some other species. Yet as we have seen, the divine license to 'subdue the earth' is retracted already in primordial time, and the prophets later confirm that the restoration of a peaceable created order is not a task that humans can handle by themselves. Only God can restore such a comprehensive covenant. Any implication that humans can subdue the earth by means of their own power would appear, from Hosea's perspective, as an arrogant fantasy.

'Children of Ham' as Empire Builders

If the initial divine command to 'subdue the earth' has been misused in the history of colonialism, this is even more true of the narratives concerned with the 'children of Ham'. After Cain's descendents retreat into urban life, we next hear of a 'man of the land (*adamah*)' in Gen. 9.20, when Noah plants a vineyard after the flood. Noah's character is in some senses the inverse of Cain's, and the fresh relationship with the land is foreshadowed in Noah's birth speech: 'He will give us consolation in the labour and toil (*'itsabon*) of our hands from the land which Yahweh cursed' (5.29). This speech refers back to the consequences of eating the forbidden fruit in the Garden of Eden in 3.17: 'the land is cursed because of you; through toil (*'itstsabon*) you will eat of it'. After the original expulsion from Eden, as we have seen, Cain's actions increase his alienation from the land. Noah's vineyard marks a re-connection with the land which is thematically the reversal of Cain's alienation from it.[11] The ark builder has cared for every species of animal, and he lays claim to being a keeper of the soil as well. The righteous Noah is the ecological ideal.

Yet even in the celebration of Noah's vineyard, new problems arise. Noah becomes drunk on some of his wine and lies naked in his tent. 'Ham, the father of Canaan' sees his father's nakedness, and informs his two brothers, Shem and Japheth (9.22). The logic of the story is obscure, but according the Hebrew text Shem and Japheth take elaborate steps not to look on their father's nakedness, and when Noah wakes he pronounces a curse not on Ham but on Canaan. Canaan will become a slave 'to his brothers', says Noah (v. 25). The logic is unclear not just because the nature of the crime is not spelled out, but because Noah's curse presumes that Canaan is the brother of Shem and Japheth, rather than Ham. Many scholars argue that the confusion between Ham and Canaan must be the result of editorial

---

11.   See Frank Spina, 'The "Ground" for Cain's Rejection', *Zeitschrift für die alttestamentliche Wissenschaft* 104 (1992), pp. 319–32.

changes designed to link the curse on Canaan with the 'sons of Ham'. Thus, it may be that v. 22 originally read 'Canaan saw his father's nakedness and told his two brothers outside' but the verse has been supplemented to read '*Ham, the father of* Canaan, saw his father's nakedness…' This is speculation, but it resolves the problem of why the original curse was directed at Canaan. Such a solution does not, however, resolve the question of why all the descendants of Ham should be implicated in the curse.

At this point in primordial time, of course, the characters are not just individuals but ancestors who represent whole people groups. The relationship between acts and consequences is different from what we find in ordinary history. The question of whether guilt can be passed across generations receives a variety of answers in biblical theology (Ezekiel 18 asserts, for example, that it cannot be transferred), but from the editors' point of view in Genesis 9 the consequences of Ham's sin fall apparently on his son, Canaan, yet everyone in Ham's lineage is somehow also drawn into the 'Hamitic' sphere of guilt.

According to 10.6–20 the descendants of Ham encompass no ordinary lineage, since it includes people spread from North Africa to Mesopotamia, with a range of ethnic backgrounds and languages. This reference to a multiplicity of languages is repeated for each group of descendants from Japheth (10.5), Ham (10.20) and Shem (10.31), in spite of the fact that the narrative in the next chapter begins with 'Now the whole earth had one language' (11.1). Clearly, the editors were not so much concerned here with a strict chronology—which would have placed ch. 11 before ch. 10—but more with thematic connections, such as the connection between the cities founded by Nimrod in '*the land of Shinar*' (10.9) and the Tower of Babel being built in '*the land of Shinar*' (11.2). What then connects the Hamites, and Nimrod in particular, with the builders of the Tower?

Although a number of suggestions have been made, including the infamous tradition that Hamites are the black peoples, only one view seems to deal adequately with the complexity of the edited material. What unites the 'lineage' of Ham is not an ethnic unity but social and economic patterns of life[12]: the Hamites are builders of cities and empires, whereas the peoples of Shem are characterized more by a rural life, less stratified in structure. The Ham lineage mentions in particular the cities of the 'great warrior' Nimrod (10.8–12), Uruk, Accad, Ashur, Calah, and Nineveh, all of which were major capitals at different times. Canaan can be linked with Egypt (10.6, 15–20) in the sense that the 'Canaanites' are here understood as people

---

12. B. Oded, 'The Table of Nations (Genesis 10): A Socio-Cultural Approach', *Zeitschrift für die alttestamentliche Wissenschaft* 98 (1986), pp. 14–31.

from the city-states who in the late Bronze Age were under the sway of Egyptian imperial rule. The 'Israelites' are linked to the 'children of Shem', on the other hand, through the perception that their origins lay in rural life. In short, Genesis is foreshadowing the social history of the exodus stories.

The Israelite 'bondage to Egypt' is a literary theme that is expressed not just in the Exodus narratives about a group of slaves in Egypt, but also in *the social reality of late Bronze Age Palestine where the rural populations were subject to Egyptian rule in the form of Canaanite city states.* The details of this social history will be explained in especially in Chapter 4 below, but here the key issue is to understand why the builders of cities and empires should be subject to the curse of Ham/Canaan.

While traditional tensions between urban and rural life can be illuminated perhaps by social theory, the text of Genesis provides its own explanation in the story of Noah's violation by Ham/Canaan. In the very act of celebrating his re-connection with the earth, Noah's weakness is in some sense exploited. Just as the curse of Cain was expressed with poetic justice as resistance coming from the violated land, so also this curse is fitting: slavery is a just punishment for a crime of dominance. The narrative in 9.20–24 at least makes clear that the perpetrator, Ham/Canaan, had taken advantage of Noah's weakened state, and his brothers had not. The point is not that Shem or Japheth possess a superior culture; it is rather that a crime in primordial time explains some aspect of the story-tellers' social reality. The forced labour of 'Canaanites' can be explained in relation to Noah's curse.[13] We will explore the probable historical background for this idea in subsequent chapters, but here some brief points need to be made.

We can conclude that the editors of the primordial history in Genesis 9–11 intended to link Ham and Canaan under Noah's curse. The story of the Tower of Babel was to be seen as just one illustration of what city and empire builders are like, and the reader is reassured that Ham/Canaan deserve the poetic justice which emerges in Noah's prediction. A close reading of these chapters would suggest that the 'children of Ham' are those empire builders who are guilty of crimes of dominance. *Colonizers* would be the ones who stand under Noah's curse, not the Indigenous peoples whose connection with the land was swept aside. Thus it is not just that colonizers of modern history misconstrued these chapters in Genesis to serve their own interests. Rather, they *inverted* what the editors were setting out to do, and failed to see that the biblical texts potentially deprived them of legitimacy.

---

13.   See Günter Wittenberg, 'Let Canaan Be his Slave', *Journal of Theology for Southern Africa* 74 (1991), pp. 46–56, 53; cf. L. Rost, *Das kleine Credo und andere Studien zum Alten Testament* (Heidelberg: Quelle & Meyer, 1965), p. 47.

Concluding Reflections

Postcolonial and ecological studies have raised serious questions about the damaging effects of biblical creation theology in modern history. It has often been claimed that rather than encouraging humans to attune themselves to nature, the Bible's injunction to 'subdue' the earth has given license both to an instrumental attitude to the natural world and to the displacement of Indigenous people with different attitudes to land. Historically, one would have to say that this was not true of the early centuries of Christianity when it spread west into Europe, and it is certainly not true of the Celtic forms of Christianity within which the rhythms of creation played a very significant role. But with the rise of modern philosophies in Europe—which drew sharp distinctions between mind and matter[14]—the biblical traditions were often re-configured in line with the modernist vision of nature.

We need to recognize, however, that divisions between culture and nature are peculiarly Western phenomena; there are no significant divisions of this kind in most other cultures.[15] A key problem identified in recent development literature is that in spite of the widespread discrediting of the 'civilizing missions' in colonial history, Western ideals of science, progress and 'transferable technology' are still being exported to other cultures with damaging effects on local forms of knowledge. Most non-Western cultures see society as interconnected with nature, with cultural diversity being clearly linked to biodiversity. Traditional knowledges tend to provide multiple uses for the diversity of plants and animals, while the Western dichotomy of culture and nature has tended to promote more 'efficient' mono-cultural patterns of agriculture, reducing the environment to the rationality of markets. There is a growing sense in development studies that the 'transferable technology' approach has undermined bio-cultural diversity, and local forms of traditional knowledge need to be taken much more seriously if major environmental issues are to be addressed.

In a recent collection of essays entitled *Decolonizing Knowledge*, this environmental perspective is still linked to a critique of Christian theology, even though faith has long ceased be a constituent element of secular ideologies in Western culture. Frédérique Apffel-Marglin argues, for example, that Christian theology conditioned the Western habit of sharply distinguishing between humans and other living beings. In this connection, she refers

---

14.   See Charles Taylor, *Sources of the Self: The Making of Modern Identity* (Cambridge, MA: Harvard University Press, 1989), p. 149; Frédérique Apffel-Marglin, 'Introduction: Rationality and the World', in F. Apffel-Marglin and S. Marglin (eds.), *Decolonizing Knowledge: From Development to Dialogue* (Oxford: Clarendon Press, 1996), p. 4.

15.   See, e.g., Apffel-Marglin, 'Rationality and the World', p. 9.

to the influential biologist J.B.S. Haldane, who moved in the 1960s from Britain to India because he sensed that the cultural climate there would be more favourable to the development of his biological research. In one of his essays, interestingly, he does refer to this sharp distinction between humans and other species in Christian theology, but he goes on to say 'this may well be a perversion of Christianity. St Francis seems to have thought so'.[16]

The argument in this chapter shows at least that the creation theologies of the Hebrew Bible need not have been construed in ways that set human beings sharply apart. Certainly, the idea that humans were made in the 'image of God' is not attributed to other animals, but in terms of blood, 'spirit' and 'life', humans are not unique in these primordial narratives. Both humans and animals are made from the earth, and in this sense we all belong to the same lineage system or 'earth community'. There is a special responsibility given to humans in creation theology, but in the Hebrew Bible this is not a license for violence and dominance, nor a sanctification of a particular civilization. It is more a recognition of human power, and not just the power of kings. In the broader context of Genesis 1–11, human responsibility is more a matter of caring for the earth than of subduing it. Even the prophetic visions of redemption envisage that humans are part of the larger created order. In these respects, Aboriginal cultures are more in tune with the Bible than what is found in Christian theologies shaped by European modernism and colonialism. A postcolonial eco-theology will therefore embody, as I argue in Chapter 10 below, a *hospitality* to the created order that both protects biodiversity and has a clearer sense of human fragility.[17]

It is also evident from our discussion to this point that biblical resistance to monarchy and to imperial domination was sometimes couched in terms that derived from monarchic and imperial ideologies. The democratizing impetus in Genesis 1, for example, retained the underlying logic of monarchic 'rule', and the poetic justice at work in the 'curse of Ham' inverted the fates of oppressor and oppressed while retaining the discourse of slavery. We will return to this issue of 'mimetic circulation' at several points in subsequent chapters, and it will emerge as one of the key ironies being explored in postcolonial studies.

---

16. Apffel-Marglin, 'Rationality and the World', p. 28; cf. Francis Zimmerman, 'Why Haldane Went to India', in Apffel-Marglin and Marglin, *Decolonizing Knowledge*, p. 287, quoting from Haldane's essay 'The Unity and Diversity of Life' (1959).

17. Cf. Deborah Bird Rose, *Reports from a Wild Country: Ethics for Decolonisation* (Sydney: UNSW Press, 2004), p. 214: 'Ethics for decolonisation actually call us into greater vulnerability as well as greater connectivity'.

Ancestors and their Gifts

'Do not move an everlasting boundary stone, set up by your ancestors (*'avot*)'.

Proverbs 22.28

'Do not move your neighbour's boundary stone, set up by your predecessors in the inheritance you receive in the land Yahweh your *'elohim* is giving to you to possess'.

Deuteronomy 19.14

Biblical theology often presumes some elements of contemporary culture in the ancient world, but then reshapes these elements in light of fresh understandings. To take one straightforward example from a dialogue in Gen. 14.18–22, an Indigenous priest names the Creator as 'El Elyon' (usually translated 'God Most High'), and Abram replies by calling God 'Yahweh El Elyon', assimilating the peculiarly Israelite name of God 'Yahweh' to the Indigenous name. Abram's perspective implies an 'inclusive monotheism' since the different divine names are presumed to be pointing to the same God. The high god El in Canaanite religion is seen in Genesis 14 to be none other than Israel's God, and unlike the criticism often directed at other Canaanite gods (especially Baal and Asherah) there is no explicit critique of El in the Bible.[1]

Having spent some years as a missionary in China in the 1920s, the British scholar H.H. Rowley proposed an analogy between the way that God was re-named in Israelite history and the way in which biblical translations in China also adopted a traditional name for God, 'Shang Ti'. Rowley defended this Chinese translation on the grounds that Moses also established a link between a new name for God, Yahweh, and the names of ancestral deities: 'God also said to Moses, "I am Yahweh. I appeared to Abraham, to Isaac and

---

1. Ugaritic texts contain more than five hundred references to El. See further Mark Smith, *The Early History of God: Yahweh and the Other Deities in Ancient Israel* (San Francisco: Harper & Row, 1990), esp. pp. 16–20; W. Herrmann, 'El', in K. van der Toorn, B. Becking, P. van der Horst (eds.), *Dictionary of Deities and Demons in the Bible* (Leiden: Brill, 1995), pp. 521–33.

to Jacob as El Shaddai [God Almighty], but by my name Yahweh I did not make myself known to them' (Exod. 6.2).[2]

This text in Exodus also presents a problem, however, since it implies that the ancestor Abraham did not know the name Yahweh, when Genesis 14 suggests that he did. This problem leads to a whole host of questions about how the biblical texts and biblical theology are related to the history of Israelite religion that lies behind them. The purpose of this chapter is to focus on the place of *ancestral* religion in ancient Israel, and to explore the relationship between the ancestors and the arrival of Yahweh. Clearly, ancestral religion was not simply swept aside—as it frequently was under modern colonial regimes—but the ancestors were understood in a variety of ways.

A fresh appreciation of ancestral religion is crucial, I would argue, to the formulation of a postcolonial approach to the Bible. The issues at stake here are particularly relevant in contexts where Christianity has been linked with the colonizing culture, for example, in contexts such as Australia and North America, where Christian missionaries have been accused of cultural genocide.[3] In light of this history, it is simply astonishing that Indigenous Christians today are still able to assert that Aboriginal spirituality and Christian faith are not incompatible.

Deborah Bird Rose has, however, recently described an example in northern Australia of how religious conflict between a traditional Aboriginal 'culture way' and a Christian 'church way' are diametrically and tragically opposed. Rose's social description takes its starting point from Marcel Gauchet's thesis in *The Disenchantment of the World* that 'primitive religions', free of the influence of states, represent the pinnacle of religious connectivity, whereas Christianity is the fulfilment of 'disenchantment', a fracturing of

2. H.H. Rowley, *The Missionary Message of the Old Testament* (London: Carey Press, 1944), pp. 15–16. Cf. Lamin Sanneh's discussion of the process by which Zulu biblical translations came to adopt the traditional name for God, *uNkulunkulu* (*Translating the Message* [Maryknoll: Orbis, 1989], pp. 171–72).

3. See Djiniyini Gondarra's reference to 'spiritual genocide' in his essay 'Aboriginal Spirituality and the Gospel', in Anne Pattel-Gray (ed.), *Aboriginal Spirituality: Past, Present, Future* (Melbourne: HarperCollins, 1996), p. 42. Cf. also the reference to 'cultural genocide', in Rainbow Spirit Elders, *Rainbow Spirit Theology* (Melbourne: Harper Collins Religious, 1997), p. 51. For similar arguments from Native American Christians, see George E. Tinker, *Missionary Conquest: The Gospel and Native American Cultural Genocide* (Minneapolis: Fortress Press, 1993).

the connections with kin and country.[4] The irony in Rose's account is that the Christian missionaries in this case were themselves Indigenous, reflecting the fact that Aboriginal Christians have differing attitudes towards the indigenization of Christian faith and practice.

It is perhaps a sign of the times that two other recent works by non-Indigenous authors have been concerned to articulate some reversals of this process of 'disenchantment' and social fracturing: David Tacey's *ReEnchantment: the New Australian Spirituality* engages in cultural criticism on a grand scale, linking ecospirituality to Aboriginal reconciliation. Ivan Jordan's *Their Way: Towards an Indigenous Warlpiri Christianity* offers self-critical reflections on two decades of living among the Warlpiri people in central Australia, who now have adapted traditional corroborees, art, and music for use in Christian worship.[5] In some respects, these recent books are echoing arguments advanced by many Indigenous Christians over the last decades, as indicated by the collection of essays edited by Anne Pattel-Gray, *Aboriginal Spirituality: Past, Present, Future*.[6]

In this chapter, I will examine some biblical traditions that might bear on these recent discussions, focusing on the loss and retrieval of ancestral religion in ancient Israel and Judah. Admittedly, this is an area of research that is fraught with conflicting hypotheses, and even if we could achieve a measure of consensus, many scholars would distinguish quite sharply between the history of Israelite religion and the theology found in the biblical texts.[7] Nevertheless, I will argue that there are some striking analogies between the cultural disenchantment within colonized Indigenous communities and the rise of Deuteronomic theology in ancient Judah. Before drawing out the significance of these analogies (both the similarities and the differences), it will also be necessary to examine the complex changes within Israelite religion during the seventh century BCE.

---

4.   Deborah Bird Rose, 'Pentecostal Missionaries and the Exit from Religion', paper delivered at the Bible and Critical Theory Seminar, Melbourne, June 2004, drawing on M. Gauchet, *The Disenchantment of the World: A Political History of Religion* (Princeton: Princeton University Press, 1999). A different version of Rose's argument appears in her *Reports from a Wild Country: Ethics for Decolonisation* (Sydney: UNSW Press, 2004), pp. 149–62.

5.   David Tacey, *ReEnchantment* (Sydney: HarperCollins, 2000); Ivan Jordan, *Their Way* (Darwin: Charles Darwin University, 2003).

6.   See above n. 3 and cf. James Treat (ed.), *Native and Christian: Indigenous Voices on Religious Identity in the United States and Canada* (New York: Routledge, 1996).

7.   See Mark G. Brett, 'Canonical Criticism and Old Testament Theology', in A.D.H. Mayes (ed.), *Text in Context* (Oxford: Oxford University Press, 2000), pp. 63–85.

Ancestors and the Innovations of Deuteronomy

A number of historical studies have suggested that the Assyrian invasion of Judah in 701 BCE resulted in the mass deportation of a significant segment of the rural population, leaving the society dependant upon initiatives from Jerusalem.[8] This invasion under the Assyrian king Sennacherib undermined the old clan system that was the matrix of social identity, legal judgment, land tenure and local forms of religious practice. According to this historical hypothesis, Sennacherib's deportations were interpreted by Jerusalem theologians as Yahweh's judgment on the rural worship practices, and religion was therefore centralized under king Hezekiah in the one cult of Yahweh, which had already assimilated El as a divine name but which now interpreted all the rural cults as the 'foreign' practice of Aboriginal Amorites.[9]

In the popular Israelite religion of the previous century, Yahweh had been worshipped in various parts of the country alongside the Canaanite gods like Baal and Asherah. This has been confirmed by archaeologists, and it is asserted by the Book of Hosea. But it seems that the centralizing Jerusalem theologians of the seventh century insisted that the legitimate cult of Yahweh/El belonged solely in Jerusalem, and ancestral religion had to accommodate to this vision.

Baruch Halpern has described the outcome of this innovation as a process of alienation from land, gods, kin and tradition: 'Hezekiah deconsecrated the land' and 'assaulted the resonance of its timeless ancestral associations'.[10]

> For Hezekiah's purposes, it had been essential to amputate the ancestors, those responsible for the bestowal of rural property to their descendants: they, and they alone, consecrated the possession of land.[11]

---

8.   This argument has been advanced especially by Baruch Halpern in many publications, but see especially his essay 'Jerusalem and the Lineages in the Seventh Century BCE', in B. Halpern and D.W. Hobson (eds.), *Law and Ideology in Monarchic Israel* (Sheffield: Sheffield Academic Press, 1991), pp. 11–107. Halpern's work has been affirmed, e.g., by Mark S. Smith, *The Origins of Biblical Monotheism: Israel's Polytheistic Background and the Ugaritic Texts* (New York: Oxford University Press, 2001), pp. 163, 286 n.106; Bernard M. Levinson, *Deuteronomy and the Hermeneutics of Legal Innovation* (New York: Oxford University Press, 1997), pp. 148–49.

9.   Halpern, 'Jerusalem and the Lineages', pp. 78, 81, 86, 91; 'The Baal (and the Asherah) in Seventh-Century Judah: YHWH's Retainers Retired', in R. Bartelmus et al. (eds.), *Konsequente Traditionsgeschichte: Festschrift für Klaus Baltzer* (Göttingen: Vandenhoeck & Ruprecht, 1993), pp. 115–54; so also B.M. Levinson, *Hermeneutics of Legal Innovation*, pp. 148–49.

10.   Halpern, 'Jerusalem and the Lineages', p. 82; cf. p. 84.

11.   Halpern, 'Jerusalem and the Lineages', p. 74.

This interprets the historical process in harsh terms, but it seems that Assyrian imperial aggression had dislodged the ancestral ties, with the result that communal solidarity and land tenure could be re-constructed around a more centralized theology: land was to be seen as a gift from the national God Yahweh, rather than from localized ancestors. This, at least, is how the Jerusalem theologians of the seventh century saw the world.

The over-riding of ancestral religion may be discerned particularly in some of the traditions of Deuteronomy, and recent studies have convincingly dated several chapters in this book in relation to Assyrian material from the seventh century BCE. In particular, Deuteronomy 13 and 28 seem to be based on models derived from the 'vassal' treaties of Sennacherib's successor, king Esarhaddon (i.e., treaties with states absorbed within the Assyrian empire).[12] In particular, Deut. 13.2–10 subversively 'mimics' Assyrian treaty material, ironically, in order to demand exclusive loyalty to Yahweh rather than to the Assyrian king.[13] In one Assyrian text, the potential sources of threat are listed in an order that begins from the obvious outsider, the 'enemy', then moves to the 'ally', family members, prophets and anyone else. The Deuteronomic author, on the other hand, puts the prophetic threat first, then moves to family members, with much greater focus on the possibility of conflict within the most intimate family relationships, specifying not just 'brother' but 'full brother' ('the son of your mother'), not

---

12.   Influential work from this perspective includes William Moran, 'The Ancient Near Eastern Background to the Love of God in Deuteronomy', *Catholic Biblical Quarterly* 25 (1963), pp. 77–87; Moshe Weinfeld, *Deuteronomy and the Deuteronomic School* (Oxford: Clarendon Press, 1972), pp. 81–126. Deut. 28.20–44 appropriates, in particular, the list of curses in VTE §56. See Simo Parpolo and Kazuko Watanabe (eds.), *Neo-Assyrian Treaties and Loyalty Oaths* (State Archives of Assyria, 2; Helsinki: Helsinki University Press, 1988), p. 49, and the discussion in Hans Ulrich Steymans, *Deuteronomium 28 und die adê zur Thronfolgeregelung Asarhaddons: Segen und Fluch im Alten Orient und in Israel* (OBO, 145; Göttingen: Vandenhoeck & Ruprecht, 1995), pp. 119–41. See also Eckart Otto, *Das Deuteronomium: Politische Theologie und Rechtsreform in Juda und Assyrien* (Berlin: de Gruyter, 1999). Parallels with the earlier Hittite treaties pale into insignificance by comparison.

13.   Otto, *Politische Theologie*, pp. 14, 364–65. Norbert Lohfink uses the term 'counter-propaganda', in Lohfink, 'The Strata of the Pentateuch and the Question of War', in his *Theology of the Pentateuch* (Edinburgh: T. & T. Clark, 1994), 194. Cf. the idea of 'mimicry' in postcolonial studies—adopting genres from a dominant culture and turning them to native advantage (Homi Bhabha, *The Location of Culture* [London: Routledge, 1994], pp. 102–22).

just wife, but 'the wife of your bosom'.[14] This comparison can be appreciated more readily when the texts are set out side by side:

Vassal Treaty of Esarhaddon §10

If you hear any evil, improper, ugly word which is not seemly nor good to Ashurbanipal, the great crown prince designate, son of Esarhaddon, king of Assyria, your lord, either from the mouth of his *enemy* or from the mouth of his *ally*, or from the mouth of *his brothers, his uncles, his cousins, his family, members of his father's line,* or from the mouth of *your brothers, your sons, your daughters,* or from the mouth of a *prophet, an ecstatic, an enquirer of oracles,* or from the mouth of any human being at all; you shall not conceal it but come and report it to Ashurbanipal, the great crown prince designate, son of Esarhaddon, king of Assyria.[15]

Deuteronomy 13.1–9 (Hebrew 13.2–10)

[2]If there should arise among you *a prophet or dreamer of dreams* who provides a sign or portent, [3]and if the sign or portent come true—concerning which he had spoken to you, saying, 'Let us go after other gods (whom you have not known) so that we may worship them', [4]Do not listen to the oracles of that *prophet or that dreamer of dreams*; for Yahweh your God is testing you, to know whether you love Yahweh your God with all your heart and all your being... [6]And that prophet or that dreamer of dreams shall be killed, for he fomented apostasy against Yahweh your God, who brought you out of Egypt and redeemed you from slavery... [7]If *your brother, the son of your mother, or your son, or your daughter or the wife of your bosom, or your friend who is as your own self,* entices you secretly, saying, 'Let us go and worship other gods'—whom neither you nor your fathers have known, [8]some of the gods of the peoples who are round about you...—[9]do not assent to him or listen to him!

In one of the most comprehensive analyses of comparisons such as these, Eckart Otto suggests a quite specific dating of core Deuteronomic texts between 672 and 612 BCE, dates which frame the period between Esarhaddon's treaties and the fall of Nineveh, marking the end of Assyrian imperial influence. Otto argues persuasively that these biblical texts had the specific purpose of subversively opposing Assyrian hegemony.[16] The adaptation of Assyrian ideology was a bold strategy, asserting Yahweh's authority

---

14.　Noted by Bernard Levinson, 'Textual Criticism, Assyriology, and the History of Interpretation: Deuteronomy 13.7 as a Test Case in Method', *Journal of Biblical Literature* 120 (2001), pp. 238–41.

15.　Parpolo and Watanabe, *Neo-Assyrian Treaties*, pp. 33–34.

16.　Otto, *Das Deuteronomium*, p. 14.

above the obvious power of the Assyrian empire, but in the process demanding the strictest loyalty to Yahweh and over-riding even the loyalty due to
an individual's family. We may infer from the heightening of these 'intimate
enemies' in Deuteronomy 13 that the perceived social threat came not just
from 'foreigners' but from the closest family obligations.

The removal of the ancestor cults was apparently just one aspect of
Deuteronomy's program of reform. But the overall strategy was not so
much to revoke the previous traditions as to assert a new interpretation of
older Israelite identity and law, claiming continuity within change. Thus,
for example, the old festivals were re-established with the new principle of
centralization, celebrating not 'in any town' but at a single site: 'the place
Yahweh will choose as a dwelling for his name'. In contrast, the older law in
Exodus suggested that an altar of earth could be built 'in *every* place' where
Yahweh's name is 'remembered'.

Exodus 20.24 (Hebrew 20.21)

> You need make for me only an altar of earth and sacrifice on it your
> burnt offerings and your offerings of well-being, your sheep and your
> oxen; in *every place* (*kol ha-maqom*) where I cause my name to be
> remembered I will come to you and bless you.

Deuteronomy 12.5–6

> You shall seek *the place* (*ha-maqom*) that Yahweh your God will
> choose out of all your tribes as a dwelling for his name. You shall go
> there, bringing your burnt offerings and your sacrifices, your tithes
> and your donations, your votive gifts, your freewill offerings, and the
> firstlings of your herds and flocks.

The early festival calendar in Exod. 23.14–17 accordingly contains no
hint of restriction to just one worship site, and similarly, in the calendar in
Leviticus, the festivals take place 'in all your settlements' (Lev. 23.14, 21,
31; cf. 6.31).[17] Centralization of worship in Jerusalem, and the exclusion of
other worship sites, is Deuteronomy's program for orthodoxy.

In other traditions, we find a diversity of worship sites. 1 Samuel 20.6,
for example, speaks of a sacrifice taking place in Bethlehem for David's
clan without any suggestion from the narrator that this is unorthodox.[18]
Similarly, according to 1 Sam. 9.12–13, Samuel presides happily at a sacrifice at the 'high place' (*bamah*) near Ramah, although from Deuteronomy's

---

17. See Jacob Milgrom, *Leviticus 17–22* (New York: Doubleday, 2000),
pp. 1503–14.
18. See further, Karel van der Toorn, *Family Religion in Babylonia, Syria and Israel*
(Leiden: Brill, 1996), pp. 211–18.

point of view such 'high places' should not exist, and they are accordingly destroyed in the reforms of Hezekiah and Josiah (2 Kgs 18.4; 23.5–9). Deuteronomy envisaged a religion under central organization in Jerusalem, and this implied an exclusion of all rival gods and 'names', including local-ized ancestor worship. Many recent studies have concluded that it was ancestral religious practices that lie behind the prohibition in Deut. 16.22 of the sacred pillar called a *matsebah*.[19]

Deuteronomy's perspective on the *matsebah* is clearly different from the views we find in the ancestral narratives of Genesis, and in the older nar-ratives of Samuel, where such pillars could be erected without any sense of impropriety. Genesis 35.20 says that Jacob set up a pillar (*matsebah*) mark-ing Rachel's tomb. 2 Samuel 18.18 uses the same term *matsebah* to refer to a pillar that Absolom sets up so that his name may be remembered. This may well echo a practice known from neighboring Ugarit and Sam'al, where it was the duty of a son to set up a pillar at which to 'remember' or to 'invoke the name' of his father, and the poignancy of 2 Sam. 18.18 is that Absolom has no son to perform these rites. These examples probably reflect the traces of older forms of family religion.

The book of Genesis, in particular, preserves a pattern of religious prac-tice that is clearly different from Mosaic traditions, and many scholars agree that this distinctive pattern reflects family cults, rather than the offi-cial religion of the state.[20] Without attempting to describe the historical developments of Israelite religion in detail, Walter Moberly sets out the distinctiveness of ancestral religion over against the ethos of Deuteronomy in his book *The Old Testament of the Old Testament: Patriarchal Narratives and Mosaic Yahwism*. He notes, for example, that Deut. 16.21 prohibits the juxtaposition of altars and trees, presumably because it is wary of the tree symbolism associated with the Canaanite goddess Asherah, but the narrators of Genesis express no such anxiety; Abram builds altars in two

---

19.   T.J. Lewis, *Cults of the Dead in Ancient Israel and Ugarit* (Atlanta: Scholars Press, 1989), pp. 118–20; E. Bloch-Smith, *Judahite Burial Practices and Beliefs about the Dead* (Sheffield: Sheffield Academic Press, 1992), pp. 113–14, 122–26; A. Cooper and B.R. Goldstein, 'The Cult of the Dead and the Theme of Entry in the Land, ' *Biblical Interpretation* 1 (1993), pp. 285–303; van der Toorn, *Family Religion*, pp. 206–235; Smith, *Origins of Monotheism*, pp. 68–70.

20.   An earlier exponent of this view emphasizes that the patterns in Genesis reflect not so much 'a preliminary stage' as a 'substratum' of Yahweh religion, a family religion that demonstrates notable similarities with other ancient Near Eastern religious prac-tices (Rainer Albertz, *A History of Israelite Religion in the Old Testament Period*, I [London: SCM Press, 1994], p. 29, building on his pioneering work in *Persönliche Frömigkeit und offizielle Religion* [Stuttgart: Calwer Verlag, 1978]).

places where it seems that sacred trees already exist (Gen. 12.6–7; 13.18).
Moberly emphasizes that ancestral religion is open and inclusive, with virtually no evidence of antagonism with the Indigenous people.[21] There is
no specialized priesthood, and no distinctive customs like Sabbath or food
laws. As already noted, the Canaanite divine name El Elyon is shared with
the Indigenous priest of Salem (Gen. 14.18–20). Ancestral religion does
not have exclusivist emphases, and it lacks the language of holiness, which
is found in the Yahwism of Exodus. In short, it lacks the antagonistic spirit
of Deuteronomy.[22]

Studies of vocabulary associated with ancestor cults have thrown new
light on some old problems, such as the plural form *'elohim*—customarily
translated 'God' or 'gods' depending on the context. It seems that the term
'elohim might in some cases also refer to 'divinized' ancestors of the underworld, or 'spirits', a usage that explains peculiar references to the 'holy ones
who are in the earth' (Ps. 16.2), and to the dead Samuel in the context
of 'gods [*'elohim*] coming up from the earth' (1 Sam. 28.14).[23] Elizabeth
Bloch-Smith argues, for example, that the *'elohim* referred to in Gen. 28.22,
31.52–54 and 46.1 are actually ancestral deities,[24] and this is quite clearly
the case in Laban's speech in Gen. 31.30. In the context of this narrative,
Jacob has stolen the 'household gods' (*teraphim* in 31.19), but Laban calls
these 'household gods' *'elohim* in his speech to Jacob: 'Even though you had
to go because you longed greatly for your father's house, why did you steal

---

21.   The only exception perhaps is Gen. 35.2, 4, which Moberly takes to be evidence
of Yahwist influence, yet even this text does not attribute idolatry to Canaanite influence. See Walter Moberly, *The Old Testament of the Old Testament* (Minneapolis: Fortress
Press, 1992), pp. 88–89.

22.   Moberly speaks of the 'ecumenical bonhomie' of Genesis in *The Old Testament*,
p. 104; cf. Gordon Wenham, 'The Religion of the Patriarchs', in A.R. Millard and
D.J. Wiseman (eds.), *Essays on the Patriarchal Narratives* (Leicester: IVP, 1980),
pp. 157–88; Claus Westermann, *Genesis 12–36* (Minneapolis: Augsburg, 1985), p. 68:
'There is not so much as a single sentence which rejects Canaanite religion or morality';
Norman Habel, *The Land is Mine* (Minneapolis: Fortress Press, 1995), pp. 115–33.

23.   It is possible that these *'elohim* of the earth do not include Samuel himself, and
we should note that supernatural beings of the underworld need not be thought of as
powerful, like Baal or Asherah. At least in Isa. 14.9, they are represented as 'weak'.
Isa. 8.19 refers to consulting the ancestors (*'ovot*) in the context of necromancy;
cf. the 'ancestor spirits' (*'ovot*) in 1 Sam. 28.3 and van der Toorn's interpretation in
Family Religion, pp. 221–222, 318; see also Brian B. Schmidt, 'Memory as Immortality',
in A.J. Avery-Peck and J. Neusner (eds.), *Judaism in Late Antiquity*. Part 4. *Death,
Life-After-Death, Resurrection and the World-to-Come in the Judaisms of Antiquity* (Leiden:
Brill, 2000), pp. 87–100.

24.   Bloch-Smith, *Burial Practices*, pp. 122–23.

my *'elohim.'* Although *teraphim* is normally translated as 'household gods', Karel Van der Toorn has argued convincingly that they should be seen more precisely as ancestral icons.[25]

The dead were often seen in family religion as benefactors of their descendants, particularly in the bequest of ancestral land. When Naboth refers to 'the inheritance of my fathers' in 1 Kgs 21.3, for example, he is referring to his ancestral estate, and his reluctance to sell the land to the king may be illuminated by the parallel expression in 2 Sam. 14.16 'the inheritance of *'elohim'*. This 'inheritance' can be seen as traditional land that is inalienable because it is a gift of divinized ancestors. Such an interpretation conforms to the school of interpretation which links kin groups, localized worship practices and traditional forms of land tenure.[26] Religious practices for the dead may well have served the welfare of the ancestors who originally owned the land but, at the same time, these practices would also have re-asserted the descendants' moral rights to the inheritance. In line with this understanding, Alan Cooper and Bernard Goldstein have discerned a literary pattern behind ten different biblical narratives, linking deified ancestors (*'elohim*), the possession of land, and the setting up of a *matsebah*, stele or altar. Their argument suggests that the presence of these stones or pillars established the 'real or symbolic presence of deified ancestors', which in turn 'manifests an assertion of ownership in perpetuity'.[27]

The narratives of Joshua 24 and Exod. 23.20–24.11, which share this pattern, assert that foreign *'elohim* must not be venerated and their *matsebot* should be broken down (Exod. 23.24). Joshua sets up a 'large stone' instead (Josh. 24.26–27). It seems that the pattern of ancestral religion—to set up a pillar as a reflection of land tenure—is in Joshua supplanted by a

---

25. Traces of ancestral religion have also been found in personal names, such as 'Ammiel' which has been interpreted as 'my ancestor is god', and 'Eliam', meaning 'my god, the ancestor' (van der Toorn, *Family Religion*, pp. 228–30). See, however, the discussion in Jon D. Levenson, *Resurrection and the Restoration of Israel: The Ultimate Victory of the God of Life* (New Haven: Yale University Press, 2006), p. 56.

26. Herbert C. Brichto, 'Kin, Cult, Land, and Afterlife', *Hebrew Union College Annual* 44 (1973), pp. 1–54; Christopher J.H. Wright, *God's People in God's Land: Family, Land and Property in the Old Testament* (Grand Rapids: Eerdmans, 1990), pp. 151–59; T.J. Lewis, 'The Ancestral Estate (נחלת אלהים) in 2 Samual 14.16', *Journal of Biblical Literature* 110 (1991), pp. 597–612; van der Toorn, *Family Religion*, pp. 210–11; Bloch-Smith, *Burial Practices*, p. 146; Halpern, 'Jerusalem and the Lineages', pp. 57–59.

27. Cooper and Goldstein, 'Cult of the Dead', pp. 294, 297. The ten narratives are: Gen. 12.1–9; 28.10–22; 31.1–32.3; 33.18–20; 35.1–20; Exod. 23.20–24.11; Deuteronomy 27; Josh. 3.5–5.12; 8.30–35; 24; cf. the reservations expressed by Francesca Stavrakopoulou, 'Bones, Burials and Boundaries in the Hebrew Bible', paper presented at the British Society for Old Testament Studies meeting, Durham, 2006.

new pillar for Yahweh, established in opposition to the other *'elohim* who were worshipped by the ancestors (Josh. 24.14–15). According to Cooper and Goldstein, the gift of land from Yahweh 'supersedes' the gifts from the ancestors. This perspective may also be reflected in Ps. 16.2–6:

> I have said to Yahweh: You are my Lord. I have nothing of value beside you.
> As for the holy ones who are in the underworld, the mighty ones…
> I shall not bring their libation of blood, nor take their names on my lips.
> Yahweh is my allotted portion and my cup; you hold my lot.
> The lines have fallen for me in pleasant places, yea, my inheritance pleases me.[28]

While the narratives in Joshua 24 and Exod. 23.20–24.11 reflect the assimilation of the ancestral religion to the worship of Yahweh, they do not share all of Deuteronomy's perspectives. For example, Joshua establishes his *own* cultic site and writes his own 'law of *'elohim*' in Josh. 24.25–26, rather than defer to a pre-existing law of Moses (elsewhere in the book of Joshua, the law of Moses is usually presumed to be already established[29]). Several studies have pointed out that Exodus 23 envisages the destruction of Indigenous cults only, not the 'holy war' on Indigenous peoples that we find in Deut. 20.16–18. In Exodus, the prior inhabitants are said to be dispossessed by Yahweh *alone*, not by Israelite wars (a perspective on land possession that Exodus shares with Lev. 18.28 and 19.23).[30] In view of such differences between the various traditions, it would be reasonable to conclude that Yahweh's control of the land was a feature of Israelite religion independently of Deuteronomy's theology of conquest and centralization. In other words, there was more than one denomination of Yahwism.

We can infer that the Indigenous rites associated with the *matsebah* were assimilated in different ways: some traditions in Genesis and Samuel continued to use the term, but other traditions seem to avoid it. An ambiguity can also be discerned in the Hebrew phrase 'Yahweh your *'elohim*'. In Deuteronomy's perspective, this may simply mean 'Yahweh your God', but this phrase might also have implied that Yahweh incorporated the divinized

---

28. The translation follows van der Toorn, *Family Religion*, p. 210.

29. On the distinctiveness of Joshua 24, see S. David Sperling, 'Joshua 24 Re-examined', in G.N. Knoppers and J. Gordon McConville (eds.), *Reconsidering Israel and Judah* (Winona Lake: Eisenbrauns, 2000), pp. 240–58.

30. Michael Fishbane, *Biblical Interpretation in Ancient Israel* (Oxford: Clarendon Press, 1985), pp. 199–209; Baruch J. Schwartz, 'Reexamining the Fate of the "Canaanites" in the Torah Traditions', in C. Cohen, A. Hurvitz and S.M. Paul (eds.), *Sefer Moshe: The Moshe Weinfeld Jubilee Volume* (Winona Lake: Eisenbrauns, 2004), pp. 151–70.

ancestors, or 'spirits', of the land. This inclusive interpretation could have been tolerated by some Deuteronomists as long as it was seen in 'monotheistic' terms. A key doctrine in Deuteronomy 6 asserts that 'Yahweh is our *'elohim*; Yahweh is one' (6.4), and although later tradition interpreted this simply as a statement of exclusive monotheism, the earliest layers of the tradition may not have been that straightforward.[31]

Even within an old poem included in Deuteronomy itself, there are two verses that provoked perplexity amongst those who copied and edited the manuscripts in the ancient world.

Qumran version of Deuteronomy 32.8–9

When Elyon apportioned the nations their inheritance, when he divided humankind, he fixed the boundaries of the peoples according to the number of *sons of 'elohim*. Yahweh's own portion was his people, Jacob his inherited share.

Later Hebrew version of 32.8–9 (Massoretic Text)

When Elyon apportioned the nations their inheritance, when he divided humankind, he fixed the boundaries of the peoples according to the number of the *sons of Israel*. Yahweh's own portion was his people, Jacob his inherited share.

The manuscript evidence found in the Qumran caves preserves the older Hebrew form of the verses. The standard Hebrew version—the Massoretic Text—has evidently altered the text in order to reflect a more clear monotheism.[32] Yet the older version of the verses provides evidence that there was a form of Yahwism which could allow the existence of other gods outside Israel. If we read 'Elyon' as standing in poetic parallel with 'Yahweh', then the two divine names may refer to the same God, as in Gen. 14.18–20. Other nations may have their own gods, the text implies, but Jacob/Israel is the special jurisdiction of Elyon/Yahweh (as suggested also by Mic. 4.4–5, Judg. 11.24, and perhaps Deut. 4.19–20).[33] But this denomination of Yahwism could still make claims like 'Yahweh is our *'elohim*; Yahweh is one' (or possibly 'unique') insofar as Yahweh is 'one' with the *'elohim* of

---

31. On the problems of Deuteronomy 6.4, see R.W.L. Moberly, '"Yahweh is One": The Translation of the Shema', in J.A. Emerton (ed.), *Studies in the Pentateuch* (Leiden: Brill, 1990), pp. 209–15.

32. Paul Sanders, *The Provenance of Deuteronomy 32* (Leiden: Brill, 1996), pp. 154–60; Emmanuel Tov, *Textual Criticism of the Hebrew Bible* (Minneapolis: Fortress Press, 2nd edn, 2001), p. 269. On the Canaanite background to the parallel expression 'sons of *elim*' in Ps 29.1, see Frank M. Cross, 'Notes on a Canaanite Psalm in the Old Testament', *BASOR* 117 (1950), pp. 19–21.

33. Halpern, 'YHWH's Retainers Retired', pp. 146–47.

the ancestors. In the course of time, the transformation of ancestral religion into this 'inclusive monotheism' (or 'monolatry') became the standard
view.

Such a reconstruction of Israel's religious history explains how later readers came to overlook the polytheistic implications of narratives in Genesis
that speak of the *'elohim* of the ancestors. The polytheistic background to
ancestral religion comes to expression explicitly in Genesis 31, in the conflict between Jacob and Laban mentioned above. When Laban speaks in
31.53 of "*elohim* of Abraham' he invokes these *'elohim* to 'judge between us',
using the *plural* form of the verb 'to judge'. Thus, an accurate translation of
this verse would need to read: 'May the gods of Abraham…judge between
us'. Laban's perspective, therefore, is that there are several gods who are relevant to this covenant with Jacob. Jacob, on the other hand, swears by 'the
Fear of his father Isaac' (31.53), and nothing passes his lips that would need
to be read in polytheistic terms. Yet Jacob also says in 31.5 that the "*elohim*
of my father has been with me'. This is never translated as the 'gods of my
father', since it is generally understood by later tradition that the *'elohim*
of Jacob's father is/are identical with the *one* God of Israel, who is simply
referred to here using a different phrase.

These different names for God also appear in the divine promises of
land. One strand of Genesis tradition says that this land was promised by
Yahweh, and another strand says that the land was promised by *'elohim* (the
second promise tradition is reflected in Exodus 6 which, as we saw above,
claims that the ancestors did not know the name Yahweh). Neither tradition in Genesis puts significant divine conditions on keeping the land,
although Genesis 17 does insist that Abraham circumcise all the males in
his household.

Genesis 12.7

> Then Yahweh appeared to Abram and said, 'To your seed I will give
> this land'.

Genesis 17.8

> I will give to you, and to your seed after you, the land where you are
> now an alien, all the land of Canaan for an everlasting holding; and
> I will be their *'elohim*.

Deuteronomy, on the other hand, insists that the land is a gift from
Yahweh but that it can only be possessed if the Israelites keep all of Yahweh's
torah. The land promise is therefore augmented by a range of laws, and these
are often worded slightly differently from what we find in similar traditions
elsewhere in the Hebrew Bible. Thus, for example, Deut. 19.14 seems to

avoid using the term 'ancestors', perhaps making sure that land is not seen as a gift from the *'elohim* of the ancestors in any polytheistic sense.

Proverbs 22.28

Do not move an everlasting boundary stone, set up by your ancestors (*'avot*).

Deuteronomy 19.14

Do not move your neighbour's boundary stone, set up by your predecessors in the inheritance you receive in the land Yahweh your *'elohim* is giving to you to possess.

What is most significant for Deuteronomy is not that Yahweh wants to change the boundaries handed down from the ancestors, but rather, that the boundaries *were actually established by Yahweh* and not by anyone else.

In Christopher Wright's discussion of these issues, he concludes that Yahweh religion had a habit of 'taking over established culture patterns and then transforming them into vehicles of its own distinctive theology and ethics'.[34] A question arising, however, is whether Yahwism was simply imposed by the national reforms of kings like Hezekiah or Josiah. A postcolonial critic would want to investigate whether the over-writing of ancestral religion was an expression of brute monarchic force.

Even within the historical narratives influenced by Deuteronomy, however, we find significant theological defences against the abuse of monarchic power. The famous example of Naboth's vineyard demonstrates that a refusal to part with ancestral inheritance was given divine sanction by the narrators (1 Kgs 21.17–24; 2 Kgs 9.30–10.11). If the idea of national unity under Yahweh was simply an ideological mask for suppressing all aspects of the ancestral traditions, then the transfer of land between Israelites would have been consistent with the program of nationalization. What is notable about the Naboth incident is that the stubborn maintenance of ancestral land was seen to be sanctioned precisely by Yahweh: Naboth says to the king, '*Yahweh forbid* me, that I should give the inheritance of my ancestors to you' (1 Kgs 21.3).[35] Whatever the religious changes may have taken place, this episode clearly supports land rights bequeathed by the ancestors nonetheless.

---

34. Wright, *God's Land*, p. 156.

35. Cf. Brichto, 'Kin, Cult, Land', pp. 31–32; Wright, *God's Land*, pp. 158–59. The peculiar incident described in 2 Kgs 23.16, in which the bones of former priests of Bethel are disinterred and burned on the altar, appears to represent an attack specifically on the cultic site, rather than an attempt by a Southern king to usurp the land rights of Northern clans.

Moreover, Wright emphasizes that religious rites on behalf of the ancestors are only forbidden in Israel's law when such rites are connected with
'foreign' families and deities. This implies that ancestral traditions within
'Israelite' families were tolerated, and for example, the law directed
against the use of tithes in gifts for the dead proscribes exactly that—the
use of tithes, not all gifts for the dead (Deut. 26.14). Thus, Wright concludes that there is no rejection of ritual practices for the dead, or even
the use of *teraphim*, 'provided there was no question of the involvement
of other gods than Yahweh'. He distinguishes between a filial piety or veneration and actual worship of divinities, insisting that 'veneration is not
worship'.[36] On this interpretation, the national profile of Yahweh accommodated ancestral cultural practices, and it is quite possible to claim that
even within Deuteronomic tradition Yahweh's gifts of land still allowed
both for veneration of a clan's ancestors *and* for an understanding of
ancestral land tenure.

This conclusion is reinforced from a quite different theological perspective in the book of Leviticus. Lev. 25.23–24 prohibits the permanent sale
of land on the grounds that it belongs solely to Yahweh. A sceptical reader
might take this as an ideological strategy for reinforcing centralized monarchic or priestly interests over against clan authority, but the requirement
in these verses that 'You must provide redemption for the land' affirms the
right of return in the fiftieth year for families wishing to reclaim precisely
their *traditional* land (25.13). Leviticus rejects ancestor worship, and cultic practices involving the dead (Lev. 19.28, 31; 20.6, 27),[37] but this book
nowhere suggests that Yahweh underwrites the land holdings of the Crown.
On the contrary, the theology of 'redemption' in Leviticus focuses on the
restoration of 'kin and country': in the fiftieth year, when liberty (*dᵉror*)[38]
was proclaimed, everyone was to return to their family and land (25.10).

---

36. Wright, *God's Land*, pp. 156–57; Brichto, 'Kin, Cult, Land', pp. 28–29, 46–47;
Milgrom, *Leviticus 17–22*, pp. 1772–85.

37. Lewis, *Cults of the Dead*, p. 175. See further Jacob Milgrom, *Leviticus 23–27*
(New York: Doubleday, 2000), pp. 1283–91.

38. The terminology is probably related to the Akkadian term *anduraru*, meaning literally 'return to the mother'. See Weinfeld, *Deuteronomy and the Deuteronomic
School*, p. 153. On Leviticus and land theology, see further Weinfeld, *Deuteronomic
School*, pp. 225–32; Jan Joosten, *People and Land in the Holiness Code* (Leiden: Brill, 1996),
pp. 137–92, Milgrom, *Leviticus 17–22*, pp. 1404–1405.

Concluding Reflections

Genesis, Leviticus and Deuteronomy all pay respect to the ancestors, even though the monotheizing tendency of these books has absorbed the diversity of ancestral religion in very different ways. The ancestors of individual clans have been consolidated into the larger narrative, extending eventually back to Abraham. Within this process, the land rights of the clans have been preserved, and there is an important sense in which 'redemption' in the Torah is unthinkable without the 'connectivity of kin and country', to use Deborah Rose's words.[39] Regardless of the diversity of the Torah's theology and ethics, there is a common assumption that Israelite clans had indefinite claims on particular pieces of land, in spite of periods of dislocation or exile. This same kind of assumption about land can also be found in many Indigenous worldviews. Any version of theology that breaks the connections of kin and country actually seems to invert the Torah's logic of redemption.

Genesis articulates the promise of 'everlasting' landholdings to the ancestors, and Deuteronomy makes these promises the basis of its thinking about divine grace (7.7–8; 8.17–18; 9.5) while at the same time adding law observance as a condition of possessing the land. Leviticus has a slightly different view of land 'possession' which insists that Israelites have the same *theological* status as resident aliens (25.23).[40] Yet none of this is used to justify the overturning of land allotments given to 'Israelite' ancestors. Even in the prophetic literature that envisages life after the exile in Babylon, the people are redeemed *in the land* (e.g., Isaiah 35, 54; Ezekiel 36–37). In short, the biblical ideas of redemption cluster around the restoration of 'kin and country', and to suggest as colonizers sometimes did that Indigenous people need to forsake their kin and country in order to be 'redeemed', turns this biblical language into nonsense.

An analogy is suggested by Khiok-Khng Yeo when he observes that 'To advise the Chinese not to offer food and not to eat the food in ancestor worship may be implicitly advising them not to love their parents, not to practice love, and ultimately not to be Chinese'.[41] We could extrapolate from this point to say that wherever veneration of ancestors is constitutive of ethnic identity, Christians who belong to that culture will be presented

---

39.   See above, n. 4.

40.   Jacob Milgrom, *Leviticus 17–22* (New York: Doubleday, 2000), pp. 1404–1405.

41.   Yeo, '1 Corinthians 8 and Chinese Ancestor Worship', *Biblical Interpretation* 2 (1994), p. 308. For African theologies of the ancestors, see especially Temba Mafico, 'The Biblical God of the Fathers and the African Ancestors', in G. West and M. Dube (eds.), *The Bible in Africa: Transactions, Trajectories and Trends* (Leiden: Brill, 2000), pp. 481–89; Kwame Bediako, *Christianity in Africa* (Maryknoll: Orbis, 1995), pp. 216–33.

with complex theological questions. This is a significant issue in Africa, Asia and the Pacific, and especially for Indigenous Christians. If we are to learn anything from the histories of colonialism, we will need to conclude that these issues of identity have to be negotiated by the people concerned, and observers from other cultures need to hold their peace.[42]

The Choctaw theologian Steve Charleston has observed that every Indigenous nation has a *unique* covenant with the Creator, but many of the basic themes in these covenants are comparable with Israel's story: land, law, sacred places and rituals.[43] In Australia, there are ongoing debates about the ways in which Indigenous law, ritual, veneration and sacred topography can be retrieved as part of the exercise of Aboriginal Christian faith. Djiniyini Gondarra, for example, draws analogies between sacred sites in his own culture and the significance of sites like Bethel and Sinai for the construction of Jewish identity. His allusion to Bethel is especially relevant in light of the references to the Bethel *matsebah* in Gen. 35.14, 20, reflecting local forms of ancestral religion.

Even the act of translating the Bible poses significant questions for how Israelite ancestral narratives may be understood within Indigenous traditions. Vernacular translations, in particular, generate a cultural hybridity that translators cannot control.[44] If, for example, 'teraphim' should be understood as ancestral icons, then the translation of this term may elicit Aboriginal vocabulary used for ancestral icons—such as 'tjurunga' among the Aranda people. The argument presented above for the legitimacy of *teraphim* within an 'inclusive' Yahwism provides a fresh perspective on the recent reclaiming of the *tjurunga* amongst the Christian Aranda.[45] Not only are these icons significant for determining land rights, but they hold spiritual significance within Aranda identity.

---

42. See Jordan, *Their Way*, pp. 28–33, who refers to an analogy in 1 Corinthians 8.

43. Charleston, 'The Old Testament of Native America', in S.B. Thistlethwaite and M.B. Engel (eds.), *Lift Every Voice: Constructing Christian Theologies from the Underside* (San Francisco: HarperCollins, 1990), pp. 49–61; cf. Djiniyini Gondarra, *Series of Reflections on Aboriginal Religion* (Darwin: Bethel Presbytery, Uniting Church in Australia, 1996); Mark G. Brett, '*Canto Ergo Sum*: Indigenous Peoples and Postcolonial Theology', *Pacifica* 16 (2003), pp. 247–56.

44. Bediako, *Christianity in Africa*, p. 123; Sanneh, *Translating the Message*, esp. pp. 157–210. On cultural hybridity in theology, see Robert J. Schreiter, *The New Catholicity* (Maryknoll: Orbis, 1997), pp. 63–83.

45. P.G.E. Albrecht, 'Hermannsburg, a Meeting Place of Cultures', *Nungalinya Occasional Bulletin* 14 (1981); Harris, *One Blood*, pp. 891–92. On the collection of *tjurunga* for anthropological purposes, see especially Barry Hill, *Broken Song: T.G.H. Strehlow and Aboriginal Possession* (Sydney: Vintage, 2002), pp. 158–62.

By moving the 'boundary stones' of the ancestors, and thereby denying the land rights of Indigenous peoples, colonization rendered the biblical concepts of 'redemption' largely unintelligible. Expectations of redemption in the Hebrew Bible concerned the restoration of family and land, and these expectations can hardly be met by the fracturing of kin and country. What forms of restoration may today be meaningful is a matter for dialogue with Indigenous people, and this issue will be discussed in Chapter10 below, but measures taken by the churches will need to cohere with the biblical practices of redemption.[46]

One clue to reconciliation was provided some years ago at a Eucharist held in Yurrkuru (Brooks Soak, Central Australia) memorializing a massacre of Aboriginal people that took place in the area in 1928. In this meeting of sacramental cultures, the Warlpiri Elder Jerry Jangala invoked the eponymous ancestor, Jesus Christ, whom he shared with the whites at the meeting—the ancestor who also died unjustly at the hands of an empire. The Christian Eucharist thereby intersected with the traditional Indigenous invocation of the ancestors, knitting together a community who refuses to give alienation and brute force the final word. This, at least, is an interpretation of the Eucharist that will be discussed below in Chapter 9 in reflections on the apostle Paul.[47]

46. See Wright, *God's Land*, pp. 110–14.

47. See Jordan, *Their Way*, pp. 26–27; Petronella Varzon-Morel (ed.), *Warlpiri karnta karnta—kurlangu yimi Warlpiri Women's Voices* (Alice Springs: IAD Press, 1995), p. 36. On analogies between the Christian Eucharist and the Indigenous invocation of ancestors, see also Barry Hill, *Broken Song*, pp. 49, 437; T.G.H. Strehlow, *Central Australian Religion: Personal Monototemism in a Polytotemic Community* (Bedford Park: Australian Association for the Study of Religions, 1978), pp. 27, 34, 60; cf. Jürgen Moltmann, 'Ancestor Respect and the Hope of Resurrection', *Sino-Christian Studies* 1 (2006), pp. 13–36.

4

PIGS, POTS AND CULTURAL HYBRIDS

'By origin and by birth, you are of the land of the Canaanites'

Ezekiel 16.3

'A living tradition then is an historically extended, socially embodied argument, and an argument precisely in part about the goods
which constitute that tradition'.

Alasdair MacIntyre.[1]

In the previous chapter, we examined the relationship between ancestral
religion and the worship of Yahweh, describing how the biblical traditions
forged their monotheism and established that Yahweh was 'one', in spite of
the fact that the names for God were diverse. Most surprisingly, perhaps,
Yahweh turned out to be identical not just with the *'elohim* of the ancestors
but also with El, the high god of Indigenous Canaanite religion. We may
assume that the development of Yahwist monotheism (or 'monolatry') was
controversial at the time. The explicit polemics in the Bible against other
gods—the Canaanite baals, Asherah and other 'foreign *'elohim'*—are sufficient to show that popular religion was often very different from what
ended up in scripture. While the details of historical developments cannot
be recovered, the evidence of Israel's religious diversity is quite clear in the
biblical literature, and the Canaanite identity of El is similarly indisputable.
The Hebrew Bible is somewhat less clear on how the 'inclusive' dimensions
of Yahwist monotheism came to be formed. In this chapter, we will investigate how these issues can be illuminated by archaeology and anthropology.

It should be recognized at the outset that there are deep disagreements
amongst archaeologists and historians about the details of Israel's early
history. I will attempt to incorporate a range of opinions in the discussion
that follows, but my concern is also to find as much common ground as is
possible. There would be little point in attempting to reconcile fundamentalist theologians and the most sceptical biblical scholars who believe that

---

1.   Alasdair MacIntyre, *After Virtue* (Notre Dame: University of Notre Dame Press,
1981), p. 207.

virtually nothing in the Hebrew Bible corresponds to historical events that the texts purport to represent. We may simply note that very few of the most sceptical scholars are professional archaeologists, and very few fundamentalist theologians have made contributions to biblical scholarship that are widely recognized outside their own circles. My focus will be on the broad range of opinion that lies between these two extremes in order to see what the areas of greatest consensus can contribute to an understanding of early Israelite culture.

Important recent scholarly contributions to biblical history from a self-designated 'conservative' perspective have conceded that none of the narratives concerning Israel's beginnings (the ancestral stories, the exodus from Egypt, and the conquest of Canaan) have been *proved* by archaeology.[2] The primary concern of Provan, Long and Longman's *A Biblical History of Israel* (2003), for example, is to argue that the biblical accounts are still *plausible* in light of historical research. It is also recognized in conservative scholarship (1) that the biblical texts have been 'updated' in later periods; (2) that there are enormous difficulties in dating the exodus; (3) that it is impossible to read the conquest accounts 'literally', since a host of contradictions arise as soon as such a fundamentalist approach is attempted; (4) most importantly, that the biblical narrative has to be seen in terms of the *genre* to which it belongs: ancient historiography. We cannot expect such writing to contain the standards of evidence-giving or styles of argument that we find in modern histories. In its own cultural context, biblical historiography is shaped by its own conventions of communication (e.g., hyperbole) that cannot be reduced to simple propositions about the past. K. Lawson Younger's groundbreaking work *Ancient Conquest Accounts* (1990) has been rightly influential in making this point.

Conservative scholars also tend to accept the majority scholarly opinion that key episodes in biblical narrative, such as the spectacular conquest of Jericho in Joshua 6, cannot be reconciled with *current* archaeological findings; Jericho had no walls in the Late Bronze Age—c. 1500 to 1200 BCE, the period when the conquest would have taken place—and hence the walls could not have fallen as the biblical account suggests. The characteristic conservative response to such a consensus about a seeming discrepancy is to say that the jury is still out; further research may change the picture. But it is also important to notice that many

---

2.   See Iain Provan, V. Philips Long, Tremper Longman, *A Biblical History of Israel* (Louisville: Westminster John Knox, 2003), pp. 125, 168, 192.

conservative scholars question the 'conquest' model of Israel's origins.[3] This is not just because archaeological research cannot corroborate an invasion, but also because they realize that biblical claims about these events have been misread by generations of commentators.

For example, Provan, Long and Longman emphasize that according to the book of Joshua, only three cities were actually burned—Jericho, Ai and Hazor—and so we should not expect to find archaeological evidence for the burning of numerous cities to indicate an Israelite incursion. Significant difficulties arise with even these three sites: majority opinion suggests that Jericho had no walls, as already indicated, and Ai (et Tell) was not occupied between 2400 and 1200 BCE when the 'conquest' is often said to have occurred. Only Hazor provides, therefore, a plausible case for consistency: it was destroyed several times in the Late Bronze Age, and the last time was probably during the thirteenth century, although hypotheses about the dates vary. But there is also an inconsistency between the conquest accounts in Joshua itself, however, since in relation to Hazor the livestock were spared the destruction (11.14), while in the Jericho narrative they were destroyed completely (6.21). Only the Jericho account enacts the law in Deut. 20.16 which stipulates that in the case of war in the promised land, 'everything that breathes' should be killed. (In this connection, it is also interesting to notice that although, according to Joshua 24, Joshua held a covenant ceremony in Shechem, this city is never listed in the biblical narratives as having been conquered.)

We will look more closely at the biblical laws and narratives concerned with conquest in the next chapter, but here we will take up the question of what archaeological evidence there may be for the arrival of a new people group in the Late Bronze Age. In the case of the Philistines, who arrived on the coastal plains during the twelfth century, archaeologists have been able to describe their distinct material culture—e.g., pottery and architecture—which clearly differs from previous models in the area.[4]

---

3.   Provan, Long, and Longman, *A Biblical History of Israel*, pp. 140, 167, 191; on the conventional nature of the rhetorical excesses in the book of Joshua, see K. Lawson Younger, *Ancient Conquest Accounts: A Study in Ancient Near Eastern and Biblical History Writing* (Sheffield: JSOT Press, 1990), and his critique of the conquest model in 'Early Israel in Recent Biblical Scholarship', in D.W. Baker and D.T. Arnold (eds.), *The Face of Old Testament Studies* (Grand Rapids: Baker, 1999), pp. 176–206.

4.   Lawrence Stager, 'Forging an Identity: The Emergence of Ancient Israel', in M.D. Coogan (ed.), *The Oxford History of the Biblical World* (New York: Oxford University Press, 1998), pp. 113–28; Eliezer Oren (ed.), *The Sea Peoples and their World: A Reassessment* (Philadelphia: University Museum, 2000).

In the case of the Israelites, however, it is now widely recognized that there are no features of the material culture that can clearly differentiate them from the Indigenous peoples of Canaan. The only possibility lies in the three hundred or so new settlements that arose in the central hill country at the beginning of the Iron Age, from the twelfth to the eleventh century BCE. While there is substantial agreement about the evidence for social transformation in the central hills, there is no consensus about how to explain the evidence. There is even doubt about whether the new settlements of the early Iron Age can properly be termed 'Israelite'.[5] The present chapter will attempt to interpret the controversy, and perhaps even reconcile some disagreements, while showing how the debate relates to issues of cultural interaction in colonized societies.[6]

Israel's Indigenous Origins

Standing against the tide of the extremely sceptical historical 'revisionism', two leading archaeologists—William Dever and Israel Finkelstein—have recently argued that there are many convergences between biblical narratives and archaeological reconstructions, but *not* in relation to the traditions that describe Israelite origins.[7] Given the heat of the controversy, it is surprising to notice that there is actually a broad agreement underlying the recent discussion, namely, that most of the highland population

5.   Compare the differences between two of the leading archaeologists in William Dever, 'Ceramics, Ethnicity, and the Question of Israel's Origins', *Biblical Archaeologist* 58 (1995), pp. 200–13; Israel Finkelstein, 'Ethnicity and Origin of the Iron I Settlers in the Highlands of Canaan: Can the Real Israel Stand Up?', *Biblical Archaeologist* 59 (1996), pp. 198–212. A more detailed version of Finkelstein's argument appeared as 'Pots and People Revisited: Ethnic Boundaries in the Iron Age I', in N.A. Silberman and D. Small (eds.), *The Archaeology of Israel: Constructing the Past, Interpreting the Present* (Sheffield: Sheffield Academic Press, 1997), pp. 216–37.

6.   The following section revises the argument first outlined in Mark G. Brett, 'Israel's Indigenous Origins: Cultural Hybridity and the Formation of Israelite Ethnicity', *Biblical Interpretation* 11 (2003), pp. 400–12.

7.   William Dever, *What Did the Biblical Writers Know and When Did They Know It? What Archaeology Can Tell Us about the Reality of Ancient Israel* (Grand Rapids: Eerdmans, 2001); Israel Finkelstein and Neil Silberman, *The Bible Unearthed: Archaeology's New Vision of Ancient Israel and the Origin of its Sacred Texts* (New York: Free Press, 2001).

in the early Iron Age (c, 1200 to 1000 BCE) was Indigenous.[8] Even the
recent conservative account by Provan, Long and Longman, *A Biblical
History of Israel*, concedes this point, without agreeing that *all* Israelites
were Indigenous. The archaeologist Lawrence Stager has summarized the
agreement succinctly, 'The evidence from language, costume, coiffure,
and material remains suggest that the early Israelites were a rural subset
of Canaanite culture'.[9]

There are, however, a variety of explanations for these Indigenous origins. Finkelstein argues that the majority of the highland population were
previously pastoral nomads from the area, and in some of his recent publications, he doubts whether they would have called themselves 'Israelite'.
Dever, on the other hand, advocates the view that the highland communities, which he calls 'proto-Israelite', derived in the main from sedentary
Canaanite populations. He speaks of 'displaced Canaanites' including 'an
assortment of urban refugees, social dropouts and malcontents, migrant
farmers, resedentarized pastoralists, perhaps some Shasu-like bedouin
and other immigrants from Transjordan [east of the Jordan river], and
even some newcomers from Syria and Anatolia'.[10] The key arguments for
cultural continuity rest on Dever's analysis of pottery and religious arte-
facts, while his defence of the ethnic label 'Israel' rests primarily on a
contemporary Egyptian inscription from around 1210 BCE (the Merneptah
stele, discussed below) which refers to 'Israel' as a people group. Dever
is convinced that there was a 'population explosion' in the central hill
country—from around 12,000 to at least treble that number by the end
of the eleventh century—which cannot be accounted for by Finkelstein's

8.   Provan, Long and Longman, *A Biblical History of Israel*, p. 144; cf. Paula McNutt,
Reconstructing the Society of Ancient Israel (Louisville: Westminster John Knox, 1999),
pp. 57, 63; Dever, *What Did the Biblical Writers Know?*, pp. 41, 99; Finkelstein and
Silberman, *The Bible Unearthed*, pp. 117–18. Ziony Zevit has some reservations about
the idea of Indigenous origins but finds no archaeological evidence for the immigration
of an outside group. Zevit, *The Religions of Israel: A Synthesis of Parallactic Approaches*
(New York: Continuum, 2001), esp. pp. 113–14.

9.   Stager, 'Forging an Identity', p. 102.

10.   Dever, 'Ceramics, Ethnicity', p. 211. Cf. Zevit, *The Religions of Israel*, p. 118:
'Some of the people who identified themselves as Israel during the Iron Age may very
well have coalesced out of Hapiru groups and Shasu of earlier times and some out of
the many groups of Semitic-speaking people who had some familiarity with Egyptian
culture of the eastern delta'; so also Ann E. Killebrew, *Biblical Peoples and Ethnicity: An
Archaeological Study of Egyptians, Canaanites, Philistines and Early Israel 1300–1100* BCE
(Atlanta: SBL, 2005), p. 184.

hypothesis that the majority of the new settlers were previously pastoral nomads.[11]

Finkelstein argues that over the centuries there were various waves of settlement in the highlands, and one of these waves finally developed into a state, properly to be called 'Israel' only with the rise of King Omri in the 9th century BCE.[12] What is envisaged in this longer-term perspective is an oscillation of 'sedentarization and nomadization of indigenous groups in response to changing political, economic, and social circumstances'.[13] Thus, there are widely differing views about the constituent elements of the highland population—farmers, herders, refugees and so on—but the bulk of the population is seen as Indigenous, no matter what model of settlement is proposed.

The key questions concerning the new settlers of central hill country in the twelfth and eleventh centuries are these: did they have sufficient solidarity to constitute Israelite ethnicity (as Dever argues), or did they not (so Finkelstein, in some of his more recent publications)? How and when did Israelite ethnicity distinguish itself from its Indigenous origins? The answers to these questions depend partly upon archaeological evidence and partly upon conceptual issues: what exactly is meant by 'ethnicity', and how does a distinctive ethnic group arise from its cultural antecedents? It is hardly possible to make any coherent claim about *when* Israelite ethnicity arose until these logically prior questions are addressed.

I want to provide some fresh perspectives that help to justify Dever's interpretation of the early Iron Age communities as 'proto-Israelite'.[14] First, it will be necessary to make some general 'theoretical' points. The assumption that every ethnic group has a distinctive material culture, for example, is mistaken. In the case of the Philistines, we *can* describe a distinct configuration of elements in the archaeological record, but this is not always the case. There are certainly a number of significant problems in correlating

11. Dever, *What Did the Biblical Writers Know?*, pp. 110–19; see also pp. 97–100 ('Who were the Early Israelites?'); cf. Finkelstein and Silberman, *The Bible Unearthed*, pp. 111–18. Zevit, *The Religions of Israel*, p. 93, does not accept the idea of a population explosion on this scale, and he provides different figures.

12. Finkelstein and Silberman attribute statehood to Judah only at the end of the 8th century, after the northern kingdom fell under Assyrian domination (*The Bible Unearthed*, pp. 23, 44, 150, 325).

13. Finkelstein, 'Can the Real Israel Stand Up?', p. 208.

14. Dever, *What did the Biblical Writers Know?*, p. 117, wrongly claims that Brett accepts 'the general skepticism of the revisionists' in the introductory essay, 'Interpreting Ethnicity', in *Ethnicity and the Bible* (Leiden: Brill, 1996), pp. 3–22. On the contrary, I simply indicated the difficulties in correlating material remains with ethnicity.

material remains from the twelfth and eleventh century BCE with Israelite ethnicity.

There are common arguments in the 'biblical archaeology' literature prior to the 1980s, for example, in which particular types of pottery and domestic architecture were taken to be uniquely Israelite (especially the so-called 'four-room house' and the 'collar-rim' storage jar). It was subsequently discovered that these models were not as distinctive as previously thought, and the task of correlation was thereby rendered much more difficult.[15] *Yet cultural permeability, or hybridity, is not in itself an argument against ethnicity.* Anthropological research indicates that the elements of a cultural repertoire that are maintained by an ethnic group can vary considerably; some elements will inevitably be shared with—or borrowed from—other groups, but the most significant factor is how the social boundaries are maintained.[16] Cultural traits may be shared across ethnic boundaries in highly complex ways, e.g., a single group may share a religion with people who speak a different language, while their economy may be shared with a quite different group.[17] Ethnic indicators potentially arise from a range of cultural practices and artifacts, configured in distinctive patterns and maintained by the group themselves. Moreover, these patterns are subject to re-negotiation.

Even Finkelstein seems willing to concede, however, that there is one distinctive feature in the new Iron Age settlements of the central hill country, namely, the absence of pig bones. Archaeological evidence now indicates that pig husbandry was practised in the earlier Canaanite communities of the Bronze Age (including sites in the highlands), and it continued to be practised on the coastal plains as well as in the Transjordan during the early Iron Age, *but not in the highlands.* Thus, while there are strong continuities in architecture and pottery on both sides of the Jordan in this period, the absence of pig bones is distinctive.

If this can be taken as evidence of a 'pig taboo' then it could provide a clue to an ethnic boundary at the time.[18] It is only a clue, however, since it is logically possible that there were merely practical reasons why pig husbandry was not maintained in this period, and the archaeological findings

---

15. See Stager, 'Forging an Identity', pp. 104–105.

16. Fredrik Barth (ed.), 'Introduction', *Ethnic Groups and Boundaries: The Social Organization of Culture Difference* (London: Allen & Unwin, 1969), pp. 9–38.

17. Thomas Eriksen, *Ethnicity and Nationalism: Anthropological Perspectives* (London: Pluto, 1993), p. 34.

18. Finkelstein, 'Can the Real Israel Stand Up?', p. 206, following Lawrence Stager, *Ashkelon Discovered* (Washington: Biblical Archaeology Society, 1991), pp. 9, 19; cf. Dever, *What Did the Biblical Writers Know?*, p. 113.

cannot demonstrate the cultural or religious values at stake for the highland population.[19] To speak of a 'pig taboo' is to go beyond what the evidence requires, and it certainly does not indicate Israelite uniqueness, since pork was avoided in many societies in southwest Asia during the Iron Age. The archaeologist Elizabeth Bloch-Smith accepts these points, but rightly argues that ethnicity is not so much about uniqueness as about contrast: 'Pork consumption was widespread in twelfth- and eleventh-century BCE Philistia and rare in Israel. Not eating pork distinguished Israel from its Philistine enemy during contentious times, while other peoples' dietary preferences were irrelevant'.[20]

Thus, it is not just that an ethnic group shares a configuration of cultural traits, but it is important to see this identity as relational and negotiated. Ethnicity is 'a product of contact', as Thomas Eriksen puts it in his comprehensive discussion of the relevant anthropological literature. 'If a setting is wholly mono-ethnic, there is effectively no ethnicity, since there is nobody there to communicate cultural difference to'.[21]

We must also recognize that there are degrees of ethnic unity, ranging from large ethnic communities that may share territory and political organization to ethnic 'networks' which share resources or culture without any centralized organization.[22] Thus, even if Finkelstein and Silberman are correct about the rise of an Israelite 'state' in the ninth century, this does not preclude the existence of ethnic *networks* in earlier periods. Hence, 'Israelite' networks may well have existed in the twelfth and eleventh centuries BCE, even if they lacked centralized political organization. This would accord with the biblical narratives that describe a period during which the tribes were governed by 'judges' before the rise of Israelite kings.

Dever's term 'proto-Israelite' can appear anachronistic—as if it were simply a retrospective inference from later periods, rather than a self-description used in the twelfth century. Unfortunately, there is no inscription from the early Iron Age bearing the name 'Israel' which has been recovered from the excavations in the central hill country. There is, however, good archaeological evidence to suggest that already around 1210 BCE there was a people

19.   Brian Hesse and Paula Wapnish, 'Can Pig Remains Be Used for Ethnic Diagnosis in the Ancient Near East?', in Silberman and Small, *The Archaeology of Israel*, pp. 238–70.

20.   Elizabeth Bloch-Smith, 'Israelite Ethnicity in Iron I', *Journal of Biblical Literature* 122 (2003), p. 423.

21.   Eriksen, *Ethnicity and Nationalism*, pp. 34–35.

22.   Eriksen, *Ethnicity and Nationalism*, pp. 41–45, discusses degrees of incorporation, distinguishing ethnic 'communities', which have the highest degree of incorporation, from 'networks' and 'categories'.

group in Canaan recognized as 'Israel'. As already indicated, the so-called Merneptah stele records an Egyptian military victory against this group and claims to have wiped them out:

> The princes are prostrate, saying 'Shalom' [Peace]
> Not one is raising his head among the Nine Bows.
> Now that Libya [Tehenu] has come to ruin,
> Hatti is pacified.
> The Canaan has been plundered into every sort of woe;
>   Ashkelon has been overcome;
>   Gezer has been captured;
>   Yanoam is made nonexistent;
>   The Israelites are laid waste and their seed is not.[23]

Within the larger territory of Canaan, the text designates Ashkelon, Gezer, and Yanoam as city-states, but in the case of 'the Israelites', the name is attached to a hieroglyphic symbol indicating that this was a people group. The inscription does not provide clear evidence of the size or precise location of this Israel, but at the very least, it points to an ethnic group with a low degree of incorporation, distinguishable from the city-states within Canaan.

Even Finkelstein and Silberman have conceded this point in their book *The Bible Unearthed*. Commenting on the Merneptah stele, they note that 'the Israelites emerged only gradually as a distinct group in Canaan, beginning at the end of the thirteenth century BCE'.[24] What follows from this argument is not the denial of Israelite ethnicity in the early Iron Age (as some of Finkelstein's work suggests), but rather a more nuanced understanding of what might constitute ethnicity. Niels Lemche, in an otherwise sceptical book, supplies just this nuance when he suggests that an ethnic group may be seen as 'part of a continuum of ethnic groups with overlapping borders, with probably many identities, held together by a founding myth or set of myths and narratives about how this particular group came into being'.[25]

Even given the controversial nature of the archaeological evidence, we do know that already at the end of the thirteenth century a group bearing the name 'Israel' did exist, whatever discontinuities may be discerned

---

23. The translation is from Stager, 'Forging an Identity', p. 91, except that I have rendered 'Israel' as 'the Isaelites' in order to reflect the plural in the Egyptian text. The most comprehensive study on this controversial inscription is now M.G. Hasel, *Domination and Resistance: Egyptian Military Activity in the Southern Levant, ca. 1300–1185 BCE* (Leiden: E.J. Brill, 1998).

24. Finkelstein and Silberman, *The Bible Unearthed*, p. 57.

25. Niels Lemche, *The Israelites in History and Tradition* (Louisville: Westminster John Knox, 1998), p. 20.

between that group and the later Israel of the ninth or seventh centuries BCE. This group may be reasonably linked with the new settlements in the central hill country at the beginning of the twelfth century, since the evidence of pig avoidance there at least distinguishes them from the Philistines who were settling on the coastal plains in that century. We do not, however, have any clear archaeological evidence for how early Israel distinguished itself from Indigenous groups in Canaan. Since the Canaanite divine name 'El' was incorporated within the very name 'Israel', we may infer that this group were originally worshippers of El, alongside other gods like Baal, Asherah and Anat.[26] Judg. 9.46, for example, refers to 'El of the covenant' rather than 'Yahweh of the covenant'.

The Prophets' Interpretations of Israel's Story

In Finkelstein and Silberman's critical account of Israel's history in *The Bible Unearthed*, the seventh century is a key formative period, and the Bible's traditions are not considered a reliable guide to Israel's self-understanding before that time. Yet Finkelstein and Silberman accept that some memories of an 'exodus' can be found in the prophets of the eighth century, particularly in Amos 2.10, 3.1; 9.7 and Hos. 11.1; 13.4.[27]

They claim that the pre-existing saga of the exodus from Egypt, which is 'neither historical truth nor literary fiction', was re-shaped by the momentous confrontation in the seventh century between the young Judean king, Josiah, and the imperial Pharaoh Necho. The 'ancient traditions from many different sources were crafted into a single sweeping epic that bolstered Josiah's political aims'. The foundational tradition that spoke of a confrontation between Moses and Pharaoh was shaped into a mirror of Josiah's contemporary reality. According to Finkelstein and Silberman, the exodus tradition may reflect the Semitic Hyksos occupation of Egypt and their later expulsion in 1570, since it is quite plausible to think that the story of a Semitic group rising to power in Egypt could have served as a focus of solidarity in resistance against Egyptian imperial rule in Canaan. However, there is so much anachronism, or 'updating', incorporated into the biblical material that it is now impossible to trace the genealogy of these

---

26.   Mark Smith, *The Origins of Biblical Monotheism* (Oxford: Oxford University Press, 2001), pp. 142–43; *The Early History of God* (London: Harper & Row, 1990), pp. 1–39; John Day, *Yahweh and the Gods and Goddesses of Canaan* (Sheffield: Sheffield Academic Press, 2000), pp. 226–33; Zevit, *The Religions of Ancient Israel*, pp. 611–90.

27.   Finkelstein and Silberman, *The Bible Unearthed*, p. 68.

traditions.[28] (Interestingly, for example, amongst the known Hyksos kings in Egypt we find the Semitic name 'Yaqub', and this spelling is the equivalent of the biblical 'Jacob' although the biblical narrative never claims that this ancestor was a king in Egypt.[29])

We can draw more conclusions, however, about the Yahwism of the eighth-century prophets than what Finkelstein and Silberman seem to allow. It is significant that Amos 3.15 and 6.4 refer to ivory decoration, which has so far only been found in excavated material from the ninth and eighth centuries, so it is not likely that this material in Amos was invented in later centuries. Accordingly, Dever affirms the historical authenticity of Amos's preaching, and he concludes that the exodus tradition—although not all the details found in the biblical narrative—is at least a century older than Josiah.[30] (If we see the exodus tradition as a 'foundation myth', in Lemche's terminology, it is important to note that this is an analytical term used by modern scholars, rather than an 'ethnic genre' used by ancient Israelites.[31] Any 'founding myths' shared by an Israelite population would have been *seen as* truthful, otherwise they could not have had the function of founding myths.[32])

In regards to the development of Israelite identity, it is clear that Deuteronomy includes a very sharp distinction between 'Israelites' and the previous populations of Canaan, although many archaeologists now say that this distinction cannot be demonstrated from material remains. As we noted in the previous chapter on the ancestors, Deuteronomy's distinction is clearly founded on the religious ideal of fidelity to Yahweh. Indeed, we can surmise that the label 'Canaanite' became in the course of time not so much an ethnic tag as a derogatory term used by Yahweh-El worshippers for their neighbours who continued to worship other gods.[33] Yet, as already

28.   So Finkelstein and Silberman, *The Bible Unearthed*, pp. 56–57, 69–71.

29.   William Dever, *Who Were the Early Israelites, and Where Did They Come from?* (Grand Rapids: Eerdmans, 2003), p. 10. See further, E.S. Frerichs and L.H. Lesko (eds.), *Exodus: The Egyptian Evidence* (Washington: Biblical Archaeology Society, 1993).

30.   Dever, *What Did the Biblical Writers Know?*, pp. 237–39.

31.   David Ben-Amos, 'Analytical Categories and Ethnic Genres', in D. Ben-Amos (ed.), *Folklore Genres* (Austin: University of Texas Press, 1976), pp. 215–42; Susan Niditch, *Oral World and Written Word: Ancient Israelite Literature* (Louisville: Westminster John Knox, 1996), pp. 114–16.

32.   This is accepted also by Lemche, *The Israelites in History and Tradition*, p. 96, who otherwise emphasizes the fictional nature of biblical material.

33.   Karel van der Toorn, *Family Religion in Babylonia, Syria and Israel* (Leiden: Brill, 1996), p. 328; Bernard M. Levinson, *Deuteronomy and the Hermeneutics of Legal Innovation* (New York: Oxford University Press, 1997), pp. 148–49.

noted, the archaeological evidence for Iron Age religious practices indicates that 'Israel' as a whole also worshipped Canaanite gods and goddesses, e.g., Baal, Asherah, and Anat. Thus, Deuteronomy's version of Yahwism could not have been the key element in the earlier formation of 'Israelite' self-understanding.

Nevertheless, it is important to recognize that Yahweh is not mentioned in the earliest religious texts of Canaan, and it is therefore justifiable to conclude that Yahweh was not an Indigenous god.[34] It thus becomes possible to suggest that the worship of Yahweh may have been one of the catalysts in forging a unifying ethnic identity above the level of the tribes.[35] A clear reference to the name 'Yahweh' in non-biblical material is found in a Moabite inscription of the ninth century, although earlier Egyptian texts seem to associate it with the Shasu tribes south-east of Palestine. This Egyptian material may be connected with biblical narratives linking Yahwism with 'Midianites',[36] but whatever is concluded about the origins of Yahwism, we can safely assume that the divine name 'Yahweh' entered the religious repertoire of Iron Age Palestine before the ninth century. The Moabite inscription allows us to push the arrival of Yahwism in Canaan back that far, simply on archaeological grounds.

It would be difficult to conclude much about the nature of this Yahwism without reference to biblical texts, but we could plausibly infer from the Book of Amos that some version of an exodus story was an assumption lying behind the prophetic material. Thus, one could say for example that Amos 2.10 and 3.1–2 do not themselves supply a 'founding myth', to use Niels Lemche's term, but they imply one: they imply a founding story concerning the 'children of Israel', whose exodus from Egypt is linked with the intervention of Yahweh. And these verses imply one more thing: that the implications of this founding narrative have been misunderstood by Amos' audience. Indeed, if there is any commonality amongst the prophetic texts normally dated to the eighth century, it is that the prophetic perspective is at odds with popular religion.

In particular, Amos wants to insist that the story of salvation from Egypt's oppression does not provide Israel with a divine assurance of everlasting protection in the promised land. Amos 9.7 even insists that the exodus experience is not unique to Israel: this oracle of Yahweh says 'Did I not bring Israel up from the land of Egypt, and the Philistines from Caphtor and the Arameans from Kir?' The arch-enemies of the early Iron Age,

34. This is, for example, Zevit's conclusion, *The Religions of Israel,* p. 687.
35. See Stager, 'Forging an Identity', pp. 112–13.
36. Stager, 'Forging an Identity', pp. 105–11.

the Philistines, are here given space within divine providence, a shocking suggestion for those who may have believed that Israelite landrights were exclusive. More importantly for Amos, Yahweh has expectations regarding social justice, and if they are not respected, the land will be lost. Amos does not cite any laws of Moses in order to make this point (as Deuteronomy does), but Yahweh's expectations are assumed to be valid nonetheless.

Hosea, on the other hand, is most concerned to say that the land will be lost if Israel does not act in ways which demonstrate loyalty to Yahweh *alone*; the worship of any of the other gods of Canaan is not acceptable. The bond created by the exodus story implies an exclusive loyalty:

> When Israel was a child, I loved him,
> And out of Egypt I called my son.
> The more I called them, the more they went from me;
> They kept sacrificing to the baals, and offering incense
>   to idols (Hos. 11.1–2).

Hosea sees no divine legitimation of Israel's perpetual hold on the land, but rather predicts a judgment wrought by the neighboring empires: 'They shall return to the land of Egypt, and Assyria shall be their king, because they have refused to return to me' (11.5). So both Hosea and Amos seem to be promoting novel interpretations of the exodus in ways quite unexpected by their audiences.

The controversies reflected in the Books of Amos and Hosea provide good evidence of *intra-Israelite* debate in the eighth century, a debate that seems to envisage a level of social cohesion above the level of the clan *before* Sennacharib's invasion discussed in our previous chapter. In the seventh century, Deuteronomic theologians inherited the preaching of the prophets—as well as the theological problem of how to explain the loss of the northern territories to the Assyrian empire—and constructed a 'national' unity ('Israel the people of Yahweh') by focussing on the 'brother' Israelite who shared exclusive loyalty to Yahweh. This language of kinship was used to re-shape Israelite ethnic identity in a way that was focussed on religion, rather than other cultural markers.[37] Language, architecture and pottery, for example, did not distinguish Israel from the Indigenous peoples of Canaan.

---

37. See Moshe Weinfeld's emphasis on the metaphor of 'brotherhood' in Deuteronomy, in his *Deuteronomy and the Deuteronomic School* (Oxford: Clarendon Press, 1972), pp. 225–32, especially p. 229; Bernard Levinson, *Deuteronomy and the Hermeneutics of Legal Innovation* (New York: Oxford University Press, 1997), pp. 148–49. On 'constructivist' rather than 'primordial' models of ethnicity, see Brett, 'Interpreting Ethnicity', *Ethnicity and the Bible*, pp. 12–14.

As already noted, the archaeological evidence suggests that Israel's earlier cultural identity was not focussed on exclusive loyalty to Yahweh. On the contrary, Yahweh was at first incorporated into Indigenous religious practices, and perhaps the introduction of a 'pig taboo' may have been part of this process. In contrast to the Iron Age incursion of the Philistines, the formation of Israel as a people was not characterized by the imposition of a new culture; Israelite ethnicity seems to have arisen as a split within Canaanite culture, and that helps to explain why we find many aspects of cultural hybridity in the archaeological record.[38] It seems that Israelite ethnicity was forged in the early Iron Age with an antagonism to the Philistine colonies. But in the course of time, a moderately 'inclusive' Yahwism—having linked with El and the *'elohim* of the ancestors—became progressively more exclusive, especially in the preaching of Hosea and in the laws of Deuteronomy. Israel's history was then re-interpreted in light of this more exclusive Yahwism, not just in the historiographical works influenced by Deuteronomy, but also in the later prophets.

Concluding Reflections

The debate concerning the implications of Israel's Indigenous origins has barely begun. For many religious conservatives, the key task is to hold on to the essential historical reliability of the biblical narratives, even given the recent turn in the archaeological tide. The radical 'revisionists', on the other hand, have relentlessly put forward arguments that deny historicity to biblical accounts, while most archaeologists tend to be more moderate. William Dever, for example, can see little historical value in the conquest narratives, but he still takes seriously the idea that among the early followers of Yahweh were some tribal Shasu who, under a 'sheikh-like leader with the Egyptian name of Moses', brought the name 'Yahweh' to Canaan, along with a story of liberation. This story and divine name could well have become *a formative influence amongst the Canaanites who sought liberation from Egyptian imperial rule*.[39] (The biblical narrative itself mentions that people who were not part of the Israelite kinship group also escaped from Egypt with Moses, claiming in Exod. 12.38 that 'a mixed multitude went up with them'). Certainly, someone brought the name of 'Yahweh' to Canaan, since at least this divine name was not Indigenous. And there has to be some connection between

38. On ethnic 'fission' see Erikson, *Ethnicity and Nationalism*, pp. 68–69.

39. William Dever, *Who Were the Early Israelites, and Where Did They Come from?* (Grand Rapids: Eerdmans, 2003), pp. 232–37.

this early movement and the later 'narrative extensions' of Israelite identity that shaped various groups into an enduring solidarity.[40]

A political controversy has recently arisen about the legitimacy of these 'narrative extensions', since more than one story can include the Iron Age communities of the central hill country. Palestinian archaeologists and community leaders have recently been arguing that modern Palestinians are the descendants of the ancient Canaanites and that the 'biblical archaeologists' of the early twentieth century—both Christians and Jews—conspired to displace Palestinian history.[41] Some secular Jews, on the other hand, have argued that Jews no longer need the Bible to justify their presence in the modern state of Israel, since they can now claim the status of 'natives'.[42] Both sides of the Palestinian-Israeli conflict have therefore laid claim to their Indigenous origins.

As anthropologists have made clear, even the most traditional cultures have usually borrowed from neighbouring cultures, and significant elements may be held in common with others, and in this respect ancient Israel is no different. But the key aspect in the formation of ethnic groups is the construction and *maintenance of boundaries*. Quite apart from the aspects of material culture and the worship of El that we have discussed in this chapter, the *religious* hybridity of Jews and Palestinians may be illustrated through their common adherence to traditions of Abraham, even though these scriptural roots often seem to provoke further sibling rivalries and negotiations. Interestingly, Christian and Muslim Palestinians have historically shared a festival at a shrine of Elijah near Bethlehem, yet the prophet Elijah's place in *Jewish* tradition is obscured in the complex negotiations between Christian and Muslim participants.[43] It seems

---

40.   Bloch-Smith, 'Israelite Ethnicity in Iron I', p. 405; cf. Stephen Cornell, 'That's the Story of our Life', in P. Spickard and W. Burroughs, *We Are a People: Narrative and Multiplicity in Constructing Ethnic Identity* (Philadelphia: Temple University Press, 2000), pp. 43–44.

41.   See Keith Whitelam, *The Invention of Ancient Israel: The Silencing of Palestinian History*. (London: Routledge, 1996), esp. pp. 43–45 where the discussion of 'empty land' discourse echoes the Australian ideology of terra nullius; cf. John J. Collins, 'Exodus and Liberation in Postcolonial Perspective' in his *The Bible after Babel: Historical Criticism in a Postmodern Age* (Grand Rapids: Eerdmans, 2005), pp. 53–74.

42.   This point has been made, for example, by Ze'ev Herzog, an archaeologist from Tel Aviv University, quoted in Dever, *Who Were the Early Israelites?*, p. 239; on Palestinian archaeology more generally, see Dever, pp. 237–41.

43.   G. Bowman, 'Nationalizing the Sacred: Shrines and Shifting Identities in the Israeli-Occupied Territories', *Man: The Journal of the Royal Anthropological Institute* 28 (1993), pp. 431–60. See further, Rashid Khalidi, *Palestinian Identity: The Construction of Modern National Consciousness* (New York: Columbia University Press, 1997).

that every community's story is marked by such patterns of exclusion and inclusion, and the key question is what implications are drawn from that dynamic. 'Every identity therefore is a construction', the postcolonial critic Edward Said once said, 'a composite of different histories, migrations, conquests, liberations, and so on. We can deal with these either as worlds at war, or as experiences to be reconciled'.[44]

In the histories of colonization, a key problem has been the *imposition* of ethnic identity by those who had the most power. As the Australian Aboriginal lawyer Taylor has put it, 'Our identity is an issue that should be adjudicated by us, not for us'. Her insistence on this point flows from the accumulated experience of government bias of 'white over black, or etic over emic, standpoints' in successive phases of legislation.[45] Even when native title was recognized in Australian law after 1992, white courts retained the power to define which groups were 'authentically' Aboriginal and therefore justified in asserting their connection with traditional lands. The Indigenous leader Professor Michael Dodson has criticized the persistent tendency in the Australian law and media to distinguish between 'authentic' and 'hybrid' Aborigines—expressed especially in the contrast between traditional, rural and remote communities on the one hand, and urban Indigenous people on the other. The right to self-definition, Dodson writes, 'must include the right to inherit the collective right of one's people, and to transform that identity creatively according to the self-defined aspirations of one's people and one's own generation'.[46]

This perspective from contemporary Australian politics provides an analogy for thinking about the development of Israelite religion. Israelite cultural identity was not imposed from outside in the manner of the Philistine colonists; it first developed as a fissure within Canaanite culture in the rural setting of the central hill country. In the course of time, and especially with the rise of urban centres, one group within Israel developed an understanding of El-Yahweh that made the worship of other gods incompatible with

---

44. Edward Said, *The End of the Peace Process* (New York: Pantheon, 2000), p. 142. The processes and nature of 'reconciliation' are, of course, matters that require further reflection. See Chapter 10 below.

45. Taylor, 'Who's Your Mob?—The Politics of Aboriginal Identity and the Implications for a Treaty', in Australian Institute of Aboriginal and Torres Strait Islander Studies, *Treaty: Let's Get It Right* (Canberra: Aboriginal Studies Press, 2003), p. 90. 'Emic' refers here to insider points of view, while 'etic' refers to outsiders' views—whether academic or legislative.

46. Michael Dodson, 'The End in the Beginning: Re(de)fining Aboriginality', *Australian Aboriginal Studies* 1 (1994), pp. 2–13 (5). See also Marcia Langton, 'Urbanizing Aborigines', *Social Alternatives* 12/2 (1981), pp. 16–22.

Israelite identity, even though many aspects of culture continued to be shared with Indigenous neighbours. In principle, there is nothing problematic with this development, since no ethnic group is static, and some aspects of a group's cultural history may be lost from the collective memory as a consequence of that group's choices and struggles. Unless one is to fall back on to the nostalgic 'myth of authenticity', there is no reason to assume that ancient Canaanite culture was incorrigible and that ancient Israelites were not free to develop their own self-definition in fresh religious terms.

In terms of 'postcolonial' ethics, the key issue here is whether these developments were simply imposed by the most powerful, or developed by Israelite people themselves. I argued in the previous chapter that Yahwist theology was not used to legitimate land dispossession in the interests of the Crown, since all the Torah's law codes re-affirm family ties to *ancestral* land. And with regard to the discussion in this chapter, we have no reason to doubt that the theological innovations of Amos and Hosea came from eighth-century prophets with little power, who were largely ignored until their visions of judgment came to dreadful fruition—when the Assyrian empire took violent possession of the northern kingdom of Israel.

What remains disturbing, however, is that a classic text in the seventh century, the book of Deuteronomy, proposed a theologically focussed revision of Israel's identity that included images of genocide for other people groups. This is the thorny problem that will concern us in the next chapter.

5

Deuteronomy, Genocide and the Desires of Nations

> …the Hittites, Girgashites, Amorites, Canaanites, Perizzites, Hivites and Jebusites, seven nations more numerous and stronger than you: when Yahweh your God has delivered them over to you and you have defeated them, then you must ban them completely (*hrm*). Make no treaty with them, and show them no mercy. Do not intermarry with them.
>
> *Deuteronomy 7.1–3*

> However, in the cities of these peoples Yahweh your God gives you as an inheritance, do not leave alive anything that breathes. Indeed, you will ban them completely (*hrm*).
>
> *Deuteronomy 20.16–17*

How are we to understand the biblical texts that 'ban' the prior inhabitants of Canaan? As indicated in chapter one above, these biblical directives had a significant impact in modern histories of colonization, and some of the effects on Indigenous people are still painfully evident. It would not be enough to discuss in this chapter the ancient cultural logic of the 'ban' (*herem*), or to explore the legal innovations of Deuteronomy, while ignoring this colonial history of reception—beginning with Juan Ginés de Sepúlveda's 'Treatise on the Just Causes of the War against the Indians' in 1550. Some scholars have tried to avoid the connection between the biblical *herem* and modern concepts of genocide, although there have been a number of recent discussions which face the connection more directly, partly in response to the upsurge of militant Islamist groups.[1] As we saw in the previous chapter, historians dispute the extent to which biblical conquest narratives correspond to actual events, but the theory alone has wrought monstrous damage in modern history, regardless of what conclusions we reach about events in the Bronze Age. And we should note that the United Nations *Convention on the Prevention and Punishment of the Crime of Genocide* (1948), Article II, does not restrict itself to mass killing but refers also to 'mental harm' caused

---

1. E.g., Stanley N. Gundry (ed.), *Show Them No Mercy: Four Views on God and Canaanite Genocide* (Grand Rapids: Zondervan, 2003).

by practices of cultural genocide.[2] In this chapter we will accordingly discuss a range of questions regarding the laws and narratives of conquest, without presuming any particular reconstruction of Israel's early history. The focus will be on the development of biblical *ideas* about the conquest, and then on some implications arising for postcolonial interpretation.

The Hebrew Bible's conceptions of war were not formed all at once, and as we have seen there are a number of inconsistencies in the conquest narratives. The famous destruction of Jericho, for example, presumes a relatively rare version of *herem* that does not accord with other narratives. It includes the slaughter of *livestock* along with the mass killing of men, women and children (Josh. 6.21), and this accords with the requirement of Deut. 20.16–18 regarding the conquest of the promised land: 'everything that breathes' (*kol neshamah*) was to be killed. That this requirement of *herem* should include animals is implied both in the Jericho narrative, and in 1 Sam. 15.12–19 where Saul's failure to implement the *herem* against Amalekites turns on his failure to destroy their livestock.

The majority of conquest narratives, however, do not interpret the *herem* so comprehensively. In the narrative about Ai, for example, it is said that 'the livestock and plunder of that city Israel took for themselves, as Yahweh had instructed Joshua' (Josh. 8.24–27). Joshua 11.14, similarly, describes the taking of livestock as booty without any recognition that this is contrary to the Deuteronomic law, and even claims that 'they did not leave any who breathes' (*kol neshamah*). The narrator here presumes that the very same words as those used in the law—*kol neshamah*—mean any *person* who breathes. It is very unlikely that this narrator knew of our version of the Jericho narrative, or of Saul's failure to slaughter the animals in his *herem* against the Amalekites. Any conflict between Yahweh's command to Joshua and Yahweh's command to Moses regarding the proper conduct of the *herem* would have required some explanation.

Differences such as these reflect the historical development of ideas about the conquest. One early version of the *herem*, in Num. 21.2–3 for example, sees it as a vow taken in certain circumstances, and not as a generalized law at all.[3] Moreover, the legislation in Deuteronomy is different from what we find in the older legal tradition in Exod. 23.20–33, which mentions

---

2. See Colin Tatz, *With Intent to Destroy: Reflecting on Genocide* (London: Verso, 2003).

3. Moshe Weinfeld, *Deuteronomy 1–11* (New York: Doubleday, 1991), p. 364. Cf. Weinfeld, 'The Ban on the Canaanites in the Biblical Codes and its Historical Development', in A. Lemaire and B. Otzen (eds.), *History and Traditions of Early Israel* (Leiden: E.J. Brill, 1993), pp. 142–60.

no *herem* against persons, but only the destruction of cultic objects: 'you shall not bow down to their gods, or worship them, or follow their practices, but you shall ban them completely (*hrm*) and break their pillars in pieces' (Exod. 23.24). According to the Exodus vision of the conquest, the Indigenous peoples would be driven out gradually by God alone, and not killed by Israelites:

> I will send my terror in front of you, and will throw into confusion all the people against whom you will come, and I will make all your enemies turn their backs to you… I will not drive them out in one year, or the land would become desolate and the wild animals would multiply against you. Little by little I will drive them out, until you have increased and possess the land (Exod. 23.27, 29–30).

Some scholars have suggested that Deuteronomy's understanding of the *herem* reflects an attempt to elicit further implications from the earlier laws in Exodus, but it is also necessary to see Deuteronomy as a comprehensive theological vision for its own time. Certainly Exodus 22.20 says that anyone sacrificing to other gods must be declared *herem*, but this is not yet prescription for corporate slaughter, and it is not even clear that this version of *herem* means death; it could mean excommunication or shunning, as it came to mean in later Jewish tradition.[4]

When Lev. 27.28–29 says that persons declared *herem* should be put to death, it does not follow that Leviticus is in agreement with Deuteronomy's conquest ideology. Leviticus nowhere demands that Israelites should kill Canaanites or subject them to *herem*. Leviticus 18.25–28 explains that the land itself 'vomited out' the original inhabitants on account of their sins, employing a metaphor that implies expulsion rather than destruction.[5] In short, the ambiguities of the concept of *herem* can only be resolved in particular contexts where it is further defined.

In the case of Deut. 7.1–3, it is difficult to see why it would be necessary to ban treaties or intermarriage with the prior inhabitants of Canaan if these people were meant to be completely exterminated; presumably, one

---

4.   Christa Schäfer-Lichtenberger, 'Bedeutung und Funktion von *Herem* in biblisch-hebräischen Texten' *Biblische Zeitschrift* 39 (1994), pp. 27–75; Walter Moberly, 'Toward an Interpretation of the Shema', in C. Seitz and K. Greene-McCreight (eds.), *Theological Exegesis* (Grand Rapids: Eerdmans, 1999), pp. 135–37; Richard Nelson, '*Herem* and the Deuteronomic Social Conscience', in M. Vervenne and J. Lust (eds.), *Deuteronomy and Deuteronomic Literature* (Leuven: Leuven University Press, 1997), pp. 41–46; Weinfeld, *Deuteronomy 1–11*, pp. 364.

5.   Baruch J. Schwartz, 'Reexamining the Fate of the "Canaanites" in the Torah Traditions', in C. Cohen, A. Hurvitz and S.M. Paul (eds.), *Sefer Moshe: The Moshe Weinfeld Jubilee Volume* (Winona Lake: Eisenbrauns, 2004), pp. 151–70.

could only be tempted into treaties and marriages with people who were alive. On the other hand, Deut. 20.16–18 sees the ideal conquest as implying death for 'everything that breaths'. Such tensions within Deuteronomy raise significant questions about just what kind of law book this might be, and more generally, how this kind of literature can best be interpreted.

The Historical Setting of Deuteronomy's Genocide Texts

Biblical scholars have long thought that Deuteronomy, or at least a central core of the book, was composed in seventh-century Judah. The arguments for this hypothesis were based mainly on comparisons internal to the biblical tradition. More recently, a number of studies have reinforced the hypothesis by benchmarking the dating in relation to non-biblical texts that, without question, come from the seventh century. As we saw in the discussion of ancestral religion, there are a number of striking comparisons between Deuteronomy 13 and the treaties of King Esarhaddon, suggesting that the Yahwist requirement for exclusive loyalty to Israel's God was modeled on Assyrian material, yet contested its demand for political loyalty.[6] Israel would have had first-hand knowledge of such political demands after the Assyrian conquest of the northern kingdom and their incursion into Judah in 701 BCE. What is remarkable is that the Jerusalem theologians seem to have resisted such obvious imperial power through a subversive use of 'mimicry'—a mixture of deference and critique which imitated the treaty genre precisely in order to argue *against* submission to the Assyrian gods.[7]

Deuteronomy 13 is particularly relevant to the *herem* theme, since immediately following the portion adapted from Esarhaddon's treaty (discussed in Chapter 3 above), it is said in 13.15 that even Israelites who are proven disloyal to Yahweh shall be punished by having their entire town, people *and livestock*, devoted to the ban (*herem*).

---

6.   See, e.g., 'William Moran The Ancient Near Eastern Background to the Love of God in Deuteronomy', *Catholic Biblical Quarterly* 25 (1963), pp. 77–87; Moshe Weinfeld, *Deuteronomy and the Deuteronomic School* (Oxford: Clarendon Press, 1972), pp. 81–126; Eckart Otto, *Das Deuteronomium: Politische Theologie und Rechtsreform in Juda und Assyrien* (Berlin: de Gruyter, 1999), p. 14; cf. Otto, 'Political Theology in Judah and Assyria', *Svensk exegetisk årsbok* 65 (2000), pp. 59–76.

7.   On the idea of mimicry in postcolonial studies, see Homi Bhabha, *Location of Culture* (London: Routledge, 1994), pp. 102–22.

Vassal Treaty of Esarhaddon §10[8]

If you hear any evil, improper, ugly word…the mouth of his [the king's] *ally*, or from the mouth of *his brothers, his uncles, his cousins, his family, members of his father's line*, or from the mouth of *your brothers, your sons, your daughters*, or from the mouth of a *prophet, an ecstatic, an enquirer of oracles*, or from the mouth of any human being at all; you shall not conceal it but come and report it to Ashurbanipal, the great crown prince designate, son of Esarhaddon, king of Assyria.

Vassal Treaty of Esarhaddon §12

If you are able to seize them and put them to death, then you shall destroy their name and their seed from the land.

Deuteronomy 13.7–15

[7]*If your brother, the son of your mother, or your son, or your daughter or the wife of your bosom, or your friend who is as your own self*, entices you secretly, saying, 'Let us go and worship other gods'—whom neither you nor your fathers have known, [8]some of the gods of the peoples who are round about you…—[9]do not assent to him or listen to him! Let your eye not pity him, nor shall you hold back or condone him. [10]You must surely kill him…

[12]If you hear it said about one of the cities that the Yahweh your God is giving you to live in, [13]that scoundrels from among you have gone out and led the inhabitants of the city astray, saying 'Let us go and worship other gods'…[14]If the charge is established…[15]you shall surely put the inhabitants of that city to the sword, banning it (*ḥrm*)—all who are in it and its cattle—with the edge of the sword.

The reference to capital punishment in Deut. 13.10 provides a motive for the *herem* regulation in v. 15.[9]

What is most significant about v. 15 is that it belongs to that relatively rare version of the ban that includes animals in the scope of the destruction. If Deuteronomy 13 was composed in the seventh century, and this chapter contains the distinctive concept of *herem* found also in Deut. 20.16–18 (the conquest law relating to the Indigenous people of the promised land),

---

8. The translations of VTE §10 and §12 come from Simo Parpolo and Kazuko Watanabe (eds.), *Neo-Assyrian Treaties and Loyalty Oaths* (Helsinki: Helsinki University Press, 1988), pp. 33, 34.

9. Richard Nelson notes that the polar opposite of *herem* was 'to leave survivors or to treat people, animals and objects as plunder… Not to treat as *herem* was to "spare, keep back" (חמל 1 Sam 15.3, 9, 15; Jer 51.3)' (Nelson, 'Social Conscience', p. 45). To Nelson's list of examples one could add Deut. 13.9, where 'holding back' is opposed to *herem* in the immediate context (13.15).

then we may entertain the hypothesis that both texts come from the same authors or editors. Other scholars have dated Deut. 20.16–18 in the seventh century as well, although for different reasons.[10]

The older conquest narratives seem unaware of this most comprehensive concept of the ban, and therefore their narrators are not troubled by any conflict between these narratives and what we now find in the law of 20.16–18. This is not to deny that Deuteronomy contains material that is earlier. In 21.10–14, for example, foreign women taken in battle can become wives, without mentioning any exceptions for Canaanite women.[11] On the other hand, parts of Deuteronomy seem to address an audience in exile,[12] but it does not seem likely that the Deuteronomic *genocide* texts were composed during the exile or later.

There has, however, been one recent proposal to date the genocide material much later than the seventh century, on the grounds that the *herem* texts conflict with a key moral principle in Deuteronomy: love for strangers.[13] But we have to recognize that Deuteronomy does not propose protection for all strangers in the same way. The care for 'resident aliens' or 'sojourners' (*gerim*) depends upon their relative openness to cultural assimilation, whereas unassimilated foreigners are not protected. As Richard Nelson puts it, 'Deuteronomy insists on benevolence and consideration for resident aliens and other needy and marginalized groups, but does so only on the basis of a recognition of some level of community membership and of obligations creation by shared experience'. Other strangers who have not entered into stable relationships with citizens are called 'foreigners' (*nokri/ben nekar*), and they are not to receive the same treatment.[14]

---

10.   See Norbert Lohfink, *Theology of the Pentateuch* (Edinburgh: T. & T. Clark, 1994), pp. 187–88; Alexander Rofé, 'The Laws of Warfare in the Book of Deuteronomy: Their Origins, Intent, and Positivity', *Journal for the Study of the Old Testament* 22 (1985), pp. 23–44.

11.   See especially Michael Fishbane, *Biblical Interpretation in Ancient Israel* (Oxford: Clarendon Press, 1985), pp. 199–209.

12.   For example, Deuteronomy 30.5. For further details, see Georg Braulik, 'Die Völkervernichtung und die Rückkehr Israels ins Verheissungsland: Hermeneutische Bemerkungen zum Buch Deuteronomium', in Vervenne and Lust, *Deuteronomy and Deuteronomic Literature*, pp. 33–38.

13.   See Yair Hoffman, 'The Deuteronomistic Concept of the *Herem*', *Zeitschrift für die Alttestamentliche Wissenschaft* 111 (1999), pp. 196–210.

14.   Nelson, 'Social Conscience', p. 49; for a more comprehensive discussion, see also Kent Sparks, *Ethnicity and Identity in Ancient Israel* (Winona Lake: Eisenbrauns, 1998), which proposes a similar sharp distinction between the ger and the 'foreigner' (*nokri/ben nekar*) in the Hebrew Bible. See especially the summaries on pp. 283–84, 314–19.

It is particularly relevant to note here that the eighth-century prophets expressed their concern for the marginalized by focusing on widows, orphans and the poor, without mentioning *gerim*. Only in Deuteronomy and the later prophets, Jeremiah and Ezekiel, does the concern for resident strangers become a litmus test of moral concern (e.g., Jer. 7.6; Ezek. 14.7). The best way to explain this heightened awareness from the seventh century onwards is that after the fall of the northern kingdom, there was a flood of refugees who headed south into Judah.[15] The experience of these refugees displaced by Assyrian expansion was apparently matched with Israel's story of suffering under the power of Egypt. Hence one could say that the shared experience expressed in the dictum 'Love the stranger (*ger*), because you were strangers in Egypt' (Deut. 10.19) is suffering under imperialism, but this gives rise to solidarity only through assimilation to Yahweh's rule.

One permutation of loyalty to Yahweh included the protection of *gerim*, but the *herem* extrapolates from exclusive loyalty to Yahweh to a specific class of persons or things declared *herem* which belong exclusively to Yahweh and therefore cannot be put to human use (cf. Lev. 27.28). In short, the moral conflict that we perceive between *herem* and the love of strangers was not part of Deuteronomy's logic; *herem* may simply be seen as a mutation of exclusive loyalty to Yahweh. But while it may be possible to explain Deuteronomy's conceptual consistency in regard to the love of strangers, at least two narratives in Joshua suggest that Israel's historians may still have perceived a moral problem with the idea of genocide.

We have already noted that the Jericho narrative provides the paradigm case in which the full extent of the *herem* is enacted (the killing of men, women, children and animals), yet it is precisely the Jericho story which breaks the law in one highly significant respect. An Indigenous prostitute, Rahab, is exempted from the *herem* because she demonstrates loyalty to Yahweh and to Israel (Josh. 6.21–25). In this case, a covenant was made with Rahab to save her family in return for hiding Israelite spies. There was no ambiguity about her being Indigenous, yet a covenant was made anyway, contrary to the requirement in Deuteronomy 7.2 that no covenant or treaty (*berit*) be made with the prior inhabitants of the promised land. Rahab's clan, the narrator tells us, 'has lived in Israel until this day' (6.25), indicating that the narrator tells the story from the perspective of later times. We could presume that the narrator knows the

15.   Frank Crüsemann, *The Torah: Theology and Social History of Old Testament Law* (Edinburgh: T. & T. Clark, 1996), pp. 182–85.

genocide law and needs to explain why an Indigenous group lives safely amongst the Israelites, even though Deuteronomy's vision of the future precludes this. Alternatively, the story may have been constructed precisely in order to oppose the law in Deuteronomy.

The Gibeonites in Joshua 9 provide another case where a treaty was made with a local group, although their claim that they came from a 'far country' meant that Joshua made the treaty without being aware of their Indigenous status (Deut. 20.15 permits treaties with 'distant cities'). When the Gibeonite ruse is discovered, the story puts Joshua into a quandary: should he keep to the treaty, or should he rather keep the law of Moses and kill them all? Joshua keeps his word, against a good deal of pressure from other Israelites, and the Gibeonites therefore are spared 'until this day' (Josh. 9.27). Once again, the narrator is viewing events in the distant past and attempting to explain a puzzling aspect of contemporary reality. In this case, however, the issue is not just that Indigenous people continue to live amongst the Israelites, but the fact that these people are 'hewers of wood and drawers of water' (9.27, an outcome that according to the law in Deut. 20.11 should apply only to peoples who live 'at a distance'). The narrative proposes that the Gibeonite deception provides the answer: since they lied, it seems that they bear an ongoing judgment as slaves of Israel (a notion of intergenerational punishment that coincides with Noah's curse on Ham/Canaan, discussed above in Chapter 2). 1 Kgs 9.20–21 claims, on the other hand, that other Indigenous peoples became slaves simply because the Israelites were *not able* to exterminate them.

Whatever else may be said about the conquest narratives, they point up a number of tensions between theory and practice, or more precisely, between Deuteronomy's legislative theology and Israelite experience. Deuteronomy was engaged in an ideological contest with Assyrian imperial power, and this had complex consequences for how Israel's tradition was being reinterpreted in the seventh century. The narrators of Joshua 6 and 9 provide good evidence that, for example, not everyone agreed with Deuteronomy's interpretation of *ḥerem*.

It is not that Deuteronomy was simply 'invented' at this time. The comparisons between Deuteronomy and Esarhaddon's treaties, discussed above, have suggested to some scholars that Deuteronomy can be seen as part of a 'treaty' or 'covenant' tradition which can be found not only amongst the Assyrians in the seventh century but also much earlier in the documents of the Hittite empire. The blessings in Deuteronomy 28 and the historiographic prologue in chs 1–3 seem to have more in common with earlier Hittite models, whereas the curses and the demand for loyalty in Deuteronomy 13 are derived from Assyrian models, as we have seen.[16] Similarly, the concept of *herem* is not unique to Israel, since it is found in an inscription from the ninth century, recording a Moabite victory over Israel.[17] What this indicates is that Deuteronomy is part of a long literary tradition that has drawn not only on Israelite legal precedents, but has interacted in various ways with neighboring cultures in light of new challenges and crises.[18]

Nevertheless, in light of some clues taken from postcolonial studies, my interpretation of Deuteronomy will show how the details of its 'cultural hybridity' are related to Israel's struggle against the dominant empire of the day.[19] The intention here is not to generalize about imperialism, but to study specific effects and strategies of resistance, in this case focusing on seventh-century material in Deuteronomy.[20] In the next section, we will investigate the application of one theoretical model to the *herem* texts, particularly taking up René Girard's idea of 'mimetic desire' and how it generates the need for scapegoats.

Mimetic Desire in Postcolonial Perspective

The theory of mimetic desire has been applied to a wide range of literatures, including the Bible. We will not be concerned here with the breadth

---

16. See, e.g., Weinfeld, *Deuteronomic School*, pp. 67–84; 'Deuteronomy, Book of', in D.N. Freedman (ed.), *Anchor Bible Dictionary,* II (New York: Doubleday, 1992), p. 170; George Mendenhall and Gary Herion, 'Covenant', in *ABD*, II, pp. 1180–83; Hans Ulrich Steymans, *Deuteronomium 28 und die adê zur Thronfolgeregelung Asarhaddons: Segen und Fluch im Alten Orient und in Israel* (Göttingen: Vandenhoeck & Ruprecht, 1995), pp. 119–41.

17. Sa-Moon Kang, *Divine War in the Old Testament and in the Ancient Near East* (Berlin: de Gruyter, 1989), pp. 80–84. Lawson Younger argues that Assyrian, Hittite and Egyptian conquest accounts reveal a common imperialistic ideology that is shared with the biblical conquest narratives. He notes that the ninth-century Assyrian king Assur-nasir-pal II spoke of 'total war', and his conquest accounts included the killing of young boys and girls (Younger, *Ancient Conquest Accounts* [Sheffield: Sheffield Academic Press, 1990], pp. 95–96, 235–36, 253).

18. See further Udo Rüterswörden, *Von der politischen Gemeinschaft zur Gemeinde: Sudien zu Dt. 16, 18–18, 22* (BBB, 65; Frankfurt: Athenaeum, 1987).

19. For theoretical discussions, see especially Bill Ashcroft, *Postcolonial Transformation* (London: Routledge, 2001); Bhabha, *Location of Culture*; Edward Said, *Culture and Imperialism* (New York: Random House, 1993); Leela Gandhi, *Postcolonial Theory* (St Leonards: Allen & Unwin, 1998).

20. For other examples of cultural response to the Assyrian empire, see Mark Hamilton, 'The Past as Destiny: Historical Visions in Sam'al and Judah under Assyrian Hegemony', *Harvard Theological Review* 91 (1998), pp. 215–50.

of Girard's controversial work, but will focus instead on Norbert Lohfink's specific application of the theory to Deuteronomy.[21] To begin with a summary of the basic framework of ideas is necessary. Girard adopted the classical Greek term 'mimesis' to indicate that beyond mere imitation, human beings learn *what* to desire by acquisitively desiring what we perceive others to desire. But this leads to a dangerous double-bind in which the model is 'always a potential rival and the rival is always an implicit model'.[22] The tensions inherent in this double-bind are relieved by collective violence against scapegoats, by means of which social boundaries are established that sustain the group. Religious ritual can sometimes be seen as a means for reiterating these boundaries, often without the need for repeating the actual violence.[23]

These ideas have already been applied in many different ways in biblical studies, but here I want to draw an analogy between mimetic desire and some similar ideas in postcolonial studies. Homi Bhabha has made famous the idea of 'colonial mimicry', a sly mixture of deference and critique adopted in the exercise of cultural resistance. In one of the most influential discussions of this idea, Bhabha described an example of the 'imitation' of biblical language in colonial India, in which the sacred text was appropriated in an anti-colonial mixing of borrowed and local content.[24] Other postcolonial critics have described similar examples where Indigenous people have borrowed from their colonizers in order to synthesize a new cultural hybridity that sustains their own identity (see also the discussion above in Chapter 1). This postcolonial paradigm of research intersects with Girard's ideas, attending especially to the complexities of social and economic power in the expression of mimetic desire.

21. Norbert Lohfink, 'Opferzentralisation, Säkularisierungthese und mimetische Theorie', in *Studien zum Deuteronomium und zur deuteronomistischen Literatur*, III (Stuttgart: Katholisches Bibelwerk, 1995), pp. 219–60. See also Norbert Lohfink (ed.), *Gewalt und Gewaltlosigkeit im Alten Testament* (Freiberg: Herder, 1983); James G. Williams, *The Bible, Violence and the Sacred: Liberation from the Myth of Sanctioned Violence* (New York: HarperCollins, 1991); Willard Swartley (ed.), *Violence Renounced: René Girard, Biblical Studies and Peacemaking* (Scottdale, PA: Pandora, 2000).

22. Williams, *Sanctioned Violence*, p. 8.

23. Williams, *Sanctioned Violence*, p. 11.

24. Bhabha, *Location of Culture*, pp. 102–22; cf. Elleke Boehmer, *Colonial and Postcolonial Literature* (Oxford: Oxford University Press, 1995), pp. 106–107; Mary Louise Pratt, 'Transculturation and Autoethnography: Peru 1615–1980', in F. Barker *et al.* (eds.), *Colonial Discourse / Postcolonial Theory* (Manchester: Manchester University Press, 1994), pp. 24–47; cf. Susan Hawley, 'Does God Speak Miskitu? The Bible and Ethnic Identity among the Miskitu of Nicaragua', in Brett (ed.), *Ethnicity and the Bible*, pp. 315–42; Ashcroft, *Post-Colonial Transformation*, *passim*.

Norbert Lohfink has identified a specific terminology in Deuteronomy that he links to the idea of mimetic desire: 'When you come to the land Yahweh your God is giving you, do not learn (למד) to imitate (עשׂה ב), the detestable ways of those nations' (Deut. 18.9).[25] The other significant place where this prohibition of imitation appears is in Deut. 20.17–18: 'you shall commit them to the ban—the Hittites and the Amorites, the Canaanites and the Perizzites, the Hivites and the Jebusites—as Yahweh your God has commanded, that they may not teach (למד) you to imitate (עשׂה ב), all their detestable practices'. Lohfink argues that this fear of mimetic desire in Deuteronomy suggests that we look also for the scapegoat process that Girard's model implies. What we find, however, is not an overt ritual that reiterates the founding violence or exclusion, but rather a legal discourse of *herem* that marks the exclusion of near rivals.[26]

Another important aspect of Girard's theory is that the ritual victim must be seen to be 'outside' the community, when in practice victims are usually on an ambiguous margin between 'outside' and 'inside'. And in one permutation of this marginalized position, the victim must be made to appear 'more foreign' than they actually are, in order to reconstitute the community's boundaries.[27] It seems to me that the dynamics of mimetic desire in Deuteronomy are best seen in these terms: the legal discourse excluding the Indigenous peoples arises precisely from a need—perceived by the Deuteronomic authors—to inscribe new boundaries of exclusive loyalty to Yahweh within an Israelite society which over the previous centuries had commonly worshipped other gods alongside Yahweh. Thus, Girard comments that 'there is reason to believe that the wars described as "foreign wars" in the mythic narratives were in fact formerly civil strifes'.[28] One of the functions of the scapegoating process, then, is to obscure such civil conflicts behind the text.

25.   The notion of 'learning' torah is a key motif in Deuteronomy's theology, but here it is applied to Yahweh's rivals. For the language of 'teaching/learning' (למד) and 'imitating' or 'doing according to' (עשׂה ב), see especially Deuteronomy 1.5; 4.1, 5, 10, 14; 5.31; 6.1, 7; 11.19; 17.11; 24.8; 31.19, 22; 33.10. See Lohfink, 'Mimetische Theorie', p. 258; Georg Braulik, *The Theology of Deuteronomy* (Richland Hills, TX: BIBAL Press, 1994), pp. 183–98.

26.   Lohfink, 'Mimetische Theorie', pp. 259–60.

27.   Gordon Matties, 'Can Girard Help Us to Read Joshua?', in Swartley, *Violence Renounced*, p. 90; cf. Girard, *Violence and the Sacred* (Baltimore: Johns Hopkins University Press, 1977), pp. 271–72.

28.   Girard, *Violence and the Sacred*, p. 249.

What kind of 'civil strifes', we may ask, would Deuteronomy want to obscure? As we saw in the previous chapter, there is now a significant consensus amongst archaeologists that early Israel was in fact Indigenous to Canaan. Deuteronomy's reformation of Israelite ethnic identity—centering it on a radically exclusive loyalty to Yahweh—excluded not so much 'Indigenous' peoples but intimate kin who held different religious views and practices. This is the social context that explains the link between the *herem* declared on *Israelite* towns in Deuteronomy 13 and the same unusual *herem* in Deut. 20.16–18 declared on the prior inhabitants of Canaan. What appears on the surface of Deuteronomy 20 as a program for genocide is actually part of an internal social and religious reform in the seventh century.

As we saw in the previous chapter, this ambivalence towards Israel's own Indigenous past has left a trace in Deut. 32.8–9 which refers to Elyon (the 'Most High'), the same Canaanite divine name that is used by the Indigenous priest Melchizedek in Gen. 14.19. Even a reader with no interest in the ancient textual variations is left with the problem of how the Indigenous divinity Elyon can be represented as allotting the people of Israel to Yahweh when Yahweh is said to be the only God (32.39). The most likely solution is to see Yahweh as Elyon, a process of assimilation— or inclusive monotheism—that has been almost entirely obscured by the text, but not quite. Retrospectively we could say that Yahweh has fused with El Elyon, but the other aspects of 'Canaanite' religious adherence have been represented as more foreign in order to assert a new system of ethnic boundaries.[29]

There is actually no evidence that Deuteronomy's reform movement led to mass killings of the kind demanded by its *herem* concept, whether of Canaanites or of Israelites. Whatever historical events might lie behind Josiah's reform narrative in 2 Kings 22–23, for example, we may note that although Josiah slaughters the priests of the high places in the north (2 Kgs 23.20; cf. 23.5, 24), the priests from high places in the south are exempt (2 Kgs 23.8–9). The focus of the reform is on religious objects and practices, and there is no wholesale destruction of towns. It may well be

---

29. Cf. Karel van der Toorn, *Family Religion in Babylonia, Syria and Israel* (Leiden: Brill, 1996), p. 328; Bernard Levinson, *Deuteronomy and the Hermeneutics of Legal Innovation* (New York: Oxford University Press, 1997), pp. 148–49; and our discussion in Chapter 4 above.

that the most extreme form of the ban in Deut. 13.14–16 and 20.16–18 was never taken literally in the seventh century.[30]

Concluding Reflections

The theology of Deuteronomy is in many ways open to deconstruction, since it appears that the quest to formulate an exclusivist worship of Yahweh is itself shaped by a mimetic logic that borrows from Assyrian culture while resisting foreign influence, appropriating the imperial discourses of loyalty, violence and punishment. And all this is justified by love for a God whose character is revealed in a narrative of liberation from Egyptian imperialism.

Deuteronomy produced a 'nationalist' vision in something like the modern sense—an 'imagined community' in which there was 'a deep, horizontal comradeship' established in opposition to imperial impositions. Each Israelite was seen as a 'brother' before Yahweh in a social vision that worked at times positively to urge greater solidarity, and at times negatively, to reject those who did not conform to the new homogeneity. This dynamic is not without analogies in the modern period, when nationalist ideologies have usually been generated by selectively forgetting the past, and at times, forcefully rejecting minorities.[31]

As we saw in the case of Joshua 6 and 9, however, even in the classic applications of Deuteronomy 20 in biblical narrative, the biblical authors began to imagine alternatives to genocide. If we interpret Deuteronomy as an assertion of national dignity over against the dehumanizing tendencies of empire, then it can be seen as part of an ongoing tradition that continues to debate the coherence of its own assumptions and practices. A living tradition, it must be said, is an 'historically extended, socially embodied argument, and an argument precisely in part about the goods

---

30. Moberly, 'Interpretation of the Shema', p. 37. Moberly's argument for a non-literal interpretation of 20.16–18 therefore has some validity.

31. See, e.g., Benedict Anderson, *Imagined Communities: Reflections on the Origin and Spread of Nationalism* (London: Verso, 2nd edn, 1991); Ernest Gellner, *Nations and Nationalism* (Ithaca: Cornell University Press, 1983); Eric Hobsbawm, *Nations and Nationalism since 1780: Programme, Myth, Reality* (Cambridge: Cambridge University Press, 1990); Peter McPhee, *A Social History of France 1780–1880* (London: Routledge, 1992). The analogy with modern nationalism applies even to the balance of powers in Deuteronomy that restricted the jurisdiction of the Crown. See further Mark G. Brett, 'Nationalism and the Hebrew Bible', in J.W. Rogerson, M. Davies, M. Daniel Carroll R. (eds.), *The Bible in Ethics* (Sheffield: JSOT Press, 1995), pp. 136–63.

which constitute that tradition'.[32] There are numerous examples where classic texts remain part of a tradition while being deprived of normative value.[33]

Rabbinic tradition confronted the violence of *herem* in various ways, ruling for example that it was inapplicable when populations had been 'mixed' to such a degree that it was no longer meaningful. Some rabbis were even bold enough to re-interpret Joshua's campaign in a way that flatly contradicts Deuteronomy's requirements. Leviticus Rabbah 17.6, for example, says that 'Joshua sent out three proclamations to the Canaanites: he who wishes to leave shall leave; he who wishes to make peace shall make peace; he who wishes to fight shall do so'.[34] It is the reception of the genocide texts in *Christian* tradition that has yielded the most violent consequences, notably when Christian hermeneutics was wedded to colonialism.

Yet even in contexts where colonial hermeneutics culminated in cultural genocide, some Indigenous theologians have in recent years inverted the tradition of proscribing Indigenous people by insisting that the heritage of each Aboriginal nation should be seen its own 'Old Testament'. This argument has been advanced, for example, by the Choctaw bishop Steve Charleston and, in Australia, by the Rainbow Spirit Elders.[35] While this theological move contravenes colonial praxis, it is consistent with the spirit of Deuteronomy, which asserted that Israel already had its *own* treaty and articulated this resistance by inverting the imperial model of treaty making. Both these ancient and current projects are driven by an anti-imperial assertion of dignity before God. Perhaps in this respect Deuteronomy can be followed, if not imitated.

32.   Alasdair MacIntyre, *After Virtue* (Notre Dame: University of Notre Dame Press, 1981), p. 207.

33.   On the normative role of post-biblical tradition in Judaism, see especially Benjamin Sommer, 'Unity and Plurality in Jewish Canons', in C. Helmer and C. Landmesser (eds.), *One Scripture or Many? Canon from Biblical, Theological and Philosophical Perspectives* (Oxford: Oxford University Press, 2004), pp. 108–50.

34.   Weinfeld, *Deuteronomy 1–11*, p. 384; Cf. Moshe Weinfeld, *The Promise of the Land: The Inheritance of the Land of Canaan by the Israelites* (Berkeley: University of California, 1993), pp. 91–92.

35.   Steve Charleston, 'The Old Testament of Native America', in S.B. Thistlethwaite and M.B. Engel (eds.), *Lift Every Voice: Constructing Christian Theologies from the Underside* (San Francisco: HarperCollins, 1990), pp. 49–61; Rainbow Spirit Elders, *Rainbow Spirit Theology* (Blackburn: Harper Collins Religious, 1997). Cf. Anne Pattel-Gray (ed.), *Aboriginal Spirituality: Past, Present, Future* (Melbourne: HarperCollins, 1996); Mark G. Brett, '*Canto Ergo Sum*: Indigenous Peoples and Postcolonial Theology', *Pacifica* 16 (2003), pp. 247–56.

The significance of *herem* continues to be a problem, but it never plays a role in theories of 'just war' today as it did in the sixteenth century, not least because a distinction between combatants and non-combatants has an indispensable place in any contemporary theory.[36] I will argue below that the very idea of a just war as it was developed in Catholic tradition is incompatible both with the non-violent life of Jesus and with the apostle Paul's theology of reconciliation. The New Testament, however, seems to reiterate the problem of *herem* by shifting divine violence into an apocalyptic framework. In Chapters 8 and 10, we will consider the theological and ethical resources that will be needed in order to break these cycles of mimetic circulation.

36.   See further George Wilkes, 'Judaism and the Justice of War', in P. Robinson (ed.), *Just War in Comparative Perspective* (Aldershot: Ashgate, 2003), pp. 9–23.

6

Dissident Prophets and the Making of Utopias

> Nation shall not lift up sword against nation; neither shall they
> learn war any more.
>
> *Isaiah 2.4 and Micah 4.3*

The unjust acquisition of land by colonial regimes has had devastating
effects on Indigenous peoples, and intergenerational trauma is still evident
today, along with ongoing economic marginalisation. Yet the legal codes
of the Bible protected ancestral estates, and the Israelite prophets repeatedly condemned the misappropriation of land. The Christian churches
rarely had the self-critical capacity to take up these prophetic traditions
in regard to land.[1] Even amongst those who insisted on 'literal' interpretation of the Bible, questions of social justice characteristically dissolved into
a generalized humanitarian paternalism, or into theological contrivances
that emptied the Hebrew Bible of any enduring significance (the prophets, for example, were often reduced to the single function of predicting
Jesus). In this chapter, we will look more closely at the prophetic tradition
of dissidence, beginning with the resistance to dispossession from ancestral
country, and ask why this prophetic critique had so little impact in the history of colonialism.

As indicated in Chapter 1, Christopher Columbus interpreted his own
mission in his *Book of Prophecies* (1501–1502) by drawing in particular from
Isaiah 41–66. There the 'distant islands' were waiting for their redemption,
after which the 'wealth of nations' could be brought to Jerusalem—meaning for Columbus that the king of Spain could use the wealth derived from
new colonies to conquer Jerusalem.[2] Even Bartolomé de las Casas, who
famously condemned the violence against Indigenous peoples, agreed that

---

1. For an account of the notable exceptions in Australia, see Henry Reynolds, *This Whispering in our Hearts* (St Leonards: Allen & Unwin, 1998).
2. See above, p. 14.

the 'discovery' of America had been foretold by Isaiah, apparently implying also that the extraction of gold was divinely legitimated.[3]

> For the coastlands shall wait for me, the ships of Tarshish first,
> to bring your children from far away,
> their silver and their gold with them, for the name of Yahweh your
> God' (Isa. 60.9).

Las Casas had no difficulty with the global claims of Catholicism. What he objected to was the legitimation of violent exploitation, as for example in the frequent use of Lk. 14.23 to argue that the Indians could be 'compelled' into service. Indeed, he argued from the teaching of Jesus that people could only be *invited* to faith, and that all conquests were unjust. Because he preached judgment against Spain, he was accused of libellous speech against the king and the nation.[4] Las Casas may be considered one of the earliest exponents of a minority tradition in the history of colonizations, which attempted to hold together the global claims of the later biblical prophets with their earlier critique of economic exploitation. After describing the development of this prophetic tradition, we will examine whether it is coherent in the sense presumed by Las Casas—whether it is possible to stop the global claims sliding into justifications for dispossession.

The Prophets' Critique of Land Misappropriation

I have argued in Chapter 3 that land holdings in Israel were probably understood originally as gifts from the ancestors. In the development of biblical theology, these traditional lands were seen to be ultimately the gift of the national God, Yahweh, promised initially to the ancestors of Genesis and then divided among the clans of Israel. While it is difficult to reconstruct this process historically, there is no evidence that the national God was seen as legitimating the Crown's displacement of Israelite clan landholdings. When, for example, King Ahab attempts to buy Naboth's vineyard, the king is rebuffed by the traditional owner who appeals to the divine authority above the Crown: 'Yahweh forbid me, that I should give the inheritance (*nachalah*) of my ancestors to you' (1 Kgs 21.3).

According to the subsequent narrative, the queen manipulates the law so as to have the traditional owner killed, inventing the charges that 'Naboth cursed God and the king'. Yet the story makes clear that Naboth's invocation of God amounts neither to blasphemy nor to treason. King Ahab is

---

3. Louis N. Rivera, *A Violent Evangelism: The Political and Religious Conquest of the Americas* (Louisville: Westminster John Knox, 1992), p. 236.
4. Rivera, *A Violent Evangelism*, pp. 237, 245, 255.

himself killed in the next chapter, in strange poetic justice, by a stray arrow in battle. Just as the prophet Elijah had predicted, Ahab's blood is 'licked up by dogs' in a direct parallel with Naboth's fate (1 Kgs 21.19; 22.38). The king had entered the battle in disguise, since the notoriously dissident Micaiah ben Imlah had predicted his death (22.17), and the disguise ironically re-iterates the theme of deception in the story: first, there is the false witness against Naboth, and then the four hundred false prophets in ch. 22 proclaim victory in battle. Among the many ironies in the story is that Ahab himself predicts that Micaiah ben Imlah will speak against the majority of the other prophets who foresee victory ('he never prophecies anything favourable about me' the king complains in v. 22), and indeed Micaiah eventually does exactly what the king expects. Yet Ahab engages in the battle nonetheless, hoping perhaps that a disguise would be sufficient protection against God.

The story of Naboth's vineyard is clearly designed to show that the mis-appropriation of land will eventually bring divine justice, and in this case, even if the injustice of the Crown appears to succeed in the short term.[5] The prophet Isaiah makes a similar point, but he extends the imagery of the vineyard metaphorically, suggesting that the whole land of Israel is a vineyard that has been exploited by the 'nobles' and 'the haughty' (Isa. 5.13–15).[6]

> For the vineyard of Yahweh of hosts is the house of Israel,
> and the people of Judah are his pleasant planting.
> He expected justice (*mishpat*) but he saw bloodshed (*mishpach*);
> righteousness (*tsedeqah*) but he heard a cry (*tse'aqah*).
> Woe to those who join house to house,
> who add field to field, until there is a place for no one but you,
> and you are left to live alone in the middle of the land (Isa. 5.7–8).

This passage is echoed in Isa. 3.14, again with a focus on the dominant classes: 'Yahweh enters into judgment against the elders and the princes of his people: It is you who have devoured the vineyard; the spoil of the poor is in your houses'.

---

5. This point may well have been supplemented with other nuances, especially if the text was edited after the exile. See especially, Alexander Rofé, 'The Vineyard of Naboth: The Origin and Message of the Story', *Vetus Testamentum* 38 (1988), pp. 89–104; Judith MacKinlay, *Reframing Her: Biblical Women in Postcolonial Focus* (Sheffield: Sheffield Phoenix Press, 2004), pp. 57–78.

6. See Marvin Chaney, 'Whose Sour Grapes? The Addressees of Isaiah 5.1–7 in the Light of Political Economy', *Semeia* 87 (1999), pp. 105–22; William Johnstone, 'Old Testament Expressions in Property Holding', *Ugaritica* 6 (1969), pp. 308–17.

The construction of large estates is also condemned by the prophet Micah in similar terms, except that Micah adds a specific reference to the motivation of acquisitive desire—or 'coveting':

> They covet fields and seize them,
> and houses and take them away.
>
> They oppress a man and his house,
> a man and his inheritance (*nachalah*) (Mic. 2.2).

Along with other examples, the poetic parallelism in this verse suggests a semantic overlap between house (*bayit*) and land (the inherited *nachalah*). '*Bayit*' is indeed an ambiguous term in Hebrew which may mean 'house', 'extended family' or 'inherited land', and all of these meanings are probably implied within the earlier version of the tenth commandment in Exod. 20.17, 'You shall not covet your neighbour's house'.[7]

In one of his most bitter attacks, Micah focusses his critique on the ruling classes and accuses them of behaviour tantamount to cannibalism.

> Listen, you heads of Jacob and rulers of the house of Israel
> Is it not your responsibility to know justice?
> You who hate good and love evil,
> who tear the skin from off their bones,
> who eat the flesh of my people,
> and flay their skin from off them,
> and break their bones in pieces,
> and chop them up like meat in a kettle,
> like flesh in a cauldron (Mic. 3.1–3).

The metaphor of cannibalism pierces the pretence of justice and poetically discloses the social realities of exploitation.[8]

While there is no scholarly consensus concerning the details of Israel and Judah's political economy in the eighth century, there is a broad agreement that the introduction of the monarchy brought tensions between the clan-based 'domestic economy' of the early Iron Age and the system of

---

7. Marvin Chaney, 'You shall not covet your neighbour's house', *Pacific Theological Review* 15 (1982), pp. 3–13. In the later version of the tenth commandment, Deuteronomy 5.21, '*beth*' is apparently used in a more restricted sense, and this illustrates that *beth/bayit* does not usually carry the full range of meanings. To put this point in more technical linguistic terms, semantic polyphony is not to be confused with semantic ambiguity.

8. Cf. the reference to judges as 'evening wolves' in Zeph. 3.3 and to the 'oppressive statutes' that rob the poor of justice in Isa. 10.1–2 (Joseph Blenkinsopp, *Sage, Priest, Prophet: Religious and Intellectual Leadership in Ancient Israel* [Louisville: Westminster John Knox, 1995], pp. 149–50).

patronage instituted by the monarchy.[9] In particular, the payment of taxation in kind brought a new set of demands on top of local subsistence needs, and successive years of drought still yielded debts that needed to be paid by whatever means available, whether with land or labour. Archaeological remains from the eighth century imply that divisions between rich and poor were far more significant during this time than what we find in the twelfth or eleventh century. The biblical prophets attacked this social stratification with the claim that people were not rich because God had blessed them but because the corruption and exploitation of the ruling classes were parasitic on resources of the landowning peasants.

We have some textual evidence that land could be acquired in certain circumstances: in cases where the traditional owners' debts left them no option (cf. Gen. 47.19–21), in cases where it was confiscated by the Crown (2 Sam. 9.7; 16.4; 1 Kgs 21.1–6, although the latter narrative contests the legitimacy the confiscation), and there is one recorded instance where King Omri bought land, apparently without censure, and interestingly named the place after the traditional owner (1 Kgs 16.24). But according to the biblical story that describes the introduction of kingship into Israel, Samuel had warned the people that the king's 'justice' (*mishpat*) would turn out to be a 'regime of accumulation'.[10] The Crown's view of social order would not just require taxation, but also the acquisition of sons, daughters and land: 'he will take the best of your fields, vineyards, and olive groves and give them to his underlings' (1 Sam. 8.11, 14).

The prophets proclaimed judgment not just against kings, but against all the oppressive wealthy, whose ivory-decorated 'large houses' would come to an end (Amos 3.15). The force of this judgment came to be understood primarily in terms of a divinely inspired prediction: when the Assyrian empire overran the northern kingdom, this was taken to be a fulfilment of certain prophetic oracles. While this model of prophecy as prediction continued to have influence in later centuries, it is not clear the classical prophets saw themselves primarily in this way. On the contrary, Amos 5.15 suggests that *if* the Israelites sought justice, then '*perhaps* Yahweh the God of hosts will have mercy on the remnant of Jacob'. Two texts in Jeremiah put this possibility most explicitly:

---

9.   See especially Ronald Simkins, 'Patronage and the Political Economy of Ancient Israel', *Semeia* 87 (1999), pp. 123–44; M. Daniel Carroll, *Contexts for Amos* (Sheffield: Sheffield Academic Press, 1992).

10.   The term 'regime of accumulation' is borrowed from Robert Boyer, *The Regulation School: A Critical Introduction* (New York: Columbia University Press, 1990) and deployed in biblical studies by Roland Boer, *Marxist Criticism of the Bible* (London: T. & T. Clark International, 2003), pp. 229–46.

Jeremiah 7.5–7

For if you thoroughly amend your ways and your actions, if you truly act justly with one another, if you do not oppress the stranger, the orphan, and the widow, or shed innocent blood in this place, and if you do not pursue other gods to your own harm, then I will dwell with you in this place, in the land that I gave to your ancestors for ever and ever.

Jeremiah 18.8

But if that nation, against which I have spoken, turns from its evil, I will repent of the disaster that I intended to bring on it.

The tension between the two models of prophecy—prediction and 'call to repentance'—is just one of the continuing paradoxes of the prophetic literature.[11] The call to repentance, in particular, does not seem relevant to the 'widow, orphan and stranger' who are identified as *victims* of injustice. Whether the 'sinned against' deserved to suffer national destruction is a question to which we will return, but that issue needs to be considered in light of another paradox in the prophets—the relationship between judgment and restoration.

Utopias and Redemption

Beyond the bringing of judgment, the prophets generated multiple visions of redemption and restoration. For our present purposes, it will not be necessary to engage in the debates about the history of literature's editing; it will be sufficient to note that there are contrasts between judgment and restoration to be found in all the prophetic books. Thus, for example, in the book of Amos, an earlier judgment oracle is inverted at the end of the book in a peaceful image of the future.

Judgment Oracle in Amos 5.11

Therefore because you trample on the poor and take from them levies of grain, you have built stone mansions, you will not live in them; though you have planted lush vineyards, you will not drink their wine.

Inversion in Amos 9.14

I will bring back my exiled people Israel; they will rebuild the ruined cities and live in them. They will plant vineyard and drink their wine.

---

11.   The book of Jonah renders the tension with great literary flair: the unfortunate Jonah generates extraordinary repentance in his audience but is apparently irritated by the fact that, among other things, his prediction of destruction is thereby proved false.

Micah takes up the imagery of houses and vineyards in his vision of a redeemed domestic economy: after all the swords of warfare are beaten into ploughshares, each family will sit 'under their own vine and fig tree' (Mic. 4.4). The prophetic 'utopia' intersects here with the more mundane legislation that was designed to free people periodically from their debts, allowing them to return to their own family and ancestral land. The restoration of quotidian life within the prophetic utopias arises from an imaginative practice of hope, rather than from metaphysical fantasies.[12]

Between judgment and utopia, the prophetic imagination inserts the experience of exile. Thus, the question arises of how the people were to live in the 'between' times, a question addressed for example in Jeremiah's letter to the exiles in ch. 29. Jeremiah's advice paradoxically draws on the laws relating to conquest in Deuteronomy. Daniel Smith points out, for example, that men are exempt from military service in Deut. 20.5–7 if they are engaged in the major life-projects of 'building a house', 'planting a vineyard' and 'marrying a wife'. These are precisely the projects mentioned in Jeremiah's letter to the exiles in ch. 29, where the prophet recommends that they seek the peace (*shalom*) of the city:

> Build houses and live in them;
> Plant gardens and eat what they produce.
> Take wives and have sons and daughters;
> Take wives for your sons and give your daughters in marriage
>   (Jer. 29.5–6).

Smith concludes that 'Jeremiah is not simply advising a settled existence…he uses the Deuteronomic exemptions from warfare to declare an "armistice" on the exiled community'.[13] The building of a *bayit* (house and family) is seen as quite possible in the powerless conditions of exile.

Even within the book of Deuteronomy, Georg Braulik has argued that later editing envisages a peaceable return after the exile, implicitly in accord with the visions of the prophets. For example, Deut. 30.1–10 in no way suggests that returning exiles should replicate some version of violent conquest reminiscent of Deut. 20.16–17. The military vocabulary of 7.1 is taken up in

---

12. See the discussion in M. Daniel Carroll R., 'Reflecting on War and Utopia: The Relevance of a Literary Reading of the Prophetic Text for Central America', in M.D. Carroll, D.J.A. Clines, and P.R. Davies (eds.), *The Bible in Human Society: Essays in Honour of John Rogerson* (Sheffield: Sheffield Academic Press, 1995), pp. 105–21; cf. Boer, *Marxist Criticism of the Bible*, pp. 135–47; Bill Ashcroft, 'Critical Utopias', *Textual Practice* 21/3 (2007), pp. 411–31.

13. Daniel Smith, *The Religion of the Landless: The Social Context of the Babylonian Exile* (Bloomington: Meyer–Stone, 1989), p. 135.

30.4–5 but emptied of its violent content, e.g., in both texts Yahweh 'brings' the community to the land to 'possess' it, but in the case of the exiled community addressed in 30.1–10, the call to conquest has been removed. This particular use of the term 'possess' (*yarash*) has the connotation of a return to traditional land, the scenario envisaged in a Jubilee year (Leviticus 25).[14]

Deuteronomy 7.1

When Yahweh your God *brings you* into the land you are entering *to possess* and drives out many nations before you—the Hittites, Girgashites, Amorites, Canaanites, Perizzites, Hivites and Jebusites, seven nations more *numerous* and stronger than you...

Deuteronomy 30.4–5

Even if you have been banished to the extremity of the heavens, from there Yahweh your God will gather you and bring you back. And Yahweh your God will *bring you* into the land that your ancestors *possessed*, and you will *take possession* of it. He will make you more prosperous and *numerous* than your ancestors.

Similarly, in the vision at the end of Amos (9.11–12), we find the same verb 'possess' used with a peaceable connotation to express what appears to be a reversal of earlier judgment. The prophet goes as far as to suggest that Edom will be one of the nations who will be called by Yahweh's 'name'. The narratives of Genesis suggest that Jacob (Israel's ancestor) and Esau (Edom's ancestor) were brothers but Esau was displaced from the main covenantal lineage. Here the prophet apparently sees a reversal of that situation.[15]

On that day I will raise up the booth of David that is fallen, and repair its breaches, and raise up its ruins, and rebuild it as in the days of old; in order that they may *possess* the remnant of Edom and all the nations who are called by my name, says Yahweh who does this (Amos 9.11–12).

Whatever ambiguities remain in this text from Amos, the Book of Isaiah envisages reconciliation on a grand scale, and once again this is inaugurated

---

14. For further details, see Georg Braulik, 'Die Völkervernichtung und die Rückkehr Israels ins Verheissungsland: Hermeneutische Bemerkungen zum Buch Deuteronomium', in M. Vervenne and J. Lust (eds.), *Deuteronomy and Deuteronomic Literature* (Leuven: Leuven University Press, 1997), pp. 33–38, following Norbert Lohfink, 'Die Bedeutungen von hebr. *jrs qal* und *hif*', *Biblische Zeitschrift* 27 (1983), pp. 23–24.

15. This potentially goes beyond Amos 9.7, where the Philistines and the Aramaeans are seen to have their own exodus. See further, M. Daniel Carroll R., 'Reflecting on War and Utopia', pp. 105–21.

by God *without* Israel being called on to use violence. Isaiah 2.2–4 sees all
the nations flowing up to Jerusalem with swords beaten into ploughshares
because war is a thing of the past, and Jerusalem is the attractive centre of
torah and justice (cf. Isa. 51.4 where Yahweh's torah and justice is a 'light
of the peoples').

Yet later in the book, the vindication of Israel has the residues of imperial images of victory: along with the restoration comes the exhortation to
'Enlarge the place of your tent... For you will spread abroad to the right
and to the left, and your seed will *possess* (*yarash*) the nations' (54.2–3).
This text goes on to say 'they will settle deserted towns', prompting one
commentator to comment that 'Anyone who settles or populates deserted
towns is no conqueror'.[16] An Australian reader could be forgiven for won-
dering whether this picture of an unpopulated earth carries implications of
a self-contradictory *terra nullius*, since Isaiah's vision also claims that nations
will come in chains (45.14) and kings lick the dust of Israel's feet (49.23).
It seems that the utopian vision is marked by a tension between judgment
on oppressive nations and the non-violence of Yahweh's future.

These metaphors of imperial victory provoke a postcolonial reader to
raise the ethical issue identified in the early prophetic tradition: the misappropriation of land. How is Israel's possession of the nations different from
the Ammonite sin of 'enlarging her border' (Amos 1.13) or the arrogance of
imperialist Assyria when it says 'I have removed the borders of the peoples'
(Isa. 10.13)? In both these texts, the Hebrew for 'border' (*gᵉvul*) is the same
word used to refer to the 'boundary stones' marking the ancestral landholdings of the Israelites (discussed above in Chapter 3[17]). The assumption is
that that borders—whether of clans or of nations—should not be moved.
Is this assumption over-ridden in the prophetic utopias where the expansive
borders of empires seem to be mimicked?[18]

16. Klaus Baltzer, *Deutero-Isaiah* (Minneapolis: Fortress Press, 2001), p. 437. Baltzer
also prefers here the translation 'inherit' rather than 'possess' the nations.

17. For some of the complexities in understanding *gᵉvul*, see J.W. Rogerson, 'Frontiers
and Borders in the Old Testament', in E. Ball (ed.), *In Search of True Wisdom: Essays in Old
Testament Interpretation in Honour of Ronald E. Clements* (Sheffield: Sheffield Academic
Press, 1999), pp. 116–26; cf. Francesca Stavrakopoulou, 'Bones, Burials and Boundaries
in the Hebrew Bible', paper presented at the British Society for Old Testament Studies
meeting, Durham, 2006.

18. For an analogous issue in the historical literature, cf. Rachel Havrelock, 'Two
Maps of Israel's Land', *Journal of Biblical Literature*, forthcoming, who argues that
Deuteronomistic texts often present a more expansive 'imperial' vision of Israel's exter-
nal borders than what is found in the Priestly tradition.

Or to put the question another way, how do the prophets secure the particularity of land rights once Yahweh's jurisdiction is held to be global? The question is particularly pressing—almost by logical implication—as the prophetic tradition becomes more resolutely monotheistic. If Yahweh has a global prerogative, how is this jurisdiction exercised?

Classical Prophets and the Question of Sovereignty

The eighth-century prophets were 'dissident intellectuals' who, against some of the older presumptions of orthodoxy, were well able to contemplate even the loss of national sovereignty. Their moral vision opposed the 'current assumptions cherished and propagated by the contemporary state apparatus, including its priestly and prophetic representatives'.[19] Micah, for example, focuses his critique on the upper strata of social and religious order:

> Its rulers give judgment for a bribe,
> its priests teach for a price,
> its prophets give oracles for money;
> yet they lean on Yahweh and say,
> 'Surely Yahweh is with us! No harm shall come upon us'.
> Therefore, because of you, Zion shall be ploughed as a field;
> Jerusalem shall become a heap of ruins (Mic. 3.11–12).

When Jeremiah is accused of a similar heresy, the people reject him on the grounds that the whole system of Israel's legitimate knowledge was being threatened: 'the teaching of the law by the priest will not be lost, nor will counsel from the wise, nor the word from the prophets' (Jer. 18.18). In Jeremiah 27–28, the clash between Jeremiah and Hananiah is in part a debate over the nature of sovereignty. On the side of Zion orthodoxy, Hananiah in effect takes refuge in the divine promise to king David that the dynasty in Jerusalem would be established 'for ever' (2 Sam. 7.12–16). Jeremiah, on the other hand, envisages a significant break of seventy years before the house of David would be restored by divine agency, along with the Levitical priesthood (Jer. 29.10; 33.17–18, 20–21).

The restoration of the Davidic lineage is, however, subject to a number of competing interpretations among the prophets. The poetry in Micah 5, for example, contains the vision of a Davidic figure asserting military dominance over an aggressor:

> But you, Bethlehem of Ephratha, small among Judah's clans,
> From you shall come forth for me one to be ruler in Israel.
> His origin lies in former times, in ancient days... (Mic. 5.2).

---

19.   Blenkinsopp, *Sage, Priest, Prophet*, p. 144.

> He shall stand and shepherd in the strength of Yahweh,
> In the majesty of the name of Yahweh his God.
> They shall dwell safely for then he will be great
>   to the ends of the earth.
> This shall be salvation from Assyria,
> when he comes into our land, and when he treads on our soil.
> We will set over him seven shepherds, and eight human chieftans.
> They will shepherd the land of Assyria with the sword,
> the land of Nimrod with the bared blade.

> He will deliver from Assyria,
> when he comes into our land,
> when he treads within our borders (Mic. 5.4–5).

The oracle envisages a ruler arising from Bethlehem whose 'human chieftains' will dominate Assyria 'with the sword'. But this is still operating in the realm of poetic justice, rather than on the utopian plane where swords are finally beaten into ploughshares, as envisaged in Mic. 4.3.

The book of Isaiah reflects a dramatic prophetic re-visioning when it proclaims in ch. 55 that the 'everlasting covenant' formerly made with David would now be devolved to the whole community (55.3–5). Where David was once the 'witness' ('ed) to the nations, now the community are to be the witnesses ('edim) to the nations (55.5; cf. 43.10; 44.8). Hezekiah, the Davidic king, is called 'my servant' in 37.35, but later in the book, it is Israel who is named 'my servant', the 'chosen' (41.8–9; 44.1–2, 21; 45.4). In Isa. 11.1–5 there is a vision of a future Davidic messiah who will bring justice to society and ecological utopia to the whole created order, yet when the language of these verses is reiterated in Isaiah 65 the David figure is missing:

> The wolf and the lamb shall feed together,
> the lion will eat straw like the ox;
> but the serpent—its food will be dust.
> They shall not hurt or destroy on all my holy mountain, says
> Yahweh. (Isa. 65.25)

The earlier interweaving of the David traditions with Zion/Jerusalem is here in ch. 65 teased apart, and the vision of peace on the holy mountain is articulated without reference to a king.[20]

It seems that as Yahweh's jurisdiction is globalized in the Isaiah tradition Judah's familiar constructions of sovereignty are being undermined. It is thus

---

20. See the discussion in Edgar Conrad, *Reading Isaiah* (Minneapolis: Fortress Press, 1991), pp. 143–53; Hugh Williamson, *Variations on a Theme: King, Messiah and Servant in the Book of Isaiah* (Carlisle: Paternoster, 1998), pp. 113–66.

even possible to discern here an element of continuity between the earlier prophetic threats against the nation and the utopias of the later visions.

The earlier divine promises, made to the kings in the Davidic dynasty, were apparently superseded in the course of time largely because the monarchy consistently failed to live up to expectations. Edgar Conrad's interpretation of the book of Isaiah, for example, suggests that the negative evaluation of kings is linked in part with their mortality: royal deaths are linked with the threat of enemy invasion, Conrad suggests, and Judah's security will always be fleeting if it is dependant upon human kings.[21] But even at the height of their powers, the kings regularly failed to exhibit a 'quiet' trust in Yahweh alone (e.g., Isa. 7.4; 30.15–16), preferring instead to engage in alliances with foreign monarchs or to rely on the weapons of war (e.g., 30.1–5; 31.1–3). According to Isaiah, military alliances and the accumulation of weapons all amount to idolatry, because they compromise trust in Yahweh.[22] There are only two real options: militarist power will lead to death, and quiet trust will lead to salvation:

> Alas for those who go down to Egypt for help
>   and who rely on horses,
> Who trust in chariots because they are many
>   and in horsemen because they are very strong,
> But do not look to the Holy One of Israel, or consult Yahweh…
>   the Egyptians are human, and not God;
>   their horses are flesh and not spirit (Isa. 31.1, 3).

> In returning and rest you shall be saved,
> In quietness and in trust shall be your strength.
> When Yahweh stretches out his hand,
>   the helper stumble, and the one helped will fall,
>   and they will all perish together (Isa. 30.15).

A significant feature of the utopian peaceableness in Isaiah 65, mentioned above, is that the exiles are to be restored not just to a particular city but to a wholly regenerated cosmos (65.17). The earlier judgement oracles are reversed, and the domestic economy returns as part of a regenerated earth: Jerusalem's population will 'build houses and live in them', 'plant vineyards and eat their fruit'; 'they shall not labour in vain, or bear children for calamity' (vv. 21, 23).

---

21.   Conrad, *Reading Isaiah*, p. 144.

22.   Ben Ollenburger, *Zion the City of the Great King: A Theological Symbol of the Jerusalem Cult* (Sheffield: JSOT Press, 1987); cf. O.H. Steck, 'The Jerusalem Conceptions of Peace', in P. Yoder and W. Swartley (eds.), *The Meaning of Peace* (Louisville: Westminster John Knox, 1992), pp. 49–68.

The visions of peace, justice and ecological order were part of the divinely given 'peace' (*shalom*) in all its dimensions: building, planting, marrying, the fertility of a regenerated earth, each family 'under their vine and fig tree', the removal of threats from war, and the practice of justice. All of this was seen to be inaugurated primarily by divine intervention, rather than by human agency.

Yet there was a residual issue for the Israelite theologians who inherited the increasing prophetic emphasis on divine jurisdiction, and this issue was not entirely resolved by utopian hope: did the innocent 'widow, orphan and alien' deserve the suffering of exile in the first place? The biblical traditions provide more than one answer to this question.

The Problem of Innocent Suffering

A key problem arises in 2 Kings 22–23 when King Josiah repents magnificently, and inaugurates massive reforms, yet he himself meets an untimely fate (23.29) and his southern kingdom is still crushed by the Babylonian armies. The biblical historians struggle to find an answer to this problem, and interestingly, they do not blame the ruling classes in general, as suggested by the eighth-century prophets. In fact, they do not mention social justice at all, choosing rather to focus on the religious impurity of following other gods—a surprisingly selective appropriation of the prophetic tradition.[23] And given that the reforms of Josiah dealt precisely with religious impurity, the authors and editors of Kings apparently felt compelled to attribute the disaster to another source: the accumulation of sins committed by king Manasseh (2 Kgs 23.26), a *predecessor* of Josiah.

This solution did not satisfy the historians who reconsidered these issues in Chronicles. When Chronicles re-tells the story of Manasseh's reign, it is claimed that he repented and instituted appropriate reforms (2 Chron. 33.10–17). Any suggestion of his responsibility for the fate of the southern kingdom is therefore removed, along with the implication that the exiles from Judah suffered for the sins of an earlier king. Unlike Kings, which gives weight to accumulated sins and transferable punishment, Sara Japhet argues that in Chronicles 'No sin was postponed, transferred or accumulated; each of the measures taken by God was meted to the actual perpetrators', a view that is more consistent with Ezekiel 18.[24] She suggests that 2 Chron. 36.16 has in mind the *collective guilt of the people at large* when it

---

23.   See further, Blenkinsopp, *Sage, Priest, Prophet*, pp. 156–57.

24.   Sara Japhet, 'Theodicy in Ezra–Nehemiah and Chronicles', in A. Laato and J.C. de Moor (eds.), *Theodicy in the World of the Bible* (Leiden: Brill, 2004), pp. 429–69, 465.

claims that 'they mocked the messengers of God, and disdained his words and taunted his prophets until the wrath of Yahweh against his people grew beyond remedy'. For Chronicles, the exile had to be deserved by the whole people, or the justice of God could not be accounted for.

The book of Jeremiah, similarly, reveals a sensitivity to the issue of inno-cent suffering. It is explicitly claimed that God would not have brought this destruction unless everyone were responsible:

> Run to and fro through the streets of Jerusalem.
> Look around and take note.
> Search its squares and see if you can find *one person*
> who acts justly and seeks the truth,
> so that I may pardon Jerusalem (Jer. 5.1).

The idea that the *ruling classes* alone were responsible for national destruction is apparently not acceptable to Jeremiah, and by implication, no one innocent can be found in Jerusalem. Isaiah, on the other hand, recog-nizes that there *were* some people who were 'righteous', or at least 'innocent' (*tsadiq* in 3.10), and the book addresses this problem in a number of ways.

Isaiah 1.25 speaks of a divine plan to purify the people: 'I will turn my hand against you; I will thoroughly purge away your dross and remove your impurities'. The latter part of the book, beginning with ch. 40, looks back on the judgment that has fallen and is now past: 'Speak tenderly to Jerusalem…she has received from Yahweh's hand double for all her sins' (40.2). The plan has come to fruition: 'See I have refined you, though not as silver; I have chosen you in the furnace of affliction' (48.10). Then it is sug-gested that the suffering of the people of God was only transitory; it was a passing moment that quickly gave way to the deeper reality of divine love.

> 'For a brief moment I abandoned you,
> but with deep compassion I will bring you back.
> In a surge of anger I hid my face from you for a moment,
> but with loyal love everlasting I will have compassion on you',
> says the Yahweh your Redeemer (Isa. 54.7–8).

Thus, the exile is seen as a transitional suffering, driven by the purpose of purification, and 54.9–10 go on to say that Yahweh will never again come in anger: 'my covenant of peace shall not be removed'.[25]

Isaiah also deals directly with the problem that the exile may have brought suffering for the innocent. A good case can be made for seeing

---

25. See further, Rolf Rendtorff, 'Noah, Abraham and Moses: God's Covenant Partners', in Ball (ed.), *In Search of True Wisdom*, pp. 127–36.

the 'servant' figure in chs. 40–55 as precisely that innocent group within the exiled community.

> He was oppressed and afflicted, yet he did not open his mouth;
> Like a lamb to the slaughter, and like a sheep
>   before its shearers is silent,
> so he did not open his mouth.
> By a perversion of justice he was taken away.
> Who could have imagined his future?
> For he was cut off from the land of the living,
> stricken for the transgression of my people.
> They made his grave with the wicked, and his tomb with the rich,
> although he had done no violence, and there was no deceit in his
>   mouth (Isa. 53.7–9).

As already indicated, there are a few texts where the 'servant' is called Jacob–Israel (41.8–9; 44.1–2, 21; 45.4), but one text in particular seems to distinguish the servant from the larger community:

> It is too small a thing that you should be my servant
> To raise up the tribes of Jacob and to restore the survivors of Israel.
> I will give you as a light of nations,
> That my salvation may reach to the ends of the earth (Isa. 49.6).

Rather than conclude that the servant here is not the corporate figure 'Jacob–Israel', this text can be better read as a call to the righteous *within* the community not only to restore the other exiles but to offer light to foreigners as well—creating a much more inclusive 'covenant' of people and establishing justice non-violently on all the earth (42.1–6).[26]

This servant will not 'lift his voice' or even damage 'a bruised reed', yet he suffers redemptively for others:

> Yet it was Yahweh's will to bruise him and cause him to suffer,
> and though Yahweh makes his life a guilt offering, he will see his
> offspring and prolong his days, and the will of Yahweh will prosper
> in his hand. He shall see the fruit of the travail of his life and be
> satisfied; by his knowledge my righteous servant will justify many,
> and he will bear their iniquities…(Isa. 53.10–11).

26. Kenton L. Sparks, *Ethnicity and Identity in Ancient Israel* (Winona Lake: Eisenbrauns, 1998), pp. 310–14.

In what might be termed a 'communion theodicy', the *innocent* servant himself becomes part of a sacrificial mechanism that restores the peace of the community by compensating for the sins of others.[27]

In reconsidering the significance of Isaiah's servant figure, it becomes possible to infer that the divine jurisdiction extends beyond retributive justice to encompass even those who are *not* innocent within a non-violent, multi-ethnic covenant (e.g., 42.1–6). The expectation of a future that includes the violent reinstatement of a Davidic king (as in Mic. 5.4–5) seems to have faded into the background of the prophetic tradition, to be largely—but not entirely—replaced by more eirenic international visions of utopia.

Concluding Reflections

The biblical prophets offer many different perspectives on social justice and on redemption beyond judgment. The prophetic utopias are more like a collage than a coherent set of images. Yet there are still elements of continuity within the complex dynamics of this literature. From beginning to end, the justice of God is a common theme, yet this very continuity yields the problem of how the demand for land justice in the eighth century relates to the utopian visions of Israelites taking 'possession' of other nations. As we saw in the case of Deuteronomy's conquest legislation, there is still a sense in which the hubris of empires—especially Assyria, Babylon and Persia—reproduces itself in the prophetic imagination of the ideal future.[28]

Note, however, the social class of those who are humbled enough to 'lick the dust' of Zion's feet, or bow down 'in chains'. They are either royalty (49.23) or the wealthy (45.14). There is a consistency in Yahweh's judgment against those who are proud and 'lifted up'—whether they are found in Assyria (10.12) or in Israel (2.12). Even in those cases where the empires of Assyria or Babylon have been deployed in judgment against Israel, they have no justification for their arrogance.

---

27. See the discussion in James G. Williams, *The Bible, Violence and the Sacred: Liberation from the Myth of Sanctioned Violence* (New York: HarperCollins, 1991), pp. 158–62; Antti Laato and Johannes de Moor, 'Introduction', in Laato and de Moor (eds.), *Theodicy in the World of the Bible*, pp. xlviii–liii.

28. Moshe Weinfeld, 'The Protest against Imperialism in Ancient Israelite Prophecy', in Samuel N. Eisenstadt (ed.), *The Origin and Diversity of Axial Age Civilizations* (Albany: State University of New York Press, 1986), pp. 181–82; Mark G. Brett, 'Nationalism and the Hebrew Bible', in J.W. Rogerson, M. Davies and M.D. Carroll R. (eds.), *The Bible in Ethics* (Sheffield: Sheffield Academic Press, 1995), pp. 136–63.

> Shall the axe vaunt itself above the one who wields it,
> or the saw magnify itself against the one who handles it?
> As if a rod should raise the one who lifts it up,
> Or as if a staff should lift the one who is not wood! (Isa. 10.15).

Nevertheless, we cannot avoid the difficulty that Isaiah's utopian peace is fractured at points by violent images of judgment. Isaiah 49.26, for example: 'I will make your oppressors eat their own flesh, and they shall be drunk with their own blood as with wine'.

> For the nation and kingdom that will not serve you shall perish;
> Those nations shall be utterly laid waste (60.12).

And in the same chapter, the peace seems to be more restricted in focus—within Israel's own frontiers: 'Violence shall no more be heard in your land, devastation or destruction within your borders' (60.18). Yet if the peace issuing from Zion is going to reach the ends of the earth, and 'nation shall not lift up sword against nation', then the scope of Yahweh's justice needs to be seen as global, well beyond Israel's borders.

One would need to confess that a significant tension remains between the particularity of Israel's vindication and the inclusive, non-violent invitation to the nations to bathe in God's redemptive light. Yet even the former imperial overlords, Egypt and Assyria, are invited into Yahweh's fold in Isaiah 19, after a period of judgment: 'Egypt will know Yahweh on that day... Blessed be Egypt my people, and Assyria the work of my hands' (19.21, 24). The explicit invitation to 'the foreigner' in Isa. 56.3–8 similarly has to be seen as 'something of a revolution, in which religious identity had almost totally supplanted the role of ethnicity in defining group identity'.[29] In the context of Isaiah 56, it is not even made clear whether the foreigner is a former oppressor or not.

The redemption of other nations is represented in a quite pluralistic way in Micah. The famous 'swords into ploughshares' text of Isa. 2.1–5 is repeated word for word in Mic. 4.1–4, but the Micah text has a slightly different conclusion. Instead of talking about the house of Jacob walking in the light of Yahweh, Micah concludes his version by referring to people who are not Israelites: 'All the nations may walk in the name of their gods; we will walk in the name of Yahweh our God for ever and ever' (Mic. 4.5). The action of Yahweh in Jerusalem is the catalyst for world peace in this text, but space is still left for other religious expressions. Perhaps there is a clue

---

29. Sparks, *Ethnicity and Identity*, p. 316.

here for how to avoid the implication that Zion is restored as the centre of a new empire.[30]

Whatever the tensions within the prophetic books, there is no warrant in the prophetic utopias for *any* human empire, or coalition of nations, to claim a divine warrant for violence. While there are traces of imperial imagery and violence in the vindication of Israel, all of it is seen as God's doing and not Israel's. The underlying logic is more paradoxical than a simple legitimation of Zion: God's rule is above all empires, and military solutions represent a failure of trust in Yahweh.[31]

If we consider the history of colonization in this light, then we would have to conclude that no use of force, no exploitation of the earth, no unjust actions by colonial administrations (legal or otherwise) can legitimately lay claim to the prophetic tradition. To what extent can those who have suffered innocently at the hands of modern empires find their experience addressed in this tradition? There is no single answer to this question. But the *ideal* of a justice that can restore life—in spite of shifting constructions of cultural power—is a biblical principle that no postcolonial society can do without.

One of the paradoxes of postcolonial ethics is that at least *some* ideals of peace and justice need to be globalized, or power struggles will remain unchecked. Respect for cultural diversity, for example, would need to be seen as a universal principle. Clearly, any such global framework cannot simply be the vision of single nation or ideology writ large. In his recent book *The Dignity of Difference: How to Avoid the Clash of Civilizations*, the British Chief Rabbi, Jonathan Sacks, urges a re-thinking also of religious universalism. If we are to avoid the clash of fundamentalisms, he argues, we need a vision of the God of justice who stands above us all, 'teaching us to make space for one another, to hear each other's claims and to resolve them equitably. Only such a God would be truly transcendent…capable of being comprehended in any human language, from any single point of view'.[32] However difficult it might be to put this into practice, the discipline of 'making space' corresponds to the ancient Israelite principle of respect for the land and inheritance of others.

---

30.   It is significant that within later developments of Jewish tradition, there are careful attempts to show that people do not need to become Jews in order to be acceptable to God. See Jon Levenson, 'The Universal Horizon of Biblical Particularism', in M.G. Brett (ed.), *Ethnicity and the Bible* (Leiden: Brill, 1996), pp. 143–69; Jonathan Sacks, *The Dignity of Difference: How to Avoid the Clash of Civilizations* (London: Continuum, 2nd edn, 2003).

31.   See especially, Millard Lind, *Yahweh is a Warrior* (Scottdale: Herald, 1980); Ben Ollenburger, *Zion, the City of the Great King: A Theological Symbol of the Jerusalem Cult* (Sheffield: Sheffield Academic Press, 1989).

32.   Jonathan Sacks, *The Dignity of Difference*, pp. 65–66.

EXILE AND ETHNIC CONFLICT

> Love the stranger as yourself, for you were strangers in the land
> of Egypt.
>
> *Leviticus 19.34*

After nearly three decades as the Chief Protector of Aborigines in Queensland (1914–1941), the Anglican churchman John Bleakly argued that the Christian missions had helped 'to preserve the purity of the white race'.[1] Analogous views can be found in South Africa, where S.J. du Toit's influential booklet *Nehemiah* had linked the ethnocentrism of the biblical Nehemiah with Afrikaner nationalism and apartheid policies.[2] These are just two of numerous examples where racism has been linked with Christian commitments in the shaping of colonial power, and this linkage has sometimes been sanctioned by the biblical idea of a 'chosen people' who are set apart from other nations. It is possible, however, that the most exclusive biblical theology, in Ezra and Nehemiah, had its roots historically not in strategies of social control invented by the ruling classes (as in Australia and South Africa), but rather in a pattern of cultural resistance adopted by minorities struggling with corporate survival. This might be true of Israel's exile in Babylon, as well as the subsequent period of restoration under Persian administration, and in this chapter we will examine some of the implications of this perspective.

In his book *Religion of the Landless: The Social Context of the Babylonian Exile*, Daniel Smith interprets separatist biblical theology from the sixth and fifth centuries BCE in light of modern studies of groups who have been subject to forced removal, or other forms of minority existence. These studies reveal common mechanisms for survival, ritual resistance, and frequently a tendency to marry within the group in order to secure its social boundaries.

---

1. J.W. Bleakley, *The Aborigines of Australia* (Brisbane: Jacaranda Press, 1961), p. 124.

2. See, e.g., A. du Toit, 'Puritans in Africa?', *Comparative Studies in Society and History* 27 (1985), p. 233; cf. B. Tlhagale, 'Culture in an Apartheid Society' *Journal of Theology for Southern Africa* 51 (1985), pp. 27–36.

Smith brings this sociological model to bear, for example, on the so-called Priestly literature of the Torah, found especially in Leviticus and Numbers.[3] It has often been assumed that the Priestly literature advocates an under-standing of holiness as essentially concerned with 'separating the clean and the unclean' and that this ideal was extrapolated into the social sphere as an ideal of endogamy, i.e., marrying within the Israelite kinship system. Smith adds to this picture by arguing that the endogamous ideal was shaped in conditions of exile, as a strategy of *cultural and religious resistance*, rather than as a mechanism of social control 'from above'.

One of the ingredients of this argument came from Mary Douglas's *Purity and Danger* which, in an influential discussion of Leviticus, had drawn an analogy between the ritual management of an individual's body (especially in relation to food and genital discharge) and the management of the *social* body: just as the individual was called on to draw distinctions between 'clean and unclean', so a division between Israel and other peoples had to be maintained. The analogy is indeed suggested by Lev. 20.26 as an aspect of holiness: 'You shall be holy to me; for I Yahweh have separated you from the other peoples to be mine'. Endogamy might then be interpreted as sim-ply one more example of dividing between clean and unclean.[4]

In retrospect, however, it is important to note that Mary Douglas wrote three books on Priestly literature, all of which reject the connection between its purity codes and ethnocentrism. She recognizes that her earlier theory was too quick to assimilate the biblical materials to a general theory of purity—one which rightly sees a common function of pollution rules in many societies as instruments for keeping social groups, or genders, apart. The system of defilement described in Leviticus and Numbers, on the other hand, is designed primarily to protect the *sanctuary*, rather than to organize social groups. The stranger (*ger*) is explicitly included within the system, as we shall see, and well beyond the general exhortation in Lev. 19.34 to 'love the stranger as yourself, for you were strangers in the land of Egypt'. This biblical deviation from what is generally true of purity codes is so sig-nificant for Douglas that she turned in her later work to argue the opposite

---

3.   There is a broad scholarly consensus that amongst the traditions of the Torah there is a distinct set of 'Priestly' traditions (often called 'P') that can be distinguished from other strands. There is no consensus on the dating of this literature, or its his-tory of editing. A lucid introduction to the complexity of the debate can be found in Alexander Rofé, *Introduction to the Composition of the Pentateuch* (Sheffield: Sheffield Academic Press, 1999).

4.   Daniel Smith, *The Religion of the Landless: The Social Context of the Babylonian Exile* (Bloomington: Meyer–Stone, 1989), pp. 80–83, 145; drawing on Mary Douglas, *Purity and Danger* (London: Routledge, 1966).

to what one might expect: she sees one of the main purposes of the Priestly editing as not to legitimate the equation of holiness and ethnocentrism, but precisely to *oppose* that very equation. Priestly theology, as we now have it, actually undermines ethnocentrism.[5]

This raises a significant question about the purposes of those texts in Ezra and Nehemiah that recommend the divorcing of foreign women on the grounds that they pollute the 'holy seed' (Ezra 9.1–2; cf. Neh. 9.2). Although Ezra is represented as a priest, his idea of ethnocentric holiness does not conform to what we know about the purity system in Leviticus and Numbers. The term 'holy seed' (*zera'*) does not actually appear in Priestly texts, and there is a suspicious irony in the fact that when Leviticus 15 deals with seed (*zera'*) as male seminal discharge it is regarded as *defiling*, as is menstrual discharge (*niddah*). Ezra 9.11 renders the 'peoples of lands' in terms of impure *niddah*, picking up the language of Leviticus 15, yet the seed (*zera'*) of Israel is termed 'holy'.[6]

The puzzle deepens in Nehemiah 8 where Ezra reads the law in 'the seventh month', and he initiates the Festival of Booths on the 'second day' of the month, conspicuously overlooking the Day of Atonement (or Day of Purgation, as it is called by some commentators). This is a crucial oversight since this ritual was designed precisely to purify the whole community, ostensibly Ezra's concern. According to Priestly legislation, the Festival of Booths begins on the *fifteenth* day of this month, and the Day of Atonement is held on the *tenth* (Lev. 23.26–44; Num. 29.7–38). While many attempts have been made to get round this difficulty, it seems to me that there are essentially two options: either the Priestly calendar of festivals had not yet stabilized, or the authors of Ezra–Nehemiah had reservations about it.

Why would they have had reservations? In the account of the Day of Atonement in Leviticus 16, we find a text which would have been inconvenient for an ethnocentric interpretation of Priestly tradition: 'This shall be a statute for you forever: In the seventh month, on the tenth day of the month, you shall deny yourselves and do no work, neither the native-born nor the *stranger* (*ger*) *who resides among you*. For on this day atonement shall

5.   Mary Douglas, *In the Wilderness: The Doctrine of Defilement in the Book of Numbers* (Sheffield: Sheffield Academic Press, 1993), p. 155; *Leviticus as Literature* (Oxford: Oxford University Press, 1999); *Jacob's Tears: The Priestly Work of Reconciliation* (Oxford: Oxford University Press, 2004), p. 124. Cf. Douglas, 'Responding to Ezra: The Priests and the Foreign Wives', *Biblical Interpretation* 10 (2002), pp. 1–23, revised as pp. 63–87 in *Jacob's Tears*.

6.   Claudia Camp, *Wise, Strange and Holy* (Sheffield: Sheffield Academic Press, 2000), pp. 33–34 n. 14; Harold Washington, 'Israel's Holy Seed and the Foreign Women', *Biblical Interpretation* 11 (2003), p. 435.

be made for you, to cleanse you from all your sins. You shall be clean before Yahweh' (Lev. 16.29–30).[7] This and other examples illustrate that, contrary to Ezra–Nehemiah's view, there is nothing inherently defiling about strangers in Priestly theology.

While there are severe difficulties in reconstructing the career of the historical Ezra, it does seem that the administration of Jerusalem under the Persian empire was undertaken in the fifth century BCE by 'native' leaders who adopted exclusivist points of view such as we find in the books of Ezra and Nehemiah. These books embody a particular interpretation of Israelite religion, but as Douglas has suggested, the interpretation cannot be clearly aligned with any of the biblical traditions, whether in the Pentateuch or in the prophetic books. The Jewish scholar who has written the most detailed works on Leviticus, Jacob Milgrom, states unambiguously that Leviticus has no general prohibition on intermarriage and that Ezra 9 is an exercise in 'halakhic midrash', i.e., legal imagination.[8] Leviticus 21.14 *does* stipulate that priests must marry only Israelites, and this can be regarded as the 'exception which proves the rule': if priests were to be distinguished in this way with a higher grade of holiness, then the general population were free to marry strangers.[9] Amongst the lengthy regulations on sexuality in Leviticus, nothing is said about the laity marrying foreigners. And if the account of a war against Midian in Numbers 31 can be considered a part of the 'Priestly' tradition, then it is notable that virgin women were made an exception to the ban, suggesting that they joined the community (31.18).

Daniel Smith (now Smith-Christopher) has returned to the issue of intermarriage in his recent book, *A Biblical Theology of Exile*, which is significant not just for its social-scientific insights but also for its engagement with postcolonial studies. A weakness in this work, however, arises from

7. In Israel Knohl's complex account of the 'Day of Atonement' texts, he argues that the Priestly tradition has been enhanced in its consciousness of the *gerim* by the 'Holiness School' (Knohl, *The Sanctuary of Silence* [Minneapolis: Fortress Press, 1995], pp. 27–28; cf. pp. 53, 93.

8. Jacob Milgrom, *Leviticus 17–22* (New York: Doubleday, 2000), pp. 1584–86. See further Saul Olyan, *Rites and Rank: Hierarchy in Biblical Representations of Cult* (Princeton: Princeton University Press, 2000), pp. 63–102; Christine Hayes, *Gentile Impurities and Jewish Identities: Intermarriage and Conversion from the Bible to the Talmud* (Oxford: Oxford University Press, 2002), pp. 19–44.

9. Jan Joosten, *People and Land in the Holiness Code* (Leiden: Brill, 1996), p. 85. Milgrom, *Leviticus 17–22*, p. 1820, curiously resists Joosten's conclusion without sufficient argument. On pp. 1805–1806, Milgrom indicates that the prohibition of intermarriage in Lev. 21.14 applies only to the high priest, and not even to Zadokite priests in general (as it does in Ezekiel 44.22). Cf. Hayes, *Gentile Impurities*, pp. 27–28, 230 n. 31.

Smith-Christopher's lack of attention to Mary Douglas's recent studies of the Priestly literature. For example, he reiterates his earlier argument that the key concept in Lev. 18.24–30 is pollution caused by *strangers (gerim)*,[10] overlooking the implications of v. 26 in that very section of the chapter: 'But you shall keep my statutes and my ordinances and commit none of these abominations, either the native-born or the stranger (*ger*) who resides among you'. It is the abominations that are at issue, the sinful actions, not the ethnicity of the person committing them.

Similarly, Numbers 15 stipulates offerings that are appropriate if one sins unintentionally, and then v. 29 spells out that this applies to strangers as well: 'In regard to both the native-born among the Israelites and the stranger living among them, you shall have the same law for anyone who acts in error' (cf. Num. 19.10). Once again, what defiles is the action, not the person as such, and purification is offered to both citizen and stranger alike. Thus, when Ezra 9.1–2 speak of maintaining the separation of the 'holy seed' from the surrounding peoples, these verses are proposing a 'racial' interpretation of defilement against the grain of the Priestly literature as we now have it. Whatever diversity may be discerned in the Priestly legal traditions, they never suggest that strangers inevitably defile the land, as maintained in Ezra 9.1–2, 11.[11]

This is not to say that strangers stood before Priestly law on a completely equal footing. Leviticus 24.22 seems to suggest equality ('you shall have one law for the stranger and for the native-born'), but when this requirement is repeated at the conclusion of the Priestly Passover law in Exod. 12.49, the legislation actually reveals a difference: *if* strangers wish to participate in the Passover festival they need to have their males circumcised (Exod. 12.48). The example illustrates that although strangers may have been subject to the same laws as citizens in regard to certain civil and ritual matters, a native-born Israelite would have had no choice but to participate in the Passover, whereas strangers did have a choice. The *gerim* were

> obligated to observe only the negative commandments, the prohibitions, but not the positive commandments, the performative ones. The rationale for this legal distinction rests on a theological

---

10.   Smith-Christopher, *A Biblical Theology of Exile* (Minneapolis: Fortress Press, 2002), p. 149; *Religion of the Landless*, p. 146.

11.   Kenton Sparks, *Ethnicity and Identity in Ancient Israel* (Winona Lake: Eisenbrauns, 1998), pp. 295, 318, has suggested that Ezra 6.19–21 allows for the possibility of 'proselyte' women, but it is more likely that this text simply distinguishes between returning exiles and other Judeans (presumably non-exiles) who had 'separated themselves from unclean practices'. Ezra–Nehemiah never mentions *gerim*, and unlike the Priestly legislation, never clarifies the possibility that foreigners might not commit abominations.

premise. The violation of a prohibition generates a toxic impurity that radiates into the environment, polluting the sanctuary and the land... It therefore makes no difference whether the polluter is an Israelite or a *ger*.[12]

It was only in regards to 'performative' religious law that strangers were in a different position. Unlike Israelites, for example, they were not required to bring *all* slaughtered animals to the sanctuary (Lev. 17.3) but only animals sacrificed for religious purposes (17.8–9). An implication of this legislation, according to Milgrom, was that strangers were not free to worship other gods, but neither could they be constrained to worship Yahweh.[13] This distinction in no way implies that all strangers had to be banned from the community, or that they were inherently defiling.

It might be thought that the original inhabitants of Canaan would form an exception in Priestly theology. But when Lev. 18.25–28 explains that the land 'vomited out' the original inhabitants on account of their sins, it implies not that Israel needed to take up a genocidal mission, but rather that the land was defiled precisely by particular sins.[14] These people were expelled, according to this view, on account of their actions and the ensuing pollution of the land, not on account of their 'race'. If Israelites acted in the same way, then they would suffer a similar fate. Even Deuteronomy, which appears to exclude the prior inhabitants of Canaan on ethnic grounds (along with the neighbouring Ammonites and Moabites, in Deut. 23.3–4), nowhere places an absolute ban on intermarriage. Indeed, Deut. 23.7–8 specifically opens the community to Egyptians—'for you were a stranger in their land'—while Ezra 9.1 explicitly *prohibits* marriage to Egyptians.

What is clear is that ethnic identity was disputed in the Persian period, and that the legal imagination of Ezra–Nehemiah has hardened the distinction between insiders and outsiders beyond anything that we find in previous laws. What is less clear is whether Ezra and Nehemiah have interpreted Israelite religion to serve imperial administrative interests, or whether these books can still be read as, in some sense, promoting cultural resistance 'from below'. Smith-Christopher, for example, finds evidence of a cultural resurgence amongst the disadvantaged exiles, with the nativist governors working subversively on their own religious agenda while creating the

12. Milgrom, *Leviticus 17–22*, p. 1417.
13. Milgrom, *Leviticus* (Minneapolis: Fortress Press, 2004), p. 191.
14. Baruch J. Schwartz, 'Reexamining the Fate of the "Canaanites" in the Torah Traditions', in C. Cohen, A. Hurvitz and S.M. Paul (eds.), *Sefer Moshe: The Moshe Weinfeld Jubilee Volume* (Winona Lake: Eisenbrauns, 2004), pp. 151–70.

appearance of subservience to the imperial centre.[15] Other historians see Ezra–Nehemiah as representing an elite whose religious discourse masks the social and economic interests of Persian administration. A good case has been made, for example, for seeing the fortification of Jerusalem under Nehemiah (Neh. 2.8 and 7.2) as part of a wider imperial response to an Egyptian revolt in the mid-fifth century against the Persian empire.[16]

While it may be true that Ezra and Nehemiah perceive themselves in their memoirs to be facing opposition from several directions, the texts also represent them as having significant power within the restoration community. Thus, for example, Ezra 10.8 suggests that anyone failing to attend the prescribed convocation would face severe penalties: 'by the instruction of the officials and the elders, all his property is forfeited, and he is excluded from the assembly of the exiles'. Furthermore, the letter from Artaxerxes in Ezra 7 concludes by saying that anyone who does not obey the law of Ezra's God would suffer severe consequences, including the confiscation of property (7.26).[17] A number of scholars have suggested that the prohibition against foreign marriages in Ezra–Nehemiah was a nativist initiative that also served the interests of imperial social control—however indirectly— since genealogies could be used as a way of establishing and clarifying the legitimacy of land tenure. The theological language was thereby connected to economic management.[18]

The book of Ruth illustrates some of the implications of intermarriage for a domestic economy, and this book is highly relevant to the Persian period, whether it was composed at the time or in an earlier context. The narrative establishes the legitimacy of a Moabite wife—Ruth herself—even

15. Smith, *Theology of Exile*, pp. 45, 160.

16. Kenneth Hoglund, *Achaemenid Imperial Administration in Syria–Palestine and the Missions of Ezra and Nehemiah* (Atlanta: Scholars Press, 1992), pp. 209–10.

17. See Matthew Stolper, 'Mesopotamia, 482–330 BC', in D.M. Lewis (ed.), *The Cambridge Ancient History*, VI (Cambridge: Cambridge University Press, 1994), p. 250.

18. See Joseph Blenkinsopp, 'The Social Context of the "Outsider Woman" in Proverbs 1–9', *Biblica* 74 (1991), pp. 457–73; Hoglund, *Achaemenid Imperial Administration*, pp. 207–40 and the critique of Hoglund in Charles Carter, *The Emergence of Yehud in the Persian Period* (Sheffield: Sheffield Academic Press, 1999), pp. 214–48; Tamara C. Eskenazi, 'Out from the Shadows: Biblical Women in the Post-Exilic Era'. *Journal for the Study of the Old Testament* 54 (1992), pp. 35–36); Douglas, *In the Wilderness*, pp. 216–47; T.C. Eskenazi and E.P. Judd, 'Marriage to a Stranger in Ezra 9–10', in T.C. Eskenazi and K.H. Richards (eds.), *Second Temple Studies. II. Temple Community in the Persian Period* (Sheffield: JSOT Press, 1994), pp. 266–85; Harold Washington, 'The Strange Woman of Proverbs 1–9 and Post-Exilic Judean Society', in Eskenazi and Richards, *Second Temple Studies*, II, pp. 217–42.

though Deut. 23.3 appears to exclude both male and female Moabites from the community, and Ezra 9.1 lists Moabite women as defiling.

The most intriguing element of the narrative, for our purposes, is the conversation between the two Israelite males in the final chapter. Boaz argues that if the closest male relative wants to buy the family land, then there are additional liabilities on account of Ruth and the need to maintain the name of her dead first husband. The dead man has a continuing claim on the family land, and this should not be erased. This argument from family piety has a telling effect on the closest relative, who shifts the discourse to more mundane matters. He refuses the package since it would cause 'inheritance' problems (Ruth 4.6). There is still some ambiguity left, since it is unclear whether he envisages a future struggle amongst his children, or whether his worry is that after his death or divorce Ruth might make a claim to the land in her own right. Whatever the source of his anxiety, the economic complexity was too much for him. Boaz, on the other hand, is willing to take the risk because of his relationship with Ruth. Nothing in the narrative suggests that there were theological reservations about Boaz's intermarriage; on the contrary, the concluding genealogy makes clear that Ruth became an honoured mother in the genealogy of King David (Ruth 4.17–22).

Many studies of the Persian period discuss the conflict between Ezra–Nehemiah's perspective on ethnicity and what we find in other books that were composed or edited at the time. Apart from Ruth, the radical openness of the Isaiah tradition is often recognized (as discussed in our previous chapter), and there is an increasing awareness that Chronicles has brought an inclusive ethos to its re-telling of the history of Israel and Judah.[19] In what follows, I want to focus on the editing of selected chapters from Genesis to show that this book also embodies a subtle and inclusive theology, presented through the shaping of ancestral narratives. As in the case of Ruth, we may presume that regardless of the date of composition, or editing, the audiences of the Persian period would have been looking for the relevance of the stories for their own time.

Competing Voices in Genesis 21–22

It is widely agreed that the Persian period is the most likely historical setting for the final editing of Genesis, but the implications of this

---

19. See, e.g., the influential work of H.G.M. Williamson, *Israel in the Books of Chronicles* (Cambridge: Cambridge University Press, 1977); Sara Japhet, *The Ideology of the Book of Chronicles and its Place in Biblical Thought* (Frankfurt: Peter Lang, 1980).

consensus are disputed. Recent analyses of the final editing have come to diametrically opposed hypotheses as to what might have motivated the editors. Christopher Heard's work reads the narratives of Genesis 12–36 as amounting to a series of 'dis-elections' in which the marginal characters like Ishmael are excluded from the covenant by an omniscient narrator who carries divine authority. On this account, the narrator provides divine legitimation for the editors, who are to be seen as ethnocentric mediators of Persian imperial interests.[20]

Heard's proposal forms a useful contrast to my own perspective on Genesis: we both read the 'final' text as shaped by the politics of the Persian period, and we both explore the ambiguity of the narratives in ideological terms. My hypothesis, taking a cue from post-colonial studies, is that different traditions are juxtaposed by the editors in such a way as to undermine the dominant voice, including the voice of the 'omniscient' narrator. The editors are thereby subtly resisting the ethnocentric ideology of the imperial governors in ways that can be characterized as 'intentional hybridity'.[21] What is envisaged here is *neither* an organic hybridity within which the complex pre-history of the texts are entirely unknown, *nor* a serial addition of traditions, all equally coherent and perspicuous. Rather, intentional hybridity is a blending of two or more voices, without compositional boundaries being evident, such that the voices combine into an unstable mix—sometimes speaking univocally but more often juxtaposing alternative points of view such that the authority of the dominant voice is put into question. Instead of viewing Genesis through the grid of reconstructed literary sources, this model of editing throws fresh light on the significance of the Genesis narratives in the Persian period.[22]

Genesis 21–22 evoke the issues surrounding the divorces of foreign women prescribed by Ezra–Nehemiah.[23] The property claims of the 'holy seed' who returned from Babylon, for example, could well have been made

20. R. Christopher Heard, *Dynamics of Diselection: Ambiguity in Genesis 12–36 and Ethnic Boundaries in Post-Exilic Judah* (Atlanta: Society of Biblical Literature, 2001), pp. 183–84.

21. The term is borrowed from Mikhail Bakhtin, *The Dialogic Imagination* (Austin: University of Texas Press, 1981), pp. 358–61, and the concept has affinities with Homi Bhabha's notion of 'mimicry' in *The Location of Culture* (London: Routledge, 1994).

22. For a similar approach, see Judith McKinlay, *Reframing Her: Biblical Women in Postcolonial Focus* (Sheffield: Sheffield Phoenix Press, 2004), pp. 112–36.

23. This connection is made independently both by Heard, *Diselection*, and by Mark G. Brett, *Genesis: Procreation and the Politics of Identity* (London: Routledge, 2000), drawing in particular on the work of Kenneth Hoglund, *Achaemenid Imperial Administration in Syria–Palestine*.

on the basis of genealogical connections designed to demonstrate prior ownership, and these claims would inevitably have come into conflict with those who had never gone into exile and who are represented as having inter-married with the 'people of the lands' (Ezra 9.1). My hypothesis is that this theological discourse in Ezra is a distortion of Priestly traditions, and it was opposed by the editors of Genesis. Heard's reading, on the other hand, sees Genesis as covertly supportive of ethnocentrism.

To begin with, these two chapters juxtapose the suggestion that Isaac is Abraham's 'only son' (22.2) with the recognition that there is another son, Ishmael, who is 'your seed' (21.13). Ishmael's name is ironic: although his name means 'El hears' (16.11), it seems that the divine voice represented in Genesis 22.2 does not recognize Ishmael's existence. Heard's argument follows the tradition of ignoring the contradiction in the 'omniscient narrator',[24] suggesting that the narratives advocate the dis-election of Ishmael from the covenant: even if the ambiguities of the text allow us to read Ishmael more positively and Sarah more negatively, these differences of character are irrelevant to the ostensibly omniscient voice-over that Ishmael is divinely destined for exclusion. The sight of Ishmael 'laughing' provokes Sarah to assert in 21.9–10 that Hagar's son will not share the *inheritance* of Isaac. Whether, for example, Ishmael is innocent or Sarah is malicious are details Heard deems irrelevant to the overall direction of the story.

If, however, Sarah's complaint to Abraham in Gen. 21.9–10 can be read as in some sense addressing events in the Persian period, then it is noticeable that the editors have allowed Sarah's speech to render the driving away of a foreign woman purely in economic terms. From Sarah's point of view the issue is inheritance, and there is no theological veneer obscuring this fact. Hagar and Ishmael's fate in Genesis 21 stands for the dispossession of many others who have inter-married. But do the editors of Genesis legitimate the politics of dispossession, or do they not?

Why have the editors allowed the divine voice to contradict itself within such a short stretch of text? God's positive reference to Ishmael as Abraham's seed in 21.13 is all-too-swiftly occluded by the divine command in 22.2. Moreover, the editors have chosen not to provide a simple identification of Isaac at the beginning of ch. 22 (along the lines, perhaps, of 'take your son, the son of the covenant'). Evidently the story in ch. 22 was not originally attached to the expulsion of Ishmael in ch. 21, and the editors may simply be preserving a traditional form of words in 22.2, but such an hypothesis does not exhaust the question of why the editors have

---

24. Heard, *Diselection*, pp. 135–36, touches on the possibility of an unreliable narrator, without recognizing that this possibility actually undermines his overall thesis.

structured chs. 21–22 the way they have. The idea that they have juxta-posed the stories for purely antiquarian reasons, without regard to the nar-rative tensions they have created, seems implausible. Taken together with all the other evidence of subtle editing in Genesis, the significance of ch. 22 may well be suggested by its literary context.

In both chapters, 21 and 22, Abraham is called on to sacrifice a son. In the first case, the sacrifice comes at Sarah's initiative, not God's; it is she who wants to cut off Ishmael's inheritance by sending him away, and Abraham sees Sarah's agency as evil (21.11). Commentators have observed that Sarah's oppression of Hagar, and her 'driving out', picks up vocabulary used later in the story of Israel's oppression in Egypt. Phyllis Trible sums this idea up with disturbing brevity: Hagar's experience 'prefigures Israel's story even as Sarah foreshadows Egypt's role'.[25] The 'exodus' of Genesis 21 leads Hagar, however, to wilderness borderlands and not to the conquest of Canaan, although God assures Abraham that Ishmael is his seed and that the slavewoman's son will become a 'great nation' (the same promise given to Abram in 12.2).

In ch. 22, the sacrifice of the son is God's initiative. At the highpoint of horror, a divine messenger calls out from the heavens, just as when Hagar was at breaking point in 21.16–17. In ch. 21, Hagar is sitting 'a bowshot' away from Ishmael, unable to watch her child die, and the heavenly mes-senger assures her that God has heard her son's weeping. The voice of the innocent victim is heard, as the reader would expect from the naming of 'Ishmael' earlier in 16.11 ('El hears'). In ch. 22, on the other hand, we are not told of a weeping child or parent. What is at issue, apparently, is solely the extraordinary obedience of Abraham:

> Because you have done this thing and have not held back your son, your only one, I will greatly bless you and will greatly multiply your seed, as the stars in the heavens and as the sand on the shore of the sea, and your seed shall seize the gate of their enemies. And all the nations of the earth will be blessed through your seed because you have listened to my voice (22.16–18).

This divine speech, however, still leaves some significant questions hang-ing: why is it, for example, that the editors have retained the reference to Abraham's 'only son' when the connections with the Ishmael narratives are so clear? Not only do we find the common themes linking ch. 22 to the

---

25. Phyllis Trible, *Texts of Terror* (Philadelphia: Fortress Press, 1984) p. 21; Thomas Dozeman, 'The Wilderness and Salvation History in the Hagar Story', *Journal of Biblical Literature* 117 (1998), pp. 24–43; Brett, *Genesis*, pp. 58–61; McKinlay, *Reframing Her*, pp. 132–36.

expulsion of Hagar in ch. 21, but when Abraham names the place of Isaac's deliverance 'Yahweh Yireh' ('Yahweh sees') in 22.14, this naming scene parallels Hagar's naming of God in 16.13–14 ('El who sees me'). Moreover, in both chs. 16 and 22 the naming scenes are associated with the divine deliverance of Abraham's sons, as well as with divine promises. These connections make it all the more puzzling to find that Yahweh's promises in 22.16–18 mention Abraham's 'only' son. The divine speech seems to be written within the terms of reference defined by an exclusivist ideology that would regard Isaac as the only relevant son since he is the one circumscribed by the covenant in 17.18–22. Given the numerous allusions to Ishmael in ch. 22, however, this ideology need not be identified with the final editors' point of view. It is more likely that the joining of chs.21 and 22 is designed to undermine such exclusivism.

The concluding verses of ch. 22 might seem relatively insignificant, but there are at least two elements worth noting: the reference to a journey in 22.19 and the genealogical notes in 22.20–24. After the dramatic test of faith in ch. 22, v. 19 says that Abraham returns to Beersheba, the very place where, according to 21.14, the divine promise concerning Ishmael was delivered to his mother Hagar. This geographical irony is simply too great to dismiss: Beersheba is the site where God promised that Abraham's other son would become a 'great nation'. Ishmael is the son confirmed by God as the *seed* of Abraham (21.13), and Ishmael is the son circumcised by Abraham himself, marking him with the sign of the covenant (in 17.23–27, discussed below). As the son of an Egyptian, he is the product of a foreign marriage prohibited in Ezra 9.1, but the editors of Genesis have planted numerous subversive clues to suggest that this is no impediment to divine blessing.

The second aspect of 22.19–24 worth noting is that the genealogical details provide the identity of a certain Rebekah, who is destined in ch. 24 to become Isaac's wife. Rebekah, we discover here for the first time, is the granddaughter of Abraham's brother Nahor. In line with the exclusivist ideology of the divine speeches in ch. 22, the marriage of Isaac and Rebekah is foreshadowed as endogamous. In short, Isaac's marriage is blessed by Abraham's kinship system, yet 22.19 implies that Isaac lives with his father in Beersheba, the very place where Abraham's son through a foreign marriage received a divine promise. (And the careful reader needs to ask why Rebekah is sought out for marriage in ch. 24 when God commanded Abram in Gen. 12.1 to leave not only his home but also his *kin*.)[26]

---

26.   Note also the lack of divine blessing on the wooing of Rebekah in Genesis 24. See Brett, *Genesis*, pp. 49–51, and cf. Heard, *Diselection*, pp. 28–29, who once again notes the narrator's ambiguity without recognizing that this weakens his overall argument.

In the historical setting of the Persian period, the implied connections between chs. 21 and 22 would have had quite clear social implications. The model of holiness promoted by the Ezra–Nehemiah party suggested that all foreign women should be sent away, including Egyptians (Ezra 9.1–2). The expulsion of Hagar and her son can, in this sense, be read as one paradigm of holiness. Yet, as we have seen, a careful reading of the final form of Genesis suggests that the editors thought otherwise. While not explicitly attacking the ideology of endogamy, they arranged the narratives such that Hagar and Ishmael emerge equally as recipients of divine grace, and exogamous marriages are thereby covertly defended. The exclusivist ideology of the divine speeches in ch. 22 can only pass without question if one is willing to deny the reality of Ishmael's existence and his status as Abraham's son. In effect, the editors have revealed the dishonesty of the narrow conception of covenant. The reader of Genesis in the Persian period is thus invited not to succumb to the paradigm of holiness suggested by Ezra 9.1–2.

Nevertheless, the detail and the drama of Genesis 22 cannot simply be dismissed as exclusivist ideology. There is a theological profundity in the chapter that deserves further reflection. By this point in the narrative, we should remember, Isaac has become the focus of all Abraham's hopes for blessing and fame (21.12). If a test of faith is to be a test of self-interest, it will need to address the son who represents that self-interest, Isaac. The editors seem to have used the narrative of Genesis 22, even with its exclusivist ideology, to address the most rigorous question for piety: will Abraham follow God's instructions only because the rewards of progeny and land are so desirable, or is God intrinsically worthy of obedience? The question is never framed in such philosophically abstract terms, but by putting the life of Isaac at risk, the narrative has indeed evoked precisely this issue (cf. the parallel issue in Job 1.9).

In effect, the editors have placed two tests of faith side by side in Genesis 21 and 22. The first, the sacrifice of Hagar and Ishmael, is the kind of test proposed by the imperial governors of the Persian period. Yet this test does not actually touch the core issue of self-interest: if the quest for purity is simply a means to gain rewards, then God has not been honoured as intrinsically worthy but only as the giver of desirable goods—notably *land*. Genesis 22, on the other hand, implies that the only true test for disinterested piety would be to sacrifice Isaac—the medium through which all the future gifts of progeny and land would be grasped. The subtle juxtapositions of Genesis 21–22 question the motivation for dispossessing foreign women. Responsibility towards foreign wives returns as a viable ethic, and indeed, as one that stands firmly within the older legal traditions of Israel: 'You shall not wrong or oppress a stranger, for you were strangers in Egypt' (Exod. 22.21).

As we have seen above, this ethic was also underwritten by Priestly texts such as Lev. 19.34, which exhorts the native-born to 'love the stranger as yourself, for you were strangers in the land of Egypt'. It will therefore be interesting to explore the common hypothesis that there was a Priestly literary source also within Genesis—not just in Leviticus and Numbers—and to observe how the issue of ethnicity is treated in this tradition.[27] It will become evident that both Priestly material and the final form of Genesis share a common resistance to the idea of a 'holy seed'.

Priestly Ethnocentrism in Genesis?

In Gen. 27.46, Rebekah complains to her husband about the possibility that her son might marry a Hittite woman: 'If Jacob takes a wife from among the women of the land, from the Hittite women like these, what will life mean to me?' It is often assumed that this text reflects the ethnocentric attitude of a Priestly author (at work in Gen. 26.34–35 and 27.46–28.5) who endorses not only Rebekah's endogamous marriage but her pursuit of the same ideal for Isaac. But there are many ways to interpret these ambiguous narratives, whether in literary or historical terms. Jacob Milgrom, for example, points out that the aversion to exogamous marriage in this text may well reflect an ethnic sentiment, but this should not be confused with a developed codification of marriage law or a theology of purity.[28]

It might be thought that the Priestly covenant tradition in Genesis 17 would resolve this issue, but even the 'sign of the covenant' in this text is highly ambiguous: every male of the household is to be circumcised, both those born in the household and those bought from 'any foreigner—those who are not of your *seed*' (Gen. 17.9–14). Abraham accordingly circumcises every male of his household, including the foreigners, beginning with his son Ishmael, born to an Egyptian woman (Gen. 17.23–27).

Between these two sections lies the most problematic part of the chapter, vv. 15–22. First, there is a parallel promise to Sarah: her name is changed (just as Abraham's was in v. 5), and it is said that she will become the mother of nations and of kings, just as Abraham is to become the father of nations and kings (v. 6). An innovation here is that although Abraham was promised descendants as numerous as the dust of the earth (13.16) and the

---

27. My assumption in the following discussion is that we have sufficient reason to identify the work of a Priestly school in the Torah, but we do not have sufficient reason to suppose that the 'final' form of Genesis also comes from the later activity of this school, as some have suggested.

28. Milgrom, *Leviticus 17–22*, p. 1585.

stars of the sky (15.5), this extraordinary fecundity could still be interpreted within the framework of the single 'great nation' mentioned in 12.2. Now that Abraham and Sarah are set to become the father and mother of many nations, it is no longer possible to restrict this covenantal promise to the people of Israel. The catch for Abraham, however, is that if Sarah's inclusion within the covenant means that she herself must have a son, then the status of Hagar's son is thrown into question. Abraham therefore intercedes on Ishmael's behalf (v. 18), only to be assured that Hagar's son will become a 'great nation', but outside the covenant with Sarah's son (vv. 19–21). This divine reassurance in vv. 19–21 is precisely what makes the conclusion of the chapter so problematic: if circumcision is the sign of the covenant (v. 11), and the covenantal line is to go through Isaac—not through Ishmael—why have the editors so blithely placed vv. 23–27 at the end of the chapter, recording the faithful circumcision of the son excluded from the covenant?

A standard response to this kind of problem is to reconstruct the layers of the text so that the first layer of the narrative is seen to be coherent, while the clumsy additions have rendered the final text illogical. This kind of interpretative response leaves one of the most interesting questions unexplained: why would anyone want to add a contradiction to a text? It seems much more likely that the editors had a specific purpose in view, but that this purpose could not be conveyed by overt reasoning since the issue at stake lay at the heart of a dominant ideology of the Persian period. The apparently simple 'obedience' of Abraham in 17.23–27 is exploiting the tensions within the final text: the circumcision of Ishmael contradicts the exclusivism of vv. 19–21 by holding to the inclusivist ideology of 17.9–12. If every male of the household is to be circumcised, as suggested in the first part of the chapter, then that should include Ishmael. Moreover, if Ishmael is to be the father of a 'great nation' (v. 20), then that is in some sense the fulfillment of the promise that Abraham is to be the father of many nations (v. 5). In short, the divine blessing on the seed of Abraham is not restricted to a binary logic of 'pure' and 'impure' descendants.[29]

The rite of circumcision is much more inclusive than one might have thought. Any reader familiar with the narrow interpretation of the 'holy seed' in Ezra 9.1–2, for example, would have been struck by the wording of Gen. 17.12:

---

29. See Albert de Pury, 'Abraham: The Priestly Writer's "Ecumenical" Ancestor', in S. L. McKenzie, T. Romer, H. H. Schmid (eds.), *Rethinking the Foundations* (Berlin: Walter de Gruyter, 2000), pp. 163–81.

> For the generations to come every male among you who is eight days
> old must be circumcised, including those born in your household or
> bought with money from a foreigner—he who is not of your seed.

If this text is implying that *all* slaves are to be bought from foreigners,
then it seems to presume the legal background of Lev. 25.39–46, rather
than Deut. 15.12–15 (the Deuteronomic slave law permits the buying of
Hebrew slaves, but the Levitical law resists this, permitting only the pur-
chase of foreign slaves). But whatever the legal presumption, Genesis 17 is
clearly envisaging that foreigners could be circumcised, and in this sense,
the covenant is seen as broader than Israelite kinship. It would include
those born outside the line of Ezra's 'holy seed'.

Indeed, in the setting of the Persian period, circumcision could no longer
have the same significance as it had during the exile: the Babylonians
did not practise circumcision, and therefore the rite would have been a
distinctive mark of minority identity for Israelites living in Babylon, but
the distinctiveness of this mark of the covenant would have been lost as
soon as the Israelites moved back to the promised land. As indicated by
a text in Jeremiah, Israel's neighbours also practised circumcision, including the Egyptians, Edomites, Ammonites, Moabites and 'all who live in
the desert' (Jer. 9.25–26). If we can include the Ishmaelites amongst these
desert-dwellers (cf. Gen. 21.20–21), then the people listed in Jeremiah 9
include not just the exclusive people of the covenant but also all peoples
represented in Genesis as related to Abraham. Ezra 9.2, we should remember, prohibits intermarriage specifically with Egyptians, Ammonites and
Moabites, three of the peoples listed in Jer. 9.25–26 as circumcised.

In short, the logic of ethnic exclusivism in Ezra 9.2 cannot be based on
the sign of the covenant in Genesis 17, and Ezra once again stands opposed
to the Priestly traditions. Many attempts have been made to date the various layers of Genesis 17, but for our present purposes it is not necessary to
propose a detailed theory of editing. If Genesis 17 was largely completed by
exiles in Babylon (with circumcision acting as a unique mark of cultural difference and resistance), then in the Persian period it would have provided
a ready-made source of opposition to Ezra's idea of the holy seed. If, on
the other hand, the editing was not complete until the fifth century, then
the possibility arises that this chapter was deliberately shaped in opposition
to Ezra–Nehemiah.[30]

---

30.   This would accord with Rolf Rendtorff's suggestion that some Priestly texts relat-
ing to 'strangers' have been edited in opposition to Ezra and Nehemiah. See Rendtorff,
'The *Ger* in the Priestly Laws of the Pentateuch', in Mark G. Brett (ed.), *Ethnicity and the
Bible* (Leiden: E.J. Brill, 1996), pp. 77–88.

Concluding Reflections

The preceding discussion should, I think, count *against* the theory of the Pentateuch's formation that suggests it was authorized by the Persian administration for the purposes of local rule in the province of 'Yehud' (as Judah is called in the Aramaic sources from the period).[31] This theory gained some credence from, for example, the extravagant representation of the emperor Cyrus as a 'messiah' in Isa. 45.1, but recent historical studies have positioned such appreciative language against the larger background Persian imperial interests. In particular, as already noted, the fortification of Jerusalem under Nehemiah has been seen as part of a wider military and economic strategy designed to consolidate the western holdings of the empire. So a key question remains: how was political power actually configured in fifth-century Yehud, and what difference does this make to our interpretation of 'ethnocentric' holiness in the period?

Daniel Smith-Christopher suggests that the books of Ezra and Nehemiah can themselves be interpreted as examples of 'cultural resistance', and he even sees the imperial warrants in Ezra 1–7 as prudent statements of deference that mask more subtle forms of subversive resistance. This approach is inspired in particular by the anthropologist James Scott, whose book *Domination and the Arts of Restistance: Hidden Transcripts* provides ground-breaking work on the varieties of covert resistance.[32]

The key problem with applying this anthropological perspective to Ezra–Nehemiah is that the horizon of solidarity in these books seems to include only the returning exiles, so that the people of Judah who never went into exile are represented as 'people/s of the land/s'. The 'covert resistance'—if indeed it is resistance—is not just to the empire. There is a binary contrast between 'the children of the exile' (e.g., Ezra 4.1; 6.19–20; 8.35; Neh. 7.5–73) and everyone else, so that Judeans who never went into exile were classified as foreigners along with Moabites, Egyptians or Samarians. The exiles were identified with Israel as such, and all others were mired in the 'land unclean (*niddah*) with the pollutions peoples of

---

31. See the critical discussion in James W. Watts (ed.), *Persia and Torah: The Theory of Imperial Authorization of the Pentateuch* (Atlanta: Scholars Press, 2001); Gary N. Knoppers and Bernard M. Levinson, *The Pentateuch as Torah: New Models for Understanding its Promulgation and Acceptance* (Winona Lake: Eisenbrauns, 2007).

32. James Scott, *Domination and the Arts of Resistance: Hidden Transcripts* (New Haven: Yale University Press, 1990); Smith-Christopher, *Theology of Exile*, pp. 22–23; 34–45. Cf. Brett, *Genesis*, pp. 8, 17.

the lands, with their abominations which have filled it from end to end' (Ezra 9.11).[33]

If we were looking for sociological analogies between Ezra and Nehemiah's exclusivist 'Israel' and modern case studies, then a number of possibilities have been suggested beyond Smith-Christopher's focus on groups subjected to forced removals. In Palestine under the British Mandate of the 1930s and 1940s, for example, the Chief Rabbinate's administration of marriages was frequently contested by Eastern European orthodox rabbis (*Haredim*) who denied Jewish identity to non-orthodox Jews—although in this case the British colonial authority was on the side of the Chief Rabbinate. The analogy, if it holds, would be between Ezra and the exclusivist *Haredim*, who were more concerned with an intra-Jewish struggle over religious identity than with colonial administration.[34] The main difficulty with the analogy is that Ezra 1–7 is so clearly concerned with imperial warrants, which the *Haredim* were not.

I want to suggest another analogy from the twentieth century that may be at least as significant in throwing light on the dynamics of the Persian period. I have in mind a comparison with anti-colonial movements that have promoted a 'nativist' agenda—that is, an *overt* program of reinstating 'Indigenous cultural tradition' which is presented as unsullied and uniquely 'authentic'.[35] Recent studies have described a range of examples where nativism has functioned as an oppositional discourse in the formation of post-colonial states. Arising as critiques of the West, these examples demonstrate ironically that national identities were produced within territorial borders defined by the colonial powers, rather than by pre-colonial cultures, and within these borders, native elites produced fictive unities between the present and the past.

33. Sara Japhet, 'People and Land in the Restoration Period', in Georg Strecker (ed.), *Das Land Israel in biblischer Zeit* (Göttingen: Vandenhoeck & Ruprecht, 1983), pp. 112–15; Joseph Blenkinsopp, *Ezra–Nehemiah*, p. 108; H.G.M. Williamson, 'The Concept of Israel in Transition', in Ronald Clements (ed.), *The World of Ancient Israel* (Cambridge: Cambridge University Press, 1989), p. 155.

34. T.C. Eskenazi and E.P. Judd, 'Marriage to a Stranger in Ezra 9–10', pp. 272–85; Smith-Christopher, 'The Mixed Marriage Crisis in Ezra 9–10 and Nehemiah 13', in Eskenazi and Richards, *Second Temple Studies*, II, pp. 257–58.

35. See the introductory discussion in Mehrzad Boroujerdi, *Iranian Intellectuals and the West: The Tormented Triumph of Nativism* (Syracuse: Syracuse University Press, 1996), pp. 1–19. Nehemiah's administration has also been interpreted in terms of a nativist cultural revitalization by D. Tollefson and H.G.M. Williamson in 'Nehemiah as Cultural Revitalization: An Anthropological Perspective', *Journal for the Study of the Old Testament* 56 (1992), pp. 41–68.

A frequently observed irony at work in nativist social visions is that they have often been blind to particular groups within their own society. For example, in *Producing India: From Colonial Economy to National Space*, Manu Goswami has argued that 'territorial nativism' identified 'upper-caste Hindus as the organic, original, core nationals with an intimate and unmediated relationship with the imagined nation'. Muslims accordingly became problematic within this territory.[36] Similarly concerned with the inbuilt blindness of nativist ideology in India, Partha Chatterjee argues in his influential *Nationalist Thought and the Colonial World* that the transition from the colonial to the post-colonial Indian state was effected without substantive structural transformation; it reiterated the capitalist assumptions of the West and authorized the continued marginalisation of particular social groups.[37]

My main point here is not that modern examples like these might provide a direct analogy with Persian period Yehud, but rather, that they illustrate the myriad complexities and layering of colonial power and resistance to it. Postcolonial and 'subaltern studies' have repeatedly shown how the dichotomy of oppressor/oppressed does not illuminate the capillaries of power. It is not just that Ezra and Nehemiah might afford examples of both accommodation and resistance (as suggested by Smith-Christopher) but we can expect that their own vision and practice will have generated its own series of responses, including the Priestly perspectives in the Torah.

To return to the Australian context once again, nativist discourses have had multiple ambiguous functions in recent politics and law, and one highly significant example of this relates to the effects of the 'Mabo' decision of the High Court. In this landmark decision, native title rights and interests were importantly identified as 'inherent', rather than 'granted' by the Crown. But instead of seeing an inherent system of traditional rights as implying a sovereign system of law (as in North America), the federal parliament set about providing new legislation that would begin to restrict the possibilities of native title.

The *Native Title Act* of 1993 raised a whole new set of questions about the ways in which Indigenous polities could be recognized in Australia, and jurisprudence since the Mabo judgment has tended to recognize the

---

36. Manu Goswami, *Producing India: From Colonial Economy to National Space* (Chicago: Chicago University Press, 2004), pp. 10, 283–85. cf. Daniele Conversi, 'Conceptualizing Nationalism', in D. Conversi (ed.), *Ethnonationalism in the Contemporary World* (London: Routledge, 2002), p. 10.

37. Partha Chatterjee, *Nationalist Thought and the Colonial World* (Minneapolis: University of Minnesota Press, 1986), p. 168; *The Nation and its Fragments: Colonial and Post-Colonial Histories* (Princeton: Princeton University Press, 1993).

legitimacy of native land title but only by making it inaccessible to many Indigenous people: in order to be recognized under this legislation, a local Indigenous community is required to demonstrate a continuous observance of traditional law and custom, in spite of the effects of colonisation. The cunning in this strategy is that it recognizes 'authentic' Indigenous groups while denying justice to those who have suffered the most dislocation under the so-called 'tides of history'.[38] This is just one example of a widespread tendency in the Australian law and media to distinguish between 'authentic Aborigines' on the one hand and culturally hybrid ones on the other, and in this case the discourse stems not from native elites but from non-Indigenous groups who have seized on nativist discourses for their own purposes.

Postcolonial interpretation needs to be vigilantly aware of the complex effects of power at work in the reproduction of nativist discourses. The exclusivist biblical theology in Ezra and Nehemiah *may* have had its roots in a pattern of cultural resistance adopted by minorities struggling with corporate survival, but these discourses could easily have been co-opted for a range of other political purposes. The modern comparisons I have mentioned do not provide direct analogies, but they illustrate the complexities and layering of colonial power and resistance to it.

38. Hannah McGlade, 'Native Title, "Tides of History" and our Continuing Claims for Justice', in Australian Institute of Aboriginal and Torres Strait Islander Studies, *Treaty: Let's Get It Right* (Canberra: Aboriginal Studies Press, 2003), pp. 118–36; cf. Elizabeth Povinelli, *The Cunning of Recognition* (Durham: Duke University Press, 2002), pp. 37, 265.

Jesus, Non-violence and the Christ Question

> In the beginning was the *tjukurpa*.
>
> *John 1.1*

We noted in Chapter 1 that Mahatma Gandhi was an advocate of Jesus' teaching. Gandhi insisted that religious conversion was problematic, since it tore the fabric of social relations, but he was sufficiently moved by the 'Sermon on the Mount' in Matthew 5 to provide a fresh inter-pretation of non-violence within Hinduism.[1] This hybrid mix of Jesus' sermon and Hindu spirituality shaped Gandhi's advocacy of a mass movement against British rule in India. In an intriguing circulation of biblical influences, the Baptist minister Martin Luther King Jr was later inspired by Gandhi's example to lead his own non-violent strug-gle against the American legacies of the 'curse of Ham'. I will argue in this chapter that although the historical Jesus exercised his resistance to Roman rule more covertly, Gandhi and King laid legitimate claims to the political implications of the Gospels and to the significance of Jesus' non-violence.

The broad sweep of history that is sometimes called 'the Second Temple period'—stretching for seven centuries from the re-building of the temple in Jerusalem under Persian administration to its destruction by the Romans in 70 CE—is a period of shifting imperial tides and spasmodic Jewish revolts. For example, in the final decades of the fourth century BCE, Syria-Palestine changed hands seven times as the successors to Alexander the Great wres-tled over their competing interests in the area. In the first part of the second century, persecution of the Jews provoked the Maccabean Revolt which led to a brief period of independence. When Simon Maccabee conquered the Jerusalem citadel and took power as a high priest, he was understood to be assuming the mantle of the Phinehas in Num. 25.1–15 whose violent

---

1. M.M. Thomas, *The Acknowledged Christ of the Indian Renaissance* (London: SCM Press, 1969), pp. 198–209; Ashis Nandy, *The Intimate Enemy: Loss and Recovery of Self under Colonialism* (Delhi: Oxford University Press, 1983), pp. 51–57.

religious zeal earns him an 'eternal priesthood' (see 1 Macc. 2.54; Sir. 45.23–24).

While the Maccabean priesthood held power for only a few years, the memory of their victories lived on into the Roman period, being celebrated especially in the festival of Hanukkah. Successive Roman administrations in Galilee and Judea met with resistance in various forms and responded with bloody repression. Jesus of Nazareth lived and died within the four decades of social conflict between the death of Herod the Great in 4 BCE to the end of Pontius Pilate's governorship in 36 CE—the latter apparently recalled to Rome because of his use of disproportionate force against a group of Samaritans who had formed around one of their prophets. A number of revolts are recorded in subsequent decades, including the Jewish War of 66–70, which culminated in the destruction of the Jerusalem temple, and the rebellion led by Simon bar Kokhba (132–35 CE). This was, arguably, an age of revolt.

It was also an age of deep social divisions between the ruling classes—both Roman and Jewish—and the majority peasant population who produced the agrarian resources upon which ancient Middle Eastern societies were based. Rome typically exercised its rule through local elites whose interests could be aligned with those of the empire. Peasants were required to pay tribute to Rome and its local representatives, as well as to provide the tithes demanded by the high priestly houses in Jerusalem. The total amount of tribute payable could be as much as forty percent of crops and herds each year.[2]

This tributary peasant economy forms the background to the parables of Jesus that focus on debt. In his pithy narratives and teachings, Jesus provides an alternative to the contemporary Jewish practice that had found ways to circumvent the ancient requirements to cancel all debts in the seventh or 'Sabbatical', year (Exod. 22.25; Deuteronomy 15). The rabbis had introduced a legal mechanism called the *prosbul* whereby a person could swear before a court that a debt would indeed be repaid, regardless of the Sabbatical year. Against this practice, which locked peasants into poverty, Jesus saw debt as an opportunity for forgiveness. When he recommends the prayer 'Forgive us our debts as we forgive our debtors', he draws no distinction between economic and 'spiritual'

2. Richard Horsley, *Galilee: History, Politics, People* (Valley Forge: Trinity Press International, 1995), pp. 216–21.

debts. Forgiveness potentially becomes a daily practice, rather than a Sabbatical exception to ordinary life.[3]

Similarly, the ancient scriptural requirement to restore ancestral lands in the fiftieth year, the year of 'Jubilee', is reinterpreted in the Gospels as one way of understanding the coming 'kingdom of God'. The Gospel of Luke highlights this at the beginning of Jesus' public activities by suggesting that a prophetic text referring to 'the year of the Lord's favour' (the Jubilee) is on the verge of fulfilment. The narrative describes a scene in a synagogue where Jesus reads from Isaiah 61, a prophetic oracle that alludes to the idea of Jubilee in using the key word 'release' (*dᵉror* in Hebrew and *aphesis* in Greek):

The scroll of the prophet Isaiah was handed to him. Unrolling it, he found the place where it is written:

> The Spirit of the Lord is on me,
> Because he has anointed me to preach good news to the poor.
> He has sent me to proclaim *release* to the captives
> and recovery of sight for the blind,
> to set at liberty those who are oppressed,
> to proclaim the year of the Lord's favour.

> Then he rolled up the scroll, gave it back to the attendant and sat down. The eyes of everyone in the synagogue were fixed on him, and he said to them, 'Today this scripture is fulfilled in your hearing' (Lk. 4.17–21, quoting from Isa. 61.1–2).

The legal idea of the Jubilee is poetically amplified in Isaiah's oracle and then again slightly modified in Luke's rendering of the story. The use of the term *dᵉror* 'release' in Isaiah 61.1 echoes the Jubilee legislation:

> You shall hallow the fiftieth year, and proclaim release (*dᵉror*) throughout the land to all its inhabitants. It shall be a Jubilee for you, when each of you shall return to your ancestral inheritance and each of you shall return to your family (Lev. 25.10).

Isaiah 61 takes up the older law and absorbs it within a prophetic vision of restoration—Israel returning from exile, confident that her debts of sin have been paid. The cancellation of debts is subsumed within the broader eschatological expectations supplied by Isaiah, but questions of interpretation

---

3.   William R. Herzog, *Jesus, Justice and the Reign of God* (Louisville: Westminster John Knox, 2000), pp. 107–108; on the *prosbul*, see Jacob Neusner, *The Rabbinic Traditions about the Pharisees before 70*. I. *The Masters* (Leiden: E.J. Brill, 1971), pp. 217–20; Martin Goodman, *The Ruling Class of Judea: The Origin of the Jewish Revolt against Rome, A.D. 66–70* (Cambridge: Cambridge University Press, 1987), p. 58.

arise when the prophetic poetry is rendered into Greek within the Gospel of Luke. The verbal associations that would have been conveyed in the Hebrew texts may have been diluted among readers who, in the course of time, engaged with this story in Greek and encountered a more ambiguous terminology for 'release' or 'forgiveness': *aphesis* instead of *dᵉror*.[4] The concrete meanings of *dᵉror* in Hebrew texts were apparently overlaid in Christian tradition with a more 'spiritualized' connotation of forgiveness.

It would be a mistake, however, to infer that debt release was seen by the historical Jesus in narrow spiritual terms, dissociated from the oppressive economic conditions of peasant life. The fact that Matthew's version of the Lord's prayer has 'forgive us our debts' (6.12) rather than Luke's 'forgive us our sins' (11.4) probably illustrates not so much a spiritualization on Luke's part as the breadth of associations carried by the term 'sin'. This is implied by Luke's continuing with 'for indeed, we ourselves forgive our every debtor'.[5] It is likely that when Jesus spoke about God's eschatological sovereignty he had in mind both a praxis of cancelling debts/sins and an intervention of God who would forgive sins and restore economic order, necessarily supplanting the rule of Rome. Centuries before, the prophetic tradition had linked the cancellation of sins with a healing and regeneration of the society—symbolized for Isaiah as a return from exile to a fertile Judah (Isaiah 40–55)—and it is this regeneration that Jesus spoke about as evidence of the kingdom of God.[6]

The cancellation of debt is actually a more common discourse in the Gospels than the cancellation of sins. And the language of 'salvation' is more often associated with healings.[7] The explanation of Jesus' name in Mt. 1.21—'for he will save his people from their sins'—raises a question about the nature of these sins. The common presumption that narrowly religious matters are in view here is quite unjustified. The classical prophetic tradition of Israel was at pains to make precisely the point that social sins are at least as grievous as any other sin. And as we have seen, the prophets go as far as to suggest that religious practices are invalidated by the oppression and exploitation of the poor. As Warren Carter rightly puts it, sinfulness is

4. Sharon Ringe, *Jesus, Liberation, and the Biblical Jubilee* (Philadephia: Fortress Press, 1985), pp. 23–45.

5. See Raymond E. Brown, 'The Pater Noster as an Eschatological Prayer', *Theological Studies* 22 (1961), pp. 199–200.

6. N.T. Wright, *Jesus and the Victory of God* (Minneapolis: Fortress Press, 1996), pp. 269–74.

7. John Carroll, 'Sickness and Healing in the New Testament Gospels', *Interpretation* 49 (1995), pp. 130–42.

'simultaneously political, economic, social, religious and moral'.[8] This key
tenet of the prophetic tradition would be lost if salvation was conceived in
a narrowly religious way.

The healing narratives embody one aspect of the broader pattern of
regeneration within the kingdom of God. It is not just that the healings
demonstrate divine power, but at the same time they raise questions about
alternative claims to power. In the story of the paralysed man in Mk 2.1–12,
for example, Jesus mediates a divine forgiveness which leads to healing, but
in so doing he competes with the authority of the temple hierarchy and,
more indirectly, with other hierarchies of the imperial order.[9] The scribes
who witness this event accuse Jesus of blasphemy, asking 'Who can forgive
sins but God alone?' (2.7), but we may infer that the objection is at least
in part masking their own social interests; the healing is evidence of divine
presence, and the temple no longer has to be seen as the centre of that presence. What is implicit in this healing story becomes explicit in Jesus' prediction that the temple will be destroyed (Mk 11.15–18 and parallels).

John Dominic Crossan has provided a concise summary of the terrible
ironies inherent here in the interplay of economic, social and religious factors. We know that illness can be correlated with economic factors in various ways, but the religion of the day linked sickness and sin:

> Since the religiopolitical ascendency could not blame excessive
> taxation, it blamed sick people themselves by claiming that their
> sins had led to their illnesses. And the cure for sinful sickness was,
> ultimately, in the Temple. And that meant more fees, in a perfect
> circle of victimization.[10]

Accordingly, in Mk 11.15–19 when Jesus confronts the traders and
pilgrims in the temple, he is challenging the whole system of payment of
fees for sacrificial animals (addressing both 'those who sold and those who
bought'), once again taking up the Israelite prophetic tradition that rejected
the temple's sacrificial system as the focus of divine concern.

In Mk 11.17 we find Jesus citing from two prophetic texts (Isa. 56.7 and
Jer. 7.11) in his confrontation in the temple:

8.   Warren Carter, *Matthew and Empire: Initial Explorations* (Harrisburg: Trinity Press
International, 2001), p. 79.

9.   William R. Herzog, *Jesus, Justice and the Reign of God*, p. 253. Cf. Edwin K.
Broadhead, 'Mark 1, 44: the Witness of the Leper', *Zeitschrift für die neutestamentliche
Wissenschaft* 83 (1992), pp. 257–65.

10.   John Dominic Crossan, *The Historical Jesus: The Life of a Mediterranean Peasant*
(San Francisco: HarperCollins, 1991), p. 324.

> Is it not written, 'My house will be called a house of prayer for all
> nations'? But you have made it 'a cave of bandits'.

The analogies between Jesus' symbolic action in the temple and these
earlier prophetic messages are significant. In the wider context of Isaiah
56, the prophet criticizes the conventional hierarchies of purity even to
the extent that the prophetic word overrules legal prescriptions found in
the Torah. Where, for example, Deut. 23.1 had excluded eunuchs from the
temple, Isa. 56.3–4 accepts them. The overturning of the moneychangers'
tables in Mark 11, one could say, carries a symbolic resonance with Isaiah's
overturning of the purity codes.

There may also be an additional level of irony in Jesus' quotations in Mk
11.17, however, since his reference to 'a cave of bandits' may be a double
allusion not only to Jeremiah's concerns about the temple (Jer. 7.11) but
also to the banditry of Jesus' own day. Jesus seems to imply that in the eyes
of God there is little difference between the structural violence of the temple and living a violent and opportunistic life on the fringes of social order.[11]
Jesus' judgement on the oppressive practices in the temple is analogous to
Jeremiah's assertion that divine concern is focussed more on the 'widow,
orphan and alien' than it is on the making of sacrifices. Concern for the
most vulnerable emerges as a higher priority for faith than formal religious
practice.

Despite the symbolic violence of overturning tables, Jesus in fact embodies and espouses a 'non-violent social revolution' that challenges all the
conventional constructions of power and order, not just the temple.[12] The
term *basileia* in Greek (normally translated 'kingdom') commonly referred
to empires,[13] so when Jesus instructs his disciples to pray for the arrival of
a '*basileia* of God' in the historical context of Roman rule (Mt. 6.10) this
could hardly have been seen as politically irrelevant. The language inevitably contests the imperial claim to sovereignty. That God's will should be
done 'on earth, as it is in heaven' suggests a universal perspective that competes with Roman religion and its ideological legitimation of the emperor
as Lord of the earth.

Instead of leading a violent revolt, however, Jesus emerges as prophet
of the Galilean peasantry, whose praxis demonstrates indirectly just who
is mediating divine power and how that power should be understood. The
exorcism story in Mk 5.1–20, for example, implies its point through word

---

11. Herzog, *Jesus, Justice and the Reign of God*, pp. 138–43.
12. Richard Horsley, *Jesus and the Spiral of Violence: Popular Jewish Resistance in
Roman Palestine* (San Francisco: Harper & Row, 1987), pp. 147–66.
13. For examples, see Warren Carter, *Matthew and Empire*, p. 62.

choices that are heavy with ambiguity: the story identifies a 'legion' of demons which Jesus 'vanquishes' by causing them to enter a 'troop' of pigs who then drown in the sea. The terminology plays on the Roman 'legions' who become, in this narrative analogy with the Exodus story, the 'troops' of Pharaoh who drown in the Sea of Reeds.[14]

Similarly, the genealogy at the beginning of Matthew's Gospel implies that God's purposes are sustained historically in a curious Jewish lineage that includes foreign women and Judean kings, rather than in the emperors who were sanctioned by imperial Roman religion. Matthew 1.17 claims that there were fourteen generations from Abraham to David (the paradigm of Judean kings), another fourteen generations to the exile, and a further fourteen generations from the exile to 'Christ'. The narrator of Matthew here foreshadows for the readers that Jesus is 'the Christ'—*christos* in Greek translating *mashiach* in Hebrew—who will fulfil the messianic expectations articulated in the Hebrew scriptures. In several key oracles which are reinterpreted in the New Testament, Israel's prophets envisaged the reversal of the exile and the reassertion of divine sovereignty under the *mashiach*/Christ.

Matthew's introductory chapter implies a political contest with Rome, for example in v. 23, when Jesus' birth is seen as the fulfilment of the 'Emmanuel' prophecy in Isaiah. The language of fulfilment reinterprets the ancient prophecy in messianic terms:

> The young woman will be with child and will give birth to a son, and they will call him 'Immanuel', which means 'God with us' (Isa. 7.14 cited in Matthew 1.23).

The literary context of Isa. 7.14 is quite clear: two kingdoms to the north of Judah are threatening to invade, and Isaiah offers a sign in the form of a child's name: 'Emmanuel'. The prophecy asserts that before the child is weaned, the threat from the two kingdoms will evaporate. The re-use of this prophecy in Matthew's Gospel has a similar function: God's presence in the child Jesus will become the answer to the military threat presented by Rome. And according to Matthew's version of events, King Herod certainly perceives a political threat and therefore seeks to have Jesus killed.

The fact that Herod does not succeed is given a paradoxical twist at the end of the Gospel when, at the crucifixion, some Roman soldiers come to identify Jesus as the 'Son of God' (27.54). In Roman theology of the

---

14.   Howard Clark Kee, 'The Terminology of Mark's Exorcism Stories', *New Testament Studies* 14 (1968), pp. 232–46; Ched Myers, *Binding the Strong Man: A Political Reading of Mark's Story of Jesus* (Maryknoll: Orbis, 1988), pp. 190–94.

day, 'Son of God' was a title used especially of emperors.[15] So precisely at the moment when it seems that the empire at last succeeds in asserting its violent dominance, such power is disclosed as ultimately worthless. As the Gospel makes clear in many places, Jesus' alternative community has got nothing to do with tyrannical rule (Mt. 20.25).

Nothing in the life and death of Jesus corresponds to the violent motifs generated by Israel's messianic imagination. Matthew 2.6 does cite from Micah 5 and thereby reads Jesus as the fulfilment of that prophetic promise. But in Micah, the poetry suggests an imperial invasion which is then repelled as Israel's own empire asserts dominance over its aggressor:

> But you, Bethlehem of Ephratha, small among Judah's clans,
> From you shall come forth for me one to be ruler in Israel.
> His origin lies in former times, in ancient days... (Mic. 5.2).
>
> He shall stand and shepherd in the strength of Yahweh,
> In the majesty of the name of Yahweh his God.
> They shall dwell safely for then he will be great
>   to the ends of the earth.
> This shall be salvation from Assyria,
> when he comes into our land, and when he treads on our soil.
> We will set over him seven shepherds, and eight human chieftans.
> They will shepherd the land of Assyria with the sword,
> the land of Nimrod with the bared blade.
> He will deliver from Assyria,
> when he comes into our land,
> when he treads within our borders (Mic. 5.4–5).

Micah envisages a ruler arising from Bethlehem whose 'human chieftains' will dominate Assyria 'with the sword', yet retaliation with the sword is notably missing from the praxis of Jesus. The very meaning of messianic theology is under reconstruction in the Gospels, and one indication of this process are the texts such as Mk 8.30 in which Jesus prevents his disciples from making messianic claims on his behalf. The idea of the messiah is apparently being re-defined as non-violent (although this redefinition accords with broader developments within the prophetic tradition, as I have interpreted them in Chapter 6 above).

The theme of non-violence appears repeatedly in the parables and teachings, and not just in relation to the meaning of the title 'messiah/Christ'. In a less obvious example, it is conceivable that an earlier version of the parable recorded in Mk 12.1–12 contemplates the possibility of revolt only to

---

15. Tae Hun Kim, 'The Anarthrous *uios theou* in Mark 15.39 and the Roman Imperial Cult', *Biblica* 79 (1998), pp. 221–41.

dismiss the option as unrealistic. The parable sets up a scene of social conflict in which a wealthy landlord acquires a vineyard and lets it out to tenants while he travels abroad. In the economy of the day, this kind of investment was the prerogative of the elite, while the dependant labourer 'tenants' would have been in this situation most often as a result of debt slavery and dispossession from their land. The actions of the labourers described in the narrative escalate from ejecting the owner's emissaries to killing the son of the landlord, implicitly setting out options for violent resistance. The question 'What will the owner of the vineyard do?' (12.9) already implies the futility of these actions. Peasant revolts are inevitably crushed: 'He will come and kill those tenants and give the vineyard to others'.

Mark's version of the parable has already been developed allegorically by the Gospel writer in such a way that the recalcitrant tenants stand for the Jewish leaders in Jerusalem, and the 'beloved son' is Jesus himself who is to meet death at their hands, or rather, Roman hands. This allegory coheres with a 'post-Easter' view of events to such an extent that earliest version of the story has probably been overlaid with a layer of interpretation generated by the early church. One of the problems with this allegorical reading is that it creates a troublesome picture of God as a violent, absentee landlord—a theological problem to which we will return below.[16] Parables are, however, by their very nature susceptible of multiple interpretations.

William Herzog has provided a particularly illuminating possibility for understanding this parable in a pre-Easter historical setting. He suggests that there is special significance in the wording in v. 7 which refers to the 'heir' (*kleronomos*) of an 'inheritance' (*kleronomia*). The terminology carries a deep resonance with the narratives and laws describing the allotment of land as an 'inheritance' to the tribes and families of Israel. The tenants could lay claim to the tradition of prophetic critique that indicted the wealthy for 'adding field to field' as they expanded their estates and dispossessed the traditional owners (Isa. 5.8; Mic. 2.2). From this perspective, the tenants could be seen as taking divine judgment into their own hands, with sanctions ostensibly provided by scripture such as when it describes the punishment of Ahab for taking the ancestral landholding of Naboth's vineyard. Herzog puts the predicament of the tenants this way:

---

16. Barbara E. Reid, 'Violent Endings in Matthew's Parables and Christian Nonviolence', *Catholic Biblical Quarterly* 66 (2004), p. 253. See also W.D. Davies and Dale C. Allison, *Matthew*, III (Edinburgh: T. & T. Clark, 1997), p. 178.

'How can they reclaim their honourable status as heirs if violent revolts always end in futility? Are there other ways to assert their claims?'[17]

In answer to such questions, Herzog argues that the opposition to Rome and its agents is expressed in the Gospels with the subtle indirectness—the 'hidden transcript'—that is characteristic of chronic peasant resistance rather than spasmodic revolts.[18] Immediately following the parable of the tenants in Mark 12, for example, the question of resistance is implicitly raised once again in a question about whether Jews should pay tax to Caesar. Jesus feigns obedience with the language of compliance while, at the same time, contesting imperial authority: 'Jesus said to them, "Give to Caesar what is Caesar's and to God what is God's"'.

The parallel narratives that contain this story (Mk 12.13–17; Mt. 22.15–22; Lk. 20.20–26) suggest that Jesus is being goaded by the Pharisees and 'Herodians' into exposing the underlying resentment against the Roman poll tax, the *kensos*. When Jesus calls for a *denarius* in this story, he is not calling for an ordinary coin; the coin's inscription laid claims to the emperor's divinity, linking Roman power to its cult.[19] The Pharisees and Herodians inadvertently confess that they have conceded too much by the very act of carrying the coin and thereby being in a position to provide it for inspection. Instead of pointing out that Jesus has begged the question of what exactly would belong to Caesar, Luke is able to say, 'And astonished by his answer, they become silent'. The silence arises from the fact that Jesus' antagonists have incriminated themselves.

This kind of exchange is characteristic of the kind of resistance Jesus recommends. His approach often provokes shame, but he does not promote violence. The Sermon on the Mount in Matthew 5 presents a number of examples in vv. 38–42. Instead of accepting an ideal of retributive justice— 'eye for eye, and tooth for tooth' (Exod. 21.24)—Jesus presents alternatives. While translations of 5.39 sometimes read 'Do not resist an evil person', a better translation would be 'Do not retaliate', and what follows are examples of non-violent resistance.

'If someone strikes you on the right cheek, turn to him the other also' (5.39). What is implied here is striking with the back of the right hand,

17. William Herzog, *Parables as Subversive Speech* (Louisville: Westminster/John Knox, 1994), p. 113; cf. James D. Hester, 'Socio-Rhetorical Criticism and the Parable of the Tenants', *Journal for the Study of the New Testament* 45 (1992), pp. 27–57.

18. William Herzog, 'Onstage and Offstage with Jesus of Nazareth: Public Transcripts, Hidden Transcripts, and Gospel Texts', in Richard Horsley (ed.), *Hidden Transcripts and the Arts of Resistance* (Semeia Studies, 48; Atlanta: Society of Biblical Literature, 2004), pp. 41–48.

19. Herzog, *Jesus, Justice and the Reign of God*, pp. 219–32.

widely considered an insult in the Graeco-Roman world. To turn the other cheek would have been seen as a provocative gesture and an implicit challenge to be treated with dignity—to be struck as an equal. The second case is similar: if someone demands an outer tunic, and you give him your inner garment as well, your resultant nakedness would shame the oppressor and observer rather than yourself. In the third case, Jesus recommends that 'If someone forces you to go with him one mile, go with him two miles' (5.41). Walking a second mile would clearly exceed the Roman rules relating to this kind of compulsory public service (the *angareia*), thereby shaming the oppressor through a symbolic heightening of their power and implicitly challenging them to break their own law.[20]

In presenting his teachings, Jesus is constantly contesting the dominant interpretations of Israel's scriptures maintained by the high priestly families in Judea and by the Pharisees whose influence extended north into Galilee. This pattern of conflict in the Gospels is not an indication of narrowly religious concerns. Rather, the religious leaders spoken about as 'Pharisees', 'Sadducees', 'chief priests' and 'scribes' belong to elite and retainer groups. The interpretation of the Torah amongst these groups established standards of purity that were, for the most part, impossible for peasants to achieve. The Pharisees held that even outside the temple—for example, in relation to the domestic consumption of food—Jews were required to maintain standards comparable to the priesthood. In order to be 'clean', all food had to be tithed to the temple, whether it was domestically grown or bought in the marketplace. Purity strictures applied equally to the pots in which food was prepared and to the dishes on which it was served. All those who ate together similarly had to be in a state of purity, a requirement that Jesus regularly transgressed by eating with 'tax collectors and sinners' (e.g., Mk 2.15–17 and 7.1–23).

Jesus' offensive eating habits become the focus for a number of Gospel traditions. His politics of eating works symbolically to include precisely those who would be excluded by Pharisaic ideals. This reversal of conventions applies especially to his parabolic depiction of grand banquets to which the most unlikely guests are eventually invited, while the expected guests refuse to attend (e.g., Lk. 14.15–24). This reversal of expectations is not to be explained in terms of some nascent conflict between 'Judaism' and 'Christianity', which would be completely anachronistic, but rather in

---

20. See Hans Dieter Betz, *The Sermon on the Mount* (Minneapolis: Fortress Press, 1995), pp. 280–91; Walter Wink, 'Neither Passivity nor Violence', in W.M. Swartley (ed.), *The Love of Enemy and Nonretaliation in the New Testament* (Louisville: Westminster/John Knox, 1992), pp. 102–25.

terms of a fundamental tension between rulers and the ruled. Jesus takes the side of the poor and excluded in pronouncing judgement on the temple, its priests and the lay Pharisaic exponents of priestly models of purity. The parable presents an invitation to join the feasting within God's kingdom, but those 'otherwise preoccupied (such as with expanding their own property holdings) would find themselves excluded'.[21]

Ironically, it may well be the case that the Pharisees embodied their own form of solidarity and communal resistance to the imperial system. It has been suggested that they sought to preserve a clear Jewish identity, in the face of manifold threats, by focussing on the domestic sphere where a measure of self-determination was still possible.[22]

In some respects, there is an analogy here between the purity concerns expressed in Ezra and Nehemiah and the domestic concerns of the Pharisees. In both cases, elite Jewish groups promoted social visions that were blind to other groups within their own society. Sociologically minded New Testament scholarship has recently been concerned to highlight Jesus' solidarity with peasant groups and the poor, and more generally with people who were chronically marginalized by the purity codes, but the analogy with Ezra and Nehemiah points once again to the layering of imperial power and the complex ironies of resistance to it.

The analogy with Ezra and Nehemiah also suggests that we give some attention to the puzzles in the Gospels regarding Jesus' attitude to 'the nations/gentiles'. While nineteenth-century Christian missions were founded on the commission at the end of Matthew's Gospel to go into 'all the world and make disciples of the nations', this conclusion to the Gospel stands in some contrast to Jesus' encounter with the 'Canaanite' woman (or the 'Syro-Phoenician woman as she is called in the parallel story in Mk 7.24–30, which is more likely to have been her own self-description). The earlier traditions of Matthew represent Jesus as focused on 'the lost sheep of the house of Israel' (10.6 and 15.24). He responds only reluctantly to the foreign woman who Matthew identifies as 'Canaanite', no doubt precisely to evoke the ancient antipathies for Canaanites in the Torah. She represents 'primally unfinished business', as Jim Perkinson puts it.[23]

21.   Horsely, *Jesus and the Spiral of Violence*, p. 180.

22.   Anthony Saldarini, *Pharisees, Scribes and Sadducees in Palestinian Society* (Wilmington: Glazier, 2001), p. 213.

23.   Jim Perkinson, 'A Canaanite Word in the Logos of Christ', *Semeia* 75 (1996), p. 79. See further, Judith McKinlay, *Reframing Her: Biblical Women in Postcolonial Focus* (Sheffield: Sheffield Phoenix Press, 2004), pp. 96–111.

In both Mark and Matthew's versions of this story, Jesus implies that the woman is a 'little dog' (*kunarion*). An Australian reader may flinch at this point, recalling the colonial history of comparing Indigenous people with animals. But the woman twists the attempt at exclusion back on itself, suggesting a domestic scene where the puppies do indeed eat the scraps from the table. She re-inscribes herself within the sphere of the discourse that had been designed to exclude her, with the effect that her desire is answered. Her daughter is healed.

Some commentators worry that the Canaanite woman loses her dignity by, in effect, domesticating herself within the world as Jesus constructs it. But that judgment picks up on only half the story, since arguably it is the world of Jesus that is reconstructed more dramatically through this exchange. The faith of the 'Canaanite' woman has effectively deconstructed Jesus' ethnocentric presumptions to such an extent that in the development of Matthean tradition the Gospel comes to be prefaced with an introductory genealogy that includes four foreign women, and the conclusion provides a mission discourse that contemplates disciples from any nation.

Jesus' self-understanding is revealed in this narrative to be constitutively dialogical—willing to be shaped in conversation with the other. A greater danger is to arise much later in the history of biblical interpretation when the outcome of this conversation with the Canaanite woman is converted into a gospel that admits of no dialogical transformation. As we saw above in Chapter 1, it was characteristic of nineteenth-century missions to see themselves as in no need of such enrichment from Indigenous peoples.

Perhaps more problematic for the interpretation of the Gospels, however, is the fact that the non-violent resistance that Jesus embodies in his practice is potentially overshadowed by traumatic visions of divine judgment. Take, for example, the glimpse of eternal torture suggested by Mk 9.42–48, or the eagles gathered with the corpses at the coming of the 'Son of Man' in Matthew 24.28. In the case of Matthew 24, it may be that the apocalyptic language simply provides a set of metaphors for envisaging the demise of Rome, as Warren Carter suggests, with v. 24 alluding to Roman eagle emblems scattered among fallen imperial troops.[24] But as in the case of Mark 9, the rhetorical excess still seems to rest on the foundations of violent divine judgment:

> If your eye causes you to sin, pluck it out. It is better for you to enter the kingdom of God with one eye than have two eyes and be thrown into hell, where 'their worm does not die, and the fire is not quenched' (Mk 9.47–48).

---

24. Warren Carter, *Matthew and Empire*, p. 87.

God is envisaged to be acting with all the brute force that the historical Jesus relinquished. The triumph of divine *basileia* is conceived, apparently, through the symbolic heightening of imperial power.

A number of the Jesus traditions, however, make this contradiction paradoxical. For example, a speech in Mark's Gospel rejects the language of 'lordship':

> You know that those who are regarded as rulers of the Gentiles lord it over them, and their high officials exercise authority over them. It shall not be so with you. Instead, whoever wants to become great among you must be your servant, and whoever wants to be first must be slave of all (Mk 10.42–44 and Mt. 20.25–27).

If this paradox of the last being first is characteristic of the reign of God, then it is too simple to claim—as, for example, Warren Carter does—that 'the overthrow of imperial power co-opts and imitates the very imperial worldview that it resists. For Rome and God, the goal is the supreme sovereignty of the most powerful'.[25] It is quite clear from some of the Jesus traditions that the sovereignty of God is disclosed precisely in the renunciation of sovereignty, hardly an imitation of Rome's politics.

Another approach to this problem becomes possible if one distinguishes between the prophetic words of the historical Jesus, on the one hand, and the recollection of those sayings after the destruction of Jerusalem around 70 CE. A number of New Testament scholars have challenged the picture of an End-of-the-World Jesus by arguing that the texts that *do* possess an apocalyptic tone were not actually part of earliest traditions, since 'kingdom of God' language (as opposed to some of the 'Son of Man' sayings) usually communicates no apocalyptic content at all.[26] For example, when the kingdom of God is compared to leaven that is 'hidden' in flour, the image implies an agent that quietly works through the dough (Lk. 13.20–21). The comparison does not suggest a sudden and dramatic divine intervention, but rather, a covert transformation of the social order.

John Dominic Crossan has concluded that the early Gospel traditions are well aware of apocalyptic eschatology, but they are shaped precisely

---

25. Warren Carter, *Matthew and Empire*, p. 89; cf. p. 171.

26. See, for example, Marcus Borg, 'A Temperate Case for a Non-Eschatological Jesus', *Forum* 2 (1986), pp. 81–102; Robert Miller (ed.), *The Apocalyptic Jesus: A Debate* (Santa Rosa, CA: Polebridge Press, 2001).

in order to reject it. This seems to be the force of the following saying in Luke:

> The kingdom of God is not coming with things that can be observed; nor will they say, 'Look, here it is!' or 'There it is!' For, in fact, the kingdom of God is among you' (Lk. 17.20–21).[27]

While some scholars have attempted systematically to eliminate eschatological perspectives from their representations of the historical Jesus, a more plausible approach carefully defines the meaning of 'eschatology' in ways that are more compatible with Israel's earlier prophetic tradition than with the apocalypticism that took hold in Hellenistic times. N.T. Wright, for example, articulates this approach:

> Eschatology is the climax of Israel's history, involving events for which end-of-the-world language is the only set of metaphors adequate to express the significance of what will happen, but resulting in a new and quite different phase within space-time history.[28]

From this point of view, the historical Jesus is more a radical exponent of the prophetic traditions that engage with the present in light of the justice of God, without yet drawing on apocalyptic visions of history's collapse and ultimate divine judgment.

The New Testament visions of eschatological violence—which may not be part of the early Jesus traditions—arguably recapitulate a theology of *conquest*, transposed to the end of history, with the empire of God finally trumping any human construction of power and authority. An analogy might suggest itself here with Deuteronomy's theology of the 'ban' (discussed above in Chapter 5) in that judgment in these New Testament texts is seen to fall also on an unrepentant Israel.

Moreover, just as Deuteronomy 13 envisages punishment for any family members who compromise their exclusive loyalty to Yahweh, so also the teaching of Jesus at times opposes the 'family of God' to flesh-and-blood kin. In the one significant case where Jesus paradoxically claims to bear 'a sword' (Mt. 10.34), this is a metaphor for division within families as some become his disciples and others do not.[29]

There are, however, distinct limits to any analogy between apocalyptic judgment and Deuteronomy's violent ban on the Canaanites: if a literal

---

27. See John Dominic Crossan, *The Birth of Christianity* (San Francisco: Harper, 1999), pp. 305–16 ('Negating Apocalyptic Eschatology').

28. Wright, *Jesus and the Victory of God*, p. 208.

29. Mt. 10.35–38 and the parallel in Lk. 12.51–53 which eliminates the reference to a 'sword'.

sword is involved at all in Matthew 10, the disciples of Jesus are seen to be its victims rather than its bearers.[30] The disciples are instructed, for example, not to be afraid 'of those who kill the body but cannot kill the soul' (Mt. 10.28). When Luke describes Jesus' arrest, one of the disciples is rebuked for using a sword to cut off the ear of the high priest's slave. Instead of encouraging violent resistance, Jesus *heals* the injured slave (Lk. 22.49–51).[31]

The New Testament's representation of apocalyptic judgment could, however, be seen as in one way resolving a tension that had arisen in the prophetic traditions which saw successive empires acting as agents of divine judgment. The prophetic literature reflects an anxiety about the scenario where evil empires are punished by other empires who subsequently reveal themselves to be equally evil. Thus, for example, Assyria is first conceived as Yahweh's agent acting against Israel and then condemned for its own hubris (Isa. 10.1–19). As we saw in Chapter 6 above, the problem emerges most acutely in Jer. 5.1 where it is seen that the destruction of Judah would be unjust if there is any collateral damage to innocent persons. The idea that the *ruling classes* alone were responsible for national destruction is apparently not acceptable to Jeremiah, and by implication, no one wholly innocent can be found.

> Run to and fro through the streets of Jerusalem.
> Look around and take note.
> Search its squares and see if you can find *one person*
> who acts justly and seeks the truth,
> so that I may pardon Jerusalem (Jer. 5.1).

While the issue of divine judgment remains a vexed matter for theology, one conclusion in relation to the Gospels is clear: nothing in the Jesus traditions, whether 'early' or 'late', can provide a sanction for colonial violence. If final judgment is God's business alone, then human agencies are necessarily excluded.[32] No legitimate claim can be laid on a divine calling to do violence, even as part of a program of 'just war'.

---

30. Richard B. Hayes, *The Moral Vision of the New Testament* (San Francisco: HarperCollins, 1996), p. 333.

31. See Brendan Byrne, 'Jesus as Messiah in the Gospel of Luke: Discerning a Pattern of Correction', *Catholic Biblical Quarterly* 65 (2003), pp. 89–90: 'While the cutting off of the ear is mentioned in all four gospels and, in each version, receives a rebuke, only in Luke is the disciple's action elaborated in this way, and only in Luke is it reversed by Jesus' healing touch. The combined force of the two "sword" episodes [in 22.38 and 22.47–53] serves to reinforce the impression that Jesus' way is not that of physical violence, let alone armed revolt'.

32. Barbara E. Reid, 'Violent Endings in Matthew's Parables and Christian Nonviolence', *Catholic Biblical Quarterly* 66 (2004), p. 253.

Some postcolonial biblical scholars will find this kind of conclusion unsatisfactory, since they rightly insist that the discourses of the Gospels have in fact been drawn into colonialist violence, regardless of what may have been the case around the time of Jesus. And to make matters worse, it has been argued that the spirituality of John's Gospel becomes all-too-useful within colonial ideology, since it undermines the religious connections to particular territories or sacred sites, thus opening up a conception of space that is available for conquest and occupation. Jesus' conversation with the Samaritan woman in John 4 provides a paradigm example:

> 'Sir', the woman said, 'I can see that you are a prophet. Our fathers worshipped on this mountain, but you Jews claim that the place where we must worship is in Jerusalem.' Jesus declared, 'Believe me woman, a time is coming when you will worship the Father neither on this mountain nor in Jerusalem… God is spirit, and his worshippers must worship in spirit and in truth' (4.19–21, 24).

This 'spiritual' undermining of the sacred sites that were maintained by Samaritans and Jews alike could be interpreted, in the course of time, to be destroying the legitimacy of all territorially based religious traditions and opening the way to global religious pretensions (a thesis which has some analogies with the Deuteronomic imposition of uniformity in Israelite worship, discussed in Chapter 3 above, over against the multifarious locations of ancestral religion). Ironically, the most 'other worldly' of the canonical Gospels resonates, according to some critics, with the later imperial projects.[33]

In response to this postcolonial critique, I want to make a number of points. First, John's language can be read in its own historical setting as a discourse that counters the claims of Rome, and this underlying motivation should not be overlooked. As Fernando Segovia has argued, the Fourth Gospel lays claim to a higher authority in a divine 'counter-empire'.[34] All existing structures and mediators are relativized in this light, including the powers associated with the Jewish temple. The followers of Jesus had no

---

33.   Tod D. Swanson, 'To Prepare a Place: Johannine Christianity and the Collapse of Ethnic Territory', *Journal of the American Academy of Religion* (1994), pp. 241–63; cf. Musa Dube, 'Savior of the World but Not of This World: A Postcolonial Reading of Spatial Construction in John', in R.S. Sugirtharajah (ed.), *The Postcolonial Bible* (Sheffield: Sheffield Academic Press, 1998), pp. 118–35.

34.   Fernando Segovia, 'The Counterempire of God: Postcolonialism and John', *Princeton Seminary Bulletin* 27/2 (2006), pp. 82–99; 'The Gospel of John', in F.F. Segovia and R.S. Sugirtharajah (eds.), *A Postcolonial Commentary on the New Testament* (London: T. & T. Clark International, forthcoming).

'worldly' power to impose their convictions on anyone; that possibility only came to fruition centuries later when Christians acquired powers of state.

Biblical *texts* do not impose an ideology of themselves; they are drawn into ideological contests by particular agencies and formations of power. And even when all the hermeneutical agency seems to be weighted on one side, there are notable cases where biblical interpretation runs counter to the dominant colonial ideology.

As discussed in Chapter 1, for example, Maori biblical interpreters in Aoteroa New Zealand deliberately identified themselves as 'Jews' precisely because they wanted to oppose the dominant reading of the Bible proposed to them by Christian missionaries and colonial administrators. Such are the ironies of hermeneutics. Postcolonial interpreters of the Bible who extrapolate from the texts themselves—independently of what actual historical agents did with the texts—are adopting an approach that paradoxically overlooks the social and historical dynamics within which all interpretation is formed.

It is also is significant to note that, according to Johannine theology, God does not engage with the world abstractly. As was the case with Israel's theology of election, divine 'love of the world' retains the character of particularity. John 1.1–18 avoids the framework of messianic expectation supplied by Jewish tradition, and instead grounds Jesus' identity in cosmic origins: 'In the beginning was the Word (*logos*), and the Word was with God and the Word was God' (Jn 1.1). But this alternative Christology goes on to assert precisely the idea of *incarnation*, which undermines any rigid dualism between God and the world—the Word becomes flesh and 'dwells' in the world, not only full of grace and truth but also fragility and particularity. Whatever one makes of the other-worldly spirituality of the Fourth Gospel, the particularity of incarnational theology does not fit easily with the abstraction of space as conceived within colonial ideologies.

Concluding Reflections

To the extent that Johannine theology undermines traditional connections to ancestral country and sacred sites, it seems to move in a different direction from the earlier Gospel traditions that resist imperial dispossession from Israel's inherited lands and resources. Yet this tension between the four canonical Gospels may be eased to some extent if John's reticence towards sacred sites is seen to be a product of Jesus' critique of the temple and of the economic hierarchies that it represented at the time.

Jeffrey Staley has recently responded to the critiques of 'spiritual' detachment in John by emphasizing that the cultural *location* of the symbols in the Fourth Gospel partially constitutes their meaning. Quoting from Michael

Keith's and Steve Pile's *Place and the Politics of Identity*, Staley suggests an analogy between incarnation in John and the 'multiple spatialities' in post-modern geography that illustrate that 'the metaphoric and the real do not belong in separate worlds':

> the ground we stand on becomes a mongrel hybrid of spatialities; at once a metaphor and a speaking position, a place of certainty and a burden of humility, sometimes all of these simultaneously, some-times all of them incommensurably.[35]

I have no intention here of unpacking the intricacies of this theory-laden language, except to note that postmodern geography as it is described here is recovering some pre-modern themes.

This recovery bears some striking similarities, for example, to what has been called 'complex space' in recent theological discussions—the idea that societies encompass a range of communal contexts, 'intermediate bodies' with overlapping jurisdictions and loyalties that stand between individu-als and governing political powers. The idea of complex 'storied' space has been contrasted with the construction of 'smooth' or 'simple space' in the early modern era when, as William Cavanaugh puts it, there was

> an enfeebling of local common spaces by the power of the center, and a simultaneous parochialization of the imagination of Christendom into that of the sovereign state.[36]

Among other things, this would suggest that it is not so much the Gospel of John that was a catalyst for 'smooth space' ideology as was the mod-ern construction of state sovereignty. Clearly, the social location of reading communities plays a decisive role in how conceptions of space are under-stood in biblical interpretation.

The idea of spatial hybridity is suggestive of some recent attempts to explore the ways in which sacred and storied topography can be retrieved as part of Indigenous Christian praxis. The Choctaw theologian Steve Charleston has no difficulty saying, for example, that God became incar-nate within the people of Israel, and consequently their story is of primary

---

35. Jeffrey L. Staley, 'Dis Place Man', in Dube and Staley (eds.), *John and Postcolonialism*, pp. 42–43, referring to Michael Keith and Steve Pile, *Place and the Politics of Identity* (New York: Routledge, 1993), p. 23.

36. William T. Cavanaugh, 'Killing for the Telephone Company: Why the Nation-State is Not the Keeper of the Common Good', *Modern Theology* 20 (2004), pp. 251, 243–74; see especially John Milbank, *The World Made Strange: Theology, Language, Culture* (Oxford: Basil Blackwell, 1977), pp. 268–92; and cf. Michel de Certeau's discussion of storied space in *The Practice of Everyday Life* (Berkeley: University of California Press, 1984), pp. 115–30.

importance within the making of Christian identity.[37] But to say that Jesus is 'the Christ' is to interpret the meaning of his life in a particular location, beginning with the particular cultural mix of the first century—including the mixture of Judaism and Hellenism which yielded the language of *logos* to describe the being of Jesus as *antecedent* to Jewish expectations of a messiah. In the contemporary making of Christian identity, Jesus Christ is also Choctaw, Navajo, Cherokee and so on, and still becoming 'Christ' in dialogue with *these* antecedent Indigenous cultures—still becoming *intelligible* within a productive cultural hybridity.[38]

The humble business of biblical translation illustrates these issues quite clearly. To take an Australian example, when the Pitjantjatjara New Testament interprets the *logos* of Jn 1.1–18 as *tjukurpa*, the term encompasses a range of possible meanings, including the Aboriginal Dreaming or Law.[39] Here the meaning of *logos* is only comprehended in juxtaposition with the particularity of Pitjantjatjara sacred sites, which are themselves examples of 'multiple spatialities' that join the metaphorical and the real. Vernacular translation of the Bible necessarily generates a cultural hybridity that the translator cannot control. The notion that biblical texts will of themselves assert a particular ideology, regardless of the multiple agencies of interpretation or formations of power, does not take account of this complexity.

The study of the Gospels might be said to illustrate a point made by Homi Bhabha in one of his most frequently cited essays:

> If the effect of colonial power is seen to be the *production* of hybrid-
> ization rather than the noisy command of colonialist authority

---

37.   Charleston, 'The Old Testament of Native America', in S.B. Thistlethwaite and M.B. Engel (eds.), *Lift Every Voice: Constructing Christian Theologies from the Underside* (San Francisco: HarperCollins, 1990), pp. 49–61. Cf. David H. Turner, 'The Incarnation of Nambirrirrma', in T. Swain and D.B. Rose (eds.), *Aboriginal Australians and Christian Missions* (Bedford Park: Australian Association for the Study of Religions, 1988), p. 479.

38.   See John Wilcken, 'Christology and Aboriginal Religious Traditions', *Australian Catholic Record* 75 (1998), pp. 184–94, who relates this issue to the idea of the 'pre-existent Christ' behind the Jesus of history. Cf. Lamin Sanneh's discussion of how kinship language of the Yoruba was used to describe the 'cosmic Christ' (*Translating the Message* [Maryknoll: Orbis, 1989], pp. 182–84).

39.   See the wide-ranging discussion in Roland Boer, *Last Stop before Antarctica: The Bible and Postcolonialism in Australia* (Sheffield: Sheffield Academic Press, 2001), pp. 150–79, along with my critical review in *St Mark's Review* 192 (2003), pp. 43–44. For a parallel argument linking the *logos* of John 1.1–18 with a Native American 'Corn Mother' Christology, see Clara Sue Kidwell, Homer Noley, and George Tinker, *A Native American Theology* (Markyknoll: Orbis, 2001), pp. 76–84.

> or the silent repression of native traditions, then an important
> change of perspective occurs. It reveals the ambivalence at the
> source of traditional discourses on authority and enables a form
> of subversion.[40]

We may conclude from this chapter that the Gospels each illustrate their own forms of subversion of 'traditional discourses of authority', although these examples of subversive mimicry were themselves co-opted by successive Christian empires from Emperor Constantine onwards. It would be difficult to assert, however, that those later colonial discourses cohere with the most distinctive features of the Jesus traditions.

One would be justified in concluding that Mahatma Gandhi stood closer in some respects to the dynamics of Jesus' life and teaching than did his British colonial antagonists. Not only did Gandhi stand for the dignity of local culture (the local 'inheritance'), as does any postcolonial theology, but he also stood for a localized and anti-imperial economy. Postcolonial theology needs to regain this economic dimension of the early Gospel traditions. Rather than advancing simply an anti-imperial economy, however, the next two chapters will raise more complex possibilities for 'hybrid economies' within which the redemptive dimensions of local traditions may be combined with global networking.

---

40. Homi K. Bhabha, 'Signs Taken for Wonders: Questions of Ambivalence and Authority under a Tree outside Delhi, May 1817', *Critical Inquiry* 12 (1985), p. 65.

Paul and Hybrid Christian Identities

In Christ there is neither Jew nor Greek, slave nor free, male and female.

Galatians 3.28

In this chapter, we will examine Paul the radical interpreter of Judaism in the context of the imperial Roman regime under which he was eventually executed. As in the case of Gospels, I will argue that what is articulated in the apostle's letters is not a new religion, but a new social imagination that inevitably conflicts with the practices of empire. In Paul's case, however, the axis around which his theology turns is not the life and teachings of the historical Jesus, but rather, the death and resurrection of the cosmic Christ. Pauline ethics establish the priority of solidarity 'in Christ' and the construction of communities that embody cultural diversity, rather than conformity to an homogenous system of law. A key issue for Paul—and the focus of his 'conversion'—is how Gentiles come to share in the life of Israel 'by faith' without, at the same time, subjecting themselves to the dictates of Jewish ethnicity.

At the outset, it is worth noting an irony in the recent shift away from reading Paul through the Protestant lenses. Martin Luther is often credited with an interpretation of the Pauline letters which suggests that salvation is determined primarily by the 'existential' faith of the believer, rather than by the maintenance of religious law or tradition. Among the effects of this emphasis in the sixteenth century was not simply an opposition to Judaism, but also a diminishing of the metaphysical sanctions claimed by the hegemonic Catholic church. The Reformation then provided one set of ideological resources for the political changes that were to see nation states emerge eventually as modernity's ideal of government.

Protestantism was a major catalyst in the Western history of ideas leading up to modernity. There is a distinctly Protestant tint, for example, to the view that moral authority needs to be disengaged from all traditions and external standards because it is ultimately the 'inner voice' that determines our ethical convictions. The philosopher Charles Taylor has built a thorough case demonstrating that the common ground between Protestantism and modernity is in many respects more significant than the obvious differences between them.[1] To cut a long story short, the letters of the apostle Paul have been implicated in a number of disparate intellectual movements since the Reformation, and the extraordinary historical effects of the letters have far exceeded his own imaginings.

On the other hand, there has also been a strong tradition of using Paul's writings to sanction particular forms of oppression, notably in colonial defences of slavery. To mention just one of many examples, in a scholarly essay on 'Slavery in the Light of Divine Revelation' in 1860, the American theologian Thornton Stringfellow drew warrants not just from the Hebrew Bible but also from such texts as 1 Cor. 7.20–24 in the King James Version:

> Let every man abide in the same calling wherein he was called. Art thou called being a servant? Care not for it: but if thou mayest be made free, use it rather. For he that is called in the Lord, being a servant, is the Lord's freeman: likewise also he that is called, being free, is Christ's servant. Ye are bought with a price; be not ye the servants of men. Brethren, let every man, wherein he is called, therein abide with God.

Stringfellow regarded this text as 'applicable alike in all countries and at all stages of the church's future history', and accordingly 'each one should remain in the state in which he was called', including slaves.[2] The fact that Paul's epistles could be put to such purposes illustrates their ambiguous history of effects. Our discussion in this chapter will not attempt to dispel this ambiguity, but rather, I will propose an approach to Paul that locates the tensions in his thought against the political background of the Roman empire.

We need to acknowledge that letters are occasional writings not well suited to systematic theology, and indeed Paul's epistles in are full of examples of rhetorical argument addressed to particular communities under particular circumstances. Nevertheless, it is possible to describe some characteristic emphases in spite of the tensions that arise as a result of the contingencies of each letter.

---

1.   See especially Charles Taylor, *Sources of the Self: The Making of the Modern Identity* (Cambridge: Cambridge University Press, 1990).

2.   Thornton Stringfellow, 'The Bible Argument: Or, Slavery in the Light of Divine Revelation', in E.N. Elliot (ed.), *Cotton is King, and Pro-Slavery Arguments. Comprising the Writings of Hammond, Harper, Christy, Stringfellow, Hodge, Bledsoe and Cartwright on this Important Subject* (Augusta, GA: Pritchard, Abbott & Loomis, 1860), pp. 481–82.

Political Implications of a Cosmic Christ

When he writes to the Corinthian assembly 'I resolved to know nothing among you except Jesus Christ and him crucified' (1 Cor. 2.2) the claim is not so much literal as a rhetorical statement of priorities that reappears at many points in Paul's correspondence. Taken literally, the claim would be perplexing. In some respects, there was nothing distinctive about Jesus' death; his crucifixion simply reiterates the pattern of thousands of other deaths. This kind of execution was commonplace, especially for slaves, and it was designed to be a brutal instrument of imperial terror. For example, in urging a court to crucify four hundred slaves on the grounds that one of them had murdered their master, the Roman lawyer Gaius Cassius asserted that such people could never be restrained 'but by terror'.[3]

Paul's elliptical comment about 'knowing nothing' except the crucifixion of Jesus is part of his rhetorical strategy, which obscures certain aspects of the argument temporarily. A crucial underlying premise is that *force is not the ultimate reality*. As Neil Elliot puts it, 'This is an insight possible for Paul only in light of the resurrection, for the crucifixion alone would only rehearse, not expose, the logic of founding violence'. The death *and* resurrection of Christ, interpreted in cosmic terms, constitute the core of Paul's writings.[4]

The cosmic interpretation of Jesus' slave-death is, in the wider context of Paul's letters, designed to counter the claims of any worldly power. In this paradigm case, imperial terror fails to serve its oppressive purpose. It is not that Paul wants to condemn a particular miscarriage of justice, as other first-century writers do. Flavius Josephus, for example, records that Pilate was sent to Rome to answer charges that he had slaughtered unarmed Samaritan refugees in Tirathana (*Antiquities* 18.85–89). This is mentioned in Josephus' history without the implication that the incident undermined Roman legitimacy as such. In the case of Jesus, Pilate's crime was not a local injustice. According to Paul, the implications were 'apocalyptic': this particular death begins to unmask 'the powers of this world'. If the 'rulers of this age' understood the hidden spiritual reality, then 'they would not have crucified the Lord of glory' (1 Cor. 2.6–8).

---

3. Tacitus, *Annals* 14.42–45, quoted in G.E.M. de Ste Croix, *The Class Struggle in the Ancient Greek World, from the Archaic Age to the Arab Conquests* (Ithaca: Cornell University Press, 1981), p. 409. See further, Martin Hengel, *Crucifixion* (London: SCM Press, 1977).

4. Neil Elliot, 'The Anti-Imperial Message of the Cross', in R. Horsley (ed.), *Paul and Empire* (Harrisburg, PA: Trinity Press International, 1997), p. 181; cf. J. Christiaan Beker, *Paul the Apostle* (Philadelphia: Fortress Press, 1980), pp. 194–98, 205–208.

The reference to Jesus as the 'Lord of glory' adopts vocabulary which would have been understood in both religious and political terms, as illustrated by the hymns that were composed to honour the emperors in the first century. Modern readers who have become accustomed to distinguishing between political and spiritual matters have often failed to appreciate the political connotations of this language of worship, which appears prominently in Paul's writings and in the book of Revelation. The imperial ruler was variously called 'Lord' (*dominus*), 'holy one' (*sacer*), 'glory of the earth' (*terrarum gloria*), 'salvation' (*salus*), 'our Lord and God, Lord of the earth, Lord of the world' (*dominus et deus noster, dominus terrarum, dominus mundi*). The language of praise that saturates the New Testament is derived therefore not just from the Hebrew scriptures; it also sets up a dissonance with the vocabulary of the Roman court and cult. The cosmic claims of the imperial hymns were implicitly contested by Paul's apocalyptic views.[5]

It has sometimes been suggested that Paul's thinking cannot be characterized as 'apocalyptic' since the letters do not embody the characteristic concerns of apocalyptic literature (biblical examples of which are the books of Daniel and Revelation). Paul does not speculate, for example, on the timetable for the world's end, or provide descriptions of the heavens, angels and demons. But the key issue here is not whether the epistles as a genre of writing might fulfil criteria that belong to another genre of literature known as 'apocalypse'; the question is whether the convictions that underlie apocalyptic literature have shaped Paul's arguments. To avoid a merely terminological confusion, it may be more accurate to describe these convictions as 'cosmic' rather than 'apocalyptic'.

Clearly, he is aware of some of the speculations about the architecture of the heavens, since he claims to have been caught up to 'the third heaven' himself. Paul's own spiritual experience in this regard is said to defy articulation, and in any case, is of lesser value than the experience of grace in weakness (2 Cor. 12.1–10). His argument does not imply that the tours of the heavens in apocalyptic literature are entirely mistaken, but rather, that the cosmic visions described in the apocalypses are to be reinterpreted in light of Christ's weakness and crucifixion.

What Paul provides is a 'Christological' reinterpretation of ideas that had already been expressed in the Jewish apocalypses. In Daniel, for example,

---

5.   David Aune, *Revelation* (Waco: Word Books, 1997), p. 317, referring in particular to Rev. 4.11; 5.12–13; 6.10; 7.12; 12.10; 13.10; 19.1, 6. See especially the imperial hymns written by Statius and Martial discussed in Kenneth Scott, *The Imperial Cult under the Flavians* (Stuttgart: Kohlhammer, 1936) and Friedrich Sauter, *Der römische Kaiserkult bei Martial and Statius* (Stuttgart: Kohlhammer, 1934).

the empires of this world are symbolically represented in dreams and visions as giving way to each other in relentless succession until such time as

> the God of heaven will set up a regime that will never be destroyed, nor shall its sovereignty be left to another people. It will break in pieces all those kingdoms and bring them to an end, but it will endure for ever (Dan. 2.44).

For Paul, the cosmic struggle will come to an end when Christ 'has destroyed every regime, authority and power' (1 Cor. 15.24) and when *every* knee bows 'in heaven and on earth and under the earth' (Phil. 2.10).

Daniel is even willing to praise a Babylonian king as one who has been given 'dominion and power and might and glory', only to point out that this sovereignty is for a limited time (2.37–39). It is not that history will end or the earth be destroyed; it is rather that all the *temporary* sovereignties are to be superseded by a divine sovereignty.[6] Later in the book, Daniel's vision encompasses even the overcoming of death itself, in divine vindication of those who suffer at the hands of a king who desecrates the Jerusalem temple in the course of his program of persecution (Dan. 11.31; 12.1–2). Similarly in 1 Corinthians, when every regime is finally taken over by Christ, death itself is the final enemy to be destroyed (15.26).

Paul's choice of particular words often carries significant political implications. The Greek term *parousia*, for example, is used six times in Thessalonians with reference to Christ's apocalyptic 'arrival', and elsewhere in Paul only once (in 1 Cor. 15.23–24 where all powers submit to Christ in his second coming, as we have seen). Helmut Koester points out that *parousia* is not used in pre-Christian apocalyptic literature with this meaning, but it was characteristic terminology for the arrival of a king or emperor. In short, the letters to the Thessalonians are describing Christ's appearance in judgment in manner that implies a contest of power and authority with the Roman imperial order.

This is precisely the contestation that seems to be implied by1 Thess. 5.3, where Paul adopts a phrase that is well known in Roman propaganda—*pax et securitas*—but unknown in the Septuagint, the Greek version of the Old Testament:

> While people are saying 'peace and security' (*eirenē kai asphaleia*), destruction will come on them suddenly.

The term *aspheleia* ('security') is never used in the Greek version of the Old Testament to render *shalom*, the common Hebrew word for peace. Take

---

6.   John Goldingay, *Daniel* (Waco: Word Books, 1989), p. 60.

for example a text from the book of Jeremiah that articulates the similar theme of false peace:

> They have healed the wound of my people lightly, saying 'peace,
> peace' where there is no peace (Jer. 6.14).

The Hebrew text has '*shalom, shalom*' where there is no '*shalom*', and the Greek version has '*eirenē, eirenē*' where there is no '*eirenē*'. The term *aspheleia* translates other Hebrew terms that are used to express the 'security of cities' or 'safe conduct' guaranteed by treaties or military protection. Koester rightly concludes that in using the phrase *eirenē kai asphaleia*, 1 Thess. 5.3 is not alluding so much to the false peace articulated by Jeremiah but to the delusion of *pax et securitas* discourse and to Rome's impending destruction.[7]

In the case of 1 Thessalonians, the threat to Rome is more of a 'hidden transcript' than it is elsewhere in Paul's letters. But even in 1 Cor. 15.24 and Phil. 2.10 the prognosis for the imperial order has to be *inferred*. If Christ will in the end destroy 'all dominion, authority and power' and 'every knee will bow' to him, whether on earth or in the heavens, then we must presume that this universal scope includes the imperial powers indicted in apocalyptic tradition. These powers were seen as possessing both spiritual and physical aspects, without drawing a sharp distinction between the two dimensions.

This may not, however, have been the conclusion drawn by some of Paul's followers, since a number of later texts in the New Testament appear to indicate that the eschatological victory is primarily over the *heavenly* powers. For example, it is possible to detect in Ephesians the beginnings of a narrow spiritual conception of 'the powers', and by implication perhaps, a qualified perception of Christ's present sovereignty:

> For our struggle is not against enemies of blood and flesh, but against
> the rulers, against the authorities, against the cosmic powers of this
> present darkness, against the spiritual forces of evil in the heavenly
> places (Eph. 6.12).

Yet at other points, in both early and late letters, one finds a cosmic conception of Christ whose sovereignty is undivided and whose being sustains both the heavens and the earth:

> Indeed, even though there may be so-called gods in heaven or on
> earth—as in fact there are many gods and many lords—yet for

---

7.   Helmut Koester, 'Imperial Ideology and Paul's Eschatology in 1 Thessalonians', in Horsley (ed.), *Paul and Empire*, pp. 158–62; cf. Ernst Bammel, 'Ein Beitrag zur paulinischen Staatsanschauung', *Theologische Literaturzeitung* 85 (1960), col. 837.

us there is one God, the Father, from whom are all things and for whom we exist, and one Lord, Jesus Christ, through whom are all things and through whom we exist (1 Cor. 8.5–6).

> He is the image of the invisible God, the firstborn of all creation;
> for in him all things in heaven and on earth were created, things
> visible and invisible, whether thrones or dominions or rulers
> or powers—all things have been created through him and for
> him… For in him all the fullness of God was pleased to dwell, and
> through him God was pleased to reconcile to himself all things,
> whether on earth or in heaven, by making peace through the blood
> of his cross (Col. 1.15–16, 19–20).

Whatever differences may exist between the earlier and later Pauline epistles, there are a number of key issues in this literature that any post-colonial reading of the New Testament must address. In particular, I will focus on the discourse about the 'governing authorities' in Rom. 13.1–7, the paradoxical discussions of slavery, and Paul's distinctions between the ethics appropriate in the domestic sphere, or within the Christian community, as opposed to public contexts. A discussion of these topics will provide the necessary background for a fresh evaluation of Christian colonial ideology measured in Pauline terms.

The Governing Authorities in Romans 13

Romans 13.1–7 are some of the most difficult verses in the Pauline tradition to understand. This text seems to conflict with the apocalyptic expectations, already discussed, that include the demise of the Roman empire. As we have seen in 1 Cor. 2.8, 'the rulers of this age' are arrayed against God, and they have unknowingly crucified 'the Lord of glory'. Certainly, the dramatic symbolism in Revelation 13 depicts Rome as 'the beast' that opposes God and coerces worship of the emperor (Rev. 13.12). Yet Paul seems to endorse the authority of 'the state' in Romans 13 without reservation, which is at the very least ironic considering he was himself to be executed under the emperor Nero:

> Let every person be subject to the governing authorities; for there is
> no authority except from God, and those authorities that exist have
> been instituted by God. Therefore whoever resists authority resists
> what God has appointed, and those who resist will incur judgement.
> For rulers are not a terror to good conduct, but to bad. Do you wish
> to have no fear of the authority? Then do what is good, and you will
> receive its approval; for it is God's servant for your good. But if you
> do what is wrong, you should be afraid, for the authority does not
> bear the sword in vain; it is the servant of God to execute wrath on
> the wrongdoer (Rom. 13.1–4).

There are a number of clues in the surrounding context that suggest that this passage need not be taken purely at face value. First, the passage immediately preceding this one exhorts the assembly in Rome not to respond to evil with violent retaliation:

> Beloved, never avenge yourselves, but leave it to the wrath (*orgē*) of God; for it is written, 'Vengeance is mine; I will repay, says the Lord'. (Rom. 12.9)

Yet in the next breath, the earthly authority is said to bear the sword as 'the servant of God to execute wrath (*orgē*) on the wrongdoer' (13.4). It would seem to follow that the congregation—the *ekklēsia*[8]—cannot execute divine anger on a wrongdoer, but the state can. The followers of Christ would be excluded from being 'the servant of God' in this particular respect.

Another exhortation to the *ekklēsia* in 13.8 raises a similar issue, where Paul says '*owe* no one anything except love (*agapē*)'. In the immediately preceding verse, he has stated that his reader 'owes' tax to some, 'fear' to some, and 'honour' to others. The conventional ways of acknowledging authority—through taxation, fear, and honour—seem to be undermined by the claim in 13.8 that, fundamentally, it is really only the most indiscriminate form of love (*agapē*) that is owed to anyone.

A possible way to escape contradiction would be to suggest that payment of tax, fear and honour are all forms of *agapē*, but this approach is implausible since it would reduce *agapē* to a merely conventional system of ethics. We know from several other texts, which will be discussed below, that Paul sees 'the body of Christ' in *opposition* to the conventional systems of honour and status in the Graeco-Roman world. And he goes on to remind his readers of the fragility of the current conventions by referring to their apocalyptic situation: 'Besides this you know what hour it is...the day is at hand' (Rom. 13.11–12).

These puzzles in the immediate literary context of Rom. 13.1–7 only increase when we turn attention to the historical context of the letter. In contrast to the rhetoric of previous emperors who laid claim to their *pax* through war, examples of Nero's propaganda suggest that, under his rule, swords have been reduced to merely symbolic functions. According to the encomium found in the writings of Calpurnius Siculus, for example, this emperor 'has broken every maddened sword-blade', with his peace

---

8. The term *ekklēsia* is a common Greek word for a civic 'assembly' rather than a narrowly religious term. 'Church' is therefore a potentially misleading translation.

'knowing not the drawn sword' (*Eclogue* 1.45–65).[9] As Neil Elliot has argued, the overt message of Romans 13 does indeed caution against rebellion, but the prudently hidden message may be more complex. Paul's claim that the authorities 'do not bear the sword in vain' suggests that he does not succumb to Nero's ideology of the unbloodied, idle sword.

It is important to remember that in earlier apocalyptic tradition, the empires can be given 'dominion and power and might and glory' for a limited time (Dan. 2.37–39). Also, in the prophetic oracles of earlier centuries, it is not uncommon to find an empire designated as the 'servant' of Yahweh, even bringing judgement against Israel. Assyria, for example, is first seen as Yahweh's agent and then condemned for its own hubris (Isa. 10.1–19). Nebuchadnezzar, the Babylonian king, is seen as Yahweh's 'servant' for a period of judgment against Jerusalem (Jer. 27.6), and Cyrus the Persian king is designated a 'shepherd' who brings about the restoration of Jerusalem (Isa. 44.28). In this respect, there is nothing new in Paul's claim in Rom. 13.1 that authorities are 'instituted by God'.

The complex mixture of tradition, deference and paradox in Romans 13 is however suggestive, according to Neil Elliot, of the more cautious form of covert resistance that in modern anthropological studies has been termed the 'hidden transcript'. Elliot finds a first-century parallel to this concept in Philo's admonition to his readers in *De specialibus legibus* to avoid 'untimely frankness' and to adopt defiant speech only 'under circumstances that allow it' (2.92–94). The admonition follows on immediately from his discussion of Abraham's deference to the Hittites in Gen. 23.7 which Philo interprets to be motivated by fear rather than by respect: 'he feared their power at the time and their formidable strength and cared to give no provocation' (*Spec. leg.* 2.90). Inserted between this interpretation of Abraham's motives and Philo's admonition to avoid 'untimely frankness', we find this comparison:

> Again, do not we too, when we are spending time in the marketplace, make a practice of standing out of the path of our rulers and also of beasts of carriage, though our motive in the two cases is entirely different? With the rulers it is done to show them honour, with the animals from fear and to save us from suffering serious injury from them (*Spec. leg.* 2.91).

9. Neil Elliot, 'Romans 13.1–7 in the Context of Imperial Propaganda', in Horsley, *Paul and Empire*, pp. 201–204; J.W. Duff and A.M. Duff (eds.), *Minor Latin Poets* (Cambridge: Cambridge University Press, 1954), pp. 222–23.

The distinction between rulers and brutes is deconstructed, without explicitly saying so, by the *immediately preceding* interpretation of Abraham acting out of fear. [10]

Similarly, Paul seems to articulate the most accommodating deference to rulers in Rom. 13.1–7 while implicitly questioning Nero's ideology of the unbloodied sword, requiring followers of Jesus to prosecute no punishment of evil (12.9), and insisting that they 'owe' no one anything except love (13.8). The ambiguity is as complex as Jesus' question-begging recommendation regarding taxation: 'give to Caesar what belongs to Caesar and to God what belongs to God'. Just as Caesar's coins claim divine qualities for the emperor, so the 'governing authorities' in Romans 13 exercise vengeance when it properly belongs to God alone (12.9). While it must be conceded that this 'deconstructive' reading of Paul's intentions in Romans 13 does not enjoy a scholarly consensus, it is worth noting that there are several other difficult texts in Paul's letters that may be illuminated in a similar way, including the passages relating to slavery.

Slaves and Lords

Take for example the passage from 1 Corinthians that was claimed as support for the cause of slave owners in the nineteenth century, here rendered in a modern translation:

> Let each of you remain in the condition in which you were called. Were you a slave when called? Do not be concerned about it. Even if you can gain your freedom, make use of your present condition now more than ever. For whoever was called in the Lord as a slave is a freed person belonging to the Lord, just as whoever was free when called is a slave of Christ. You were bought with a price; do not become slaves of human masters. In whatever condition you were called, brothers and sisters, there remain with God (7.20–24).

Does Paul imagine that serving two masters is an easy balance of power to achieve? Or has an axe been laid at the base of the tree when he says 'do not become slaves of human masters'? Clearly, there is no incitement to slave rebellion here, but could this text be suggesting a deconstructive perspective within which, in the fulness of time, slavery would have no place in the church—that the church would move towards a paradoxical utopia wherein the liberated can only 'belong to the Lord'? If that scenario

---

10. Elliot, 'Strategies of Resistance and Hidden Transcripts in the Pauline Communities', in Horsley, *Hidden Transcripts and the Arts of Resistance*, pp. 113–17; E.R. Goodenough, *An Introduction to Philo Judaeus* (Oxford: Blackwell, 2nd edn, 1962), p. 57.

can be detected in the text, the followers of Paul who wrote Colossians and Ephesians excluded it, as we shall see.

The Israelite legal traditions had struggled with a similar issue and ended up drawing a distinction between Israelite and non-Israelite slaves, precisely because all Israelites belong to God:

> Because the Israelites are my slaves, whom I brought out of the land of Egypt, they shall not be sold as slaves are sold. You shall not rule over them with harshness, but shall fear your God. As for the male and female slaves whom you may have, it is from the nations around you that you may acquire male and female slaves. You may also acquire them from among the strangers residing with you, and from their families that are with you, who have been born in your land; and they may be your property. You may keep them as a possession for your children after you, for them to inherit as property 'for ever'. These you may treat as slaves, but as for your fellow Israelites, no one shall rule over the other with harshness (Lev. 25.42–46).

These verses provide the reasoning that lies behind the requirement that, unlike other slaves, all *Israelite* debt-slaves are to be released in the Jubilee year (25.41).[11] This differs from the manumission law in Deut. 15.12–18, which requires Israelite men and women to be released from slavery in the seventh year, the Sabbatical year, but both sets of laws establish the expectation of manumission.

It would seem to be a small, logical step to move from Jesus' radical reinterpretation of Jubilee tradition (discussed above in Chapter 8) to infer that slavery should not exist within the communities who seek to embody the kingdom of God. Yet neither the Gospels nor Paul take this step in unambiguous terms. Instead, the theological arguments are generally accommodated to the institutional arrangements of slavery—except in the congregational context of the gathered *ekklēsia*.

Thus, for example, the letter to the Colossians exhorts slaves to obey their master or 'lord' *as if* they were serving God, regardless of how the human lord may behave. Masters are required to act justly, and a wrongdoer will be judged, but not by the slave:

---

11. Bernard Lewis has pointed out that Islam 'prohibited the enslavement not only of freeborn Muslims but also freeborn non-Muslims living under the protection of the Muslim state'. It is precisely this ruling that motivated the importation of slaves: 'This gave rise to a vast expansion of slave raiding and slave trading in the Eurasian steppe to the north and in tropical Africa to the south of the Islamic lands' ('The Crows of the Arabs', in H.L. Gates [ed.], *'Race', Writing and Difference* [Chicago: Chicago University Press, 1986], pp. 111–12); cf. David Goldenberg, *The Curse of Ham: Race and Slavery in Early Judaism, Christianity and Islam* (Princeton: Princeton University Press, 2003), p. 200.

> Slaves, obey your earthly lords [*kyrioi*] in everything, not only while
> being watched and in order to please them, but wholeheartedly,
> fearing the Lord [*kyrios*]. Whatever your task, put yourselves into it,
> as done for the Lord and not for human beings, since you know that
> from the Lord you will receive the inheritance as your reward; you
> are slaves to the Lord Christ. For the wrongdoer will be paid back
> for whatever wrong has been done, and there is no partiality. Lords,
> treat your slaves justly and fairly, for you know that you also have a
> Lord in heaven (Col. 3.22–4.1).

If there is a counter-cultural suggestion in this passage, it would lie in the
claim that slaves have an inheritance. Legally speaking, slaves did not hold
property and therefore had no inheritance; they were themselves property
and could be inherited. A hidden theological premise in Colossians 3 is
spelt out more fully in Galatians where Paul says to the *ekklēsia*: 'So then
you are no longer a slave, but rather a son; and if you are a son, you are also
an heir by God's act of adoption' (4.7).

This premise makes more sense in the context of Graeco-Roman law
than that it does as an extrapolation of Jubilee tradition. Paul does not
presume a Sabbatical or Jubilee theology in which manumission may be
expected, with the effect that a former slave could return to the family
and ancestral inheritance (as in Lev. 25.41). On the contrary, the apostle
presumes that slaves are alienated from their kinship structures and have
no inheritance rights.[12] That condition of alienation, however, is overcome by divine adoption into the body of Christ, which is effected by faith
and baptism into Christ:

> You are all children of God through faith in Christ Jesus. For all of
> you who were baptized into Christ have clothed yourselves with
> Christ. There is neither Jew nor Greek, slave nor free, male and
> female; for all of you are one in Christ Jesus. And if you belong
> to Christ, then you are Abraham's offspring, heirs according to the
> promise (Gal. 3.26–29).

Yet this transformation into Christ's body seems to have yielded little
effect in terms of underlying social structures. Ethnicity, class and gender
remain relatively constant constructions of social order, in spite of their
spiritual irrelevance.

Colossians 3.11, for example, makes a radically egalitarian claim for the
church and then reiterates the most conventional of ethical requirements:

---

12. See Orlando Patterson, *Slavery and Social Death* (Cambridge, MA: Harvard
University Press, 1982), pp. 38–45; Jennifer A. Glancy, *Slavery in Early Christianity*
(Oxford: Oxford University Press, 2002), p. 133.

'Here there is no longer Greek and Jew, circumcised and uncircumcised, barbarian, Scythian, slave and free; but Christ is all and is in all'. The same chapter exhorts slaves to obey their 'earthly lords in everything', as we have seen above, requiring a similar code of obedience from women and children (Col. 3.18–4.1).

It may be that these household codes in the later Pauline literature represent a growing conservatism within the churches. It may equally be the case that the later household codes simply make more explicit the dominant attitudes of previous decades relating to proper conduct in the domestic sphere.[13] The earlier letters do however contain stronger statements of reciprocity in the case of husbands and wives, for example, in the letter to the Corinthians:

> For the wife does not have authority over her own body, but the husband does; likewise the husband does not have authority over his own body, but the wife does (1 Cor. 7.4).

Paul's letter to Philemon regarding the slave Onesimus involves a hint of the manumission theme, but this brief and personal exchange is notoriously heavy with ambiguity:

> I am appealing to you for my child, Onesimus, whose father I have become during my imprisonment. Formerly he was useless to you, but now he is indeed useful both to you and to me. I am sending him, that is, my own heart, back to you. I wanted to keep him with me, so that he might be of service to me in your place during my imprisonment for the gospel; but I preferred to do nothing without your consent, in order that your good deed might be voluntary and not something forced. Perhaps this is the reason he was separated from you for a while, so that you might have him back for ever, no longer as a slave but as more than a slave, a beloved brother—especially to me but how much more to you, both in the flesh and in the Lord (Phlm 9–16).

If Onesimus were a runaway slave, as some commentators have suggested, Paul does not give him the benefit of asylum accorded by the Torah:

> Slaves who have escaped to you from their owners shall not be given back to them. They shall reside with you, in your midst, in any place they choose in any one of your towns, wherever they please; you shall not oppress them (Deut. 23.15–16).

Paul's reticence in his letter to Philemon was hardened into policy by the early church when, for example, the Council of Chalcedon in 451 CE

---

13.   Glancy, *Slavery in Early Christianity*, p. 141.

forbade monasteries to accept slaves without first securing their master's permission (Canon 4).[14]

While early Christianity did little damage to the institutional arrangements of slavery, this is not to say that Christian attitudes to slaves are entirely lacking in distinctiveness. In the early second century, the governor of a province of Asia Minor reports that 'with the assistance of torture' he sought information about the Christian movement from two women slaves 'who were styled ministers' (*diakonoi*), 'but I could discover nothing more than depraved and excessive superstition'.[15] The torture of slaves was commonplace, and no legal redress was available to them, but what is remarkable in this text is its acknowledgement of the leadership role granted to these slavewomen.

This, and a great deal of other evidence, points to early Christian congregations being composed of mixed social groups, and although Paul on occasion criticizes a community's failure to live up to their spiritual standards, there is little doubt that the ideals within the church itself were far more egalitarian than what is evidenced in the surrounding culture. Paul repeatedly contravenes conventional indicators of honour and status by celebrating the 'weak' and the 'lowly' as God's agents who shame the strong (e.g., 1 Cor. 1.27–28). Accordingly, he chastises the Corinthians for celebrating the Lord's Supper so that 'one remains hungry and another gets drunk', humiliating those who have nothing (1 Cor. 11.21–22).

Even within the domestic sphere, hierarchical structures seem to be paradoxically 'subverted' at points, while simultaneously being maintained.[16] What happens to the master-slave paradigm when Paul recommends to the Galatians that they be 'slaves of one another' (5.13)? And what is the impact on the conventional household code of Eph. 5.21–6.9 when it is suggested, by way of introduction in 5.21, that the members of the community should 'be subject to one another out of reverence for Christ'? This cannot be construed as a revolutionary egalitarianism, but there is no license in the 'love patriarchalism' of these biblical texts for domestic abuse or violence.[17] As was suggested in the case of Rom. 13.8–10, love of 'the other' is

14. Glancy, *Slavery in Early Christianity*, p. 90. See further, John Byron, 'Paul and the Background of Slavery: The *status quaestionis* in New Testament Scholarship', *Currents in Biblical Research* 3 (2004), pp. 116–39.

15. Pliny the younger, *Epistulae* 10.96, cited in Glancy, *Slavery in Early Christianity*, p. 130.

16. Richard B. Hays, *The Moral Vision of the New Testament* (San Francisco: HarperCollins, 1996), p. 64.

17. The term 'love patriarchalism' was coined by Elizabeth Schüssler-Fiorenza, *In Memory of Her* (New York: Crossroad, 1983), p. 218.

a principle that potentially deconstructs every pattern of authority while it simultaneously embodies a 'fulfilment of the law'.

Agapē, Diversity and Solidarity

In 1 Corinthians 8 and 10, Paul explores another complex question relating to cultural accommodation—the question of eating meat offered to idols— and he once again proposes that love (*agapē*), in the context of ecumenical solidarity, provides the answer. He begins by noting that idols are ultimately vacuous, and once a person *knows* this, it may appear that there is no reason to avoid meat that has been offered to them. This seems to be the kind of knowledge that characterizes 'the strong' in Corinth, whereas 'the weak' have consciences that are still troubled by the contagion of idols (8.1–8). Paul's message to 'the strong' is to take care with the exercise of their free-dom. While freedom from the law may in principle mean that 'everything is permissible', not everything 'builds up' the community that is seeking the good of 'the other' (10.23; cf. 1 Cor. 8.1; Rom. 14.19). Accordingly, the apostle suggests that the strong should not partake of sacrificial food *in the temple* of a pagan god:

> For if anyone with a weak conscience sees you, who possess knowl-edge, eating in the temple of an idol, might they not be encouraged to eat that which has been sacrificed to idols? (8.10).

Nevertheless, Paul argues that in the marketplace or in domestic contexts there is no impediment to eating such meat, especially where the question of conscience has not been explicitly raised (10.25–30).[18] Questions of cul-tural accommodation, therefore, are not resolved by universal rules, applied without regard for context. Nor is freedom regarded as an absolute value for Paul. Rather, freedom is properly constrained by love, and it becomes the resource that enables the apostle to be 'a Jew to the Jews' and 'a Gentile to the Gentiles' (9.19–22). Thus, 1 Cor. 9.19 could even be translated, '*Because* I am free with respect to all, I have *made myself a slave* to all so that I might win more of them'.[19]

This metaphor of slavery is then supplemented with an athletic trope in 1 Cor. 9.24–27, where Paul ironically juxtaposes the indignity of the slave with the honour of the successful athlete:

---

18. Richard Hays, *First Corinthians* (Louisville: John Knox, 1997), p. 135.

19. Wolfgang Schrage, *Der Erste Brief an die Korinther*, II (Zurich: Benziger Verlag, 1995), pp. 338–39.

> Do you not know that in a race the runners all compete, but only
> one receives the prize? Run in such a way that you may win it.
> Athletes exercise self-control in all things; they do it to receive a
> perishable garland, but we an imperishable one. So I do not run aim-
> lessly, nor do I box as though beating the air; but I punish my body
> and enslave it, so that after proclaiming to others I myself should
> not be disqualified.

The borrowing of Hellenistic athletic imagery—precisely when naked athletic contests had been so offensive to Jews—provides an illustration of the way in which Paul is constructing a hybrid Christian identity which is neither purely Jewish nor purely Gentile.[20] Another example is provided by his argument against the imposition of Jewish law on Gentiles in Galatians 5, where Paul appropriates a catalogue of virtues and vices which—with the exception of *agapē*—is already well known in Hellenistic philosophy (5.19–23).[21]

In seeking to be less 'ethnocentric', his monotheism is compelled to be less prescriptive of Jewish identity markers and more accommodating of the surrounding Hellenised cultures. Paul envisages the body of Christ making space for diverse ethnicities 'not by erasing ethnic and cultural differences but by *combining these differences into a hybrid existence*'.[22] Accordingly, Paul is able to circumcise Timothy, whose mother was Jewish (Acts 16.1–3; cf. Rom. 3.1–2), although he resists circumcision for Gentiles in Galatians along with other requirements of the Torah. It is not that he resists only the ceremonial law while retaining the ethics, as has often been supposed; as he says in Gal. 5.18, 'If you are led by the Spirit, then you are not under law'.

The signature theme in Gal. 3.28, 'In Christ there is neither Jew nor Greek, slave nor free, male and female', implies a limiting of the hegemonic religious control that Jewish identity once possessed for Paul, and a validation of Gentile ethnicities within the household of faith. When status indicators are declared irrelevant, there is a consequential loss of

---

20. See Victor J. Pfitzner, *Paul and the Agon Motif* (Leiden: Brill, 1967), pp. 188–89, 194; Robert Paul Seesengood, 'Hybridity and the Rhetoric of Endurance: Reading Paul's Athletic Metaphors in a Context of Postcolonial Self-Construction', *The Bible and Critical Theory* 1/3 (2005), pp. 1–23; cf. Troels Engberg-Pedersen, *Paul and the Stoics* (Edinburgh: T. & T. Clark, 2000), pp. 33–44, 294.

21. Hans Dieter Betz, *Galatians* (Philadelphia: Fortress Press, 1979), pp. 281–83.

22. Sze-kar Wan, 'Does Diaspora Identity Imply Some Sort of Universality? An Asian-American Reading of Galatians', in Fernando Segovia (ed.), *Interpreting beyond Borders* (Sheffield: Sheffield Academic Press, 2000), pp. 126–27.

status for free men, and a corresponding increase for women and slaves.[23]
In this respect, the hymn in Phil. 2.5–8 is more relevant for the 'strong'
than it is for the 'weak':

> Let the same mind be in you that was in Christ Jesus,
> who, though he was in the form of God,
> did not regard equality with God
> as something to be exploited,
> but emptied himself [*kenosis*],
> taking the form of a slave,
> being born in human likeness.
> And being found in human form,
> he humbled himself
> and became obedient to the point of death—
> even death on a cross.

We may conclude, then, that the Pauline vision entails the 'self-emptying'
of the strong (*kenosis*) and the 'building up' of the weak (*oikodomē*), a social
imagination that characterizes life 'in Christ'.[24] Yet this vision also assumes
a considerable accommodation to surrounding cultures, in some cases to
the extent that it seems to conflict with the signature themes of Paul's gospel. Christian ethics do not emerge from the Pauline literature as *distinct*
from the surrounding cultural environment; rather the literature suggests
that Christian identity will always be culturally hybrid, constrained only by
the 'meta-norms' of solidarity in Christ and love of others. As David Horrell
has suggested, meta-norms provide the framework within which cultural
norms, values and customs 'can be articulated and practised'.[25] Measured
against those Pauline meta-norms, however, the particular prescriptions of
the 'household codes' emerge as, at best, examples of cultural hybridity, and
at worst, examples of incoherent syncretism.

---

23. Cf. Antoinette Wire, *The Corinthian Women Prophets* (Minneapolis: Fortress
Press, 1990), pp. 62–71.

24. On the 'construction' of community through love (verb *oikodomein* or noun
oikodomē), see especially 1 Cor. 14.3–5, 12, 17, 26; Rom. 14.19; 15.2; 2 Cor. 12.19;
13.10; 1 Thess. 5.11.

25. David Horrell, *Solidarity and Difference* (London: T. & T. Clark International,
2005), pp. 99–100, 274. Horrell follows Seyla Benhabib in defining a meta-norm as 'one
which determines the moral framework within which other norms, values and customs
can be articulated and practised'. See Benhabib, *Situating the Self* (Cambridge: Polity
Press, 1992), p. 45.

Body and Spirit

In his influential book *A Radical Jew: Paul and the Politics of Identity*, Daniel Boyarin argues that Paul's account of solidarity in Christ reflects an accommodation to Hellenism that has gone too far:

> Paul was motivated by a Hellenistic desire for the One, which among other things produced an ideal of a universal human essence beyond difference and hierarchy. This universal humanity, however, was predicated (and still is) on the dualism of the flesh and the spirit, such that while the body is particular, marked through practice as Jew or Greek, and through anatomy as male or female, the spirit is universal.[26]

Boyarin's particular concern is with the compromise of Jewish identity, and we will return to this issue below. Here, however, I want to suggest that a dualism of spirit and body is disturbingly confirmed in the chilling logic of Ignatius, Bishop of Antioch, around the end of the first century who opposed the use of church funds to redeem slaves:

> Do not be haughty to male or female slaves, yet do not let them be puffed up. Let them rather endure slavery to the glory of God, that they may obtain a better freedom from Christ. Let them not desire to be set free at the church's expense, that they be not found the slaves of desire. [27]

Clearly, Ignatius feels compelled to combat something that was actually taking place, but such an argument only makes sense when, with Hellenistic reasoning, spirit and body have been sharply distinguished; spiritual slavery has rendered the embodied distress of slavery as being of secondary importance. As we saw in Chapter 3, this kind of split thinking has severed the theology of salvation from its roots in the Hebrew Bible where redemption for slaves meant restoration to kin and ancestral country.

It is by no means clear, however, that Paul himself promotes such split thinking. Ignatius' interpretation is made possible, in part, because unity in Christ is for Paul decisively a matter of the body. In Phil. 3.10, he talks about 'knowing Christ' through participation in his suffering. This idea is reiterated in several other texts such as Col. 1.24 and 1 Pet. 4.13, and in a different way by 2 Cor. 11.23–30 where Paul provides a catalogue of bodily hardship as evidence of his commitment to Christ before *contrasting* this with a mystical experience in 'the third heaven' (2 Cor. 12.1–10).

---

26.   Daniel Boyarin, *A Radical Jew: Paul and the Politics of Identity* (Berkeley: University of California Press, 1994), p. 7; cf. p. 52.

27.   Quoted in Glancy, *Slavery in Early Christianity*, pp. 151–52; cf. p. 129.

In response to Boyarin, the Croatian theologian Miroslav Volf summarizes this point well: 'The Pauline move is not from the particularity of the body to the universality of the spirit, but from separated bodies to the community of interrelated bodies'. Accordingly, Volf argues that 'the body of Christ lives as a complex interplay of differentiated bodies—Jewish and gentile, female and male, slave and free—of those who have partaken of Christ's self-sacrifice'.[28]

This point, however, is heavily ambiguous when read in light of the histories of Christian colonial expansion, since a 'community of suffering' can just as easily underwrite an oppressive social order as oppose it. The Christian religion has provided rich resources for reinforcing unjust social and economic structures through the sanctification of injustice. 1 Peter 2.18–21 provides a case in point:

> Slaves, accept the authority of your masters with all deference, not only those who are kind and gentle but also those who are harsh. For it is to your credit if, being aware of God, you endure pain while suffering unjustly. If you endure when you are beaten for doing wrong, where is the credit in that? But if you endure when you do right and suffer for it, you have God's approval. For to this you have been called, because Christ also suffered for you, leaving you an example, so that you should follow in his steps.

Solidarity in Suffering

In some historical circumstances of oppression, explicit resistance can only be muted, or take the form of 'hidden transcripts', and solidarity in suffering is the only viable strategy for survival. In other circumstances, prophetic resistance may be possible. In his book *Torture and the Eucharist*, for example, William Cavanaugh discusses more recent experience in Chilé during the 1980s when the Catholic Church gradually extracted itself from an accommodation to the State and its oppressive practices under General Pinochet. Elements of that accommodation can be traced back to a colonial agreement between the Spanish Crown and the Church, but subsequent theological thought had only hardened the demarcation between 'temporal' and 'spiritual' jurisdictions.[29]

Cavanaugh's central argument is that torture and the Eucharist are competing exercises of social imagination: torture seeks to dismember every

28. Miroslav Volf, *Exclusion and Embrace* (Nashville: Abingdon Press, 1996), pp. 47–48.

29. William T. Cavanaugh, *Torture and Eucharist: Theology, Politics, and the Body of Christ* (Oxford: Blackwell, 1998), p. 124.

social body which stands between the individual and the State, isolating the individual in space and time, while the Eucharist does the opposite. It knits together into one body the pain of the world. A watershed event in the Church's capacity to embody the social imagination of the Eucharist came in May 1980 when the Catholic bishops' Permanent Committee issued a document entitled 'I am Jesus, Whom You Are Persecuting', alluding to the conversion experience of the apostle Paul (Acts 9.5).[30] The bishops then moved to excommunicate torturers. This is one of the many examples where the church has orientated its praxis around a cosmic Christ whose suffering expresses solidarity with victims, not in order to provide an opiate for suffering, but rather, to take a prophetic stand against oppressive power.

Another example is provided by the South African *Kairos Document* (1985), which shaped the church's resistance to apartheid. Opposition theologians condemned the 'State Theology' of the apartheid regime which 'canonizes the will of the powerful' by misusing biblical texts for their own purposes, including 'the use of Rom. 13.1–7 to give absolute and "divine" authority to the State'.[31]

Some interpreters still doubt, however, whether this kind of emancipatory impetus can be discerned in the writings of Paul, even in his most deconstructive moments. Reading in the wake of nineteenth-century conflation of Christianity and 'civilization', and earlier examples of the use of force in colonial settlement, pogroms against Jews, or the Crusades, it is especially relevant here to reflect on Paul's comments on the 'governing authorities'. It would not be enough to provide a subtle reading of Rom. 13.1–7 and conclude (rightly in my view) that the idea of a 'Christian state' would be oxymoronic from the perspective of Pauline theology.

There is an imperialism inherent in the theology of a cosmic Christ which takes on a new significance when it is transformed from a strategy of resistance in the early Christian centuries into a means of legitimating the holy Roman empire. After Constantine, when the monopoly of force was extended from the metaphysical to the political domain, the 'relativising' of Jewish identity within Pauline theology was open to abuse.

30.   Cavanaugh, *Torture and the Eucharist*, pp. 15, 116, 280.
31.   Robert McAfee Brown (ed.), *Kairos: Three Prophetic Challenges to the Church* (Grand Rapids: Eerdmans, 1990), p. 29.

Concluding Reflections: Tolerance is Not Assimilation

According to the Jewish scholar Daniel Boyarin, when Paul reduced distinctively Jewish practices such as circumcision and food laws to matters that pertain only to Jews, his tolerance amounts to *intolerance*; the essential particularities of identity are 'reduced to a matter of taste'.[32] Boyarin is quite willing to recognize the limitations of Jewish ethnocentrism in certain circumstances, as well as the necessity of cultural hybridity in ethnic identity. But he has a justifiable suspicion of Christian tendencies towards 'coercive universalism', especially as it came to be expressed by Christian empires. He has his own reformation of Judaism in mind:

> somewhere in the dialectic between the Pauline universalized human essence and the rabbinic emphasis on Israel a synthesis must be found, one that will allow for stubborn hanging on to ethnic, cultural specificity but in a context of deeply felt and enacted human solidarity. For that synthesis, Diaspora provides the model, and only in conditions of Diaspora can such a resolution be attempted. Within the conditions of Diaspora, many Jews discovered that their well-being was absolutely dependent on the principles of respect for difference.[33]

Although Judaism has historically revolved around a tension between ideas of genealogical descent and ideas of divinely given territory, Boyarin's proposal implies that genealogy should be given priority over possession of territory, and ethnicity should be separated from all forms of political hegemony. He reclaims the perspective of Rabbinic Judaism that renounced the land until the final redemption and provided the Diaspora model of solidarity without coercion. Boyarin also goes a step further: noting that the Bible makes no claim to Israel's autochthony, he relentlessly draws out the consequences in his model for the

> renunciation of sovereignty, autochthony, indigeneity (as embodied politically in the notion of self-determination), on the one hand, combined with a fierce tenacity in holding onto cultural identity, on the other.[34]

The model of Diaspora has also enjoyed a revival amongst those who are attempting to wrest Christian theology from the ideology of Christendom, and it is no accident that this entails a reconsideration of Christian

---

32. Boyarin, *A Radical Jew*, p. 32.
33. Boyarin, *A Radical Jew*, p. 257.
34. Boyarin, *A Radical Jew*, p. 259.

dependence on Judaism. An influential theologian in this connection has been John Howard Yoder, whose collection of essays in *The Jewish–Christian Schism Revisited* is indicative of arguments that he presented over many years. Yoder sees an analogy between Diaspora Judaism and the pacifist left-wing churches of the Reformation:

> Occasionally privileged after the model of Joseph, more often emigrating, frequently suffering martyrdom non-violently, they were able to maintain identity without turf or sword, community without sovereignty. They thereby demonstrated pragmatically the viability of the ethic of Jeremiah [Jer. 29.4–7] and Jesus. In sum, the Jews of the Diaspora were for over a millennium the closest thing to the ethic of Jesus existing on any significant scale anywhere in Christendom.[35]

As we noted above in relation to *kenosis*, however, it is worth reflecting on whether the Diaspora principle can be universalized without attention to particular circumstances. For example, 'territory' is not such a negotiable item in the construction of the social identity of *Indigenous* Christians.[36] Certainly in the Australian context, it is difficult to see how they could renounce any claim to sovereignty over traditional lands and still remain Indigenous. As we have seen, the historical presumption that Aboriginal people could sever ties with their traditional lands proved all too convenient for colonial interests. The state-sponsored policies of assimilation, the calculated severing of kin and country, have analogies with Cavanaugh's description of torture as seeking to *dismember every social body that stands between the individual and the State*.

One of the key challenges for a postcolonial faith can be articulated in Pauline terms. The 'strong' or dominant groups, in Australia for example, who have habitually seen the land as *terra nullius*, will need to make space for the particular identities of the 'weak' and marginalized. In the first instance, it would be non-Indigenous Australian Christians who need to

---

35. John Howard Yoder, *The Jewish–Christian Schism Revisited* (Notre Dame: Shalom Desktop, 1996), p. 60; cf. Daniel Smith-Christopher, *A Biblical Theology of Exile* (Minneapolis: Fortress Press, 2002), pp. 189–203; Douglas Harink, *Paul among the Postliberals: Pauline Theology beyond Christendom and Modernity* (Grand Rapids: Brazos Press, 2003), pp. 151–207.

36. See Patrick L. Dodson, Jacinta K. Elston and Brian F. McCoy, 'Leaving Culture at the Door', *Pacifica* 19/3 (2006), p. 254, and compare Kevin Vanhoozer's critique of the theological requirement of 'a kind of *kenosis*' of anything distinctive to a culture in his essay, 'One Rule to Rule Them All?', in C. Ott and H.A. Netland (eds.), *Globalizing Theology: Belief and Practice in an Era of World Christianity* (Grand Rapids: Baker Academic, 2006), p. 100.

appropriate a self-understanding as a Diaspora group. The self-limiting and space-making practices of *'kenosis'* are not simply reducible to an existential attitude, or to a civic rhetoric of multiculturalism; in many areas of Australia, *kenosis* will imply 'giving up' land that properly belongs to the First Nations. Certainly, churches who preach a theology of exile and Diaspora will need to provide this language with some economic coherence—especially the Australian churches with historic grants of land from the Crown who are therefore beneficiaries of Aboriginal dispossession. A 'decolonizing' church will be exploring how a diversity of cultural values can be embraced by the Pauline 'meta-norms', beginning with an embracing (rather than an assimilation) of the distinctive land-based cultural values of the first Australians.

Another set of issues arise, of course, where those 'others' do not freely join in the solidarity offered by the body of Christ. What does Paul's multicultural vision mean for the Jews, or members of other religious traditions, who remain unconvinced by the Christian gospel? This is an issue that will be considered in a much broader theological framework in our next chapter, but a number of points can be briefly introduced at this stage.

First, Paul is able to detect the grace of God at work even in Israel's *unbelief*, so that he is able to say in Romans 11 that Jews are loved on account of their ancestors, since God's gifts are 'irrevocable'. As a consequence, unbelief is in fact no obstacle to the universal offer of divine grace (Rom. 11.29–32). Paul draws this argument to conclusion by suggesting that the church is to witness to that divine grace but must draw back from the pretence of understanding or controlling it:

> O the depth of the riches and wisdom and knowledge of God!
>> How unsearchable are his judgements and how inscrutable his
>> ways!
> 'For who has known the mind of the Lord?
> Or who has been his counsellor?'
> 'Or who has given a gift to him,
> to receive a gift in return?' (Rom. 11.33–35, citing Isa. 40.13).

John Barclay infers from this argument that 'Paul partially deconstructs his own Christological exclusivism by the pervasive appeal to the grace of God'.[37]

---

37.   John M.G. Barclay, '"Neither Jew nor Greek": Multiculturalism and the New Perspective on Paul', in M.G. Brett (ed.), *Ethnicity and the Bible* (Leiden: Brill, 1996), p. 213. Cf. Jacques Derrida's reference to 'negative theology' as the *'kenosis* of discourse', in Jacques Derrida, *On the Name* (Stanford: Stanford University Press, 1995), p. 50.

Romans 11 opens up a number of questions as to the nature of an 'inclusive' Christology and monotheism. As we saw in Chapter 3, 'El' was an Indigenous Canaanite name for God which, by a process of historical fusion, became another name for Yahweh, the one God of Israel. The concept of inclusive monotheism accommodates this historical fact, even though the self-perceptions of Israelite identity—as constructed generally in Deuteronomic theology—came to deny it. But at many points, Israelite theologians themselves called into question their own ability to articulate the mysteries of God—for example, in Isa. 40.13, the text that Paul reiterates in Rom. 11.34. The very question 'For who can know the mind of the Lord?' necessarily disables a privileged human grasp on divine reality.

An inclusive Christology would take a less anthropocentric approach to understanding faith, consistent with the growing number of scholars who interpret the key phrase *pistis christou* (for example in Rom. 3.22 and Gal. 3.22) as 'faithfulness *of* Christ', rather that 'faith *in* Christ'. The emphasis then falls on the reality of God's cosmic action in Jesus Christ, and participating in it through the mystery of Spirit, rather than on establishing a threshold test for salvation.[38]

This is not to deny that Christian identity turns on the revelation of God in Jesus of Nazareth. It does not follow, however, that the cosmic Christ can be exhaustively grasped through faith in the historical Jesus. Romans 8.22 says that 'all creation has been groaning' in anticipation of redemption, and Paul goes on to say that human participation in this wider process is so far beyond our knowledge that the Spirit necessarily 'intercedes for us with groans that words cannot express' (8.26). This is another indicator of the limits of human perception.

An inclusive Christology would infer from Rom. 8.26 that the full reality of the cosmic Christ remains unknown, but it would at least explore the relationship between the cosmic Christ in the New Testament and the independent witness to the Creator in the Hebrew Bible. Beyond that, it may ask whether the intimations of 'natural theology' in the Hebrew Bible—the disclosure of the divine in creation itself—would be compatible with the engagement of other religious traditions with the same Creator Spirit (cf. Rom. 2.12–16). Such questions suggest an agenda for postcolonial theology, rather than a 'biblical theology' narrowly conceived. The Bible itself provides no systematic guidance on

---

38. See Richard Hays, '*Pistis* and Pauline Christology: What Is at Stake?', in Elizabeth Johnson and David M. Hay (eds.), *Pauline Theology*, IV (Atlanta: Scholars Press, 1997), pp. 35–60; Harink, *Paul among the Postliberals*, pp. 25–65.

how to evaluate the diversity of its voices, and as we shall see in the next chapter, the answers provided in Western Christian tradition will be inadequate in non-Western contexts.[39] In addressing these wider issues, the Pauline literature will necessarily take its place alongside other theological perspectives.

39. This point has long been stressed by 'contextual' theologians. For recent discussions, see for example Kevin Vanhoozer, 'One Rule to Rule Them All?', in Ott and Netland, *Globalizing Theology*, pp. 85–126; Gerald O. West, 'Contextual Bible Study in South Africa: A Resource for Reclaiming and Regaining Land, Dignity and Identity', in G.O. West and M.W. Dube (eds.), *The Bible in Africa: Transactions, Trajectories and Trends* (Leiden: E.J. Brill, 2000), pp. 594–610.

Postcolonial Theology and Ethics

> He has brought down the mighty from their thrones
> and lifted up the lowly.

Luke 1.52

The preceding chapters have illustrated the multiple ironies at work when the Bible has been appropriated within colonial discourses, since the biblical traditions were themselves shaped by voices subject to the shifting tides of ancient imperial powers. Indeed, among the soundings we have taken in the biblical tradition, the resistance to empire has been a constantly reiterated theme. In re-reading these traditions, we have critically examined 'the contestation of meaning, the shaping of the imagination and the changing power relations' as any postcolonial theology will need to do.[1] But beyond the mere description of identity politics, why should such interpretive work be undertaken? What are the assumptions that lie behind postcolonial critique, and—apart from taking sides in cultural conflicts long past—what purposes does it serve?

The fact that such 'practical' questions are raised at the outset of this chapter is already indicative of a certain pragmatic tone in postcolonial studies. For example, instead of providing a purely descriptive history of ancient Israel and early Christianity, this book has approached the historical issues in light of questions raised by colonial uses of the Bible many centuries later, focussing on the themes of indigeneity and dispossession. It does not follow, however, that the discussion has been flagrantly anachronistic, or that it has explored particular biblical texts only 'because of the effect they have on us, not because of the source they came from'.[2] But it is clear that the history of those effects (especially the deleterious effects)

---

1. Kwok Pui-lan, *Postcolonial Imagination and Feminist Theology* (Louisville: Westminster John Knox, 2005), p. 205.

2. Richard Rorty, 'What is Religion's Future after Metaphysics?', in Santiago Zabala (ed.), *The Future of Religion: Richard Rorty and Gianni Vattimo* (New York: Columbia University Press, 2005), pp. 60–61.

provides good reason to re-examine the sources and contexts from which biblical texts emerged.

A leading proponent of postcolonial studies, the Palestinian literary critic Edward Said, regularly drew a sharp distinction between 'worldly' and 'theological' criticism in part because he rejected the colonial violence that has been underwritten by the Western tradition of metaphysics.[3] I have tried to show that such a sweeping dismissal of theology is not justified by a careful reading of the Bible. We do not have to wait for the recent attacks on metaphysics to encounter theological criticism of colonialism.[4] In numerous expressions of liberation theology and postcolonial biblical studies the Christian canon has been put into question. The outcome, however, is rarely the banishing of religion; more frequently, it amounts to the immanent *critique* of religion—which on some accounts is theology in its most adequate form.[5]

Schubert Ogden, for instance, has noted that many scholars would distinguish between *religion* as a first-order activity of referring to transcendent reality or God (in ritual activities, for example) and *theology* as critical reflection on a particular religion. Thus, 'biblical theology' might be conceived as a discipline of critically reflecting on the history of Israelite religion and early Christianity. Yet Ogden articulates a more comprehensive brief for theology: he wants to say that it is not just critical reflection on 'religion' narrowly defined; it also engages with cultural, political or economic matters within which religion is embedded. Thus, while Christian theology may reflect upon the explicit expressions of biblical faith in order to articulate 'doctrine', it may also include critical reflection on the social and cultural frameworks within which that faith is expressed. In other words, theology on this account would include precisely the kind of literary criticism Edward Said understood to be 'worldly', and this is necessarily the case with postcolonial theology.

In one controversial attempt to articulate the nature of Christian theology in more 'worldly' terms, George Lindbeck has described doctrine as a

---

3. See the detailed discussion in William D. Hart, *Edward Said and the Religious Effects of Culture* (Cambridge: Cambridge University Press, 2000).

4. Among many other studies, see R.S. Sugirtharajah, *The Bible and the Third World: Precolonial, Colonial and Postcolonial Encounters* (Cambridge: Cambridge University Press, 2001); Gustavo Gutiérrez, *Las Casas: In Search of the Poor of Jesus Christ* (Maryknoll: Orbis, 1993); Henry Reynolds, *This Whispering in our Heart* (St. Leonards: Allen & Unwin, 1998).

5. Schubert Ogden, 'Theology and Biblical Interpretation', *Journal of Religion* 76 (1996), pp. 175, 172–88; cf. Gerald West, *The Academy of the Poor: Towards a Dialogical Reading of the Bible* (Sheffield: Sheffield Academic Press, 1999).

kind of 'grammar' of religious language. In *The Nature of Doctrine*, he rejects
the idea that doctrinal theology might merely be a cognitive exercise,
reducible to a list of propositions about religious practice, and he also rejects
the picture of theology as simply the religious crust that forms over more
personal, existential attitudes and experience. Over against both the propo-
sitional and existential approaches, he suggests that religious statements
need to be viewed as part of a 'total pattern of speaking, thinking, feeling
and acting', much as interpretative anthropologists would view a culture. In
the case of the Christian religion, Lindbeck argues, the world is interpreted
through the lenses supplied by its scriptures.

It is not my intention here to engage with the commentaries on
Lindbeck's complex proposals, but I do want to reflect on one much discussed illustration of his views which is highly relevant to the task of postcolonial theology:

> The crusader's battle cry "*Christus est dominus*" ["Christ is Lord"],
> for example, is false when used to authorize cleaving the skull of
> the infidel (even though the same words in other contexts may
> be a true utterance). When thus employed, it contradicts the
> Christian understanding of Lordship as embodying, for example,
> suffering servanthood...a primarily cognitive-propositional theory
> of religion...is unable to do justice to the fact that a religious sys-
> tem is more like a natural language than a formally organized set of
> explicit statements, and that the right use of this language, unlike
> a mathematical one, cannot be detached from a particular way of
> behaving.[6]

Lindbeck is not here conflating theology with ethics. He is, rather, arguing that the very *intelligibility* of religious statements is derived from wider
traditions of speaking and acting.

Lindbeck's judgment on the crusader's battle cry—which is very much
in tune with my reading of the non-violent Christ—is obviously a retrospective critique and one which would not have enjoyed a broad consensus in medieval times, with the notable exception of St Francis of Assisi.
Crusader idelogy generated a 'pattern of speaking, thinking, feeling and
acting' that took centuries to untangle. It was rejuvenated by Christopher
Columbus, for example, and by the theologians of the day who defended
a 'just war' against the Indigenous peoples of South America, as well as
their reduction to slavery. As we saw in Chapter 1, Columbus's own *Book
of Prophecies* interpreted Isaiah 41–66 as justification for taking wealth

---

6.   George Lindbeck, *The Nature of Doctrine: Religion and Theology in a Postliberal Age*
(Philadelphia: Westminster Press, 1984), p. 64.

from the Americas to enable the king of Spain to conquer Jerusalem and rebuild the temple, thus reiterating crusader theology.[7]

One of the features of natural languages is that they are quite capable of embodying contradictions, but Lindbeck's argument suggests that the Christian religion as a 'cultural-linguistic system' cannot tolerate certain kinds of contradictions—contradictions that go to the very grammar of the culture, as it were. One might infer from his argument that while every religious tradition encompasses historically extended debates about the contents of that tradition, wherever Christian faith and practice has become so deeply contradictory that a non-violent Jesus Christ is said to provide sanctions for crusader or colonialist violence, then that expression of Christian faith has lost any intelligible claim to truthfulness.

I suggested in Chapter 3 that a similar point can be made about a Christian theology of salvation that so completely reverses the logic of redemption in the Hebrew Bible that it tolerates, or even promotes, the dispossession of Indigenous people from their traditional country. The scale of the contradiction in this case is, once again, so great that the tradition has arguably lost any intelligible claim to truthfulness.[8] Among the horrors recorded by Native American scholars, for example, Jace Weaver has described the Trail of Tears of 1838 when thousands of Cherokees died as they were force-marched from their homelands in Georgia to present-day Oklahoma. The Christian Cherokees sang hymns in their own language as they walked, including poignant lines such as 'Guide me, Jehovah, as I am walking through this barren land'.[9]

An early example of Indigenous Christians engaging with the contradictions of colonial theology can be found in the work of William Apess, a nineteenth-century Pequot Indian who became a Methodist. Apess both absorbed and contested the values of the colonizers' version of American civil religion, which regularly excluded Native Americans from moral or

---

7. See above, p. 14.

8. Cf. Anthony C. Thiselton, *The Two Horizons* (Grand Rapids: Eerdmans, 1980), p. 233, who argues from a philosophical point of view that the intelligibility of Christian language about redemption is dependent upon models provided in the Hebrew Bible.

9. Jace Weaver, 'From I-Hermeneutics to We-Hermeneutics: Native Americans and the Post-Colonial', in Laura Donaldson (ed.), *Postcolonialism and Scriptural Reading* (Semeia, 75; Atlanta: Scholars Press, 1996), p. 153. See Vicki Rozema (ed.), *Voices from the Trail of Tears* (Winston–Salem, NC: John F. Blair, 2003).

legal concern.[10] Apess responded with an *expanded* version of American
national identity, founded on his colour-inclusive Methodism, calling for
a re-examination of the discourses of civil liberty and equality. Resisting
the tradition of configuring Native Americans as 'Canaanites', Apess
adopted the synthesis of scriptural and Enlightenment discourse and turned
it against his colonizers. In effect, he re-inscribed his Native American
identity precisely within the sphere of the colonizing discourse that had
excluded it. Apess stands at the beginning of a long American tradition
of critical theology, emanating from minority groups, which contest the
patterns of 'speaking, thinking, feeling and acting' that have fallen short of
what Christian hospitality demands.

A necessary feature of postcolonial theology will be the advocacy of
practices of repentance that not only confess to the collusion of Christianity
and colonialism but, as a consequence, *resolutely resist new temptations to
exercise mastery over others* (a proposal that, in some respects, runs parallel to the renunciation of political hegemony in the Diaspora theology advocated by Daniel Boyarin and John Howard Yoder—discussed
above in Chapter 9). As the Catholic philosopher Gianni Vattimo has
suggested, Christian praxis needs to be reconstituted around the *kenosis*
suggested by Phil. 2.7 and to embody 'an essential inclination to assert
its truth through weakening' or 'self-emptying'.[11] While this approach
clearly addresses the hubris of crusader and colonial violence, one could
still enquire whether *kenosis* provides a sufficiently fruitful starting point
for the other theological concerns that have been identified in critiques
of colonial discourse. I want to suggest that it does.

The German theologian Jürgen Moltman has long argued that incarnational *kenosis* should be correlated with *creation* theology in that both
reveal the self-limiting life of God, and that it is therefore crucial to see
kenosis not as a temporary anomaly in the life of Christ but as characteristic of the Trinitarian life that makes space for the whole created
order (and a parallel point can be made about divine self-limitation in

10.   William Apess, *On our Own Ground: The Complete Writings of William Apess,
A Pequot* (ed. B. O'Connell; Amherst: University of Massachusetts Press, 1992);
Laura Donaldson, 'Son of the Forest, Child of God: William Apess and the Scene of
Postcolonial Nativity', in C.R. King (ed.), *Postcolonial America* (Urbana: University of
Illinois Press, 2000), pp. 201–22. In an infelicitous reflex of earlier times, a recent dis-
cussion of Deuteronomy's influence on American political thought in the 18th century
neglects to mention how Native Americans were affected. See G.E. Connor, 'Covenants
and Criticism', *Biblical Theology Bulletin* 32 (2002), pp. 4–10.

11.   Gianni Vattimo, *Belief* (Cambridge: Polity Press, 1999), pp. 39, 49. On Philippians
2 and *kenosis*, see Chapter 9 above.

the Jewish concept of *tzimtzum*).[12] As was indicated in Chapter 2 above, this perspective on divine hospitality to the whole of creation will inevitably be an essential feature of postcolonial theology. In the modern period, the injunction in Genesis 1 to 'subdue' the earth was interpreted as a sanction for instrumental attitudes to the natural world and to the displacement of Indigenous people whose attitudes to land were regarded as unproductive. But with increasing awareness of environmental crises, the tables are now turning. Rather than subduing the earth, we need to cultivate new habits of *making space* for the natural order, and creation theology can provide a significant framework for kenotic hospitality in this environmental mode.

Feminist and postcolonial critics have, however, placed a question mark over kenotic theology by pointing out that it has more relevance in contexts where human subjects have power and resources that might be given up.[13] A related issue arises where the survival of fragile Indigenous cultures is being advocated in an intellectual environment where postmodernists scorn the very notion of culture as a coherent reality. As Marshall Sahlins has put it, 'Just when so many people are announcing the existence of their culture, advanced anthropologists are denying it'.[14] Promoting the *kenosis* of fragile cultures, or selves, may simply provide a new theological means to reinforce injustice and dispossession.

12.   Jürgen Moltman, 'God's Kenosis in the Creation and Consummation of the World', in J. Polkinghorne (ed.), *The Work of Love: Creation as Kenosis* (Grand Rapids: Eerdmans, 2001), pp. 137–51. On the analogy between *kenosis* and the concept of *tzimtzum* in Jewish mysticism, see Moltmann, *God in Creation: An Ecological Doctrine of Creation* (London: SCM Press, 1985), pp. 86–87. Cf. Gershom Scholem, *Major Trends in Jewish Mysticism* (New York: Schocken Books, 1946), pp. 260–65.

13.   See Sarah Coakley, 'Kenosis and Subversion: On the Repression of "Vulnerability" in Christian Feminist Writing', in D. Hampson (ed.), *Swallowing a Fishbone?* (London: SPCK, 1996), pp. 82–111; Sze-kar Wan, 'Does Diaspora Identity Imply Some Sort of Universality? An Asian-American Reading of Galatians', in Fernando Segovia (ed.), *Interpreting Beyond Borders* (Sheffield: Sheffield Academic Press, 2000), pp. 107–33; cf. Graham Ward, 'Kenosis and Naming: Beyond Analogy and towards *allegoria amoris*', in P. Heelas (ed.), *Religion, Modernity and Postmodernity* (Oxford: Blackwell, 1998), pp. 233–57.

14.   Marshall Sahlins, *How 'Natives' Think about Captain Cook, for Example* (Chicago: Chicago University Press, 1995), p. 13. Sahlins follows Isaiah Berlin in arguing that the self-conscious use of 'culture' as an anti-colonial strategy originated in Germany in the late 18th century, in defiance of the global pretensions of English and French models of 'civilization'. See Isaiah Berlin, *Vico and Herder* (New York: Vintage Books, 1976), and especially Herder's comment, 'Only a real misanthrope could regard European culture as the universal condition of our species' (quoted in Sahlins, *Captain Cook*, pp. 11–12).

As was indicated above in Chapter 9, however, the theology of the apostle Paul does not necessarily lead to this conclusion. When status indicators like 'male' or 'free citizen' are declared irrelevant 'in Christ', then there is a consequential loss of status for free men, and a corresponding increase for women and slaves that is the necessary condition of a *mutual* 'self-giving'.[15] Similarly, moving beyond ethnocentrism, Paul is less prescriptive of Jewish identity markers and more accommodating of surrounding cultures 'not by erasing ethnic and cultural differences but by *combining these differences into a hybrid existence*' within the community of Christ's followers.[16] Accordingly, *kenosis* does not imply self-extinction, but rather, it makes space within the divine economy for the 'strangers' who invited into the hospitality of God. One could see here an analogy with the prophetic ethic, discussed in Chapter 6 above, of making space for others.

It would therefore be a misunderstanding of *kenosis* to construe it simply as an ascetic religious requirement of self-abnegating submission to divine sovereignty. Indeed, what we discover in the biblical traditions about the character of divine sovereignty is firstly the kenotic hospitality of creation, which permits extraordinary freedoms within the space sustained by an underlying order, and secondly, the compassion of Yahweh who repeatedly makes room for the failures of Israel. The *human* side of this relationship between Israel and Yahweh includes a good measure of self-assertion—embodied, for example, in the psalms of lament, the complaints of Jeremiah and the arguments of Job. As in any relationship constituted by love, the practice of biblical faith presents a *dialectic* of self-regard and self-abandonment.

As Walter Brueggemann has observed, the Hebrew Bible envisages a similar dynamic on the *divine* side between self-regard (represented especially by the discourse of holiness) and the vulnerability of divine risk. God enters into a pathos-filled relationship with Israel, risking solidarity in a way 'which seems regularly to qualify, if not subvert, Yahweh's sovereignty and self-regard'. In his *Old Testament Theology*, Brueggemann argues that

> the dominant Christian tradition has not fully appreciated the way
> in which the dialectic of assertion and abandonment in the human

15.   Antoinette Wire, *The Corinthian Women Prophets* (Minneapolis: Fortress Press, 1990), pp. 62–71. Cf. John D. Zizioulas, *Communion and Otherness: Further Studies in Personhood and the Church* (London: T. & T. Clark, 2006), p. 68.

16.   Sze-kar Wan, 'Does Diaspora Identity Imply Some Sort of Universality?', pp. 126–27. It must be noted here that Jewish ethnocentrism does not logically entail cultural imposition since non-Jews are understood to have their own pathway to God within the inclusive scope of Noachic covenant. See further Jon D. Levenson, 'The Universal Horizon of Biblical Particularism', in M.G. Brett (ed.), *Ethnicity and the Bible* (Leiden: Brill, 1996), pp. 143–69.

person is a counterpart to the unsettled interiority of Yahweh's sovereignty and fidelity. It seems to me that the classical Christian tradition must relearn this aspect of the interaction of God and human persons from its Jewish counterpart.[17]

Thus, even though Yahweh is seen to make laws both for Israel and the whole created order (laws which themselves mutate between the various legal codes and are sometimes contested the prophets and historians), one trajectory of biblical theology does not simply replicate imperial patterns of dominance and submission, but rather *constitutes the divine 'counter-empire' as kenotic hospitality.*

In this connection, it is worth noting that the imperative of *philoxenia* (love of strangers) as it is expressed in Heb. 13.2 provides a distinctive motivation: 'for by so doing some people have entertained angels without knowing it'. There is a reference here, no doubt, to the story of Abraham and Sarah in Genesis 18 welcoming three strangers who are later iden- tified as God. The obscurity of the divine presence is, indeed, a biblical theme that is played out in many different ways, such as in Amos' rebuke to Israelites who imagine that God has effected only one exodus (Amos 9.7), as well as in Mt. 25.31–46 which suggests that a criterion of divine judge- ment is responsiveness to an anonymous Christ who is embodied in the poor and oppressed. The common theme in all these texts is the hiddenness of God.

In the parable of the sheep and the goats in Matthew 25, 'the righteous' are as ignorant of Christ's presence as 'the unrighteous', since both groups ask essentially the same question: 'Lord, when did we see you hungry or thirsty or a stranger or needing clothes or sick or in prison?' (Mt. 25.37–38, 44). As is frequently the case with the eighth-century prophets, the practice of justice suggested here proves to be more fundamental than overt prac- tices of worship. Moreover, as Francis Watson puts it,

> the scandalous message of this text is that the distinction between righteous and unrighteous is unrelated to the distinction between church and world, and the final criterion will be the Christ secretly

---

17. Walter Brueggemann, *Old Testament Theology: Testimony, Dispute, Advocacy* (Minneapolis: Fortress Press, 1997), pp. 459, 296. For a strong statement of the nexus between human and divine action, see Emmanuel Levinas's essay on 'Kenosis and Judaism', in his *In the Time of the Nations* (Bloomington: Indiana University Press, 1994), pp. 114–32.

present among the oppressed rather than the Christ openly acknowledged within the community.[18]

This observation demonstrates the invalidity of any exclusivist models of the church that implicitly, or explicitly, prescribe a sharp separation of 'sacred' and 'secular' spaces or actions (since the secular may, against all expectations, reveal itself as sacred).

The parable of the sheep and the goats in Matthew 25 also lends some qualified support to Emmanuel Levinas's enigmatic conception of being 'under obligation to the other' without supposing that any prior metaphysical warrant is required to underwrite that obligation. As Hilary Putnam puts it, 'I am commanded without experiencing a commander'. In *Otherwise than Being*, Levinas describes the call of the Infinite as one that cannot be 'thematized' or subjected to conceptual mastery:

> The ego stripped...of its scornful and imperialist subjectivity, is reduced to the 'here I am' as a witness of the Infinite, but a witness that does not thematize what it bears witness of, and whose truth is not the truth of representation, is not evidence.[19]

While Jesus' parable arguably retains a metaphysical warrant for hospitality, the *secrecy* of Christ's presence amongst the oppressed implies that no limit can be placed on the praxis of solidarity. Accordingly, Mt. 25.21–46, Gen. 18.1–15 and Amos 9.7, each in different ways undermine controlling representations of the 'other'. Paul's argument in Romans 11 may be added to this list since, as we saw, it requires the church to refrain from attempts to control divine grace, highlighting instead the unknowable mystery of

18.   Francis Watson, 'Liberating the Reader', in Watson (ed.) *The Open Text: New Directions for Biblical Studies?* (London: SCM Press, 1993), p. 71; Leonardo Boff, *Jesus Christ Liberator: A Critical Chistology for our Time* (Maryknoll: Orbis, 1978), p. 95; Gustavo Gutierrez, *Theology of Liberation* (Maryknoll: Orbis, 1973), pp. 114–16. Even if this parable is referring to members of the body of Christ, it is suggesting that human wisdom is not sufficient to determine who are members and who are not.

19.   Emmanuel Levinas, *Otherwise than Being, or, Beyond Essesnce* (trans. A. Lingis; Dordrecht: Kluwer, 1991), p. 146; cf. Hilary Putnam, 'Levinas and Judaism', in S. Critchley and R. Bernasconi (eds.), *The Cambridge Companion to Levinas* (Cambridge: Cambridge University Press, 2002), p. 39. For a lucid entry into Levinas's work, see especially Simon Critchley, 'Introduction' to *The Cambridge Companion to Levinas*, pp. 1–32.

God. (We may also see in Paul's argument a reformulation of the Israelite antipathy to the making of divine images.[20])

In recent cultural studies, Levinas's influential moral philosophy has helped to shape a justifiable scepticism towards practices of 'representation', as did Edward Said's influential work *Orientalism*. In this ground-breaking book, Said indicted the distortions inherent in 'Orientalist discourse' that constructed recurrent images of Europe's cultural Other:

> dealing with it by making statements about it, authorizing views of it, describing it, by teaching it, ruling over it: in short Orientalism as a Western style for dominating, restructuring, and having authority over the Orient.[21]

The examples provided by Said provoked a flood of similar studies of colonial discourse and its uses, and those studies were sometimes linked with the inference that only participants *within* a particular tradition or group could be its spokespersons. Some years after the publication of *Orientalism*, Said himself saw this as a regrettable outcome of his work that limited genuine conversation and gave rise to what he called 'parochial dominations' over human experience.[22] In particular, he had in mind the fragmenting effects of identity politics in academic life, while acknowledging that these dynamics mediate the fragmentations of the wider world in more or less complex ways.

Postmodern attacks on representation have cut both ways, however, not just undermining 'Othering' discourses but also *self*-representation. Dwight Furrow, for example, is rigorously deconstructive when he argues that

> the self, whether we understand it individually or collectively, is a topography of lost and missing pieces cobbled together by a systematically distorted narrative of the remains. The quest for social

---

20.   See Ronald S. Hendel, 'Aniconism and Anthropomorphism in Ancient Israel', in K. van der Toorn (ed.), *The Image and the Book* (Leuven: Peeters, 1997), pp. 205–28. It is also worth noting here that the theology of icons in Orthodox Christianity is opposed to naturalistic representation, and is not therefore wholly incompatible with aniconic theology. See, e.g., Anastasios Kallis, 'Presidency at the Eucharist in the Context of the Theology of Icons: Questions about the Ecclesial Representation of Christ by the Priesthood', *Anglican Theological Review* 84 (2002), pp. 713–29.

21.   Edward Said, *Orientalism: Western Conceptions of the Orient* (Harmondsworth: Penguin, 1978), pp. 1–3.

22.   Edward Said, 'Orientalism Reconsidered', in *Reflections on Exile, and Other Literary and Cultural Essays* (London: Granta, 2000), p. 215. See further Anselm Kyonsuk Min, *The Solidarity of Others in a Divided World: A Postmodern Theology after Postmodernism* (London: T. & T. Clark International, 2004).

> identity is just one more vain search for the solace of origins, perpetually contested and itself the source of injustice.[23]

As in the case of Levinas' ethics, this strand of postmodernism appears to render not just the business of representation problematic, but also the very notion of cultural or religious identity (even 'minority' identity)—whether that identity is conceived in individual or collective terms.

Yet postcolonial studies rarely go this far, often attempting instead to recuperate subjugated voices that have been unjustly excluded from the 'systematically distorted narratives' constructed by colonial powers. This necessarily requires the risky business of representation, although in a manner that seeks to be more inclusive—necessarily addressing the economic and political inequities that lie behind cultural production. In the present work, for example, I have attempted to reconstruct the contours of Israelite family religion before it was over-written by the Deuteronomic theology that tended to elevate a 'national' level of identity over clan identities, in the process rendering some groups of Israelites as Canaanite 'others' because they did not accept the Deuteronomic version of exclusive monotheism.

One might argue that beyond a purely descriptive approach to historical study, such recuperation of subjugated discourses can be motivated by an emancipatory ethic that is founded on a well-established principle of modernity: every voice deserves to be heard. This is, for example, the approach taken by the philosophical school of 'discourse ethics' associated in particular with the work of Jürgen Habermas. This school, which advocates principles of equal treatment and procedural justice, begins with 'the universalist idea that every subject in his or her individuality should get the chance of an unconstrained articulation of his or her claims.'[24] Habermas is potentially relevant for postcolonial ethics in that he provides a rigorous analysis of 'systematically distorted communication' in Western tradition, of which colonial discourse may be considered a prime example.

23.   Dwight Furrow, *Against Theory: Continental and Analytic Challenges in Moral Philosophy* (London: Routledge, 1995), 192, cf. 65.

24.   Axel Honneth, 'The Other of Justice: Habermas and the Ethical Challenge of Postmodernism', in S.K. White (ed.), *The Cambridge Companion to Habermas* (Cambridge: Cambridge University Press, 1995), p. 307. See further Jürgen Habermas, *Moral Consciousness and Communicative Action* (trans. C. Lenhardt and S. Weber Nicholsen; Oxford: Polity Press, 1990); *Justification and Application* (trans. C. Cronin; Oxford: Polity Press, 1993); 'Israel and Athens, or to Whom Does Anamnestic Reason Belong? On Unity in Multicultural Diversity', in D. Batstone *et al.* (eds.), *Liberation Theologies, Postmodernity, and the Americas* (London: Routledge, 1997), pp. 243–52.

'Universal' vs 'Communitarian' Ethics

The complexity and abstractness of the philosophical debates surrounding Habermas's work should not be allowed to obscure the particular context from which it emerges. This is a philosophy that addresses the legacy of Nazism in Germany—the elevation of 'blood and soil' identity in the most violent form of nationalism—and this context needs to be borne in mind when considering the implications of key terms like 'universality'. As Habermas once commented in an interview,

> What, then, does universalism mean? That one relativizes one's own form of existence in relation to the legitimate claims of other forms of life, that one attribute the same rights to the strangers and the others, along with all their idiosyncrasies and incomprehensibilities, that one not insist on generalization of one's own identity, that the realm of tolerance must become endlessly larger than it is today: all this is what moral universalism means today.[25]

In some respects, this view represents a secular version of kenotic hospitality comparable with the ethics of the apostle Paul.[26] Ethics becomes focused on the business of making space for everyone to participate, regardless of the power that an individual may exercise.

On the other hand, some critics are suspicious of projects that rely on universal principles, even where the principle of universality is designed specifically to unseat the dominant voices within a culture. In particular, communitarian ethicists have criticized the *individualist* premises that lurk behind German 'discourse ethics'. In elevating the ideal that every individual voice should be heard, every representation of a *collective* self is rendered suspicious on the grounds that it is a potentially distorting formation of power. In Habermas's case, the individualist element is indebted to modernism, but as we have already acknowledged, individualism is also one of the legacies of Protestant attacks on tradition. There is a Eurocentric bias in individualist thought, whether that is expressed in philosophical or theological terms.

Of course, Protestant individualism is hardly a feature of biblical thought, and communitarian ethics today has many Protestant, Jewish and Catholic exponents. Prominent among these is Charles Taylor, a Catholic philosopher whose work on the 'politics of difference' has considerable relevance beyond the Canadian context where Taylor is situated. A common starting

---

25. Jürgen Habermas, 'Interview with J.M. Ferry', *Philosophy and Social Criticism* 14 (1988), p. 436.

26. David Horrell, *Solidarity and Difference: A Contemporary Reading of Paul's Ethics* (London: T. & T. Clark International, 2005), pp. 282–84.

point for this school of thought is the question whether liberal individualism allows for the *collective* right of cultural survival, or whether indeed the liberal principle of toleration is intolerant towards collectivities. In so far as liberalism attempts to accommodate this question, it is usually via the notion of multiple cultures that are allowed to flourish under certain 'universal' conditions of citizenship that are constituted democratically.

As minority groups know all too well, liberal democracies are in practice swayed decisively by the majority of a state's population, i.e., by those who carry democratic power. In Australia, for example, Aboriginal people can never dominate elections as a group. Their very right to vote in national elections did not exist until 1962, and the impediments to their participation in political life could only be overcome by moral persuasion of the non-Indigenous majority. Similarly, commenting on the situation in Sri Lanka, Uyangoda notes that 'we have had the Westminster type of democracy, which allowed an ethnic community with a numerical majority to control political power and resources'.[27] One of the key questions in postcolonial politics is how *moral persuasion* in political life is to be understood, especially in circumstances where democratic power is unevenly distributed. This is arguably no less an issue in postcolonial states where political divisions are constructed along ethnic or tribal lines, than it is in states where divisions can be articulated in 'racial' terms—as in Australia.

It is just this kind of question that German 'discourse ethics' seeks to address in that it envisages the social distortions of power being overcome by the requirements of procedural justice. Clearly, this approach draws a distinction between procedural *ideals* and the realities of politics, but it is questionable whether even this ideal has the potential to deliver decolonizing effects for multicultural states. While the model does contain a principle of equal treatment, and more importantly, it requires actual conversation amongst all those affected by political decisions, it does so in a manner that seeks to bracket the particularities of cultural identity.

Habermas, for example, attempts to distinguish on the one hand between universalizable norms and justice, on the one hand, and values or ends shaped by particular cultural identities on the other. Those universalizable norms

> require a break with all of the unquestioned truths of an established, concrete ethical life, in addition to distancing oneself from the contexts of life with which one's identity is inextricably interwoven.[28]

27. Jayadeva Uyangoda, 'Understanding Ethnicity and Nationalism', *Ecumenical Review* 47/2 (1995), p. 191. Cf. Peter Worsley, *The Three Worlds: Culture and World Development* (London: Weidenfeld & Nicolson, 1984), p. 243.

28. Habermas, *Justification and Application*, p. 12.

The assumption here is that particular cultural identities are not sufficiently rational; the univeralizing discourse of political morality has become the *logos* that mediates between social differences. Translating this into Australian political life, for example, it would seem that Indigenous people could only participate in the political process to the extent that they renounce the particularities that make them Indigenous. In short, this seems to be a sophisticated version of the assimilationist policies that have wrought so much damage in Australian history. Difference-blind liberalism colludes with the legal and poetic imagination of our past, so that now the public space emerges as a *terra nullius* managed by the discursive reasoning of democracy, rather than the by the civilizing mission of the nineteenth century.[29]

Current political expressions of liberalism also fit too neatly with contemporary manifestations of capitalism. As Hardt and Negri have argued in their much-discussed book *Empire*, a new version of economic empire is quietly undermining state-bounded concepts of sovereignty. Global flows of capital do not need to annex or conquer particular territories in any overt sense, but rather, they move in the 'smooth space' of global markets, purporting to set populations free from their 'specifically coded territories'.[30] In effect, these movements of capital ideally treat the entire globe as *terra nullius*.[31]

Globalized capital has a more subtle system of victimization that, instead of maintaining face-to-face forms of oppression or slavery, exercises dominance at a distance and excuses gross economic inequities in the name of market efficiency. As Jacques Derrida puts it in *The Gift of Death*:

> The structure of the laws of the market that [civilized] society has instituted and controls, because of the mechanism of external debt and other similar inequities, that same society *puts to death* or (failing to help someone in distress accounts for only a minor difference) *allows* to die of hunger and disease tens of millions of children…without any moral or legal tribunal ever being considered

29. Cf. Veronica Brady, 'Mabo: A Question of Space', *Caught in the Draught: On Contemporary Australian Culture and Society* (Sydney: Angus & Robertson, 1994), pp. 13–29.

30. Michael Hardt and Antonio Negri, *Empire* (Cambridge: Harvard University Press, 2000), pp. 186, 326–27.

31. Even in current theories of development, Western ideals of science, progress and 'transferable technology' are continuing to reduce local forms of knowledge to the rationality of markets. See Frédérique Apffel-Marglin, 'Introduction: Rationality and the World', in F. Apffel-Marglin and S. Marglin (eds.), *Decolonizing Knowledge: From Development to Dialogue* (Oxford: Clarendon Press, 1996), pp. 4–9.

competent to judge such a sacrifice, the sacrifice of others to avoid
being sacrificed oneself.[32]

A pressing question for Western churches is whether the long, dark history of tolerating slavery has been transformed into an accommodation of
less perspicuous forms of economic compulsion.

Hardt and Negri have in some respects overstated their case, since there
are indeed notable exponents of neo-classical economics who are arguing
that local forms of regulation are critical—both to market performance and
to the implementation of social and economic rights.[33] But Hardt's and
Negri's *Empire* also registers a significant question for exponents of 'cultural
hybridity'—a theme that has played a significant role not only in this book
but also in postcolonial studies more generally.

Instead of seeing a binary opposition between colonizer and colonized,
and focussing on anti-colonial responses in terms of that binary opposition, the tendency in *post*colonial studies in recent years has been to
see power as dispersed and complex. Resistance from subaltern groups
may be constituted by cultural borrowings and by hybrid 'mimetic effects',
even when that resistance is expressed in terms of 'nativist' recoveries
of Indigenous tradition.[34] Hardt and Negri argue that the affirmation of
hybrid and plastic identities is easily accommodated to the interests of de-
territorialised markets. The danger in postmodern theories is this: 'with
their heads turned backwards, that they tumble unwittingly into the arms
of the new power'.[35] Plasticity is indeed a key characteristic of a consum-
erist economy, as Zygmunt Bauman points out:

> Ideally, nothing should be embraced by a consumer firmly, nothing
> should command a commitment forever, no needs should be ever
> seen as fully satisfied, no desires considered ultimate. There ought

32.   Jacques Derrida, *The Gift of Death* (Chicago: Chicago University Press, 1995),
p. 86.
33.   See, for example, Amartya Sen, *Identity and Violence* (New York: W.W. Norton,
2006), pp. 120–48; Jonathan Sacks, *The Dignity of Difference: How to avoid the Clash
of Civilizations* (London: Continuum, 2nd edn, 2003), pp. 105–24; Albino Barrera,
Economic Compulsion and Christian Ethics (Cambridge: Cambridge University Press,
2005), pp. 199–200. Cf. the discussion of Hardt and Negri in Catherine Keller, 'The
Love of Postcolonialism', in C. Keller, M. Nausner and M. Rivera (eds.), *Postcolonial
Theologies: Divinity and Empire* (St Louis: Chalice Press, 2004), pp. 221–42.
34.   A classic work in this regard is Homi Bhabha, *The Location of Culture* (London:
Routlege, 1994); cf. Stephen D. Moore and Fernando Segovia (eds.), *Postcolonial Biblical
Criticism: Interdisciplinary Intersections* (Edinburgh: T. & T. Clark International 2005).
35.   Hardt and Negri, *Empire*, p. 142.

to be a proviso 'until further notice' attached to any oath of loyalty
and any commitment.[36]

The ideal consumer is always ready for the next permutation of fashion,
or commodity fetish, rather than being burdened by traditional products or
identities.

Communitarian Identities and Cultural Hybridity

There is a substantial issue here as to whether the endless plasticity of postmodern cultures is in any way equipped to withstand the tides of Empire.
On the other hand, deliberate retreats into class conflict or frozen identities
are in danger of replicating the 'parochial dominations' that Edward Said
spoke against. What is needed are forms of communitarian praxis that *are*
capable both of maintaining identifiable traditions and being open to others. It is arguable, however, that this balance is precisely what characterizes
a tradition in good order. A similar point has been made about the dynamic
nature of ethnicity, for example in Fredrik Barth's classic essay in *Ethnic
Groups and Boundaries* where he argued that criteria for group membership
may be constantly changing:

> So when one traces the history of an ethnic group through time,
> one is not simultaneously, in the same sense, tracing the history of
> 'a culture': the elements of the present culture of that ethnic group
> have not sprung from the particular set that constituted the group's
> culture at a previous time, whereas the group has a continual organ-
> izational existence with boundaries (criteria of membership) that
> despite modifications have marked off a continuing unit.[37]

Our discussion above of the forging and revisions of Israelite identity, provide an illustration of Barth's argument. The culture of 'Israel' was repeatedly contested and revised, without losing an ongoing sense of ethnicity.

There is a famous image of hermeneutics as a 'fusion of horizons'—the
transformative encounter between different historical periods, traditions
or cultures. As several chapters in this book have made clear, the classic
texts of the Bible themselves embody many examples of the absorption
and contestation of different cultures—Canaanite, Assyrian, Hellenistic,
Roman and so on—constituting various 'fusions of horizons'. Those of us
who inherit the biblical tradition cannot justifiably presume that foreign

36. Zygmunt Bauman, *Work, Consumerism and the New Poor* (Buckingham: Open
University, 1998), p. 25.

37. Fredrik Barth, (ed.), *Ethnic Groups and Boundaries: The Social Organization of
Culture Difference* (London: Allen & Unwin, 1969), p. 38.

cultures have nothing to teach us; that has been a central and flawed assumption of colonial theological discourses. As Charles Taylor has persuasively argued, if we presume that other cultures have nothing important to say, then we deprive ourselves of a significant strategy for testing the validity of own convictions. The maintenance of a living tradition necessarily includes the capacity to reflect on its own values and purposes and to pass those convictions on to new generations. Genuine conversation with other cultures are not just enriching but necessary:

> What has to happen is what Gadamer has called 'fusion of horizons'. We learn to move in a broader horizon, within which what we have formerly taken for granted as the background to valuation can be situated as one possibility alongside the different background of the formerly unfamiliar culture.[38]

It is important to note that Taylor's account of multiculturalism does not amount to a plurality of monocultures. Nor does it presume that all cultures are equally valuable. The latter presumption is both condescending in that it offers a pre-emptive judgment of worth, without actually engaging with the other, and paradoxically ethnocentric in suggesting that we already have the standards to make such judgments. Authentic judgments of value allow the possibility that in actually engaging with the other our original standards may be transformed.[39]

This book illustrates, for example, a number of fundamental shifts in the biblical literature in ways of understanding God's relationship with the world, the identity of Israel, the demands of divine justice and conceptions of salvation. Many of these shifts arose through inter-cultural contacts. Similarly, post-biblical developments within Jewish and Christian traditions reflect historically-extended and socially-embodied arguments about the patterns of 'speaking, thinking, feeling and acting' that are entailed by the development of those traditions, and sometimes those patterns are as much dependant on cultural (or sub-cultural) affiliations as they are on the interpretation of scriptural canons.[40]

Leaving to one side, for the moment, the broader ethical implications of interpreters' social locations, certain aspects of biblical interpretation

---

38.   Charles Taylor, 'The Politics of Recognition', in A.Gutman (ed.), *Multiculturalism and 'The Politics of Recognition'* (Princeton: Princeton University Press, 1992), p. 67. Cf. the reformulation of 'catholicity' in Miroslav Volf, *Exclusion and Embrace: A Theological Exploration of Identity, Otherness, and Reconciliation* (Nashville: Abingdon Press, 1996), pp. 48–55.

39.   Taylor, 'Recognition', pp. 67, 70.

40.   Cf. Sen, *Identity and Violence*, p. 67.

are necessarily 'ethnocentric', no matter how narrowly exegesis may be conceived. For example, in spite of the frequently expressed (and logically vague) exhortation for biblical scholars to analyze a text 'in its own terms', the interpretation of foreign or ancient texts requires at some point that cross-cultural comparisons and contrasts are made with the interpreter's own culture.[41] Insofar as the interpreter's own culture is an ineluctable feature of cross-cultural understanding, one would have to admit that a certain kind of ethnocentrism is unavoidable: either one 'goes native', in which case no *cross*-cultural understanding has been achieved, or one attempts to describe the 'other' in terms which would be intelligible within the interpreter's own culture. This does not mean that cross-cultural understanding needs to find simple corresponding concepts, but rather, that interpretation will often need to work with 'perspicuous contrasts' in order to avoid cultural *imposition*.

It is a characteristic weakness of biblical exegesis in the modern Western tradition, however, that although it has dignified itself with the rhetoric of objectivity, it has frequently been blind to its own cultural assumptions. African scholars such as Temba Mafico and Kwame Bediako have pointed out, for example, that there are enough analogies between the biblical world and traditional, tribal societies to suggest that some biblical concepts may be more readily intelligible in Africa than in modern Europe. This was suggested above in Chapter 3, in the discussion of ancestor traditions.[42] It is becoming more evident that scholarly discourses themselves have histories and socio-economic locations. Fernando Segovia has rightly observed that the cultural studies movement, for example, has unmasked the 'enduring construct of a universal and informed reader' that required all readers

41. See Charles Taylor, 'Understanding and Ethnocentricity', in *Philosophy and the Human Sciences* (Cambridge: Cambridge University Press, 1985), pp. 116–33; David Hoy, 'Is Hermeneutics Ethnocentric?', in J.F. Bohman, D.R. Hiley, and R. Shusterman (eds.), *The Interpretive Turn: Philosophy, Science, Culture* (Ithaca: Cornell University Press, 1991), pp. 155–75.

42. See especially Temba Mafico, 'The Biblical God of the Fathers and the African Ancestors', in G. West and M. Dube (eds.), *The Bible in Africa: Transactions, Trajectories and Trends* (Leiden: Brill, 2000), pp. 481–89; Kwame Bediako, *Christianity in Africa* (Maryknoll: Orbis, 1995), pp. 216–33.

to divest themselves of constitutive identity factors and 'to interpret like Eurocentric critics'.[43]

It does not follow from this point, however, that historical critical studies as they have been conceived in the West have no value outside their own social domains; rather, it follows that they need to be more self-critical (more kenotic, to put this in theological terms) and more open to conversation with biblical interpretation in non-Western contexts.

If, however, this hermeneutical hospitality is interpreted in terms of a universal principle requiring that all voices must to be heard equally, then we need to register a qualification. Jacques Derrida argued in several of his works, for example, that there are basically two different types of moral concern and that they are fundamentally in conflict: one is the solidarity of justice which aims to treat everyone equally, while the second is constituted by an infinite care for the irreducibly particular other. The conflict between the two versions of moral concern is revealed by the fact that a form of care that is *boundless* would be compromised if it were constrained by a principle of equal treatment.

Derrida follows Levinas in objecting to the idea that ethics must be understood in terms of abstract universal norms (the approach taken by Habermas), and argued on the contrary that ethics begins in a respect for 'absolute singularity'. Levinas says, for example, that 'Ethics as the conscience of a responsibility towards the other…does not lose one in the generality; far from it, it singularizes, it posits one as a unique individual'.[44]

In *The Gift of Death*, Derrida provides a startling re-reading of the binding of Isaac in Genesis 22 that sets out a conflict of obligations. Sacrifice, far from being the exception, 'is the most common event in the world' Derrida suggests.[45] We do not recognize its ubiquity, because we are normally attuned to local—rather than universal—forms of duty and ethics. When,

---

43.   See Segovia, '"And they began to speak in other tongues": Competing Modes of Discourse in Contemporary Biblical Criticism', in F.F. Segovia and M.A. Tolbert (eds.), *Reading from this Place*. I. (Minneapolis: Fortress Press, 1995), pp. 29–30. Cf. Jon D. Levenson, *The Hebrew Bible, the Old Testament and Historical Criticism* (Louisville: Westminster/John Knox, 1993), pp. 95, 98, 122.

44.   Jacques Derrida, *The Gift of Death* (trans. D. Willis; Chicago: Chicago University Press, 1995), p. 78, citing Emmanuel Levinas, *Noms propres* (Montpellier: Fata Morgana, 1976), p. 113. Christian attempts to overcome the tension between the particularity of love and the universality of justice through a conception of saintly *agape* cannot be sustained. Cf. Terry Veling, 'In the Name of Who? Levinas and the Other Side of Theology', *Pacifica* 12 (1999), pp. 275–92; Michael Wyschogrod, *The Body of Faith: Judaism as Corporeal Election* (Minneapolis: Seabury–Winston, 1983), pp. 58–65.

45.   Derrida, *The Gift of Death*, p. 85.

for example, justice is habitually domesticated within nationalist ideologies, we fail to see its most radically international demands. Yet, Derrida writes:

> By preferring my work, simply by giving it my time and attention, by preferring my activity as a citizen or as a professorial and professional philosopher, writing and speaking here in a public language, French in my case, I am perhaps fulfilling my duty. But I am sacrificing and betraying at every moment all my other obligations: my obligations to the other others whom I know or don't know, the billions of my fellows...who are dying of starvation or sickness...every one being sacrificed to every one else in this land of Moriah that is our habitat every second of every day.[46]

Derrida sets before us a paradox that cannot be resolved by logic but only by deliberation and decision: either we address our local forms of obligation and duty, in which case we compromise universal obligations, or, we address the *other* others, beyond our local forms of commitment, in which case we compromise our local duties.[47]

A postcolonial theology will need to inhabit this tension not just as a predicament for individual Christians, but by means of a reconstructed understanding of 'catholicity'. The praxis that is needed would include not just activating global networks of ecclesial communication, but also the development of kenotic hospitality that draws no distinction between sacred and secular experience of suffering. If time and space separate us from the suffering of others, then we must seek to overcome that distance through a 'Eucharistic' catholicity that knits together the pain of the world. A postcolonial church will be orientated around a cosmic Christ whose suffering expresses solidarity with victims, not in order to provide a narrowly religious opiate for suffering, but rather, to generate prophetic action against oppressive power and coercive economic conditions.

A kenotic hospitality will also need to be open to hearing the Spirit of God speak through other religious traditions.[48] As already indicated, this suggestion does not imply that every religious tradition is equally valuable, or equally immune to critique, since such assumptions are implicitly ethnocentric and undermine the need for actual conversation; an evaluative framework has already been presumed, and a transformative encounter is

46. Derrida, *The Gift of Death*, p. 69.

47. See further, Mark G. Brett, 'Abraham's "Heretical" Imperative: A Response to Jacques Derrida', in Charles Cosgrove (ed.), *The Meanings We Choose: Hermeneutical Ethics, Indeterminacy and the Conflict of Interpretations* (London: T. & T. Clark International, 2004), pp. 167–78.

48. See Denis Edwards, *Breath of Life: A Theology of the Creator Spirit* (Maryknoll: Orbis, 2004), pp. 59–65.

not necessary. Nor am I recommending here the Western academic model of 'comparative religion' that is a procedurally neutral activity undertaken from Olympian heights, and within which the very category of 'religion' is a truncated Western product.[49]

In this book we have encountered many expressions of 'inter-religious dialogue' in the scriptures, even if the dynamics of the debate have been somewhat hidden from view behind the received canonical texts. But this is a dialogue that embodies the life a tradition as it comes to terms with new experiences and challenges, consequently adapting the previous ways of speaking about life before God. One expression of this is the inclusive monotheism discussed above in Chapter 3. A similar dynamic is found within Indigenous communities who adopt Christianity and who, as a result, re-evaluate their ways of relating to older traditions. This process of re-evaluation has too often been dominated by missionary theologies that pre-empt the outcomes on the basis of aggregated cultural prejudices derived from Western tradition (although as many authors have pointed out, 'Western' tradition is itself a overly simplified category[50]).

As was indicated in Chapter 3, Indigenous theology can often be characterized in terms of cultural hybridity. Sometimes this is described as 'inculturation' although there are limits to this idea if it simply amounts to the translation of evangelistic ideas into language that is intelligible within the 'target' culture. As Australian Aboriginal theologian Graham Paulson has put it,

> If evangelization means the telling of the story of the gospel as it was acculturated in the western world, and translated into the subcultures of denominational religious institutions, then Aboriginal and Torres Strait Islander peoples have been very well evangelized. But if the process of evangelizing includes the telling of the biblical stories in ways which connect with our deepest spiritual expectations, evoking practices in tune with our own cultures, then we were not well evangelized at all.[51]

Paulson goes on to speak of the redemptive analogies that may be possible between Aboriginal and Christian spirituality if people engage with the possibilities of cultural hybridity.

---

49. Richard King, *Orientalism and Religion: Postcolonial Theory, India and 'the Mystic East'* (London: Routledge, 1999), pp. 50–52.

50. See, for example, Jack Goody, *The Theft of History* (Cambridge: Cambridge University Press, 2007); Peter Van der Veer, *Imperial Encounters: Religion and Modernity in India and Britain* (Princeton: Princeton University Pres, 2001).

51. Graham Paulson, 'Towards an Aboriginal Theology', *Pacifica* 19 (2006), pp. 310–11.

To say that Jesus is 'the Christ' is to interpret the meaning of his life within the particular cultural mix of the first century, including the mixture of Judaism and Hellenism which yielded the language of *logos* to describe the 'being' of Jesus as antecedent to Jewish expectations of a messiah. Just as biblical theology in the first century envisaged Jewish and gentile identities being reconciled within the body of the *ekklēsia*, so today, Jesus is still becoming 'Christ'—answering the 'deepest spiritual expectations'—to the extent that Indigenous identities are still being reconciled within the church. Reconciliation does not imply the extinction of previous identities, but rather, the embodiment of a culturally hybrid solidarity expressed through adapted patterns of 'speaking, thinking, feeling and acting'. The body of Christ is a catholic community of interrelated bodies, making space for diverse ethnicities, without projecting a final reconciliation that amounts to the denial of actual bodies or the erasure of 'complex space' (as discussed in Chapter 8 above).[52]

In the Australian context, there have been particular difficulties in reconciling non-Indigenous cultural patterns of *individualism* with the social collectivities of traditional Indigenous societies. I have suggested in this book that Christians need to recover some of the Israelite conceptions of 'redemption' that can be more closely correlated with the communitarian ethos of Indigenous cultures. Redemption in Israel usually implied *restoration to kin and country*, and this was the case up until contacts with Greek culture crystallized earlier images of hope into concepts of resurrection. Postcolonial Christian theology needs to recover these older concepts of redemption in order to articulate fresh understandings of resurrection. In this respect, Israelite and Jewish traditions could provide much needed conversation partners, both for Indigenous and non-Indigenous Christianity.[53]

I am not suggesting here that Indigenous Christians in Australia are uniformly engaged in the task of recovering their ancestral traditions. On the contrary, this issue is highly contentious, and to mention just one example from the 1990s, the intra-Indigenous disputes surrounding 'secret women's business' on Hindmarsh Island in South Australia illustrate some of the divisions that have surfaced, in this case, in complex legal and political debates over whether a bridge could be built from the island to the mainland.

52. Volf, *Exclusion and Embrace*, pp. 51–52, 109–10.

53. See especially Jon D. Levenson, *Resurrection and the Restoration of Israel: The Ultimate Victory of the God of Life* (New Haven: Yale University Press, 2006); Ben Ollenburger, '"If Mortals Die, Will They Live Again?" The Old Testament and Resurrection', *Ex Auditu* 9 (1993), pp. 29–44. Note, for example, the restoration to traditional land envisaged in Ezekiel 37.14 in the context of resurrection metaphors.

This story has been chronicled by Margaret Simons in her book *The Hindmarsh Island Affair: The Meeting of the Waters*. Simons argues that there were two groups of Christian women who were the protagonists on the Aboriginal side—one group who thought that the ancestral traditions had come to an end, and the other who thought they needed to be preserved. Simons reports prayers being said and hymns being sung in meetings of the women who sought to defend their old obligations. 'Jesus is Lord', a woman prayed at one of those meetings. 'He had given this country to the Ngarrindjeri to look after. Would he please help them to protect it'. Another Ngarrindjeri woman said this:

> Those old women saw to it that their own things that had to be done there—things we still regard as sacred, in spite of everything—passing on the teaching to the right people—that had to go on. I never saw any contradiction in that for me—I still serve the Lord Jesus and didn't He say 'in my father's house there are many mansions'? I'm sure, still, that there's a mansion there for our old beliefs.[54]

A long-term missionary among the Ngarrindjeri, George Taplin, recorded in his diary his distress at finding 'a singular but undoubted fact to me that as soon as the natives become pious and cast off their old superstitions they begin to suffer in health and sometimes die'. In his early years at the mission, he found only one reason probable, which was 'the dread of witchcraft which preys on the mind'.[55] Taplin stayed at the Point McLeay mission in Ngarrindjeri country for twenty years, learning the language and much of the culture that would have been available to males, although he also attempted to suppress male initiations. The insight that physical illnesses could be a consequence of assaults on a people's identity was apparently not available to him. But in the course of time, even he had intimations of the cultural determinants of well-being when he observed in a letter to the Department of Aborigines in 1870 that the healthiest Aborigines were the ones who adhered to the old customs and avoided European habits.[56]

Taplin's early prejudices about 'witchcraft' prevented him from engaging in a more careful process of observation that may have illuminated traditional practices in terms of their broader patterns of 'speaking, thinking,

---

54. Margaret Simons, *The Hindmarsh Island Affair: The Meeting of the Waters* (Sydney: Hodder, 2003), p. 356; cf. pp. 162, 215, 422. The allusion to Jn 14.2 is taken up in Kwame Anthony Appiah, *In my Father's House: Africa in the Philosophy of Culture* (London: Methuen, 1992). See also Marion Maddox, 'How Late Night Theology Sparked a Royal Commission', *Sophia* 36/2 (1997), pp. 111–35.

55. Cited in Simons, *Meeting of the Waters*, p. 22.

56. Quoted in John Harris, *One Blood* (Sutherland: Albatross, 1990), p. 358.

feeling and acting'.[57] Instead of making such pre-emptive judgments, postcolonial theology will need to be more patient in reflecting on the forms of cultural hybridity that Indigenous Christianity presents.[58] But, as already indicated, it is not just a matter of postcolonial *reflection* on how inequitable distributions of power and resources affect thoughts and actions, but also a question of strategies to overcome those inequities.

I will restrict myself, in these concluding comments, to the issue of 'reconciliation' between Indigenous and non-Indigenous people in the Australian context. Some of the recent debate turns on *repentance* in the form of apologies, and some of it turns on the question of a *treaty* (or 'covenant', to use the other common translation of the Hebrew term *berit* discussed in Chapter 5 above). In biblical theology, there are conceptual linkages between both repentance and 'covenant' since both entail the ongoing shaping of behaviour and not just one-off events. In Lk. 19.1–10, for example, a repentant tax collector returns half of his possessions to the poor and promises to pay people he has cheated four times the original amount. An *agape* ethic will always go beyond the general requirements of justice, but it should never sink *below* them.

In the Australian context we would surely need to conclude that in order to address the wrongful extinguishment of Indigenous land title by the Crown, a treaty would *at least* need to provide the 'just terms' compensation established by the Constitution since 1901. This was the shared conclusion of three High Court judges in the *Mabo* case when they considered the issue of compensation, and only the most perverse reasoning has been allowed to obscure that conclusion.[59] Given the structural inequities of native title in current Australian law, a treaty should also establish the legislative changes that will be necessary to implement the UN *Declaration on the Rights of Indigenous Peoples* (2007).

A leading anthropologist, Peter Sutton, recently argued that both apologies and treaties represent mistaken aspirations within the reconciliation movement. He proposes that such large scale public processes might be seen

57. Cf. E.E. Evans-Pritchard, *Nuer Religion* (Oxford: Oxford University Press, 1956), p. 189; Robert Kenny, *The Lamb Enters the Dreaming: Nathanael Pepper and the Ruptured World* (Melbourne: Scribe, 2007), pp. 153.

58. See, e.g., Mabiala Justin-Robert Kenzo, 'Religion, Hybridity, and the Construction of Reality in Postcolonial Africa', *Exchange* 33/3 (2004), pp. 244–68; Terence Ranger, 'Christianity and the First Peoples: Some Second Thoughts', in P. Brock (ed.), *Indigenous Peoples and Religious Change* (Leiden: Brill, 2005), pp.15–32. Kathryn Tanner, *Theories of Culture: A New Agenda for Theology* (Minneapolis: Fortress 1997), pp. 27, 40–41.

59. See for example *Mabo v Queensland [No. 2]* (1992) 175 CLR 1, 111 (Deane and Gaudron JJ) and the discussion in Lisa Strelein, *Compromised Jurisprudence: Native Title Cases since Mabo* (Canberra: Aboriginal Studies Press, 2006), pp. 20–23.

as reconciliation in a 'sacramental' model, when in fact a 'pietist' model is more realistic—one in which reconciliation takes place at the level of personal relationships.[60]

Sutton's argument can be compared with a paper written some years ago by the political scientist Judith Brett.[61] What Sutton characterizes as a contrast between sacramental and pietistic reconciliation is roughly analogous to a contrast that Brett constructs between between Catholic and Protestant approaches to Indigenous politics. These contrasts are heuristic fictions, but it is certainly the case in Australia that Catholics have played leading roles in developing strategies for public reconciliation—as have Jews.

Brett's argument is that the Catholic ethos has a sacramental presumption that individuals are always embedded in social networks, and the idea of reconciliation is shaped accordingly—treaties and covenants between groups become thinkable. The Protestant ethos, on the other hand, is constituted by the individual's struggle against tradition and is thereby affiliated with the individualist philosophy of liberalism. The liberal tradition in Australian politics has accordingly found it difficult to conceive of the idea that treaties with Indigenous people might be necessary.

Sutton's paper takes the pietist approach, even down to a concluding poem by John Donne that focusses on an individual's identification with Christ, on the point of death, conceived as an exchange of the 'crown of thorns' with 'his other Crowne'. The final verse in Donne's poem 'Hymn to God, my God, in my Sickness' reads:

> So, in His purple wrapp'd recieve mee Lorde,
> By these his thornes give me his other Crowne;
> And as to others soules I preach'd thy word,
> Be this my text, my sermon to my owne.
> Therefore that he may raise the Lorde throws down.

Biblical theologies of the 'Crowne', on the other hand, imagine the people of God contesting the sovereignty of successive empires—Egyptian, Assyrian, Persian, Hellenistic, Roman. Arguably none of that contestation is conceived in the individualist terms that we find in Donne's poem. Against Donne's 'Hymn to God' we may set the hymn sung at Eddie Mabo's funeral in 1996, when the Torres Strait Islander choir celebrated with a hymn about

60.   Peter Sutton, 'On Feeling Reconciled', public lecture delivered at the Australian Catholic University, Melbourne, 13 June, 2007. Available at http.//wwwling.arts.kuleuven. be/fll/eldp/sutton/index.html

61.   Judith Brett, 'The Treaty Process and the limits of Australian Liberalism' AIATSIS Seminar Series, 4 June, 2001. Available at www.aiatsis.gov. au/_data/assets/ pdf_file/5446/Brett.pdf

Moses. 'Koiki led the people of Murray islands from the bondage of *terra nullius*', it was explained.[62]

> Mama namarida Mose mara memegle e naose gair mara omaskir Israil le.
> You sent Moses your servant to lead the people of Israel from Egypt.

A postcolonial faith, as in the traditions of Moses and the Prophets, will continually make the concept of sovereignty problematic, but not in such a way as to dissolve social and economic justice into an individualized messianism.

As we have seen in previous chapters, however, postcolonial critics have identified the ways in which the 'counter-empire' of God is sometimes conceived—as in the liturgical discourses of 'Lord', 'power' and 'glory'—in language that is all too similar to the discourses of ancient empires.[63] On this issue, I want to take Lindbeck's reflection on the grammar of *Christus est dominus* one step further.

To say that 'Christ is Lord' is implicitly to deny that any other *dominus* has a competing validity, including an empire or state that promotes Christianity in its public discourse.[64] The theological grammar of this claim is derived from the traditions of Israel that established Yahweh's prerogative over every empire or nation, including Israel. In this respect, the opposition to Adolf Hitler in the Barmen Declaration of 1934 is comparable to the implied opposition to the Assyrian empire in the book of Deuteronomy (discussed in Chapter 5 above). Yet unlike Deuteronomy, the European theology that grew out of the Barmen Declaration, and which is associated especially with the name of Karl Barth, was thoroughgoing in its rejection of nationalism in part because such an approach provided a clear opposition to Nazism.[65]

---

62. Merrill Findlay, 'Eddie Mabo Comes Home.' *The Age*, 1 June, 1996.

63. See, for example, the critique in Clara Sue Kidwell, Homer Noley and George E. "Tink" Tinker, *Native American Theology* (Maryknoll: Orbis, 2001), pp. 67–70.

64. At this point I would also see a tension between *Christus est dominus* and the *plenum dominium*, the 'full beneficial' title in Australian law claimed by the Crown to underpin every land tenure. See for example *Mabo v Queensland [No. 2]* (1992) 175 CLR 1, 90–91 (Deane and Gaudron JJ) and 60 (Brennan J).

65. Barth particularly rejected the idea that German nationality could be understood as a 'second revelation'. See Doris L. Bergen, *Twisted Cross: The German Christian Movement in the Third Reich* (Chapel Hill: University of North Carolina Press, 1996), p. 21. Barth's comments were more nuanced in his *Ethics* (New York: Seabury Press, 1981), pp. 192–96, where he suggests for example that 'the ethical relevance of nationality is that we must meet God in this reality and not another' (p. 193).

Not all forms of national identity, however, need to be expunged from Christian theology, and one of the dangers of doing so is that communities of faith become isolated from public discourse. An unintended consequence of the failure to provide a public theology is that the vacuum can readily be filled by the kind of economic ideology that has been so poetically described by Hardt and Negri: the ideology that seeks to override 'specifically coded territories' in the name of a hegemonic capitalism.

Starting from a view that the divine 'counter-empire' is constituted by kenotic hospitality, postcolonial public theology needs to articulate more generous 'polyphonic' nationalities. And to the extent that those complex identities are held together within the global context of 'deeply felt and enacted solidarity',[66] it is precisely those generous nationalities that must take action against the recent manifestations of empire that threaten to turn the world into the 'smooth space' of global capital, converting the old face-to-face coercion of slavery into more subtle forms of economic compulsion.[67] Communities of faith need to act as leaven in this process and to summon the courage of their kenotic convictions: repenting of unsustainable levels of consumption, renouncing the false security of military force, shifting resources to where they are needed, expanding the horizons of hospitality, and clasping hands against the mutating arrogances of power.

---

66. The wording here is borrowed from the dialogue with Daniel Boyarin in Chapter 9.

67. See, e.g., M. Daniel Carroll R., 'The Challenge of Economic Globalization for Theology', in C. Ott and H.A. Netland (eds.), *Globalizing Theology: Belief and Practice in an Era of World Christianity* (Grand Rapids: Baker Academic, 2006), pp. 199–212; Jeffrey Sachs, *The End of Poverty: Economic Possibilities for our Time* (New York: Penguin, 2005).

BIBLIOGRAPHY

Albertz, Rainer, *A History of Israelite Religion in the Old Testament Period*, I (London: SCM Press, 1994).

—*Persönliche Frömigkeit und offizielle Religion* (Stuttgart: Calwer Verlag, 1978).

Albrecht, P.G.E., 'Hermannsburg, a Meeting Place of Cultures', *Nungalinya Occasional Bulletin* 14 (1981).

Anderson, Benedict, *Imagined Communities* (London: Verso, 2nd edn 1991).

Anderson, Bernard, *From Creation to New Creation* (Minneapolis: Fortress Press, 1994).

Apess, William, *On our Own Ground: The Complete Writings of William Apess, a Pequot* (ed. B. O'Connell; Amherst: University of Massachusetts Press, 1992).

Apffel-Marglin, Frédérique, and S. Marglin (eds.), *Decolonizing Knowledge: From Development to Dialogue* (Oxford: Clarendon Press, 1996).

Appiah, Kwame Anthony, *In my Father's House: Africa in the Philosophy of Culture* (London: Methuen, 1992).

Ashcroft, Bill, 'Critical Utopias', *Textual Practice* 21/3 (2007), pp. 411–31.

—*Postcolonial Transformation* (London: Routledge, 2001).

Attwood, Bain, *Rights for Aborigines* (Sydney: Allen & Unwin, 2003).

Attwood, Bain and Andrew Markus, *Thinking Black: William Cooper and the Australian Aborigines' League* (Canberra: Aboriginal Studies Press, 2004).

Aune, David, *Revelation* (Waco: Word Books, 1997).

Baker, D.W. and D.T. Arnold (eds.), *The Face of Old Testament Studies* (Grand Rapids: Baker, 1999).

Bakhtin, Mikhail, *The Dialogic Imagination* (Austin: University of Texas Press, 1981).

Baltzer, Klaus, *Deutero-Isaiah* (Minneapolis: Fortress Press, 2001).

Bammel, Ernst, 'Ein Beitrag zur paulinischen Staatsanschauung', *Theologische Literaturzeitung* 85 (1960), cols. 837–40.

Barclay, John M.G., '"Neither Jew nor Greek": Multiculturalism and the New Perspective on Paul', in M.G. Brett (ed.), *Ethnicity and the Bible* (Leiden: Brill, 1996), pp. 197–214.

Barnes, J.A., 'Anthropology in Britain before and after Darwin', *Mankind* 5 (1960), pp. 369–85.

Barrera, Albino, *Economic Compulsion and Christian Ethics* (Cambridge: Cambridge University Press, 2005).

Barth, Fredrik (ed.), *Ethnic Groups and Boundaries: The Social Organization of Culture Difference* (London: Allen & Unwin, 1969).

Barth, Karl, *Ethics* (New York: Seabury Press, 1981).

Bauman, Zygmunt, *Work, Consumerism and the New Poor* (Buckingham: Open University, 1998).

Bediako, Kwame, *Christianity in Africa* (Maryknoll, NY: Orbis, 1995).

Beilharz, Peter, *Imagining the Antipodes: Culture, Theory and the Visual in the Work of Bernard Smith* (Cambridge: Cambridge University Press, 1997).

Beker, J. Christiaan, *Paul the Apostle* (Philadelphia: Fortress Press, 1980).

Ben-Amos, David, 'Analytical Categories and Ethnic Genres', in D. Ben-Amos (ed.), *Folklore Genres* (Austin: University of Texas Press, 1976), pp. 215–42.

Benhabib, Sehla, *Situating the Self* (Cambridge: Polity Press, 1992).

Bergen, Doris L., *Twisted Cross: The German Christian Movement in the Third Reich* (Chapel Hill: University of North Carolina Press, 1996).

Berlin, Isaiah, *Vico and Herder* (New York: Vintage Books, 1976).

Berndt, R.M. and C., *End of an Era: Aboriginal Labour in the Northern Territory* (Canberra: Australian Institute of Aboriginal Studies, 1987).

Berndt, R.M., *An Adjustment Movement in Arnhem Land* (Paris: Mouton, 1962).

Betz, Hans Dieter, *The Sermon on the Mount* (Minneapolis: Fortress Press, 1995).

—*Galatians* (Philadelphia: Fortress Press, 1979).

Bhabha, Homi K., *The Location of Culture* (London: Routledge, 1994).

—'Signs Taken for Wonders: Questions of Ambivalence and Authority under a Tree outside Delhi, May 1817', *Critical Inquiry* 12 (1985), pp. 144–65.

Binney, Judith, *Redemption Songs: A Life of the Nineteenth-Century Maori Leader Te Kooti Arikirangi Te Turuki* (Melbourne: Melbourne University Press, 1997).

Bird, Phyllis, *Missing Persons and Mistaken Identities: Women and Gender in Ancient Israel* (Minneapolis: Fortress Press, 1997).

Bleakley, J.W., *The Aborigines of Australia* (Brisbane: Jacaranda Press, 1961).

Blenkinsopp, Joseph, *Sage, Priest, Prophet: Religious and Intellectual Leadership in Ancient Israel* (Louisville: Westminster John Knox, 1995).

—'The Social Context of the "Outsider Woman" in Proverbs 1–9', *Biblica* 74 (1991), pp. 457–73.

Bloch-Smith, Elizabeth, 'Israelite Ethnicity in Iron I: Archaeology Preserves What Is Remembered and What Is Forgotten in Israel's History', *Journal of Biblical Literature* 122 (2003), pp. 401–25.

—*Judahite Burial Practices and Beliefs about the Dead* (Sheffield: Sheffield Academic Press, 1992).

Boehmer, Elleke, *Colonial and Postcolonial Literature* (Oxford: Oxford University Press, 1995).

Boer, Roland, *Marxist Criticism of the Bible* (London: T. & T. Clark International, 2003).

—*Last Stop before Antarctica: The Bible and Postcolonialism in Australia* (Sheffield: Sheffield Academic Press, 2001).

Boff, Leonardo, *Jesus Christ Liberator: A Critical Christology for our Time* (Maryknoll, NY: Orbis, 1978).

Bolton, Geoffrey, *Spoils and Spoilers: Australians make their Environment 1788–1980* (Sydney: Allen & Unwin, 2nd edn 1992).

Borg, Marcus, 'A Temperate Case for a Non-Eschatological Jesus', *Forum* 2 (1986), pp. 81–102.

Boroujerdi, Mehrzad, *Iranian Intellectuals and the West: The Tormented Triumph of Nativism* (Syracuse: Syracuse University Press, 1996).

Bowman, G., 'Nationalizing the Sacred: Shrines and Shifting Identities in the Israeli-Occupied Territories', *Man: The Journal of the Royal Anthropological Institute* 28 (1993), pp. 431–460.

Boyarin, Daniel, *A Radical Jew: Paul and the Politics of Identity* (Berkeley: University of California Press, 1994).

Boyer, Robert, *The Regulation School: A Critical Introduction* (New York: Columbia University Press, 1990).

Brady, Veronica, 'Mabo: A Question of Space', *Caught in the Draught: On Contemporary Australian Culture and Society* (Sydney: Angus & Robertson, 1994), pp. 13–29.

Braulik, Georg, 'Die Völkervernichtung und die Rückkehr Israels ins Verheissungsland: Hermeneutische Bemerkungen zum Buch Deuteronomium', in M. Vervenne and J. Lust (eds.), *Deuteronomy and Deuteronomic Literature* (Leuven: Leuven University Press, 1997), pp. 33–38.

—*The Theology of Deuteronomy* (Richland Hills, TX: BIBAL Press, 1994).

Brett, Judith, 'The Treaty Process and the limits of Australian Liberalism', AIATSIS Seminar Series, 4 June, 2001. www.aiatsis.gov.au/_data/assets/pdf_file/5446/Brett.pdf.

Brett, Mark G., 'Abraham's "Heretical" Imperative: A Response to Jacques Derrida', in Charles Cosgrove (ed.), *The Meanings We Choose: Hermeneutical Ethics, Indeterminacy and the Conflict of Interpretations* (London: T. & T. Clark International, 2004), pp. 167–78.

—'Canto Ergo Sum: Indigenous Peoples and Postcolonial Theology', *Pacifica* 16 (2003), pp. 247–56.

—'Israel's Indigenous Origins: Cultural Hybridity and the Formation of Israelite Ethnicity', *Biblical Interpretation* 11 (2003), pp. 400–12.

—'Review of Roland Boer, *Last Stop before Antarctica*', *St Mark's Review* 192 (2003), pp. 43–44.

—*Genesis: Procreation and the Politics of Identity* (London: Routledge, 2000).

—'Canonical Criticism and Old Testament Theology', in A.D.H. Mayes (ed.), *Text in Context* (Oxford: Oxford University Press, 2000), pp. 63–85.

—'Interpreting Ethnicity: Method, Hermeneutics, Ethics', in M.G. Brett (ed.), *Ethnicity and the Bible* (Leiden: E.J. Brill, 1996), pp. 3–22.

—'Nationalism and the Hebrew Bible', in J.W. Rogerson, M. Davies and M.D. Carroll R. (eds.), *The Bible in Ethics* (Sheffield: Sheffield Academic Press, 1995) pp. 136–63.

Brichto, Herbert C., 'Kin, Cult, Land, and Afterlife', *Hebrew Union College Annual* 44 (1973), pp. 1–54.

Broadhead, Edwin K., 'Mark 1,44: The Witness of the Leper', *Zeitschrift für die neutestamentliche Wissenschaft* 83 (1992), pp. 257–65.

Brown, Raymond E., 'The *Pater Noster* as an Eschatological Prayer', *Theological Studies* 22 (1961), pp. 199–200.

Brown, Robert McAfee (ed.), *Kairos: Three Prophetic Challenges to the Church* (Grand Rapids: Eerdmans, 1990).

Brueggemann, Walter, *Old Testament Theology: Testimony, Dispute, Advocacy* (Minneapolis: Fortress Press, 1997).

Byrne, Brendan, 'Jesus as Messiah in the Gospel of Luke: Discerning a Pattern of Correction', *Catholic Biblical Quarterly* 65 (2003), pp. 80–95.

Byron, John, 'Paul and the Background of Slavery: The *status quaestionis* in New Testament Scholarship', *Currents in Biblical Research* 3 (2004), pp. 116–39.

Camp, Claudia, *Wise, Strange and Holy* (Sheffield: Sheffield Academic Press, 2000).

Carroll R., M. Daniel, 'The Challenge of Economic Globalization for Theology', in C. Ott and H.A. Netland (eds.), *Globalizing Theology: Belief and Practice in an Era of World Christianity* (Grand Rapids: Baker Academic, 2006), pp. 199–212.

—'Reflecting on War and Utopia: The Relevance of a Literary Reading of the Prophetic Text for Central America', in M.D. Carroll, D.J.A. Clines, and P.R. Davies (eds.), *The Bible in Human Society: Essays in Honour of John Rogerson* (Sheffield: Sheffield Academic Press, 1995), pp. 105–21.

—*Contexts for Amos* (Sheffield: Sheffield Academic Press, 1992).

Carroll, John, 'Sickness and Healing in the New Testament Gospels', *Interpretation* 49 (1995), pp. 130–42.

Carter, Charles, *The Emergence of Yehud in the Persian Period* (Sheffield: Sheffield Academic Press, 1999).

Carter, Paul, *The Lie of the Land* (London: Faber & Faber, 1996).

Carter, Warren, *Matthew and Empire: Initial Explorations* (Harrisburg, PA: Trinity Press International, 2001).

Casas, Bartolomé de las, *The Only Way to Draw All People to a Living Faith* (ed. Helen Rand; New York: Paulist Press, 1992).

Cassuto, Umberto, *Commentary on the Book of Genesis. I. From Adam to Noah, Genesis 1–6.8* (Jerusalem: Magnes Press, [1944] 1961).

Cavanaugh, William T., 'Killing for the Telephone Company: Why the Nation-State is Not the Keeper of the Common Good', *Modern Theology* 20s (2004), pp. 243–74.

—*Torture and Eucharist: Theology, Politics, and the Body of Christ* (Oxford: Blackwell, 1998).

Certeau, Michel de, *The Practice of Everyday Life* (Berkeley: University of California Press, 1984).

Chaney, Marvin, 'Whose Sour Grapes? The Addressees of Isaiah 5:1–7 in the Light of Political Economy', *Semeia* 87 (1999), pp. 105–22.

—'You shall not covet your neighbour's house', *Pacific Theological Review* 15 (1982), pp. 3–13.

Chapman, Colin, *Whose Promised Land? The Continuing Crisis over Israel and Palestine* (Grand Rapids: Baker, 2002).

Chapman, Stephen B., 'Imperial Exegesis: When Caesar Interprets Scripture', in W. Avram (ed.), *Anxious about Empire: Theological Essays on the New Global Realities* (Grand Rapids: Brazos, 2004), pp. 91–102.

Charleston, Steve, 'The Old Testament of Native America', in S.B. Thistlethwaite and M.B. Engel (eds.), *Lift Every Voice: Constructing Christian Theologies from the Underside* (San Francisco: HarperCollins, 1990), pp. 49–61.

Chatterjee, Partha, *The Nation and its Fragments: Colonial and Post-Colonial Histories* (Princeton: Princeton University Press, 1993).

—*Nationalist Thought and the Colonial World* (Minneapolis: University of Minnesota Press, 1986).

Cherry, C., *God's New Israel: Religious Interpretations of American Destiny* (Chapel Hill: University of North Carolina Press, rev. edn 1998).

Coakley, Sarah, 'Kenosis and Subversion: On the Repression of "Vulnerability" in Christian Feminist Writing', in D. Hampson (ed.), *Swallowing a Fishbone?* (London: SPCK, 1996), pp. 82–111.

Collins, John J., *The Bible after Babel: Historical Criticism in a Postmodern Age* (Grand Rapids: Eerdmans, 2005).

Comaroff, Jean and John, *Of Revelation and Revolution: Christianity, Colonialism, and Consciousness in South Africa* (Chicago: University of Chicago Press, 1991).

Condrad, Edgar, *Reading Isaiah* (Minneapolis: Fortress Press, 1991).

Connor, G.E., 'Covenants and Criticism', *Biblical Theology Bulletin* 32 (2002), pp. 4–10.

Conversi, Daniele, 'Conceptualizing Nationalism', in D. Conversi (ed.), *Ethnonationalism in the Contemporary World* (London: Routledge, 2002), pp. 1–23.

Cornell, Stephen, 'That's the Story of our Life', in P. Spickard and W. Burroughs, *We Are a People: Narrative and Multiplicity in Constructing Ethnic Identity* (Philadelphia: Temple University Press, 2000), pp. 41–53.

Cosgrove, Charles, 'Towards a Postmodern Hermeneutica Sacra', in C.H. Cosgrove (ed.), *The Meanings We Choose: Hermeneutical Ethics, Indeterminacy and the Conflict of Interpretations* (London: T. & T. Clark, 2004), pp. 39–61.

Crossan, John Dominic, *The Birth of Christianity* (San Francisco: Harper, 1999).

—*The Historical Jesus: The Life of a Mediterranean Peasant* (San Francisco: HarperCollins, 1991).

Crüsemann, Frank, *The Torah: Theology and Social History of Old Testament Law* (Edinburgh: T. & T. Clark, 1996).

Davies, W.D. and Dale C. Allison, *Matthew*, III (Edinburgh: T. & T. Clark, 1997).

Day, John, *Yahweh and the Gods and Goddesses of Canaan* (Sheffield: Sheffield Academic Press, 2000).

Derrida, Jacques, *On the Name* (Stanford: Stanford University Press, 1995).

—*The Gift of Death* (Chicago: Chicago University Press, 1995).

Dever, William, *Who Were the Early Israelites, and Where Did They Come from?* (Grand Rapids: Eerdmans, 2003).

—*What Did the Biblical Writers Know and When Did They Know it? What Archaeology can tell us about the Reality of Ancient Israel* (Grand Rapids: Eerdmans, 2001).

—'Ceramics, Ethnicity, and the Question of Israel's Origins', *Biblical Archaeologist* 58 (1995), pp. 200–213.

Dharmaraj, J.S., *Colonialism and Christian Mission: Postcolonial Reflections* (Delhi: ISPCK, 1993).

Djiniyini Gondarra, 'Aboriginal Spirituality and the Gospel' in Anne Pattel-Gray (ed.), *Aboriginal Spirituality: Past, Present, Future* (Melbourne: HarperCollins, 1996), pp.

Dodson, Michael, 'The End in the Beginning: Re(de)fining Aboriginality', *Australian Aboriginal Studies* 1 (1994), pp. 2–13.

Dodson, Patrick L., Jacinta K. Elston and Brian F. McCoy, 'Leaving Culture at the Door' *Pacifica* 19 (2006), pp. 249–64.

Donaldson, Laura, 'Son of the Forest, Child of God: William Apess and the Scene of Postcolonial Nativity', in C.R. King (ed.), *Postcolonial America* (Urbana: University of Illinois Press, 2000), pp. 201–22.

Douglas, Mary, *Jacob's Tears: The Priestly Work of Reconciliation* (Oxford: Oxford University Press, 2004).

—'Responding to Ezra: The Priests and the Foreign Wives', *Biblical Interpretation* 10 (2002), pp. 1–23.

—*Leviticus as Literature* (Oxford: Oxford University Press, 1999).

—*In the Wilderness: The Doctrine of Defilement in the Book of Numbers* (Sheffield: Sheffield Academic Press, 1993).

—*Purity and Danger* (London: Routledge, 1966).

Dove, Thomas, 'Moral and Social Characteristics of the Aborigines of Tasmania', *Tasmanian Journal of Natural Science* 1/4 (1842), pp. 247–54.

Dozeman, Thomas, 'The Wilderness and Salvation History in the Hagar Story', *Journal of Biblical Literature* 117 (1998), pp. 24–43.

Dube, Musa, 'Savior of the World but Not of This World: A Postcolonial Reading of Spatial Construction in John', in R.S. Sugirtharajah (ed.), *The Postcolonial Bible* (Sheffield: Sheffield Academic Press, 1998), pp. 118–35.

Duff, J.W. and A.M. Duff (eds.), *Minor Latin Poets* (Cambridge: Cambridge University Press, 1954).

Edwards, Denis, *Breath of Life: A Theology of the Creator Spirit* (Maryknoll, NY: Orbis, 2004).

Elias, Norbert, *The Civilizing Process* (Oxford: Blackwell, 1994).

Elliot, Neil, 'Strategies of Resistance and Hidden Transcripts in the Pauline Communities', in R. Horsley (ed.), *Hidden Transcripts and the Arts of Resistance* (Semeia Studies 48; Atlanta: Society of Biblical Literature, 2004), pp. 97–122.

—'The Anti-imperial Message of the Cross', in R. Horsley (ed.), *Paul and Empire* (Harrisburg, PA: Trinity Press International, 1997), pp. 167–83.

—'Romans 13:1–7 in the Context of Imperial Propaganda', in R. Horsley, (ed.), *Paul and Empire* (Harrisburg, PA: Trinity Press International, 1997), pp. 184–204.

Engberg-Pedersen, Troels, *Paul and the Stoics* (Edinburgh: T. & T. Clark, 2000).

Equiano, Olaudah, *The Interesting Narrative and Other Writings* (London: Penguin, [1789] 1995).

Eriksen, Thomas, *Ethnicity and Nationalism: Anthropological Perspectives* (London: Pluto, 1993).

Eskenazi, T.C., 'Out from the Shadows: Biblical Women in the Post-Exilic Era', *Journal for the Study of the Old Testament* 54 (1992), pp. 25–43.

Eskenazi, T.C., and E.P. Judd, 'Marriage to a Stranger in Ezra 9–10', in T.C. Eskenazi and K.H. Richards (eds.), *Second Temple Studies. II. Temple Community in the Persian Period* (Sheffield: JSOT Press, 1994), pp. 266–85.

Evans, R., K. Saunders, and K. Cronin, *Race Relations in Colonial Queensland: A History of Exclusion, Exploitation and Extermination* (St Lucia: University of Queensland Press, 2nd edn 1988).

Evans, W.M., 'From the Land of Canaan to the Land of Guinea: the Strange Odyssey of the "Sons of Ham"', *American Historical Review* 85/1 (1980), pp. 15–82.

Evans-Pritchard, E.E., *Nuer Religion* (Oxford: Oxford University Press, 1956).

Fejo, Wali, 'The Voice of the Earth: An Indigenous Reading of Genesis 9', in N. Habel and S. Wurst (eds.), *The Earth Story in Genesis* (Sheffield: Sheffield Academic Press, 2000), pp. 140–46.

Findlay, Merrill, 'Eddie Mabo Comes Home.' *The Age*, 1 June, 1996.

Finkelstein, Israel and Neil Silberman, *The Bible Unearthed: Archaeology's New Vision of Ancient Israel and the Origin of its Sacred Texts* (New York: Free Press, 2001).

Finkelstein, Israel, 'Pots and People Revisited: Ethnic Boundaries in the Iron Age I', in N.A. Silberman and D. Small (eds.), *The Archaeology of Israel: Constructing the Past, Interpreting the Present* (Sheffield: Sheffield Academic Press, 1997), pp. 216–37.

—'Ethnicity and Origin of the Iron I Settlers in the Highlands of Canaan: Can the Real Israel Stand Up?', *Biblical Archaeologist* 59 (1996), pp. 198–212.

Finkelstein, Norman G., *Image and Reality of the Israel–Palestine Conflict* (London: Verso, 1995).

Fishbane, Michael, *Biblical Interpretation in Ancient Israel* (Oxford: Clarendon Press, 1985).

Francis, Robert, 'From Bondage to Freedom', unpublished paper, August 2007.

Frerichs, E.S. and L.H. Lesko (eds.), *Exodus: The Egyptian Evidence* (Washington, DC: Biblical Archaeology Society, 1993).

Furrow, Dwight, *Against Theory: Continental and Analytic Challenges in Moral Philosophy* (London: Routledge, 1995).

Gandhi, Leela, *Postcolonial Theory* (St Leonards: Allen & Unwin, 1998).

Gardner, Anne, 'Ecojustice: A Study of Genesis 6.11–13', in N. Habel and S. Wurst (eds.), *The Earth Story in Genesis*, pp. 117–29.

Gauchet, M., *The Disenchantment of the World: A Political History of Religion* (Princeton: Princeton University Press, 1999).

Gellner, Ernest, *Nations and Nationalism* (Ithaca: Cornell University Press, 1983).

George E. Tinker, *Missionary Conquest: The Gospel and Native American Cultural Genocide* (Minneapolis: Fortress Press, 1993).

Girard, René, *Violence and the Sacred* (Baltimore: Johns Hopkins University Press, 1977).

Glancy, Jennifer A., *Slavery in Early Christianity* (Oxford: Oxford University Press, 2002).

Goldenberg, David, *The Curse of Ham: Race and Slavery in Early Judaism, Christianity and Islam* (Princeton: Princeton University Press, 2003).

Goldenberg, Robert, *The Nations That Knew Thee Not: Ancient Jewish Attitudes toward Other Religions* (New York: New York University Press, 1998).

Goldingay, John, *Daniel* (Waco: Word Books, 1989).

Goldstein, B.R and A. Cooper, 'The Cult of the Dead and the Theme of Entry in the Land,' *Biblical Interpretation* 1 (1993), pp. 285–303.

Gondarra, Djiniyini, *Series of Reflections on Aboriginal Religion* (Darwin: Bethel Presbytery, Uniting Church in Australia, 1996).

Goodenough, E.R., *An Introduction to Philo Judaeus* (Oxford: Blackwell, 2nd edn, 1962).

Goodman, Martin, *The Ruling Class of Judea: The Origin of the Jewish Revolt against Rome, A.D. 66–70* (Cambridge: Cambridge University Press, 1987).

Goody, Jack, *The Theft of History* (Cambridge: Cambridge University Press, 2007).

Goswami, Manu, *Producing India: From Colonial Economy to National Space* (Chicago: Chicago University Press, 2004).

Gowan, Donald, *Eschatology in the Old Testament* (Edinburgh: T. & T. Clark, 1986).

Gundry, Stanley N. (ed.), *Show Them No Mercy: Four Views on God and Canaanite Genocide* (Grand Rapids: Zondervan, 2003).

Gutiérrez, Gustavo, *Las Casas: In Search of the Poor of Jesus Christ* (Maryknoll, NY: Orbis, 1993).

—*Theology of Liberation* (Maryknoll, NY: Orbis, 1973).

Habel, Norman and Shirley Wurst (eds.), *The Earth Story in Genesis* (Sheffield: Sheffield Academic Press, 2000).

Habel, Norman, *The Land is Mine* (Minneapolis: Fortress Press, 1995).

Habermas, Jürgen, 'Israel and Athens, or to Whom Does Anamnestic Reason Belong? On Unity in Multicultural Diversity', in D. Batstone *et al.* (eds.), *Liberation Theologies, Postmodernity, and the Americas* (London: Routledge, 1997), pp. 243–52.

—*Justification and Application* (trans. C. Cronin; Oxford: Polity Press, 1993).

—*Moral Consciousness and Communicative Action* (trans. C. Lenhardt and S. Weber Nicholsen; Oxford: Polity Press, 1990).

Haller, W., *The Elect Nation: The Meaning and Relevance of Foxe's Book of Martyrs* (New York: Jonathan Cape, 1963).

Halpern, Baruch, 'The Baal (and the Asherah) in Seventh-Century Judah: YHWH's Retainers Retired', in R. Bartelmus *et al.* (eds.), *Konsequente Traditionsgeschichte: Festschrift für Klaus Baltzer* (Göttingen: Vandenhoeck & Ruprecht, 1993), pp. 115–54.

—'Jerusalem and the Lineages in the Seventh Century BCE', in B. Halpern and D.W. Hobson (eds.), *Law and Ideology in Monarchic Israel* (Sheffield: Sheffield Academic Press, 1991), pp. 11–107.

Hamilton, Mark, 'The Past as Destiny: Historical Visions in Sam'al and Judah under Assyrian Hegemony', *Harvard Theological Review* 91 (1998), pp. 215–50.

Hardt, Michael and Antonio Negri, *Empire* (Cambridge: Harvard University Press, 2000).

Harink, Douglas, *Paul among the Postliberals: Pauline Theology beyond Christendom and Modernity* (Grand Rapids: Brazos Press, 2003).

Harries, Patrick, 'The Roots of Ethnicity: Discourse and the Politics of Language Construction in South-East Africa', *African Affairs* 87 (1988), pp. 25–52.

Harris, John, *One Blood: 200 Years of Aboriginal Encounter with Christianity* (Sutherland, NSW: Albatross, 2nd edn 1994).

Harris, Marvin, *The Rise of Anthropological Theory* (London: Routledge & Kegan Paul, 1968).

Harrison, Peter, '"Fill the Earth and Subdue It": Biblical Warrants for Colonization in Seventeenth Century England', *Journal of Religious History* 29 (2005), pp. 3–24.

Hart, William D., *Edward Said and the Religious Effects of Culture* (Cambridge: Cambridge University Press, 2000).

Hasel, M.G., *Domination and Resistance: Egyptian Military Activity in the Southern Levant, ca. 1300–1185 BCE* (Leiden: E.J. Brill, 1998).

Hastings, Adrian, *The Construction of Nationhood: Ethnicity, Religion and Nationalism* (Cambridge: Cambridge University Press, 1997).

Havrelock, Rachel, 'Two Maps of Israel's Land', *Journal of Biblical Literature*, forthcoming.

Hawley, Susan, 'Does God Speak Miskitu? The Bible and Ethnic Identity among the Miskitu of Nicaragua', in M.G. Brett (ed.), *Ethnicity and the Bible* (Leiden: E.J. Brill, 1996), pp. 315–42.

Hayes, Christine, *Gentile Impurities and Jewish Identities: Intermarriage and Conversion from the Bible to the Talmud* (Oxford: Oxford University Press, 2002).

Hays, Richard, '*Pistis* and Pauline Christology: What Is at Stake?', in Elizabeth Johnson and David M. Hay (eds.), *Pauline Theology*, IV (Atlanta: Scholars Press, 1997), pp. 35–60.

—*First Corinthians* (Louisville: John Knox, 1997).

—*The Moral Vision of the New Testament* (San Francisco: HarperCollins, 1996).

Head, Lyndsay, 'The Pursuit of Identity in Maori Society: The Conceptual Basis of Citizenship in the Early Colonial Period', in A. Sharp and P. McHugh (eds.), *History, Power and Loss: Uses of the Past—A New Zealand Commentary* (Wellington: Bridget Williams, 2001), pp. 97–121.

Heard, R. Christopher, *Dynamics of Diselection: Ambiguity in Genesis 12–36 and Ethnic Boundaries in Post-Exilic Judah* (Atlanta: Society of Biblical Literature, 2001).

Hendel, Ronald S., 'Aniconism and Anthropomorphism in Ancient Israel', in K. van der Toorn (ed.), *The Image and the Book* (Leuven: Peeters, 1997), pp. 205–28.

Hengel, Martin, *Crucifixion* (London: SCM Press, 1977).

Hepburn, Samantha, 'Feudal Tenure and Native Title: Revising an Enduring Fiction', *Sydney Law Review* 27/1 (2005), pp. 49–86.

Herrmann, W., 'El', in K. van der Toorn, B. Becking and P. van der Horst (eds.), *Dictionary of Deities and Demons in the Bible* (Leiden: Brill, 1995), pp. 521–33.

Herzog, William, 'Onstage and Offstage with Jesus of Nazareth: Public Transcripts, Hidden Transcripts, and Gospel Texts', in R. Horsley (ed.), *Hidden Transcripts and the Arts of Resistance* (Semeia Studies, 48; Atlanta: Society of Biblical Literature, 2004), pp. 41–48.

—*Jesus, Justice and the Reign of God* (Louisville: Westminster John Knox, 2000).

—*Parables as Subversive Speech* (Louisville: Westminster/John Knox, 1994).

Hesse, Brian and Paula Wapnish, 'Can Pig Remains be Used for Ethnic Diagnosis in the Ancient Near East?', in Silberman and Small, *The Archaeology of Israel*, pp. 238–70.

Hester, James D., 'Socio-Rhetorical Criticism and the Parable of the Tenants', *Journal for the Study of the New Testament* 45 (1992), pp. 27–57.

Higginbotham, Carolyn R., *Egyptianization and Elite Emulation in Ramesside Palestine: Governance and Accommodation on the Imperial Periphery* (Leiden: E.J. Brill, 2000).

Hill, Barry, *Broken Song: T.G.H. Strehlow and Aboriginal Possession* (Sydney: Vintage, 2002).

Hobsbawm, Eric, *Nations and Nationalism since 1780: Programme, Myth, Reality* (Cambridge: Cambridge University Press, 1990).

Hoffman, Yair, 'The Deuteronomistic Concept of the *Herem*', *Zeitschrift für die alttestamentliche Wissenschaft* 111 (1999), pp. 196–210.

Hoglund, Kenneth, *Achaemenid Imperial Administration in Syria–Palestine and the Missions of Ezra and Nehemiah* (Atlanta: Scholars Press, 1992).

Honneth, Axel, 'The Other of Justice: Habermas and the Ethical Challenge of Postmodernism', in S.K. White (ed.), *The Cambridge Companion to Habermas* (Cambridge: Cambridge University Press, 1995), pp.

Horrell, David, *Solidarity and Difference: A Contemporary Reading of Paul's Ethics* (London: T. & T. Clark International, 2005).

Horsley, Richard (ed.), *Hidden Transcripts and the Arts of Resistance* (Semeia Studies 48; Atlanta: Society of Biblical Literature, 2004).

—*Paul and Empire* (Harrisburg, PA: Trinity Press International, 1997).

Horsley, Richard, *Galilee: History, Politics, People* (Valley Forge, PA: Trinity Press International, 1995).

—*Jesus and the Spiral of Violence: Popular Jewish Resistance in Roman Palestine* (San Francisco: Harper & Row, 1987).

Hoy, David, 'Is Hermeneutics Ethnocentric?', in J.F. Bohman, D.R. Hiley, and R. Shusterman (eds.), *The Interpretive Turn: Philosophy, Science, Culture* (Ithaca: Cornell University Press, 1991), pp. 155–75.

Jackson, Helen Hunt, *A Century of Dishonour* (Cambridge: Cambridge University Press, 1885).

Japhet, Sara, 'Theodicy in Ezra–Nehemiah and Chronicles', in A. Laato and J.C. de Moor (eds.), *Theodicy in the World of the Bible* (Leiden: Brill, 2004), pp. 429–69.

—'People and Land in the Restoration Period', in Georg Strecker (ed.), *Das Land Israel in biblischer Zeit* (Göttingen: Vandenhoeck & Ruprecht, 1983), pp. 112–15.

—*The Ideology of the Book of Chronicles and its Place in Biblical Thought* (Frankfurt: Peter Lang, 1980).

Johnstone, William, 'Old Testament Expressions in Property Holding' *Ugaritica* 6 (1969), pp. 308–17.

Joosten, Jan, *People and Land in the Holiness Code* (Leiden: Brill, 1996).

Jordan, Ivan, *Their Way: Towards an Indigenous Warlpiri Christianity* (Darwin: Charles Darwin University, 2003).

Kaggia, Bildad, *Roots of Freedom 1921–1963: The Autobiography of Bildad Kaggia* (Nairobi: East African Publishing House, 1975).

Kallis, Anastasios, 'Presidency at the Eucharist in the Context of the Theology of Icons: Questions about the Ecclesial Representation of Christ by the Priesthood', *Anglican Theological Review* 84 (2002), pp. 713–29.

Kang, Sa-Moon, *Divine War in the Old Testament and in the Ancient Near East* (Berlin: de Gruyter, 1989).

Kee, Howard Clark, 'The Terminology of Mark's Exorcism Stories', *New Testament Studies* 14 (1968), pp. 232–46.

Keith, Michael and Steve Pile, *Place and the Politics of Identity* (New York: Routledge, 1993).

Keller, C., M. Nausner and M. Rivera (eds.), *Postcolonial Theologies: Divinity and Empire* (St Louis: Chalice Press, 2004).

Kenny, Robert, *The Lamb Enters the Dreaming: Nathanael Pepper and the Ruptured World* (Melbourne: Scribe, 2007).

Kent, James, *Commentaries on American Law* (Boston: Little, Brown, 11th edn, 1867).

Kenzo, Mabiala Justin-Robert, 'Religion, Hybridity, and the Construction of Reality in Postcolonial Africa', *Exchange* 33 (2004), pp. 244–68.

Khalidi, Rashid, *Palestinian Identity: The Construction of Modern National Consciousness* (New York: Columbia University Press, 1997).

Kidd, R., *The Way We Civilize: Aboriginal Affairs—The Untold Story* (St Lucia: University of Queensland Press, 1997).

Kidwell, Clara Sue, Homer Noley and George E. "Tink" Tinker, *Native American Theology* (Maryknoll, NY: Orbis, 2001).

Killebrew, Ann E., *Biblical Peoples and Ethnicity: An Archaeological Study of Egyptians, Canaanites, Philistines and Early Israel 1300–1100 BCE* (Atlanta: Society of Biblical Literature, 2005).

Kim, Tae Hun, 'The Anarthrous *uios theou* in Mark 15:39 and the Roman Imperial Cult', *Biblica* 79 (1998), pp. 221–41.

King, Richard, *Orientalism and Religion: Postcolonial Theory, India and 'the mystic East'* (London: Routledge, 1999).

Knohl, Israel, *The Sanctuary of Silence* (Minneapolis: Fortress Press, 1995).

Knoppers, Gary N. and Bernard M. Levinson, *The Pentateuch as Torah: New Models for Understanding its Promulgation and Acceptance* (Winona Lake: Eisenbrauns, 2007).

Koester, Helmut, 'Imperial Ideology and Paul's Eschatology in 1 Thessalonians', in Horsley (ed.), *Paul and Empire*, pp. 158–62.

Langton, Marcia, Odette Mazel, Lisa Palmer, Kathryn Shain and Maureen Tehan (eds.), *Settling with Indigenous Peoples* (Sydney: Federation Press, 2006).

Langton, Marcia, 'Urbanizing Aborigines', *Social Alternatives* 12/2 (1981), pp. 16–22.

Lemche, Niels P., *The Israelites in History and Tradition* (Louisville: Westminster John Knox, 1998).

Levenson, Jon D., *Resurrection and the Restoration of Israel: The Ultimate Victory of the God of Life* (New Haven: Yale University Press, 2006).

—'The Universal Horizon of Biblical Particularism', in M.G. Brett (ed.), *Ethnicity and the Bible* (Leiden: Brill, 1996), pp. 143–69.

—*The Hebrew Bible, the Old Testament and Historical Criticism* (Louisville: Westminster/ John Knox, 1993).

Levinas, Emmanuel, *In the Time of the Nations* (Bloomington: Indiana University Press, 1994).

—*Otherwise than Being, or, Beyond Essence* (trans. A. Lingis; Dordrecht: Kluwer, 1991).

—*Noms propres* (Montpellier: Fata Morgana, 1976).

Levinson, Bernard M., 'Textual Criticism, Assyriology, and the History of Interpretation: Deuteronomy 13:7 as a Test Case in Method', *Journal of Biblical Literature* 120 (2001), pp. 238–41.

—*Deuteronomy and the Hermeneutics of Legal Innovation* (New York: Oxford University Press, 1997).

Lewis, Bernard, 'The Crows of the Arabs', in H.L. Gates (ed.), '*Race*', *Writing and Difference* (Chicago: Chicago University Press, 1986), pp. 111–12.

Lewis, T.J., 'The Ancestral Estate (נחלת אלהים) in 2 Samuel 14:16', *Journal of Biblical Literature* 110 (1991), pp. 597–612.

—*Cults of the Dead in Ancient Israel and Ugarit* (Atlanta: Scholars Press, 1989).

Lind, Millard, *Yahweh is a Warrior* (Scottdale, PA: Herald Press, 1980).

Lindbeck, George, *The Nature of Doctrine: Religion and Theology in a Postliberal Age* (Philadelphia: Westminster Press, 1984).

Lohfink, Norbert, *Studien zum Deuteronomium und zur deuteronomistischen Literatur*, III (Stuttgart: Katholisches Bibelwerk, 1995).

—*Theology of the Pentateuch* (Edinburgh: T. & T. Clark, 1994).

—*Gewalt und Gewaltlosigkeit im Alten Testament* (Freiberg: Herder, 1983).

—'Die Bedeutungen von hebr. *jrs qal* und *hif*', *Biblische Zeitschrift* 27 (1983), pp. 23–24.

Lonsdale, J., 'Kikuyu Christianities', *Journal of Religion in Africa* 29/2 (1999), pp. 206–29.

Lyons, Claire L. and John K. Papadopoulos (eds.), *The Archaeology of Colonialism* (Los Angeles: Getty Research Institute, 2002).

MacIntyre, Alasdair, *After Virtue* (Notre Dame: University of Notre Dame Press, 1981).

Maddox, Marion, 'How Late Night Theology Sparked a Royal Commission', *Sophia* 36/2 (1997), pp. 111–35.

Mafico, Temba, 'The Biblical God of the Fathers and the African Ancestors', in G. West and M.W. Dube (eds.), *The Bible in Africa: Transactions, Trajectories and Trends* (Leiden: Brill, 2000), pp. 481–89.

McGlade, Hannah, 'Native Title, "Tides of History" and Our Continuing Claims for Justice', in Australian Institute of Aboriginal and Torres Strait Islander Studies, *Treaty: Let's Get It Right* (Canberra: Aboriginal Studies Press, 2003), pp. 118–36.

McIntosh, Ian, *The Whale and the Cross: Conversations with David Burrumarra* (Darwin: Historical Society of the Northern Territory, 1994).

McKinlay, Judith, *Reframing Her: Biblical Women in Postcolonial Focus* (Sheffield: Sheffield Phoenix Press, 2004).

McNutt, Paula, *Reconstructing the Society of Ancient Israel* (Louisville: Westminster John Knox, 1999).

McPhee, Peter, *A Social History of France 1780–1880* (London: Routledge, 1992).

Mendenhall, George, and Gary Herion, 'Covenant', in *Anchor Bible Dictionary*, I (New York: Doubleday, 1992), pp. 1180–83.

Milbank, John, *The World Made Strange: Theology, Language, Culture* (Oxford: Basil Blackwell, 1977).

Milgrom, Jacob, *Leviticus 17–22* (New York: Doubleday, 2000).

Miller, Robert (ed.), *The Apocalyptic Jesus: A Debate* (Santa Rosa, CA: Polebridge Press, 2001).

Min, Anselm Kyonsuk, *The Solidarity of Others in a Divided World: A Postmodern Theology after Postmodernism* (London: T. & T. Clark International, 2004).

Moberly, R.W.L., '"Yahweh is One": The Translation of the Shema', in J.A. Emerton (ed.), *Studies in the Pentateuch* (Leiden: E.J. Brill, 1990), pp. 209–15.

—'Toward an Interpretation of the Shema', in C. Seitz and K. Greene-McCreight (eds.), *Theological Exegesis* (Grand Rapids: Eerdmans, 1999), pp. 135–37.

—*The Old Testament of the Old Testament* (Minneapolis: Fortress Press, 1992).

Moltmann, Jürgen, 'Ancestor Respect and the Hope of Resurrection', *Sino-Christian Studies* 1 (2006), pp. 13–36.

—'God's Kenosis in the Creation and Consummation of the World', in J. Polkinghorne (ed.), *The Work of Love: Creation as Kenosis* (Grand Rapids: Eerdmans, 2001), pp. 137–51.

—*God in Creation: An Ecological Doctrine of Creation* (London: SCM Press, 1985).

Moore, Stephen D. and Fernando Segovia (eds.), *Postcolonial Biblical Criticism: Interdisciplinary Intersections* (Edinburgh: T. & T. Clark International 2005).

Moran, William, 'The Ancient Near Eastern Background to the Love of God in Deuteronomy', *Catholic Biblical Quarterly* 25 (1963), pp. 77–87.

Morris, Benny, *Righteous Victims: A History of the Zionist–Arab Conflict, 1881–1999* (London: John Murray, 1999).

Myers, Ched, *Binding the Strong Man: A Political Reading of Mark's Story of Jesus* (Maryknoll, NY: Orbis, 1988).

Nandy, Ashis, *The Intimate Enemy: Loss and Recovery of Self under Colonialism* (Delhi: Oxford University Press, 1983).

Neale, Margo, *Urban Dingo: The Art and Life of Lin Onus 1948–1996* (Brisbane: Queensland Art Gallery, 2000).

Nelson, Richard, '*Ḥerem* and the Deuteronomic Social Conscience', in M. Vervenne and J. Lust (eds.), *Deuteronomy and Deuteronomic Literature* (Leuven: Leuven University Press, 1997), pp. 41–46.

Neusner, Jacob, *The Rabbinic Traditions about the Pharisees before 70. Part 1. The Masters* (Leiden: E.J. Brill, 1971).

Niditch, Susan, *Oral World and Written Word: Ancient Israelite Literature* (Louisville: Westminster John Knox, 1996).

—*War in the Hebrew Bible* (Oxford: Oxford University Press, 1993).

O'Connell, Barry (ed.), *On our Own Ground: The Complete Works of William Apess, a Pequot* (Amherst: University of Massachusetts Press, 1992).

Oded, B., 'The Table of Nations (Genesis 10): A Socio-Cultural Approach', *Zeitschrift für die alttestamentliche Wissenschaft* 98 (1986), pp. 14–31.

Ogden, Schubert, 'Theology and Biblical Interpretation', *Journal of Religion* 76 (1996), pp. 172–88.

Ollenburger, Ben, '"If Mortals Die, Will They Live Again?" The Old Testament and Resurrection', *Ex auditu* 9 (1993), pp. 29–44.

—*Zion the City of the Great King: A Theological Symbol of the Jerusalem Cult* (Sheffield: JSOT Press, 1987).

Olley, John, 'Mixed Blessings for Animals', in N. Habel and S. Wurst (eds.), *The Earth Story in Genesis* (Sheffield: Sheffield Academic Press, 2000), pp. 130–39.

Olyan, Saul, *Rites and Rank: Hierarchy in Biblical Representations of Cult* (Princeton: Princeton University Press, 2000).

Oren, Eliezer (ed.), *The Sea Peoples and their World: A Reassessment* (Philadelphia: University Museum, 2000).

Otto, Eckart, 'Political Theology in Judah and Assyria', *Svensk exegetisk årsbok* 65 (2000), pp. 59–76.

—'Human Rights: The Influence of the Hebrew Bible', *Journal of Northwest Semitic Languages* 25 (1999), pp. 1–14.

—*Das Deuteronomium: Politische Theologie und Rechtsreform in Juda und Assyrien* (Berlin: de Gruyter, 1999).

Parpolo, Simo and Kazuko Watanabe (eds.), *Neo-Assyrian Treaties and Loyalty Oaths* (State Archives of Assyria, 2; Helsinki: Helsinki University Press, 1988).

Pattel-Gray, Anne, *The Great White Flood: Racism in Australia* (Atlanta: Scholars Press, 1998).

—(ed.), *Aboriginal Spirituality: Past, Present, Future* (Melbourne: HarperCollins, 1996).

Patterson, Orlando, *Slavery and Social Death* (Cambridge, MA: Harvard University Press, 1982).

Paulson, Graham, 'Towards an Aboriginal Theology', *Pacifica* 19 (2006), pp. 310–11.

Pearson, G., *The Deviant Imagination* (London: Macmillan, 1975).

Perkinson, Jim, 'A Canaanite Word in the Logos of Christ', in Laura Donaldson (ed.), *Postcolonialism and Scriptural Reading* (Semeia, 75; Atlanta: Scholars Press, 1996), pp. 61–85.

Peterson, Derek, 'The Rhetoric of the Word: Bible Translation and Mau Mau in Colonial Central Kenya', in Brian Stanley (ed.), *Missions, Nationalism and the End of Empire* (Grand Rapids: Eerdmans, 2003), pp. 165–79.

Pfitzner, Victor J., *Paul and the Agon Motif* (Leiden: Brill, 1967).

Povinelli, Elizabeth, *The Cunning of Recognition* (Durham: Duke University Press, 2002).

Pratt, Mary Louise, 'Transculturation and Autoethnography: Peru 1615–1980', in F. Barker *et al.* (eds.), *Colonial Discourse/ Postcolonial Theory* (Manchester: Manchester University Press, 1994), pp. 24–47.

Provan, Iain, V. Philips Long and Tremper Longman, *A Biblical History of Israel* (Louisville: Westminster John Knox, 2003).

Pui-lan, Kwok, *Postcolonial Imagination and Feminist Theology* (Louisville: Westminster John Knox, 2005).

Pury, Albert de, 'Abraham: The Priestly Writer's "Ecumenical" Ancestor', in S.L. McKenzie, T. Romer and H.H. Schmid (eds.), *Rethinking the Foundations* (Berlin: Walter de Gruyter, 2000), pp. 163–81.

Putnam, Hilary, 'Levinas and Judaism', in S. Critchley and R. Bernasconi (eds.), *The Cambridge Companion to Levinas* (Cambridge: Cambridge University Press, 2002), pp. 33–62.

Rainbow Spirit Elders, *Rainbow Spirit Theology* (Melbourne: Harper Collins Religious, 1997).

Ranger, Terence, 'Christianity and the First Peoples: Some Second Thoughts', in P. Brock (ed.), *Indigenous Peoples and Religious Change* (Leiden: E.J. Brill, 2005), pp. 15–32.

Reid, Barbara E., 'Violent Endings in Matthew's Parables and Christian Nonviolence', *Catholic Biblical Quarterly* 66 (2004), pp. 237–55.

Rendtorff, 'Noah, Abraham and Moses: God's Covenant Partners', in E. Ball (ed.), *In Search of True Wisdom: Essays in Old Testament Interpretation in Honour of Ronald E. Clements* (Sheffield: Sheffield Academic Press, 1999), pp. 127–36.

—The Ger in the Priestly Laws of the Pentateuch', in M.G. Brett (ed.), *Ethnicity and the Bible* (Leiden: E.J. Brill, 1996), pp. 77–87.

Reventlow, H., Graf, *The Authority of the Bible and the Rise of the Modern World* (London: SCM Press, 1984).

Reynolds, Henry, *The Law of the Land* (Melbourne: Penguin, 2nd edn, 1992).

—*This Whispering in our Hearts* (St Leonards: Allen & Unwin, 1998).

Richard, Pablo, 'Biblical Interpretation from the Perspective of Indigenous Cultures of Latin America (Mayas, Kunas and Quechuas)', in Brett, M.G. (ed.), *Ethnicity and the Bible* (Leiden: E.J. Brill, 1996), pp. 297–314.

Ringe, Sharon, *Jesus, Liberation, and the Biblical Jubilee* (Philadelphia: Fortress Press, 1985).

Rivera, Louis N., *A Violent Evangelism: The Political and Religious Conquest of the Americas* (Louisville: Westminster John Knox, 1992).

Rofé, Alexander, *Introduction to the Composition of the Pentateuch* (Sheffield: Sheffield Academic Press, 1999).

—'The Laws of Warfare in the Book of Deuteronomy: Their Origins, Intent, and Positivity', *Journal for the Study of the Old Testament* 22 (1985), pp. 23–44.

—'The Vineyard of Naboth: The Origin and Message of the Story', *Vetus Testamentum* 38 (1988), pp. 89–104.

Rogerson, J.W., 'Frontiers and Borders in the Old Testament', in E. Ball (ed.), *In Search of True Wisdom: Essays in Old Testament Interpretation in Honour of Ronald E. Clements* (Sheffield: Sheffield Academic Press, 1999), pp. 116–26.

Rorty, Richard, 'What Is Religion's Future after Metaphysics?', in Santiago Zabala (ed.), *The Future of Religion: Richard Rorty and Gianni Vattimo* (New York: Columbia University Press, 2005), pp. 60–61.

Rose, Deborah Bird, *Reports from a Wild Country: Ethics for Decolonisation* (Sydney: UNSW Press, 2004).

—'Pentecostal Missionaries and the Exit from Religion', paper delivered at the Bible and Critical Theory Seminar, Melbourne, June 2004.

—'Rupture and the Ethics of Care in Colonized Space', in T. Bonyhady and T. Griffiths (eds.), *Prehistory to Politics* (Melbourne: Melbourne University Press, 1996), pp. 190–215.

—'Consciousness and Responsibility in an Australian Aboriginal Religion', in W.H. Edwards (ed.), *Traditional Aboriginal Society* (Melbourne: Macmillan, 2nd edn, 1998), pp. 239–51.

Rost, L., *Das kleine Credo und andere Studien zum Alten Testament* (Heidelberg: Quelle & Meyer, 1965).

Rowley, H.H., *The Missionary Message of the Old Testament* (London: Carey Press, 1944).

Rozema, Vicki (ed.), *Voices from the Trail of Tears* (Winston–Salem, NC: John F. Blair, 2003).

Rüterswörden, Udo, *Von der politischen Gemeinschaft zur Gemeinde: Studien zu Dt. 16,18–18,22* (Frankfurt: Athenaeum, 1987).

Sachs, Jeffrey, *The End of Poverty: Economic Possibilities for our Time* (New York: Penguin, 2005).

Sacks, Jonathan, *The Dignity of Difference: How to Avoid the Clash of Civilizations* (London: Continuum, 2nd edn, 2003).

Sahlins, Marshall, *How 'Natives' Think about Captain Cook, for Example* (Chicago: Chicago University Press, 1995).

Said, Edward, *Reflections on Exile, and Other Literary and Cultural Essays* (London: Granta, 2000).

—*The End of the Peace Process* (New York: Pantheon, 2000).

—*Culture and Imperialism* (New York: Random House, 1993).

—*Orientalism: Western Conceptions of the Orient* (Harmondsworth: Penguin, 1978).

Saldarini, Anthony, *Pharisees, Scribes and Sadducees in Palestinian Society* (Wilmington, DC: Glazier, 2001).

Sanders, Paul, *The Provenance of Deuteronomy 32* (Leiden: Brill, 1996).

Sanneh, Lamin, *Translating the Message* (Maryknoll, NY: Orbis, 1989).

Sauter, Friedrich, *Der römische Kaiserkult bei Martial and Statius* (Stuttgart: Kohlhammer, 1934).

Schäfer-Lichtenberger, Christa, 'Bedeutung und Funktion von *Herem* in biblisch-hebräischen Texten', *Biblische Zeitschrift* 39 (1994), pp. 27–75.

Schapera, I. (ed.), *David Livingstone: South African Papers 1849–1853* (Cape Town: Van Riebeeck Society, 1974).

Schmidt, Brian B., 'Memory as Immortality', in A.J. Avery-Peck and J. Neusner (eds.), *Judaism in Late Antiquity. Part 4. Death, Life-after-Death, Resurrection and the World-to-Come in the Judaisms of Antiquity* (Leiden: Brill, 2000), pp. 87–100.

Scholem, Gershom, *Major Trends in Jewish Mysticism* (New York: Schocken Books, 1946).

Schrage, Wolfgang, *Der Erste Brief an die Korinther*, II (Zurich: Benziger Verlag, 1995).

Schreiter, Robert J., *The New Catholicity* (Maryknoll, NY: Orbis, 1997).

Schüssler-Fiorenza, Elizabeth, *In Memory of Her* (New York: Crossroad, 1983).

Schwartz, Baruch J., 'Reexamining the Fate of the "Canaanites" in the Torah Traditions', in C. Cohen, A. Hurvitz and S.M. Paul (eds.), *Sefer Moshe: The Moshe Weinfeld Jubilee Volume* (Winona Lake: Eisenbrauns, 2004), pp. 151–70.

Scott, James, *Domination and the Arts of Resistance: Hidden Transcripts* (New Haven: Yale University Press, 1990).

Scott, Kenneth, *The Imperial Cult under the Flavians* (Stuttgart: Kohlhammer, 1936).

Seesengood, Robert Paul, 'Hybridity and the Rhetoric of Endurance: Reading Paul's Athletic Metaphors in a Context of Postcolonial Self-Construction', *The Bible and Critical Theory* 1/3 (2005), pp. 1–23.

Segovia, Fernando, 'The Gospel of John', in F.F. Segovia and R.S. Sugirtharajah (eds.), *A Postcolonial Commentary on the New Testament* (London: T. & T. Clark International, forthcoming).

—'The Counterempire of God: Postcolonialism and John', *Princeton Seminary Bulletin* 27/2 (2006), pp. 82–99.

—' "And they began to speak in other tongues": Competing Modes of Discourse in Contemporary Biblical Criticism', in F.F. Segovia and M.A. Tolbert (eds.), *Reading from this Place*, I (Minneapolis: Fortress Press, 1995), pp. 29–30.

Sen, Amartya, *Identity and Violence* (New York: W.W. Norton, 2006).

Sepúlveda, Juan Ginés de, *Tratado sobre las justas causas de la guerra contra los indios* (Mexico City: Fondo de Cultura Económica, 1979).

Shah, A.B., *The Letters and Correspondence of Pandita Ramabai* (Bombay: Maharashtra State Board for Literature and Culture, 1977).

Simkins, Ronald, 'Patronage and the Political Economy of Ancient Israel', *Semeia* 87 (1999), pp. 123–44.

Simons, Margaret, *The Hindmarsh Island Affair: The Meeting of the Waters* (Sydney: Hodder, 2003).

Skinner, L., 'Law and Justice for the Queensland Colony', *Royal Historical Society of Queensland Journal* 9/3 (1971–72), pp. 94–106.

Smith, Mark, *The Origins of Biblical Monotheism* (Oxford: Oxford University Press, 2001).

—*The Early History of God: Yahweh and the Other Deities in Ancient Israel* (San Francisco: Harper & Row, 1990).

Smith-Christopher, Daniel, *A Biblical Theology of Exile* (Minneapolis: Fortress Press, 2002).

Smith, Daniel, *The Religion of the Landless: The Social Context of the Babylonian Exile* (Bloomington: Meyer–Stone, 1989).

Snow, A.H., *The Question of Aborigines* (Washington, DC: Government Printing Office, 1919).

Sommer, Benjamin, 'Unity and Plurality in Jewish Canons', in C. Helmer and C. Landmesser (eds.), *One Scripture or Many? Canon from Biblical, Theological and Philosophical Perspectives* (Oxford: Oxford University Press, 2004), pp. 108–50.

Sparks, Kenton L., *Ethnicity and Identity in Ancient Israel* (Winona Lake: Eisenbrauns, 1998).

Sperling, S. David, 'Joshua 24 Re-examined', in G.N. Knoppers and J. Gordon McConville (eds.), *Reconsidering Israel and Judah* (Winona Lake: Eisenbrauns, 2000), pp. 240–58.

Spina, Frank, 'The "Ground" for Cain's Rejection', *Zeitschrift für die alttestamentliche Wissenschaft* 104 (1992), pp. 319–32.

Stager, Lawrence, 'Forging an Identity: The Emergence of Ancient Israel', in M.D. Coogan (ed.), *The Oxford History of the Biblical World* (New York: Oxford University Press, 1998), pp. 113–28.

—*Ashkelon Discovered* (Washington, DC: Biblical Archaeology Society, 1991).

Staley, Jeffrey L., 'Dis Place Man', in M.W. Dube and J. Staley (eds.), *John and Postcolonialism* (London: Continuum, 2002), pp. 32–50

Stanley, Brian, *The Bible and the Flag: Protestant Missions and British Imperialism in the Nineteenth and Twentieth Centuries* (London: Apollos, 1990).

Stavrakopoulou, Francesca, 'Bones, Burials and Boundaries in the Hebrew Bible', paper presented at the British Society for Old Testament Studies meeting, Durham, 2006.

Steck, O.H., 'The Jerusalem Conceptions of Peace', in P. Yoder and W. Swartley (eds.) *The Meaning of Peace* (Louisville: Westminster John Knox, 1992), pp. 49–68.

Steymans, Hans Ulrich, *Deuteronomium 28 und die adê zur Thronfolgeregelung Asarhaddons: Segen und Fluch im Alten Orient und in Israel* (Göttingen: Vandenhoeck & Ruprecht, 1995).

Strehlow, T.G.H., *Central Australian Religion: Personal Monototemism in a Polytotemic Community* (Bedford Park, South Australia: Australian Association for the Study of Religions, 1978).

Strelein, Lisa, *Compromised Jurisprudence: Native Title Cases since Mabo* (Canberra: Aboriginal Studies Press, 2006).

Stringfellow, Thornton, 'The Bible Argument: Or, Slavery in the Light of Divine Revelation', in E.N. Elliot (ed.), *Cotton is King, and Pro-Slavery Arguments. Comprising the Writings of Hammond, Harper, Christy, Stringfellow, Hodge, Bledsoe and Cartwright on This Important Subject* (Augusta, GA: Pritchard, Abbott & Loomis, 1860), pp. 461–91.

Sugirtharajah, R.S., *Postcolonial Reconfigurations* (London: SCM Press, 2003).

—*The Bible and the Third World: Precolonial, Colonial and Postcolonial Encounters* (Cambridge: Cambridge University Press, 2001).

—*Asian Biblical Hermeneutics and Postcolonialism* (Sheffield: Sheffield Academic Press, 1998).

Sutton, Peter, 'On Feeling Reconciled'. Public lecture delivered at the Australian Catholic University, Melbourne, 13 June, 2007. Available at http://wwwling.arts.kuleuven.be/fll/eldp/sutton/index.html.

Swanson, Tod D., 'To Prepare a Place: Johannine Christianity and the Collapse of Ethnic Territory', *Journal of the American Academy of Religion* (1994), pp. 241–63.

Swartley, Willard (ed.), *Violence Renounced: René Girard, Biblical Studies and Peacemaking* (Scottdale, PA: Pandora, 2000).

Tacey, David, *ReEnchantment* (Sydney: HarperCollins, 2000).

Tanner, Kathryn, *Theories of Culture: A New Agenda for Theology* (Minneapolis: Fortress Press, 1997).

Tatz, Colin, *With Intent to Destroy: Reflecting on Genocide* (London: Verso, 2003).

Taylor, 'Who's Your Mob?—The Politics of Aboriginal Identity and the Implications for a Treaty', in Australian Institute of Aboriginal and Torres Strait Islander Studies, *Treaty: Let's Get it Right* (Canberra: Aboriginal Studies Press, 2003).

Taylor, Charles, *A Secular Age* (Cambridge, MA: Belknap Press, 2007).

—'The Politics of Recognition', in A. Gutman (ed.), *Multiculturalism and 'The Politics of Recognition'* (Princeton: Princeton University Press, 1992), pp. 25–73.

—*Sources of the Self: The Making of the Modern Identity* (Cambridge: Cambridge University Press, 1990).

—*Philosophy and the Human Sciences* (Cambridge: Cambridge University Press, 1985).

Thiselton, Anthony C., *The Two Horizons* (Grand Rapids: Eerdmans, 1980).

Thomas, M.M., *The Acknowledged Christ of the Indian Renaissance* (London: SCM Press, 1969).

Tinker, George E., *Missionary Conquest: The Gospel and Native American Genocide* (Minneapolis: Fortress Press, 1993).

Tlhagale, B., 'Culture in an Apartheid Society', *Journal of Theology for Southern Africa* 51 (1985), pp. 27–36.

Todorov, Tzvetan, *The Conquest of America: The Question of the Other* (New York: Harper & Row, 1984).

Toit, A. du, 'Puritans in Africa? Afrikaner "Calvinism" and Kyperian Neo-Calvinism in Late Nineteenth Century South Africa', *Comparative Studies in Society and History* 27 (1985), pp. 209–40.

Tollefson, D. and H.G.M. Williamson. 'Nehemiah as Cultural Revitalization: An Anthropological Perspective', *Journal for the Study of the Old Testament* 56 (1992), pp. 41–68.

Toorn, Karel van der, *Family Religion in Babylonia, Syria and Israel* (Leiden: Brill, 1996).

Tov, Emmanuel, *Textual Criticism of the Hebrew Bible* (Minneapolis: Fortress Press, 2nd edn, 2001).

Treat, James (ed.), *Native and Christian: Indigenous Voices on Religious Identity in the United States and Canada* (New York: Routledge, 1996).

Trible, Phyllis, *Texts of Terror* (Philadelphia: Fortress Press, 1984).

Turner, David, H., 'The Incarnation of Nambirrirrma', in T. Swain and D.B. Rose (eds.), *Aboriginal Australians and Christian Missions* (Bedford Park, South Australia: Australian Association for the Study of Religions, 1988), pp. 470–84.

—*Life before Genesis: A Conclusion* (New York: Peter Lang, 2nd edn, 1987).

Uyangoda, Jayadeva, 'Understanding Ethnicity and Nationalism', *Ecumenical Review* 47/2 (1995), pp. 225–31.

Vanhoozer, Kevin, 'One Rule to Rule Them All?', in C. Ott and H.A. Netland (eds.), *Globalizing Theology: Belief and Practice in an Era of World Christianity* (Grand Rapids: Baker Academic, 2006), pp. 85–126.

Varzon-Morel, Petronella (ed.), *Warlpiri kamta kamta—kurlangu yimi Warlpiri Women's Voices* (Alice Springs: IAD Press, 1995).

Vattimo, Gianni, *Belief* (Cambridge: Polity Press, 1999).

Veer, Peter van der, *Imperial Encounters: Religion and Modernity in India and Britain* (Princeton: Princeton University Pres, 2001).

Veling, Terry, 'In the Name of Who? Levinas and the Other Side of Theology', *Pacifica* 12 (1999), pp. 275–92.

Verboom, W., 'The Netherlands as the Second Israel', in E.A.J.G. van der Borght *et al.* (eds.), *Faith and Ethnicity*, II (Zoetermeer: Meinema, 2002), pp. 93–108.

Volf, Miroslav, *Exclusion and Embrace: A Theological Exploration of Identity, Otherness, and Reconciliation* (Nashville: Abingdon, 1996).

Wan, Sze-kar, 'Does Diaspora Identity Imply Some Sort of Universality? An Asian-American Reading of Galatians', in Fernando Segovia (ed.), *Interpreting beyond Borders* (Sheffield: Sheffield Academic Press, 2000), pp. 107–33.

Ward, Graham, 'Kenosis and Naming: Beyond Analogy and towards *allegoria amoris*', in P. Heelas (ed.), *Religion, Modernity and Postmodernity* (Oxford: Blackwell, 1998), pp. 233–57.

Ward, William, *A View of the History, Literature, and Mythology of the Hindus*, III (London: Black, Kingsbury, Parbury & Allen, 1820).

Washington, Harold, 'Israel's Holy Seed and the Foreign Women', *Biblical Interpretation* 11(2003), pp. 427–37.

—'The Strange Woman of Proverbs 1–9 and Post-Exilic Judean Society', in T.C. Eskenazi and K. Richards, *Second Temple Studies*, II, pp. 217–42. [FULL DETAILS NEEDED!!!]

Watson, Francis, 'Liberating the Reader', in Watson (ed.), *The Open Text: New Directions for Biblical Studies?* (London: SCM Press, 1993), pp. 57–84.

Watts, James W. (ed.), *Persia and Torah: The Theory of Imperial Authorization of the Pentateuch* (Atlanta: Scholars Press, 2001).

Weaver, Jace, 'From I-Hermeneutics to We-Hermeneutics: Native Americans and the Post-Colonial', in Laura Donaldson (ed.), *Postcolonialism and Scriptural Reading* (Semeia, 75; Atlanta: Scholars Press, 1996), pp. 153–76.

Weiner, James F., 'Diaspora, Materialism, Tradition: Anthropological Issues in the Recent High Court Appeal of the Yorta Yorta', in *Land, Rights, Laws: Issues of Native Title*. Issues Paper 18 (2002) available at www.aiatsis.gov.au/rsrch/ntru/ntpapers/IPv2n18/pdf. Accessed 1/1/08.

Weinfeld, Moshe, 'The Ban on the Canaanites in the Biblical Codes and its Historical Development', in A. Lemaire and B. Otzen (eds.), *History and Traditions of Early Israel* (Leiden: E.J. Brill, 1993), pp. 142–60.

—*The Promise of the Land: The Inheritance of the Land of Canaan by the Israelites* (Berkeley: University of California, 1993).

—*Deuteronomy 1–11* (New York: Doubleday, 1991).

—'The Protest against Imperialism in Ancient Israelite Prophecy' in Samuel N. Eisenstadt (ed.), *The Origin and Diversity of Axial Age Civilizations* (Albany: State University of New York Press, 1986), pp. 169–82.

—*Deuteronomy and the Deuteronomic School* (Oxford: Clarendon Press, 1972).

Wenham, Gordon, 'The Religion of the Patriarchs', in A. Millard and D.J. Wiseman (eds.), *Essays on the Patriarchal Narratives* (Leicester: IVP, 1980), pp. 157–88.

West, D.C. and A. Kling (eds.), *The Libro de las profecías of Christopher Columbus* (Gainesville: University of Florida Press, 1991).

West, Gerald O., 'Contextual Bible Study in South Africa: A Resource for Reclaiming and Regaining Land, Dignity and Identity', in G.O. West and M.W. Dube (eds.), *The Bible in Africa: Transactions, Trajectories and Trends* (Leiden: E.J.Brill, 2000), pp. 594–610.

—*The Academy of the Poor: Towards a Dialogical Reading of the Bible* (Sheffield: Sheffield Academic Press, 1999).

Westermann, Claus, *Genesis 12–36* (Minneapolis: Augsburg, 1985).

Whitelam, Keith, *The Invention of Ancient Israel: The Silencing of Palestinian History* (London: Routledge, 1996).

Wilcken, John, 'Christology and Aboriginal Religious Traditions', *Australian Catholic Record* 75 (1998), pp. 184–94.

Wilkes, George, 'Judaism and the Justice of War', in P. Robinson (ed.), *Just War in Comparative Perspective* (Aldershot: Ashgate, 2003), pp. 9–23.

Williams, James G., *The Bible, Violence and the Sacred: Liberation from the Myth of Sanctioned Violence* (New York: HarperCollins, 1991).

Williamson, Hugh, *Variations on a Theme: King, Messiah and Servant in the Book of Isaiah* (Carlisle: Paternoster, 1998).

—'The Concept of Israel in Transition', in Ronald E. Clements (ed.), *The World of Ancient Israel* (Cambridge: Cambridge University Press, 1989), pp. 141–61.

—*Israel in the Books of Chronicles* (Cambridge: Cambridge University Press, 1977).

Wink, Walter, 'Neither Passivity nor Violence', in W.M. Swartley (ed.), *The Love of Enemy and Nonretaliation in the New Testament* (Louisville: Westminster/John Knox, 1992), pp. 102–25.

Wire, Antoinette, *The Corinthian Women Prophets* (Minneapolis: Fortress Press, 1990).

Wittenberg, Günter, 'Alienation and "Emancipation" from the Earth', in N. Habel and S. Wurst (eds.), *The Earth Story in Genesis* (Sheffield: Sheffield Academic Press, 2000), pp. 73–86.

—'Let Canaan Be his Slave', *Journal of Theology for Southern Africa* 74 (1991), pp. 46–56.

Worsley, Peter, *The Three Worlds: Culture and World Development* (London: Weidenfeld & Nicolson, 1984).

Wright, Christopher J.H., *God's People in God's Land: Family, Land and Property in the Old Testament* (Grand Rapids: Eerdmans, 1990).

Wright, N.T., *Jesus and the Victory of God* (Minneapolis: Fortress Press, 1996).

Wyschogrod, Michael, *The Body of Faith: Judaism as Corporeal Election* (Minneapolis: Seabury–Winston, 1983).

Yeo, Khiok-Khng, '1 Corinthians 8 and Chinese Ancestor Worship', *Biblical Interpretation* 2 (1994), pp. 294–311.

Yoder, John Howard, *The Jewish–Christian Schism Revisited* (Notre Dame: Shalom Desktop, 1996).

Younger, K. Lawson, *Ancient Conquest Accounts: A Study in Ancient Near Eastern and Biblical History Writing* (Sheffield: JSOT Press, 1990).

Zevit, Ziony, *The Religions of Israel: A Synthesis of Parallactic Approaches* (New York: Continuum, 2001).

Zizioulas, John D., *Communion and Otherness: Further Studies in Personhood and the Church* (London: T. & T. Clark, 2006).

INDEXES

INDEX OF REFERENCES

Old Testament

Genesis

1	7, 37, 183
1.21-22, 24	34, 35, 37
1.26-28	33, 35, 38
1.28	2, 20, 32, 33, 37
2.4-5	35, 36
2.15	36
2.19	35
3.14	38
3.17	39
3.23	37
4	37
4.2-3	36, 37
4.10-12	35
4.14	36
4.17	36
4.21-24	36
5.1	37
5.29	39
6.9	34
6.11-13	33 n. 3, 34
6.17	34
7.15	34
9	40
9.1	33
9.3-6	34, 35
9.7	34
9.8-17	35
9.20-27	10, 39-41
10.5-31	40
11	33
11.1-4	34, 36, 40
11.9	34
12.1, 2, 6-7, 18-27	52, 56, 122-23, 126

13.16, 18	52, 125
14	45
14.18-22	44, 52, 55, 90
15.5	126
16.11, 13-14	121-23
17	56, 127
17.8-27	56, 123, 125-26
18	185, 186
21-22	120, 121, 196
23	123
26.34-35	125
27.46-28.5	125
28.3	34
28.22	52
31.5	56
31.52-54	52, 56
32.39	90
35.11	34
35.14	60
35.20	51, 60
46.1	52
47.19-21	98
48.4	34

Exodus

6	56
12.38	75
12.48, 49	116
20.17	97
20.24	50
21.24	141
22.20	81
22.25	133
23	54
23.14-17	50

23.20-24.11	53-54, 80-81

Leviticus

6.31	50
15	114
16	114
16.29-30	115
17.3, 8-9	117
18.24-30	81, 116-17
18.28	54
19.23	54
19.28, 31, 34	58, 111, 113, 125
20.6, 26, 27	58, 113
21.14	115
23.14, 21, 26-44	50, 114
25	101, 127, 134, 163, 164
25.13, 23-24	58, 59
27.28	85

Numbers

15	116
19.10	116
21.2-3	80
25.1-15	132
29.7-38	114
31	115

Deuteronomy

4.19-20	55
6	55
6.4	55
6.25	85
7.1-3	78, 81, 85, 100-101

Deuteronomy (cont.)
7.7-8 — 59
8.17-18 — 59
9.5 — 59
12.5-6 — 50
13 — 50, 82, 86, 90, 146
13.7-16 — 83, 91
15 — 133
15.12-15 — 127
16.21 — 51
18.9 — 89
19.14 — 44, 56-57
20 — 4, 91
20.5-7 — 100
20.10-18 — 15, 54, 64, 78, 80-84, 86, 89-91, 100
21.10-14 — 84
23.1, 3-4, 7-8, 15-16 — 117, 119, 137, 165
26.14 — 58
28 — 86
30.1-10 — 100-101
32.8-9 — 55
34.6 — 26

Joshua
— 15, 53-54, 92
6 — 86, 91
6.21-25 — 64, 85
8.24-27 — 80
9 — 86, 91
11.14 — 64, 80
23 — 26
24 — 53-54, 64
24.14-15 — 54
24.26-27 — 53

Judges
9.46 — 71
11.24 — 55

1 Samuel
8.11, 14 — 98

9.12-13 — 50
28.14 — 52

2 Samuel
7.12-16 — 103
9.7 — 98
14.16 — 53
16.4 — 98
18.18 — 51

1 Kings
9.20-21 — 86
16.24 — 98
21.1-6 — 53, 57, 98
21.17-24 — 57, 96
22 — 96
22.17 — 96
22.38 — 96

2 Kings
18.4 — 51
19.30-10.11 — 57
22-23 — 90, 106
23.5-9, 26 — 51, 106

2 Chronicles
33.10-17 — 106
36.16 — 106

Ezra
— 5, 128
1-7 — 128
7.26 — 118
9 — 5, 114-19, 121, 123-24, 126-27, 129
10.8 — 118

Nehemiah
— 5
2.8 — 118
7.2 — 118
8 — 114

Job
41 — 37

41.9 — 37
41.34 — 37

Psalms
16.2-6 — 52, 54
72 — 37
104.29-30 — 34

Proverbs
22.28 — 44, 57

Isaiah
1.25 — 107
2.1-5 — 94, 102, 110
2.12 — 109
3.10 — 107
3.14 — 96
5.8 — 140
5.13-15 — 96
7.4, 14 — 105, 138
10.1-19 — 102, 109, 110, 147, 161
11.1-5 — 104
19 — 110
30-31 — 105
35 — 59
37.35 — 104
40.13 — 175, 176
41-66 — 59, 94, 102, 104, 107-10, 128, 135, 161, 180
51 — 102
53.10-11 — 108
54.2-10 — 102, 107
56 — 110, 136-37
60.12, 18 — 110
61 — 134
65 — 38, 105

Jeremiah
4.23-28 — 38
5.1 — 147

6.14	158	*1 Maccabees*		*Acts*	
7.6, 11	85, 136-37	2.54	133	16.1-3	168
9.25-26	127				
18.18	103	New Testament		*Romans*	
27-28	103, 161	*Matthew*		2.12-16	176
29-33	100, 103,	1.1-17,		3.1-2	168
	174	21, 23	135, 138,	3.22	176
			143	8.22, 26	176
Ezekiel		2.6	139	11	175, 186
14.7	85	5	132, 141	11.34	176
16.3	62	6.10, 12	135, 137	12.9	160, 162
18	40, 106	10.6, 28, 34	143, 146,	13.1-12	159, 160,
36-37	59		147		161, 162,
37.14	199 n. 53	11.29-30	13		166, 172
		15.24	143	14.19	167
Daniel		24.28	144		
2.37-44	157, 161	25.21-46	185, 186	*1 Corinthians*	
11.31	157	27.54	139	1.27-28	166
12.1-2	157	20.25-27	138, 145	2.2-8	154, 159
		28.19	23, 143-44	7.20-24	154, 162
Hosea				8	167
2.18	32, 38	*Mark*		8.5-6	159
4.3	32, 38	2	136, 142	9.19-27	167
11.1, 5	71, 74	5.1-20	137	10	167
13.4	74	7.24-30	143	11.21-22	166
		8.30	139	15.24-26	157-58
Amos		9.42-48	144		
1.13	71, 73	10.42-44	145	*2 Corinthians*	
2.10	71, 73	11	137	11.23-30	170
3.1-2	72, 98	12.1-12	139	12.1-10	156, 170
3.15	99				
5.11	72	*Luke*		*Galatians*	
6.4	73	1.52	178	3.26-29	153, 164,
9.7	101,	4.17-21	134		168
	185-86	11.4	135	4.7	164
9.11-12	99	13.20-21	145	5.13	166
9.14	99	14.15-24	95, 142	5.19-23	168
		17.20-21	146		
Micah		19.1-10	201	*Ephesians*	
2.2	97, 140	22.49-51	147	5.21	166
3.11-12	103			6.12	158
4.1-5	55, 94, 100,	*John*			
	104, 110		5	*Philippians*	
5	139	1.1-18	149	2.5-10	157-58,
5.2-5	103, 109,	4.19-24	148		169, 182
	139	14.2	200	3.1	170
			fn 54		
Sirach					
45.23-24	133				

Colossians

1.15-16,

19-20, 24   159, 170

3.11   164

3.18-4.1   164-65

1 Thessalonians

5.3   157, 158

Philemon

9-16   165

Hebrews

13.2   185

1 Peter

2.18-21   171

4.13   170

Revelation

13   159

Index of Authors

Albertz, R. 51
Albrecht, P.G.E. 60
Anderson, B. 22, 24, 91
Anderson, B.W. 34
Apess, W. 24, 181–82
Apffel-Marglin, F. 42, 43, 191
Appiah, K. 200
Ashcroft, B. 87, 88, 100
Attwood, B. 27
Aune, D. 156

Bakhtin, M. 120
Baltzer, K. 102
Bammel, E. 158
Barclay, J.M.G. 175
Barnes, J.A. 11
Barrera, A. 192
Barth, F. 68, 193
Barth, K. 203
Bauman, Z. 192–93
Bediako, K. 59, 60, 195
Beilharz, P. 9
Beker, J.C. 155
Ben-Amos, D. 72
Benhabib, S. 169
Bergen, D.L. 203
Berlin, I. 183
Berndt, R.M. 11, 30
Betz, H.D. 142, 168
Bhabha, H.K. 4, 48, 82, 87, 120, 152, 192
Binney, J. 26
Bird, P. 37
Blackstone, W. 7
Bleakley, J.W. 29, 112
Blenkinsopp, J. 97, 103, 106, 118, 129
Bloch-Smith, E. 51–53, 69, 76
Boehmer, E. 89
Boer, R. 9, 100, 151

Boff, L. 186
Bolton, G. 20
Borg, M. 145
Boroujerdi, M. 129
Bowman, G. 76
Boyarin, D. 170, 173, 204
Boyer, R. 98
Brady, V. 191
Braulik, G. 84, 89, 101
Brett, J. 202
Brett, M.G. 38, 46, 60, 65, 67, 74, 91,
    109, 120, 122, 197
Brichto, H.C. 53, 57, 58
Broadhead, E.K. 136
Brown, R.E. 135
Brown, R.M. 172
Brueggemann, W. 184–85
Byrne, B. 147
Byron, J. 166

Camp, C. 114
Carroll, M.D. 98, 100, 101, 204
Carroll, J. 135
Carter, C. 2, 118
Carter, P. 7
Carter, W. 136–37, 144–45
Casas, B. de las 14
Cassuto, U. 34
Cavanaugh, W.T. 7, 150, 171–72
Certeau, M. de 150
Chaney, M. 96–97
Chapman, S.B. 31
Charleston, S. 60, 92, 150–51
Chatterjee, P. 130
Cherry, C. 14
Coakley, S. 183
Collins, J.J. 76
Columbus, C. 14, 31

Comaroff, J. and J. 26
Conrad, E. 104, 105
Connor, G.E. 182
Conversi, D. 130
Cooper, A. 51, 53
Cornell, S. 76
Cosgrove, C. 6
Cross, F. 55
Crossan, J.D. 136, 146
Crüsemann, F. 85

Darwin, C. 11
Davies, W.D. 140
Day, J. 71
Derrida, J. 175, 191–92,
    196–97
Dever, W. 65–68, 72,
    75, 76
Dharmaraj, J.S. 22
Dodson, M. 77
Dodson, P. 174
Donaldson, L.
Donne, J. 202
Douglas, M. 113–14, 118
Dove, T. 12
Dozeman, T.
Dube, M. 148
Duff, J.W. and A.M. 161

Edwards, D. 197
Elliot, N. 155, 161–62
Engberg-Pedersen, T. 168
Equiano, O. 24
Eriksen, T. 68, 69, 75
Eskenazi, T.C. 118, 129
Evans, R. 10, 11, 18
Evans, W.M. 10
Evans-Pritchard, E.E. 201

Fejo, W. 35
Fesl, E.M.D. 31
Findlay, M. 27, 203
Finkelstein, I. 65–68, 70–72
Fishbane, M. 54, 84
Francis, R. 1
Frerichs, E.S. 72
Furrow, D. 187–88

Gandhi, L. 87
Gardner, A. 33
Gauchet, M. 46
Gellner, E. 91
Girard, R. 88–89
Glancy, J.A. 164–66, 170
Goldenberg, D. 163
Goldenberg, R. 10
Goldingay, J. 157
Goldstein, B.R.
Gondarra, D. 45, 60
Goodenough, E.R. 162
Goodman, M. 134
Goody, J. 198
Goswami, M. 130
Gowan, D. 38
Gundry, S.N. 79
Gutiérrez, G. 179, 186

Habel, N. 52
Habermas, J. 188–90
Haller, W. 14
Halpern, B. 47, 53, 55
Hamilton, M. 87
Hardt, M. 191–92
Harink, D. 174, 176
Harries, P. 25
Harris, J. 8, 10–12, 28, 60, 200
Harris, M. 11
Harrison, P. 32
Hart, W.D. 179
Hasel, M.G. 70
Hastings, A. 25
Havrelock, R. 102
Hawley, S. 26, 88
Hayes, C. 115
Hays, R. 147, 166–67, 176
Head, L. 27
Heard, R.C. 120–21, 123
Hendel, R.S. 187
Hengel, M. 155
Hepburn, S. 2, 9
Herder, J.G. 183
Herrmann, W. 4
Herzog, W. 134, 137, 140–41
Hesse, B. 69
Hester, J.D. 141

Higginbotham, C.R. 2
Hill, B. 60, 61
Hobsbawm, E. 31, 91
Hoffman, Y. 84
Hoglund, K. 118, 120
Honneth, A. 188
Horrell, D. 169, 189
Horsley, R. 133, 137, 141, 143, 162
Hoy, D. 195

Jackson, H.H. 21
Japhet, S. 106, 119, 129
Johnstone, W. 96
Joosten, J. 58, 115
Jordan, I. 60, 61

Kaggia, B. 25
Kallis, A. 187
Kang, S.M. 87
Kee, H.C. 138
Keith, M. 150
Keller, C. 192
Kenny, R. 12, 201
Kent, J. 9
Kenzo, M.J.R. 201
Khalidi, R. 76
Kidd, R. 18, 27, 28
Kidwell, C.S. 151, 203
Killebrew, A.E. 66
Kim, T.H. 139
King, R. 198
Knohl, I. 115
Knoppers, G.N. 128
Koester, H. 158

Langton, M. 77
Lemche, N.P. 70, 72
Levenson, J.D. 53, 111, 184, 196, 199
Levinas, E. 185–87, 196
Levinson, B.M. 47, 49, 72, 74, 90, 128
Lewis, B. 163
Lewis, T.J. 51, 53, 58
Lind, M. 111
Lindbeck, G. 179–81, 203
Livingstone, D. 15, 20, 21, 27
Locke, J. 19, 20
Lohfink, N. 48, 84, 88, 89, 101

Lonsdale, J. 25
Lyons, C.L. 2

MacIntyre, A. 62, 92
Maddox, M. 200
Mafico, T. 59, 195
Marshall, J. 21
Matties, G. 89
McCoy, B.F. 174
McGlade, H. 131
McIntosh, I. 30
McKinlay, J. 96, 120, 122, 143
McNutt, P.
McPhee, P. 91
Mendenhall, G. 87
Milbank, J. 150
Milgrom, J. 50, 58, 59, 115,
    117, 125
Miller, R. 145
Min, A.K. 187
Moberly, R.W.L. 51–52, 55, 81
Moltmann, J. 61, 183
Moore, S.D. 192
Moran, W. 48, 82
Myers, C. 138

Nandy, A. 22, 24, 132
Neale, M. 7
Nelson, R. 81, 83–84
Neusner, J. 134
Niditch, S. 8, 72

O'Connell, B. 24
Oded, B. 40
Ogden, S. 179
Ollenburger, B. 105, 199
Olley, J. 35
Olyan, S. 115
Oren, E. 64
Otto, E. 2, 18, 48, 49, 82

Parpolo, S. 48, 49, 83
Pattel-Gray, A. 92
Patterson, O. 164
Paulson, G. 198
Pearson, G. 27
Perkinson, J. 143

Peterson, D. 25
Pfitzner, V.J. 168
Povinelli, E. 131
Pratt, M.L. 88
Provan, I.V. 63, 64
Pui-lan, K. 178
Pury, A. de 126
Putnam, H. 186

Ranger, T. 201
Reid, B.E. 140, 147
Rendtorff, R. 107, 127
Reventlow, H. 19
Reynolds, H. 8, 9, 15–18, 20, 21, 94, 179
Richard, P. 13
Ringe, S. 135
Rivera, L.N. 13, 95
Rofé, A. 84, 96, 113
Rogerson, J.W. 102
Rorty, R. 178
Rose, D.B. 9, 11, 32, 43, 46
Rost, L. 41
Rowley, H.H. 44–45
Rozema, V. 181
Ruskin, J. 23, 31
Rüterswörden, U. 87

Sachs, J. 204
Sacks, J. 111, 192
Sahlins, M. 183
Said, E. 23, 77, 87, 179, 187
Saldarini, A. 143
Sanders, P. 55
Sanneh, L. 45, 60, 151
Sauter, F. 156
Schäfer-Lichtenberger, C. 81
Schapera, I. 15, 20, 21
Schmidt, B.B. 52
Scholem, G. 183
Schrage, W. 167
Schreiter, R.J. 60
Schüssler-Fiorenza, E. 166
Schwartz, B.J. 54, 81, 117
Scott, J. 128
Scott, K. 156
Seesengood, R.P. 168
Segovia, F. 148, 192, 196

Sen, A. 192, 194
Sepúlveda, J.G. de 12, 13, 79
Shah, A.B. 24
Silberman, N.A. 65–67, 70–72
Simkins, R. 98
Simons, M. 200
Skinner, L. 17
Smith, M.S. 44, 47, 51, 71
Smith-Christopher, D. 100, 113, 116, 118, 128, 174
Snow, A.H. 19
Sommer, B. 92
Sparks, K.L. 108, 110, 116
Sperling, S.D. 54
Spina, F. 39
Stager, L. 64, 66, 68, 73
Staley, J.L. 149–50
Stanley, B. 25
Stavrakopoulou, F. 53, 102
Steck, O.H. 105
Ste Croix, G.E.M. de 155
Steymans, H.U. 48, 87
Strehlow, T.G.H. 61
Strelein, L. 3, 201
Stringfellow, T. 154
Sugirtharajah, R.S. 22–24, 179
Sutton, P. 201–202
Swanson, T.D. 148
Swartley, W. 88

Tacey, D. 46
Tanner, K. 201
Tatz, C. 80
Taylor, L. 77
Taylor, C. 1, 42, 153–54, 189–90, 194–95
Thiselton, A.C. 181
Thomas, M.M. 24
Tinker, G.E. 29, 45, 151, 203
Tlhagale, B. 112
Todorov, T. 13
Toit, A. du 15, 112
Tollefson, D. 129
Toorn, K. van der 50–54, 72, 90
Tov, E. 55
Treat, J. 46
Trible, P. 122
Turner, D.H. 31, 151

Uyangoda, J. 190

Van der Veer, P. 198
Vanhoozer, K. 174, 177
Varzon-Morel, P. 61
Vattimo, G. 182
Veling, T. 196
Verboom, W. 14
Volf, M. 171, 194, 199

Wan, S.K. 168, 183–84
Ward, G. 183
Ward, W. 22
Washington, H. 114, 118
Watson, F. 185–86
Watts, J.W. 128
Weaver, J. 181
Weiner, J.F. 3
Weinfeld, M. 48, 58, 74, 80–82,
    85, 92, 109
Wenham, G. 52
West, D.C. 14

West, G.O. 177, 179
Westermann, C. 52
Whitelam, K. 76
Wilcken, J. 151
Wilkes, G. 93
Williams, J.G. 88, 109
Williamson, H.G.M. 104, 119, 129
Wink, W. 142
Wire, A. 169
Wittenberg, G. 36, 41
Worsley, P. 190
Wright, C.J.H. 53, 57, 61
Wright, N.T. 135, 146
Wyschogrod, M. 196

Yeo, K.K. 59
Yoder, J.H. 174
Younger, K.L. 63–64, 87

Zevit, Z. 66–67, 71, 73
Zizioulas, J.D. 184

Index of Subjects

Aboriginal (Indigenous)
    Australian Christianity 26, 30, 35 n. 6,
      46, 60, 150–51, 174, 181,
      198–201
    Burramurra, David 30–31
    Cooper, William 26
    Elcho Island 29
    Fejo, Wali 35
    Gondarra, Djiniyini 30, 60
    Jangala, Jerry 61
    Nicholls, Douglas 26
    Pattel-Gray, Anne 92
    Paulson, Graham 198
Aboriginal Protection Act (1897) 28
Aboriginal testimony 17
acquisitive desire 97
Afrikaner nationalism 112
agape 167–68, 196 n. 44
ancestral country 57, 58, 94–95, 100,
    134, 149, 170, 181, 195
angareia 142
aniconism 187
apartheid 172
Apess, William 24, 181
apocalyptic/ism 145, 146, 156–58, 160
apocalyptic violence 93, 144, 147
Aranda 60–61
Asherah 44, 47, 51, 62, 73
Australia 1–3, 8–10, 16–17, 26–29,
    174, 200
authenticity, myth of 77–78, 129, 131

Barmen Declaration 203
basileia 137, 144
berit (treaty) 82, 85–86, 201
biblical theology 176, 179, 201
Blackstone, William 7
Bleakey, John 29, 112
boundary stone/border 57, 102, 104, 110

Burrumarra, David 30–31
Buxton, Thomas 16

Calpurnius Siculus 160
    Eclogue 1.45-65 161
Campbell, J. 10
Canaanite/Canaan 10, 13, 40–41, 44, 52,
    62–66, 70, 72, 77–79, 89–92, 143–44,
    146, 176, 182, 188, 193
Carey, William 23
Casas, Bartolomé de las 13, 94, 95
catholicity 197
centralization 50, 54
Christology 185, 186, 199
        exclusive 175
        inclusive 176
civilization 2, 19, 27–29, 31, 172, 191
class 26, 98, 103, 106–107, 109, 133–34,
    143, 164
Columbus, Christopher 14, 22, 31,
    94, 180
communitarian ethics 189, 193
complex space 150, 199
conquest 26, 63–64, 75, 79–80, 102,
    109, 146
Constantine 172
Cooper, William 26
Council of Chalcedon 165
counter-empire 148, 185, 203
covert resistance 120, 124, 128, 161
Crusades/crusader 172, 180
cultural hybridity 68, 75, 88, 131, 151
cultural relativism 31
'curse of Ham'/'sons of Ham' 10, 32, 39,
    40, 43, 86, 132

deror (liberty) 58, 134–35
Day of Atonement/Purgation 114
debt 133–35, 140

democratization 38, 43
Diaspora 173–175, 182
discourse ethics 188–90
disenchantment 45–46
dispossession 78, 94–96, 102, 121,
    124, 183
dissidence/dissident 94, 103

economy 5, 21–22, 42, 94–98, 100, 118,
    121, 128, 130, 133–36, 140, 149, 152,
    171, 184, 191–93, 203–204
eco-theology 43, 106
Eipper, Christopher 28
ekklēsia 160, 163
El 44–47, 52, 62, 71–72, 75–76, 90,
    121–23, 176
Eliot, John 29
Ellis, William 18
'elohim 44, 52–57, 62, 75
Elyon 90
emic 77
encomienda 13
endogamy/endogamous marriage 113,
    115, 117, 124–25
Equiano, Olaudah 24
Esarhaddon 82–83, 86
Ethiopia 26
ethnic/ethnicity 5, 67–69, 72–73,
    74 n. 37, 75–78, 110, 116, 125,
    153, 164, 168, 173, 190, 193, 199
ethnocentric/ism 168, 173, 184, 194–95
etic 77
eucharist/ic 61, 171–72, 197
exile(s)/diaspora 9, 99–100, 107, 115,
    117, 121, 128, 138
exodus tradition 71–76, 91, 101, 122, 138
exogamous marriage 112, 115, 123

Festival of Booths 114
feudal 2, 7
Francis, Robert 1

Gandhi, Mahatma 24, 132, 152
Garden of Eden 36
genealogical connection 121
genocide 4, 45, 78–79, 82–84,
    90–92, 117

ger/gerim/stranger(s)/alien(s) 59, 84–85,
    99, 106, 112–17, 124–25, 127
    n. 30, 137
gifts/practices for the dead 58–61
Gikuyu 25
Glenelg, Lord 16
Gondarra, Djiniyini 30, 45, 60
grace 59, 124

Hagar 122–24, 126
Haldane, J.B.S. 43
Haredim 129
herem 79–87, 89–90, 92–93
Hezekiah 51
'hidden transcript(s)' 141, 158, 161–62,
    171
'high place' 50–51
'holy seed' (*zera'*) 114, 116, 120, 125–27
'holy war' 54
hospitality/kenotic hospitality 5, 43, 182,
    183–85, 189, 196, 197, 204
hybrid/hybridity 76, 77, 120, 132, 150,
    152, 168–69, 184, 192, 198, 201

'image of God' 37, 43
imperial hymns 156
inalienable right 18
indeterminacy 6
inheritance 97, 111, 121, 140, 152, 164
Isaac 121, 123–24
Ishmael 120, 121–22, 124

Jacob–Israel 108
Jangala, Jerry 61
Jericho 64
Josiah 51, 71–72, 106
Jubilee year 101, 134, 163, 164
'just war' 12, 147, 180
justice of God 107, 109–11, 146

Kaggia, Bildad 25
kairos 172
kenosis/kenotic 174–75, 182–84, 196
Kent, James 9
'kin and country' 35, 58, 59, 61,
    174, 199
King, Martin Luther Jr 24, 132
kleronomia 140

kunarion 144
kyrioi 164

land rights 59, 61, 103
Leviticus Rabbah 92
Livingstone, David 15, 20, 21
Locke, John 19
logos 132, 149, 151, 191
'love patriarchalism' 166
Luther, Martin 153
Lyell, Charles 10

Mabo judgment 3, 9, 130, 201
Mabo, Eddie 26, 202
Macaulay, T.B. 22
Manasseh 106
Maori 17, 25–27, 149, 151
Marshall, Chief Justice John 21
mashiach/messiah/Christ 138–39
matsebah 51, 53, 54
Mau Mau rebellion 25
meta-norms 169, 175
Micaiah ben Imlah 96
Midian 115
Midianites 73
mimetic 43, 91, 93, 192
mimetic desire 87, 88
mimicry 82, 88, 102, 152
Miskitu 26
monotheism 54, 62
inclusive monotheism 44, 60, 62,
    75, 176
multiculturalism 194

Naboth 96
Naboth's vineyard 57, 95, 140
nachalah 97
national allegory 14
national/nationalism 74, 91, 126,
    188–89, 204
Native American 1, 8–9, 19, 29, 150,
    181–82, 203
native title 2–3, 17, 77, 130–31
nativism/nativist 5, 128, 130–31, 192
natural law 18, 19
Nazism 203
New Zealand/Aotearoa 8, 17, 25, 149

Ngarrindjerri 200
Nicholls, Douglas 26
niddah 114, 128
Nimrod 40, 104, 139
Noachic covenant 184
non-violence/non-violent 5, 93, 102, 104,
    108–10, 132, 137, 139, 147,
    174, 180–81
North America 1, 8–9, 29, 181

oikodomē 169
omniscient narrator 120–21
Omri 67
Onus, Lin 7

Palestinians 76–77
Passover 116
Paul 5
pax et securitas 157–58
Philistine(s) 4, 64, 67, 69, 73–75, 77, 101
    n. 15
Philo, *De specialibus legibus* 2.92-94 161
pig taboo 68–69, 75
Pinochet, General 171
pistis christou 176
Pitjantjatjara 151
Polding, Bishop 15
poll tax (*kensos*) 141
possess/ion (*yarash*) 101–102, 109
Priestly tradition 5, 113–17, 121, 125,
    127, 130
primordial time 32
property 19–21, 32, 47, 53, 57–60, 77–78,
    95, 118, 143

Queen Elizabeth I 14

ruach 34–35, 43
Rebekah 123, 125
reconciliation/reconcile 1, 61, 77, 93, 159
redemption 58, 59, 61, 99, 107, 109–10,
    170, 173, 181, 199
reducción 14
Reformation 173
representation 186–88
resident alien; see *ger*
Roth, Walter 10

Ruskin, John 23, 31
Ruth 118

Sabbatical year 133, 164
sacred trees 52
Saunders, John 15
scapegoat/s 88–89
seed 122
Sennacherib 47, 74
Sepúlveda, Juan Ginés de 12, 79
servant figure 108–109
Shang Ti 44
Shechem 64
Shrine of Elijah 76
slaves/slavery 10, 13, 15–16, 25, 43,
    86, 127, 140, 145, 154–55, 163–64,
    166–69, 170–71, 192, 204
smooth space ideology 150
social Darwinism, natural selection 10–13
South Africa/n 8, 14–15, 20, 61, 112, 172
sovereign/sovereignty 3, 7, 19, 103–104,
    138, 145, 150, 157–58, 184–85, 191,
    202–203
St Francis 43, 180
Stringfellow, Thornton 154
syncretism 169

Talpin, George 200
Te Kooti 25–26, 149
teraphim 52, 58, 60

terra nullius 2, 9, 17, 20, 32, 76 n. 41, 102,
    174, 191
'tide of history' 3, 131
'tides of Empire' 193
tjukurpa 132, 151
tjurunga 60
tolerance 173, 190
torture 171–72, 174
Tower of Babel 33, 36, 41
Trail of Tears 181
treaty 85, 86, 92, 201
tzimtzum 183

UN *Declaration on the Rights of Indigenous
    Peoples* (2007) 201
utopia(s)/utopian 4, 99, 100, 101, 104,
    105, 106, 109, 162

veneration of ancestors 58, 59, 61 n. 47
violence 21, 93, 100, 147, 155. 179

Ward, William 22
Warlpiri 46, 61
Wilberforce, William 16
William of Orange 14

Yoruba 151
Yoruba Bible 25

Breinigsville, PA USA
16 February 2011
255729BV00002B/11/P

9 781906 055899